SERMONS

March – July 2020

by

NORMAN ROE

SERMONS

22 March — 5 July 2020

by

NORMAN ROE

Faith Books Ossett

2023

© Faith Books Ossett 2023

ISBN: 978-1-7393295-0-1

faithbooksossett@gmail.com

Phone: 07918 656326

.

Printed by:

4edge Limited
22 Eldon Way Industrial Estate, Hockley, Essex
SS5 4AD

CONTENTS

PUBLISHER'S FOREWORD

Norman Roe was the pastor of the two Particular Baptist churches in Ossett and Birkenhead. These sermons were preached in the Ossett chapel and relayed to Birkenhead during the UK government's first lockdown for covid in 2020. The gospel proclaimed was blessed to the hearers, old and young, at that time and, after Norman's death in September 2021, were valued as read sermons in services when there was no preacher. This book gives a permanent record for the brethren who loved to hear this ministry and highly esteemed the Lord's servant. We would desire that they be used of the Holy Spirit, if it be his will, for other needy tried sinners who love the gospel. Above all, as the sermons exalt Jesus Christ alone, they cannot but be meat, drink and joy for all to whom the Lord is precious—the altogether lovely One.

The first sermon, preached 22 March 2020, is really the best preface for this book. Here is an 80-year-old servant of the Lord, who has been preaching for nearly 60 years, confronted with the universal fear of confusion and death at that time. He reviews the Lord's help to him over the years and seems to gird up his loins, in the strength of the Lord, to give his final testimony to his faithful Saviour. And his gracious resolve was tested by severe trials, outward and inward, through those last 18 months of his life, and acutely so in the Lord's using covid to take him from this wilderness world to eternal rest and glory 10 September 2021. The truths preached in these sermons manifestly sustained him through those final months and in death itself. His last text was characteristic of his ministry. Preached 25 August 2021 at Birkenhead, it was the exhortation of Jehoshaphat: "Believe in the LORD your God, so shall ye be established; believe his prophets, so shall ye prosper." To that we would add, "Remember them which have the rule over you, who have spoken unto you the word of God: whose faith follow, considering the end of their conversation. Jesus Christ the same yesterday, and to day, and for ever."

―――――――――――

Norman's sermons have been produced in printed form in fellowship with him for over fifty years by the editor of this present book. As he got older, some stumbling in speech has made the work more difficult. We trust ours has been a devoted prayerful effort to faithfully commit his fervent pulpit ministry into writing.

All bible quotations are from the Authorised Version. Most hymn quotations are from Gadsby's Hymnbook.

1

I WILL GO IN THE STRENGTH OF THE LORD GOD

Lord's day morning 22 March 2020

> "I will go in the strength of the Lord GOD: I will make mention of thy righteousness, even of thine only. O God, thou hast taught me from my youth: and hitherto have I declared thy wondrous works. Now also when I am old and grayheaded, O God, forsake me not; until I have shewed thy strength unto this generation, and thy power to every one that is to come" (Psalm 71:16-18).

Indeed, it is in unprecedented times that we meet here this morning. I do not need to go over all the issues with which we are confronted at this present time, in the nation, amongst us also as the people of God, and in our personal lives. With all that is placed upon us and to which we desire to rightly attend, we do not want to be diverted from what should always be the chief concern of the Lord's people. And that is the worship and service of the Lord our God, in owning him and seeking still to bear witness to him who is the one and only true God as revealed in the person of the Lord and Saviour Jesus Christ. Our desire is still to testify to all that is set before us in the word of God concerning the glorious gospel of his grace. This alone addresses all the deepest needs of his people, the deepest needs of every guilty, needy sinner who is brought to cry to the Lord for mercy in all their spiritual distresses and in all the out-workings of the Lord's dealings with them in providence. In all these things, the hope and expectation of the people of God is in looking to and trusting alone in the Lord, knowing that through the grace of God we have, in the person of our Lord Jesus Christ, one who is the true rock and refuge of his people.

The psalmist could say, and surely cannot we also say in such a time as this, that the Lord has been our help, and therefore can we think that he who has helped us hitherto will now leave and forsake us? Is the Lord our God such a God as that? Is he not faithful and true, as his word ever testifies, and as borne out in all his ways and dealings with us? His love to his own knows no change and, blessed be his name, it knows no end. As he has been our help thus far, we therefore say with the psalmist, "Yea, in the shadow of thy wings will I make my refuge, until these calamities be overpast" (Ps. 57:1).

So then may we be increasingly drawn out in prayer to God, but prayer also with thanksgiving. For amidst all these things we have so much to be thankful for, and essentially in this, that the Lord our God is the same yesterday, today and for ever. The hearts of men may fail them for fear of what is coming on the earth, but surely in the Lord and Saviour Jesus Christ have not his people, as I said, a sure refuge, a blessed and glorious hope in him who "is able to do exceeding abundantly above all that we ask or think" (Eph. 3:20). It is as we sometimes sing,

> "He holds all nature in his hand;
> That gracious hand on which I live
> Does life, and time, and death command
> And has immortal joys to give."

The Lord then grant us grace in all things, and indeed at this time, to flee alone to the refuge that the gospel makes known.

Ah friends, can we even begin to question the Lord's love towards his own, when his greatness, goodness, power, and what he has accomplished are so blessedly set before us "in the word of the truth of the gospel"? (Col. 1:5). O may the Holy Spirit bring home afresh to your soul and mine this morning what the apostle could say of the Lord Jesus: "who loved me, and gave himself for me" (Gal. 2:20). As he has put away our sins by the sacrifice of himself, has brought in for us everlasting righteousness, what good thing can he, or will he, withhold from his people? And all that we may meet with can never undermine the blessed reality of the glorious hope and expectation of his people, nor the certainty of attaining unto it—not by what we are or can do, but by what Christ is, what he has done, and what he has graciously promised. "For he is faithful that promised" (Heb. 10:23).

But to come to this psalm before us this morning. Yes, it is a psalm of David. He writes out of his own experience, very evidently in the latter days of his life. He speaks of himself as being old and grayheaded. It is a very personal testimony. He again and again uses the word "I," not to exalt himself above all others, but to give his personal testimony to what he had experienced of the goodness and mercy of the Lord to him. Through the Lord's enabling grace, he sought, while he had an appointed time here on earth, never to cease bearing witness to the greatness and goodness of his God, and to testify of all the Lord had made known to him, wherein all his hope and expectation were founded.

And was it not so with all the old testament saints? What was their hope founded upon? What was their expectation? It was that God would gloriously fulfil all that he had promised in the person and finished work of the Lord Jesus Christ. They looked in believing expectation for him who was to come. In him was found their whole salvation, as it is for every sinner called by grace. It was not in their own doings, but in what God promised and fulfilled for all his people, in the person of his only begotten and dearly beloved Son. O the glorious realities of the life, sufferings, death and resurrection of our Lord Jesus Christ!

Friends, these are real things. They are not cunningly devised fables. They are the very foundation of the faith and hope of the living family of God. And at such a time as this, do we not surely need to resort more and more in prayer and praise unto the Lord our God? Do we not desire him to lead us more fully into the wonders of redeeming love and mercy, and to know the blessedness of the refuge the gospel makes known in the person and finished work of our Lord Jesus Christ?

As I said, David writes of his own experience. Here also are traced out the footsteps of the flock of Jesus Christ. But also, unquestionably, we see the footsteps of the Lord Jesus Christ as the great and good shepherd. Remember, he has walked this way before us. He was found in fashion as a man. He became obedient unto death, even the death of the cross. Behold then, in what is set before us in this psalm, the very reality of the person of our Lord Jesus Christ as God manifest in the flesh. Remember, the Lord Jesus Christ is not one who is remote or far off from us. No, as that great high priest over the house of God, he has entered into heaven itself, there now to appear in the presence of God for us. Friends, "He knoweth our frame; he remembereth that we are dust" (Ps. 103:14). Indeed, "We have not an high priest which cannot be touched with the feeling of our infirmities; but was in all points tempted like as we are, yet without sin" (Heb. 4:15). His word assures that he is able to succour them that are tempted. And surely at such a time as this, do we not need that grace which, in all its fulness and freeness, comes to us through the Lord Jesus Christ according to his purpose and founded on his promise? Ah, the apostle exhorts us to "therefore come boldly unto the throne of grace, that we may obtain mercy, and find grace to help in time of need" (Heb. 4:16).

In seeing here the footsteps of the great and good shepherd, I also want, as helped this morning, to trace out what the psalm sets before us concerning those who are brought through grace to be followers of him as the sheep of his pasture. Is not every one of them utterly helpless in themselves? Are they not wholly dependent on the shepherd? Are they not brought to realise their own helplessness and sinfulness, and their need of the grace of our Lord Jesus Christ? I trust it is so with us each increasingly, and surely at such a time as this. What have we to bring before the Lord? What have we to look to, to depend upon? Is there anything in self? Is there anything in created things, anything in the particular circumstances of this day, in the prospects that may be set before us? Even in the official announcements that may be made, what is there in those things from which we can draw help or hope of encouragement? We would not despise what man may say and seek to do according to the wisdom imparted to him. But O friend, the child of God has only one resort, only one place, one person to go to, to hear and to heed.

And so we see here in the language of the psalmist, his gracious determination, not founded on his own ability, nor his own strength, for he is conscious of his own weakness, sinfulness and need. We do not, in that sense, compare ourselves with

David, though we trust that as it was true of him and of every sinner taught by grace, our whole hope and consolation is that we are a sinner saved by grace.

The point I make is that David here expresses, as we might put it, a gracious determination with regard to himself individually and personally. And notice that he does not express it in some faltering way. In a sense, he is saying, 'I have to leave what others may or may not do. I must go the way the Lord himself has taught me and made known to me.' And by the Lord's enabling grace this was the way David had sought to pursue even up to this time of his life when he was old and grayheaded. He says, *"I will go."* O friends, may there be that same gracious determination with us: 'I will go, not looking to self, not looking to man, but looking alone to the Lord.' "I will go in the strength of the Lord God."

And is there any other resource for the people of God? Certainly there was not for David. And so likewise for ourselves. And I believe we have been increasingly brought to realise, as taught of God the Holy Spirit, that we have no resources of our own to look to and rest upon. And particularly at such a time as this are we not brought to realise our own weakness, our utter inability? As it was with Jehoshaphat, we have to say that we know not what to do, nor have we any might against this great company that cometh up against us.

We are no different, we are no better than our fellowmen. No, we are weak, poor, needy and helpless of ourselves. This is true of every servant of Jesus Christ. I have felt it very much myself personally. What am I, but an empty, polluted earthen vessel of myself? And yet by the Lord's enabling grace I trust that my concern and desire is the same as David's here—as the Lord "has helped me hitherto," still to go forward in the path he has appointed for me.

"I will go in the strength of the Lord God," that is, looking to the Lord Jesus Christ alone, seeking his enabling grace daily in utter dependence on him, with a conscious sense of one's own weakness and continual need. Friends, may that be so with each one of us, in the measure that we are taught of God the Holy Spirit.

"The strength of the Lord God." What a strength we are assured of there! For therein is a fulness of strength, not only in what the Lord imparts, but in what *he is,* as revealed to us in the person of Jesus Christ. The Lord Jesus Christ is the strength of his people, in this understanding of it: all that we need is richly treasured up in him and is made known unto his own according as their need shall be. Did not Moses of old say, "As thy days, so shall thy strength be"? (Deut. 33:25). O for grace enabling us to live a day at a time, in dependence upon him that he *will* strengthen us for what the day requires. And may we be enabled rightly, believingly, in submission to his will, to leave all future things in his hand.

We know not, and this is certainly brought home to us at this particular time, we know not what future days may unfold. Things are changing so rapidly from day to day. O friends, the consolation of the people of God is that, though we know not the future, we know him who holds the future in his hand. In all these things, in his working out his divine appointments and purposes, remember our God is sovereign. How he bears witness to that again and again in the word and in his dealings with men and nations!

"I will go in the strength of the Lord God." The psalmist is saying in effect here, 'I will go on in the way that the Lord has appointed for me. As he has helped me hitherto, so in dependence on him I still seek to pursue the path that is appointed for me even in these latter days of my life.'

We also have here the one glorious object David in gracious determination has in view the Lord enabling him: "I will make mention of *thy* righteousness, even of *thine* only." Ah, what does the psalmist mean here? What are we directed to? It is surely found in what the gospel makes known to us in the person and finished work of the Lord Jesus Christ. "I will make mention of *thy* righteousness."

Friends, are we not brought to realise this? Do we know this morning that we have no righteousness of our own? We have *nothing of ourselves* that can commend us to God. As sinners, transgressors of God's holy law, we justly deserve the condemnation it solemnly sets before us that "the soul that sinneth, it shall die" (Ezek. 18:4). And as the word solemnly declares, "God is angry with the wicked every day" (Ps. 7:11).

Ah, surely it is brought home to us that we have nothing of our own which can commend us to God? Shall I rest on my religious exercises? Shall I rest on my attempts even to do what may be considered as being done in the name of the Lord? No. Let us still seek to pursue the things which are right in the sight of God even at such a time as this—the worship and service of his name, the giving ourselves to prayer and praise, the reading and meditating on his holy word, the seeking to live as his word directs us. But friends, we cannot rest on *these* things. The righteousness which avails for us before God is not found in them. No, David realised this more and more: "I will make mention of *thy* righteousness, even of *thine* only."

No righteousness but *this* is worth mentioning. Only *his* righteousness meets the deepest needs of sinners such as you and me, the righteousness provided for sinners and saints who by divine grace are brought to believe and trust in Jesus Christ alone. *Thy* righteousness, the perfect obedience of our Lord Jesus Christ! We can never render to the law of God what it demands of us as sinners. But Jesus Christ has done that for us which we can never do for ourselves. Has he not brought in that everlasting righteousness by which God justifies the *ungodly?* Ah, and that is what we are—*ungodly.* God justifies the *ungodly* through the righteousness of Jesus Christ which is imputed to every believer through the riches of divine mercy. I will make mention of *this righteousness,* says David, and this only.

He says, "O God, thou hast taught me from my youth: and hitherto have I declared thy wondrous works." Friends, in a very humble measure, and I say that sincerely, I trust that the Lord has taught me over the years of my ministry and brought me hitherto. Ah, we have been taught some very real and painful lessons. And we still need the same divine teaching and the realisation of the Lord's mercies extended toward us. But I trust my one concern and desire has always been to declare, as David says here, "thy wondrous works," in preaching and teaching Jesus Christ and him only. It is as Paul could say when writing to the Corinthians, "I determined not to know any thing among you, save Jesus Christ, and him crucified" (1 Cor. 2:2).

He goes on also to say, "Now also when I am old and grayheaded." Friends, I can take that to myself personally, "Now also when I am old and grayheaded, O God, forsake me not." Ah forsake me not "until I have shewed thy strength unto this generation, and thy power to every one that is to come."

"Thy strength to this generation." David said, "I will go in the strength of the Lord God." Ah, the strength of the Lord's people is Jesus Christ himself and him alone. His word assures us that he alone is mighty to save.

> "With heaven and earth at his command,
>
> He waits to answer prayer."

Is not his eye ever upon his people? Friends, is he not able to deliver, save and preserve us even at such a time as this? O may the Lord grant us grace to be found looking to him only, trusting him wholly, committing our way into his hands, not only for time but also for eternity. One could say,

> "He that has made my heaven secure
>
> Will here all good provide;
>
> While Christ is rich, I can't be poor;
>
> What can I want beside?"

"Now also when I am old and grayheaded, O God, forsake me not; until I have shewed thy strength unto this generation, and thy power to every one that is to come." Friends, I trust that the desire of the psalmist here, is my desire. In all humbleness and utter dependence on the Lord, in all the issues of our present day, I would ever truly seek the welfare of the people of God and all connected with us. Above all, I desire that the Lord's name alone may have all the glory.

I will leave the remarks there this morning. May the Lord add his blessing. Amen.

2

CALL UNTO ME, AND I WILL ANSWER THEE

Lord's day evening, 22 March 2020

"Call unto me, and I will answer thee, and
shew thee great and mighty things, which
thou knowest not" (Jeremiah 33:3).

In the opening of this chapter I have read to you this evening we
see the situation that prevailed in those days of Jeremiah. He
himself was shut up in the prison. And what danger and
desolation was solemnly seen in Jerusalem and Judah through the
invasion by the armies of the Chaldeans. Furthermore, there was
the solemn and certain prophecy which the Lord had spoken
through his servant Jeremiah, that within a very short time all that
remained in Jerusalem and Judah would be overthrown and a
remnant carried into captivity in Babylon.

But the Lord here speaks through his servant the prophet a
word that was applicable to him personally and to the remnant of
the Lord's people in those days. The question might have been
asked, was there no hope in those things? Was there no light
shining in them with regard to future prospects? Indeed, the
situation was very dark and distressing. What was to be the end
of those things? What would take place in those seventy years of
captivity in Babylon which the Lord had determined? But one
thing is very evidently set before us here. The Lord had not
forgotten his people, though his hand was evident in chastening
them and in the judgments abroad in the earth at that time.

And no less so is it in the day in which we live and in the
situation in which we are found. We cannot ignore the hand of
the Lord in this affliction and the judgment of the Lord on the
nations of the earth. They may not recognize it. But I believe the
Lord's people, his true church, should bow before him in
acknowledgement that his hand is in these things and that he is
righteous and just in all he sends upon the earth in our day. O, the

Lord never acts unjustly towards the fallen sons and daughters of men. Indeed, rather we have to say that he does not deal with them immediately as their sins justly deserve.

Yet even as his judgments are abroad in the earth, surely the concern of the church and people of God should ever be to lift up their eyes and hearts unto the Lord. Surely they are to plead, as did Habakkuk concerning the Chaldean invasion, that the Lord, in the midst of deserved wrath (and let us ever acknowledge that) will be pleased to remember mercy. And friends, surely the only remedy for the situation in our day, the only hope of any deliverance, is not found in man, nor in the contingency measures placed on the nation at this time. We would not despise our rulers, for they seek to act wisely. We would pray that the Lord might grant them wisdom to act for what they consider to be for the good of the nation. But let not our trust and confidence be placed in *them*, but alone in the Lord our God.

Man is helpless. Man knows not what to do. He knows no exit strategy from this situation. Ah, how this reminds us of our helplessness. Indeed, may the Holy Spirit increasingly teach us our helplessness. Left to ourselves, how hopeless things are. But as those who profess to know and love the Lord, may we be brought low at our Saviour's feet, crying unto him that for his name's sake he would have mercy on his church and our souls personally in this trouble. O as the hand of the Lord is seen upon us, may we also see his hand in using these things for his glory in manifesting that the heavens do reign. May it be evident that it is not man who has the authority, as he may think, over the elements of earth, sky and seas, but it is God alone, the Lord our God.

Friends, though we see the hand of God in his judgments abroad in the earth, what a mercy it is that we can come here this night believing afresh by the witness of the Holy Spirit, that he is our God, our Father which is in heaven. Even in these adversities, we blessedly realise what he has revealed of himself in the precious truth of the gospel—that the Lord our God "is our refuge and strength, a very present help in [this] time of trouble" (Ps. 46:1). O what provision he has made for his people in all that the gospel makes known of pardon, peace and eternal life. If the Lord is ours, what more do we require? If we are the recipients of his pardoning love and mercy, are we not rich indeed? One says,

> "I'm rich to all the intents of bliss,
> If thou, O God, art mine."

Yes, there are matters which obviously trouble us, indeed worry us. Concerns surely abound. We are not exempt from the things to which our fellow creatures are subject at this particular time. But as believers, O may we realise more and more that the Lord is our rock and our refuge. As the psalmist testifies, "My refuge is in God" (Ps. 62:7). And our desire is the same as the psalmist in our text this morning, "Now also when I am old and grayheaded, O God, forsake me not; *until I have shewed thy strength unto this generation, and thy power to every one that is to come*" (Psalm 71:16–18).

The Lord here speaks to Jeremiah, "Call unto me, and I will answer thee." Friends, what a mercy is this word to Jeremiah, and it is the word of the Lord to us also. Our God is a prayer-hearing and a prayer-answering God. He has never yet said "unto the seed of Jacob, Seek ye me in vain" (Isa. 45:19). Brought by the Lord's mercy as a poor sinner to call on his name, have we ever been sent empty away? We may not have always received what we thought or expected, but surely we have been, and still are, the recipients of the Lord's mercies lengthened out towards us. O how deeply indebted we are to him!

What encouragement then is given us, not only at this time but at all times, to call unto him. And friends, it is no vain thing to do so when we consider who it is that tells us to call unto him. Why, he is the one, the only true God, the creator of the heavens and the earth. How often we repeat these things. Do we really believe them? Does it come into our consideration in the situation at this present time, that the Lord our God is the creator of the heavens and the earth? You know, wherever there is a gathering of the people of God, their solace and encouragement is in blessedly knowing that the heavens rule, that God has given all authority and power to our Lord Jesus Christ, the great and glorious head of the church. To him all things are, and ever will be, subject. And this will be fully manifest in that last great day when the Lord comes the second time in power and great glory.

"Call unto me, and I will answer thee." What grace is here! What power of the Lord is here displayed! He says, "Call unto me." You know, is there anything that we cannot call upon his name for? Is there any issue or situation in which the Lord is unable to hear or to help? Blessed be the Lord's name, his "hand is not shortened, that it cannot save; neither his ear heavy, that it cannot hear" (Isa. 59:1). "Call unto me." O particularly at this time may we be men and women of prayer and supplication unto the Lord our God. May he pour upon us "the spirit of grace and of supplications" (Zech. 12:10), such that, truly conscious of our great helplessness and need, we call in believing assurance on the one who:

> "With heaven and earth at his command,
> He waits to answer prayer."

What demonstrations of this are given to us in the Lord's dealings with his people as set forth in the holy scriptures. Again and again, when we look at the situations that confronted his people in their day, we see what wonders he displayed as they were brought by grace, in all their helplessness and need, to cry unto the Lord, believing and trusting in him alone.

Go again to the eleventh chapter of Hebrews. See the reality of the grace of living faith in the hearts and lives of those men and women of God. My thoughts went to Moses of whom it is said, "By faith he forsook Egypt, not fearing the wrath of the king: for he endured, as seeing him who is invisible" (Heb. 11:27). O friends, may that grace be afforded to us. May we be those who truly believe, those who by faith, to put it this way, have a gracious eyesight which, yes, beholds the situation that prevails, but above all which eyes the Saviour. And true faith is that which always goes out to him, in all our felt helplessness and need, to receive of the fulness which is in Christ Jesus our Lord.

The psalmist, in our morning's text, prayed that he might shew the Lord's strength, or as the margin renders it, "shew his arm" unto his generation. And may it ever be our concern to bear testimony to the power and love of our Lord and Saviour Jesus Christ in all his dealings with his church and people. O friend, what a blessed truth is this, that we behold our Lord Jesus Christ as the strength of his people, to uphold, keep and provide for them. Has there ever been an issue which concerns the church and people of God in which the Lord Jesus has failed them, being unable to mitigate their difficult case and circumstances? Outwardly, the path they have been brought to walk may be very distressing and trying. Look how it was for the apostle Paul when he came to the end of his life. He is imprisoned in Rome, arraigned before Nero, and he has this sad lament to make, "At my first answer no man stood with me, but all men forsook me: I pray God that it may not be laid to their charge" (2 Tim. 4:16). "Notwithstanding," he says. And friends, there is always a *notwithstanding* or *nevertheless,* as it concerns the church and people of God. "Notwithstanding the Lord stood with me, and strengthened me; that by me the preaching might be fully known, and that all the Gentiles might hear: and I was delivered out of the mouth of the lion. And the Lord shall deliver me from every evil work, and will preserve me unto his heavenly kingdom: to whom be glory for ever and ever. Amen" (2 Tim. 4: 17-18). Ah, may we know that same spirit as the apostle, in the Lord's gracious dealings *with us,* to show forth his strength and the power of his arm to deliver and save his people.

Why, what a blessed testimony we have in the truth of the gospel, that Christ has power to save to the uttermost all that come unto God by him. See it demonstrated in the very realities of the life, sufferings and death of our Lord Jesus Christ. Yes, as we read, he was crucified through weakness but he was raised in power. Look at all that Jesus Christ accomplished. He overcame sin, Satan, death, hell and the grave. What a glorious victory he has obtained, and he is still that glorious victor. And as the apostle reminds us, "we are more than conquerors through him that loved us" (Rom. 8:37).

"I will shew thee great and mighty things which thou knowest not." "Great things" can be interpreted as *hidden* things, things that are not perceived by the natural eye, but which God bears witness to in his word, and which he makes known to Jeremiah. See how we find this in the sixth verse. Ah, see that in all the desolations coming upon Jerusalem, the Lord has not forgotten the remnant of his people. He has not forgotten the covenant he had made with them. He has not overlooked the promises he had given them. "Behold," he says. Here is something to take particular notice of. "Behold, I will bring it health and cure." And the Lord declares here what *he* will do. He is not directing us to what *man* can do, or what we might expect men to do, but what *he* will do. Are not all things in his hand and under his control? "Behold, *I* will bring it health and cure, and *I* will cure them, and will reveal unto them the abundance of peace and truth."

In Psalm 71, the psalmist desired to shew forth the Lord's strength to his generation, that strength which is revealed to us in gospel days in the person of our Lord Jesus Christ, to whom all authority and power is given in heaven and earth. He is the only Saviour of sinners, to the praise of the glory of his great and holy name. Friends, not one of us who has been brought to trust in him by his grace, shall ever be brought into confusion. Ah, you may say that is a bold statement to make! But we base it upon the authority of God's word, the certainty that what he has spoken shall most surely be fulfilled. Has he saved his people with an everlasting salvation? Can then that salvation be negated? Blessed be his great and holy name—*never*. It is spoken of our Lord Jesus Christ that he cannot fail. He has not failed and never will fail in all that pertains to the temporal welfare and eternal salvation of his people. To his name be all the glory.

And the psalmist says that he desired to shew God's "power to every one that is to come" (Ps. 71:18). We see that power here displayed, the power of his grace, the wonder of his love and mercy made known to guilty, wretched and ruined sinners. "I will bring it health and cure, and I will cure them, and will reveal unto them the abundance of peace and truth." That unquestionably has blessed application to the people of God.

What is set before us here in God's dealings with the inhabitants of Jerusalem and his promises to them, has its gloriously complete fulfilment in the precious truth of the gospel, in the wonders of God's grace to the true church of Jesus Christ. "I will bring it health and cure." If we might put it this way, what was the complaint, what was the disease, what was the *root* of these distresses at Jerusalem, of which the Lord speaks by his servant Jeremiah? *It was sin*. It was man's sin and alienation from God. And be assured of this, it is the root of all that we see at the present time. The root of it is man's sin and alienation from God, that he neither acknowledges God, neither is he thankful. See how God assures us of this solemn fact when he says that his wrath "is revealed from heaven against all ungodliness and unrighteousness of men" (Rom. 1:18). The root of these things is *sin,* not merely a disease. *Sin* is ruinous, *utterly ruinous,* to fallen, sinful men and women.

And the only cure, the only provision that is made—and O the blessedness of it!—we see displayed in the power of God's grace in all he has provided in the person and work of our Lord Jesus Christ. O does not John the Baptist cry, and may we know the blessed reality of what he cried and know what it is to draw out for ourselves the blessings that flow from it: "Behold, the Lamb of God, which taketh away the sin of the world" (John 1:29). What is set forth there, embraces the one true church of God, all his elect, sinners as every one of them is, whom the Lord calls by his grace in his appointed time. The only remedy is found in the person and finished work of the Lord Jesus Christ, in his sufferings, death and glorious resurrection. There the full price was paid for the sins of his people to satisfy all the demands of God's holy justice. Friends, wrath can never take place on those who are brought to shelter beneath the precious atoning blood of the Lord Jesus Christ.

"I will bring it health and cure, and I will cure them, and will reveal unto them the abundance of peace and truth." O what abundance of peace and truth the gospel sets before us in the fulness and power of the grace of God to save to the uttermost all that come unto him through Jesus Christ. Yes, what do ruined, wretched, hell-deserving sinners find when brought in God's appointed time to call on his name in a deep sense of their utterly lost and ruined state, however far off from God they may feel to be? Do they find that God turns a deaf ear to their cry, that he takes no notice of them, indeed spurns them, has nothing to do with them? No, they find and prove to the praise of the glory of our God, that our Lord Jesus Christ is not only one mighty to save, but he still speaks to the heart of the needy, guilty sinner: "Be thou clean" (Matt. 8:3). Ah, what power and love are displayed in the cleansing efficacy of the precious atoning blood of the Lord Jesus Christ, when the sinner is brought to shelter beneath it and know its cleansing power in his soul. Such a cleansing it is! And it is that alone through which we have access unto and acceptance before God.

The psalmist said, "I am as a wonder unto many," (Ps. 71:7) and the greatest wonder to the Lord's people is that the Lord should ever look favourably upon them, ever reveal himself to them in pardoning love and mercy. The greatest wonder of all to them is that they shall be found among the living family of God, in the hope and expectation of seeing his face and being found before the throne of glory, clothed in the righteousness of Jesus Christ and washed in his precious blood.

What a testimony is given in the book of the Revelation as that question is put to John: "What are these which are arrayed in white robes? and whence came they?" "These are they which came out of great tribulation, and have washed their robes, and made them white in the blood of the Lamb. Therefore are they before the throne of God, and serve him day and night in his temple: and he that sitteth on the throne shall dwell among them … and God shall wipe away all tears from their eyes" (Rev. 7:13–17). What a glorious prospect is that for the church and people of God, for every poor sinner brought to believe and trust in the Lord Jesus Christ alone. Friend, he is able to save unto the uttermost. In him is treasured up all the fulness of grace and truth. These are not cunningly devised fables. They are glorious realities.

The Lord declares here, "Behold, I will bring it health and cure, and I will cure them, and will reveal unto them the abundance of peace and truth." O for grace to be found among the people to whom this promise is made. Surely what a mercy if there is the evidence with us, not only at this time, but in every aspect of our lives, that we are those who call upon the name of the Lord. What a work of grace is that in the soul of a sinner, which brings them to call upon the name of the Lord, crying unto him for mercy, in true confession and godly sorrow over their sins! What a work of grace it is for them to be given the believing realisation that what he has graciously promised he is most surely able to perform and will perform, to the praise of the glory of his name! They that call upon the name of the Lord shall never be brought into confusion. Our hope, our help is treasured up alone in our God and Saviour.

And surely at such a time as this, how we need more and more to realise the blessedness of fellowship and communion with our Lord and Saviour Jesus Christ. As we come before the Lord at the throne of his grace may we increasingly know union together and prayerful concern for one another as brethren. And may that be manifest in the practical outworking of it in our lives. Let us indeed love as brethren. May our lives evidence that we know and love the Lord. May we call upon his name at such a time as this, seeking that he will graciously appear for us, undertake for us, grant us delivering mercies and hear the cries of his people.

May we also see the Lord going forth in accomplishing his sovereign will. We know not what that will is, but his word assures of *one thing*—and what an application it has to our souls at this particular time. The apostle, writing to the Romans, says *"We know."* Yes, we are thankful that there are things which are not matters of speculation. *"We know* that all things work together for good to them that love God, to them who are the called according to his purpose" (Rom. 8:28). It may not appear how that can be as we view things merely from a human standpoint. But viewing it in the light of what God reveals to us in his word, does not all become clear?

"I will bring it health and cure, and I will cure them, and will reveal unto them the abundance of peace and truth." "Call unto me, and I will answer thee, and shew thee great and mighty things, which thou knowest not." O to be thus led and taught of the Lord, brought to trust in him at all times and to pour out our hearts before him. Brethren, "God is a refuge for us" (Ps. 62:8).

May the Lord add his blessing. Amen.

3

HE LAID HIS RIGHT HAND UPON ME, SAYING UNTO ME, FEAR NOT

Tuesday evening 24 March 2020

"And when I saw him, I fell at his feet as dead. And he laid his right hand upon me, saying unto me, Fear not; I am the first and the last: I am he that liveth, and was dead; and, behold, I am alive for evermore, Amen; and have the keys of hell and of death" (Revelation 1:17-18).

How this opening chapter in the book of the Revelation sets before us the greatness and glory of our Lord and Saviour Jesus Christ, as he is the one true God, God manifest in the flesh, the great and glorious head of the church! And surely all that John records here of the things he saw and heard must be a source of true encouragement and consolation to the living family of God, not only at this time, but at all times and in all circumstances in which we are found. I trust we may ever increasingly prove it to be so.

Here we are assured that our Lord Jesus Christ is "mighty to save" as his word declares. How gloriously is that set before us when we read that this Revelation is "from Jesus Christ, who is the faithful witness, and the first begotten of the dead, and the prince of the kings of the earth. Unto him that loved us, and washed us from our sins in his own blood." What a fulness is in those words! And then we look at what the Lord says here to John, when he fell at his feet as dead, overwhelmed when he beheld the risen and glorified Lord and Saviour Jesus Christ. The Lord laid his hand upon him saying, "Fear not." And friends, he speaks that *fear not,* not only to John but also to his church and people still.

What is set before us here encompassed all the brethren in those seven churches in Asia who had been brought to believe and trust alone in the Lord Jesus Christ by divine grace. But it also encompasses *everyone* who is brought by divine grace to believe and trust alone in the Lord Jesus Christ. "Fear not," he says. O is there not much to fear in our circumstances and through that sin within which does "so easily beset us"? (Heb. 12:1). Very real are the fears at this present time concerning this coronavirus and what is brought upon us in changing our whole way of life. Though I trust we are believers, yet we cannot claim we are free from the fears that human nature is subject to at such a time as this. But O, what mercy we are assured of, when the Lord speaks a "fear not." Not only does he mean what he says, but he imparts that which brings true encouragement and consolation. He lays a solid foundation for us on which we can rest. And faith which is the gift of God receives and embraces this word of our living Saviour. O what a foundation is laid in this word from the very mouth of our Lord Jesus Christ himself, for the encouragement and comfort of the people of God in life, whatever the circumstances, and also in death as well.

Yes, these are very unusual circumstances in which we are found today and meet for the service this evening. But O, the mercy is that our God is the same. All that the Lord Jesus Christ revealed to John in this Revelation to send to those churches in Asia, is living reality for his people still today. Here are not cunningly devised fables. Here are those things which are real, great and glorious, and may we be filled with wonder and adoration as was John. O to be overwhelmed—may it be so with us—*overwhelmed* with the wonder of the greatness, glory and love of the Lord Jesus Christ to sinners such as you and me!

And what does John here declare? "Unto him that loved us." Who loved us? The great and glorious Lord and Saviour Jesus Christ, described as "the faithful witness, and the first begotten of the dead, and the prince of the kings of the earth." "Unto *him* that loved us, and washed us from our sins in his own blood." O what great, glorious and wondrous things has the Lord Jesus Christ wrought out for us by his life, sufferings, death and resurrection. He has brought in everlasting righteousness for us. He has put away our sins by the sacrifice of himself. This word of God before us testifies to these things. And I trust they are sealed in your heart and mine by the gracious operations of the Holy Spirit. O may he say afresh to your soul and mine this night: "Peace be unto thee; fear not: thou shalt not die" (Judges 6:23) because full satisfaction has been given by the finished work of our Lord Jesus Christ. This delivers us from the death which we sinners justly deserve, as under the curse and condemnation of God's holy law. If friends, he has delivered us from so great a death, have we not the assurance he will deliver us now, and in all that may yet come? Shall we not then commit ourselves and our ways, wholly into his hand, and trust him alone who has delivered us from so great a death and imparted unto us spiritual and eternal life?

Look what the Lord Jesus said to Martha when those sisters were so distressed at the death of their brother Lazarus, and at what appeared to them to be the response of Jesus at that time. The Lord says to Martha, "I am the resurrection, and the life: he that believeth in me, though he were dead, yet shall he live: And whosoever liveth and believeth in me shall never die. Believest thou this?" (John 11:25–26). O friends, that same glorious Saviour and Redeemer says to *us* that, as he delivered us from so great a death, so he is our spiritual and eternal life. All that pertains to our spiritual and eternal welfare is treasured up in the person of our Lord Jesus Christ. For his believing people are *one* with him now, and will be one with him through all eternity. And if we are thus one with him, can he ever forget us, can he ever forsake one of his own? Are not his love and compassions everlasting to them in all their weaknesses, infirmities and needs? O the blessedness then of what the Lord speaks here: "Fear not."

Let us look at the circumstance of John as exiled on that isle of Patmos. Now an old man, he is severed from the brethren to whom he ministered in Asia, and is evidently in a very lonely situation. But he says, "I was in the Spirit on the Lord's day." Yes, *we* are separated from one another. In that sense, our situation is lonely. But though we are separated at present from one another, yet, as John found in that lonely place, we can never be separated from the Spirit of our Lord and Saviour Jesus Christ. We can never be severed from that great love wherewith he hath loved us.

O may we realise more of the true bond of love that binds us to one another as brethren and essentially binds us, in the riches of divine grace, to our Lord Jesus Christ, who "loved us and washed us from our sins in his own blood." During this time of separation from each other that now lies before us, may we not be left to forget one another or the welfare of the Lord's cause among us. May we be increasingly drawn out in prayer to the Lord our God who has promised to be with us. May he preserve us to glorify his name together. May we have grace to bear witness at this time to whose we are, whom we serve and in whom is our trust and confidence even in all the dangers around us. Through the Lord's mercies, may it be evident that we are those who know what it is to draw water out of the wells of salvation. O what refreshment is surely found for us in the glorious truth of the gospel, as brought to us in the ministry and reading of the word and as graciously applied by the Holy Spirit.

John, lonely on the isle of Patmos, was not forgotten. He was not forsaken. That very situation was used by the Lord. John experienced something greater and more glorious than he had ever known before. He, with Peter and James, had that glorious revelation of the Lord on the mount of transfiguration. But did not what he viewed on Patmos exceed what he saw on the mount? The point I make is that the circumstances were distressing but what blessings were in it. Jesus Christ was revealed to him afresh as he had never beheld him before. Wonders of redeeming love and mercy were opened to him.

And the Lord unfolded to him his purposes for the welfare of the churches. What searching messages did the Lord send to them by John. May this likewise be a time when the things set forth in this Revelation are unfolded to us as the people of God. Here may we see God's purposes for his own glory and for the welfare and eternal salvation of his church. For this book sets before us the full and final manifestation of the purposes of God in the whole creation, in the redemption of his people, and in the final consummation of all things.

Man fears the scourge that is now upon the nations, but a more awful and solemn judgment awaits this fallen world. The day is hastening when the Lord shall come the second time in power and great glory. See how John refers to it here. He says, "Behold, he cometh with clouds; and every eye shall see him, and they also which pierced him: and all kindreds of the earth shall wail because of him. Even so, Amen." Ah, do men think the present danger is great? Friends, how awful will be that time when he comes with clouds as described here. Then shall the ungodly say to the "mountains and rocks, Fall on us, and hide us from the face of him that sitteth on the throne, and from the wrath of the Lamb: for the great day of his wrath is come; and who shall be able to stand?" (Rev. 6:16–17).

How great is the grace which brings such sinners as you and me to know the only refuge for our souls, and to be assured that when that great last day comes it will not be a day of judgment to us. It will be a day of the glorious resurrection of the dead, when the redeemed soul and body will be re-united and live for ever with the Lord.

I have not time to dwell further upon that resurrection day. The point I make is that we may think the danger great today, but O may our whole concern and desire be to praise and thank the Lord for having delivered us from so great a death. For we have the glorious assurance, as sealed home to us by the Holy Spirit, that Jesus Christ is our all and in all. Every grace and every favour is ours and flows to us through Jesus' precious blood, "who hath loved us and washed us from our sins in his own blood."

But John says, "he laid his right hand upon me, saying unto me, Fear not." As I have said, what a revelation John is given here of the risen and ascended Lord and Saviour Jesus Christ. He gives a description, yet his language is inadequate to set forth the glory of our ascended Lord and Saviour, "the prince of the kings of the earth," the creator and upholder of all things by the word of his power. "He holds all nature in his hand." I say, can language adequately express the greatness and glory of our Lord Jesus Christ? Can it adequately express what is unquestionably set forth here of his love to his church and people?

John beholds our Lord Jesus as the true king upon his throne, as the great high priest over the house of God. And blessed be the Lord's great and holy name, he ever sits upon that throne of grace. Without doubt, these are words of encouragement and consolation to the church and people of God. But remember that in the Lord's messages to those seven churches, there is warning also. He manifests his displeasure with them and calls them to repentance and godly sorrow. He directs them to cry unto him for mercy, as well as encourages them in their walk and conversation in this fallen world and in their relationships with one another as brethren in the Lord. He also directs them to ever seek and keep in view that which is for the glory of his great and holy name. Yes, may we give ear, and heed those things. As is repeated again and again after each message to those churches, "He that hath an ear, let him hear what the Spirit saith unto the churches" (Rev. 2&3).

"And when I saw him, I fell at his feet as dead. And he laid his right hand upon me." O there is something very precious in that. *"He laid his right hand upon me."* O what a touch is that, a touch of his love, a touch that the leper experienced when he cried "Lord, if thou wilt, thou canst make me clean...And Jesus put forth his hand, and touched him, saying, I will; be thou clean" (Matt. 8:2–3). Yes, here is peace, here is gracious restoration, here is the testimony afresh of his pardoning love and mercy. Here is the very reality of that word, "who loved us." Is not that love manifest here to his servant John? "He laid his right hand upon me, saying unto me, Fear not; I am the first and the last: I am he that liveth, and was dead; and, behold, I am alive for evermore."

"I am he that *liveth.*" As I have mentioned to you so many times, we do not worship a dead Christ. We worship him that died for us but who rose again as the ever-living one. Do we not need to be established in the believing realisation of this truth, certainly in such a day as this? Our Lord Jesus Christ is the *ever-living* one, as blessedly set before us in this first chapter of the Revelation, when he proclaims, *"I am Alpha and Omega, the first and the last."* Can language be more emphatic in setting forth the sovereign power and authority of our Lord Jesus Christ? And as he ever liveth, so his people live through him, and shall live through him and with him to all eternity! We are assured of that, make no mistake about it.

"I am he that liveth, *and was dead.*" That word *"was dead"* surely directs us to Gethsemane and Calvary where he suffered and *died* for us. For what purpose? To save us from our sins. O what a price was paid there! What wonders of his love were manifest, that he who knew no sin, was made sin for us, that we might be made the righteousness of God in him. He was *dead.* Why friends, what a foundation of assurance does this lay for us. Can anything be brought against the child of God to bring them under just condemnation? What does the word of God declare? "There is therefore now no condemnation to them which are in Christ Jesus," "to them that love God…who are the called according to his purpose" (Rom. 5:1; 8:28). Their "no condemnation" is founded on the truth that Jesus *died* for them.

How can there be any condemnation of them, as they are found in Jesus Christ? There is nothing to condemn them for. All that divine justice demanded has been fully satisfied in the life and death of our Lord Jesus Christ, the surety and substitute of his people. Does God condemn them? No. "It is God that justifieth. Who is he that condemneth? It is Christ that died, yea rather, that is risen again, who is even at the right hand of God, who also maketh intercession for us" (Rom. 8:33–34).

"I am he that liveth, and was dead: and, behold, *I am alive for evermore.*" O, how this tells us that in the person of our Lord Jesus Christ we have a God who is not afar off. He is ever *near* to his people and ever *dear* to them. May we realise that more and more, especially when we are passing through the present time. O to realise more of the preciousness of Jesus Christ, that he is the refuge of our souls; he has put away our sins by the sacrifice of himself and has brought in everlasting righteousness for us. One says, "he that has made my heaven secure." And blessed be his great and holy name, heaven is secure for every believer. What good will he who has made our "heaven secure" ever deny his people? Let us then cast ourselves wholly into his hands and find rest for our souls in the unchanging love and faithfulness of our Lord Jesus Christ.

He says *"Amen."* The word "Amen" emphatically states that this person is the one and only true God. He is God manifest in the flesh, our Lord Jesus Christ, coequal with the Father and the

Holy Spirit, "Christ...who is over all, God blessed for ever" (Rom. 9:5).

And the word further says that he has "the keys of hell and of death." What an important implication does that have for us at this particular time, when death, as it were, stalks the nation and the world in the current epidemic, which many so greatly fear. Ah, the keys of hell and of death are in the hands of our Lord Jesus Christ. All can be summed up in the hymn we sometimes sing,

> "Plagues and deaths around me fly;
> Till he bids, I cannot die;
> Not a single shaft can hit,
> Till the God of love sees fit."

Friends, even if it is the Lord's purpose that death should overtake us, yet as a believer we have a glorious hope and expectation. Do we not profess that in Jesus Christ we have eternal life? We have the assurance, as the apostle could say, that to be absent from the body, is to be present with the Lord. "We know." he says. O may that truth ever be sealed in our hearts. "We *know* that if our earthly house of this tabernacle were dissolved, we have a building of God, an house not made with hands, eternal in the heavens" (2 Cor. 5:1). Glorious truth! A place is prepared for his people as he himself has declared in John fourteen: "I go to prepare a place for you" (v.2).

"The keys of hell and of death." These keys are not in the power of man, nor of the devil himself. They are in the hands of our Lord Jesus Christ. Every aspect of this fallen world, the lives of all men and women, and essentially all that concerns his church and people, are in the hands of our Lord Jesus Christ who hath "loved us, and washed us from our sins in his own blood."

"He laid his right hand upon me, saying unto me, Fear not." O may that word *"fear not"* come home afresh to us tonight, founded on what our Lord Jesus Christ has gloriously revealed here of himself as the sovereign ruler in heaven and earth.

I conclude with those words: he hath "loved us, and washed us from our sins in his own blood." I repeat that this is he who has "delivered us from so great a death" (2 Cor. 1:10). Friends, what is there to fear? Is not all that concerns us in the hands our

Lord Jesus Christ, as we are assured here? O may he speak afresh to your soul and mine tonight: "Fear thou not, for I am with thee" (Isa. 41:10), "I will not fail thee, nor forsake thee" (Heb. 13:5), "I will not leave thee, until I have done that which I have spoken to thee of" (Gen. 28:15). And the Lord is faithful that promised, blessed be his great and holy name.

The Lord add his blessing. Amen.

4

THEREFORE I WILL LOOK UNTO THE LORD

Lord's day morning 29 March 2020

"Therefore I will look unto the Lord; I will wait for the God of my salvation: my God will hear me" (Micah 7:7).

From the opening verses of this chapter it is very evident that Micah lived in times of great desolation, which caused him much distress and sorrow. The situation which prevailed in the nation at that time was brought home to him in a very personal way. Now as we consider these words of the Lord the Holy Spirit speaking through his servant the prophet, do they not have an application to the situation in which we find ourselves at this time, when we are unable to gather together as we usually do? Yet, though separated as we are, we are thankful we can come together around the word and meet at the throne of grace. Like the prophet, our eyes are drawn away from all that is of self, all that is of the creature, to look only and wholly unto the Lord our God.

When we consider the situation that prevails at this time in the nations of the world, through this virus and its sad effects upon people generally, the sickness and death, we would not be indifferent to these things. May our concern be to pray for those in authority over us, that wisdom may be granted them and the means used owned by God to mitigate the distresses. And if it be his holy will, may there be deliverance from this pestilence. Yet we would not put our confidence in man. We pray for grace to turn away from all that is of the creature, as the prophet does here, and look wholly to the Lord, depending entirely on his sovereign will and good pleasure, to give rest for our souls and bodies. Through his grace, may we have the conscious sense that he is our God, even our Father which is in heaven.

One of the most sad and distressing things for us is that in the nation as a whole, and amongst those in authority, there is no recognition of the Lord our God. There is no sense of the need for God's help, no going to him to seek his mercy to deliver us, if it is his will. In one sense, we should not be surprised that it is so, fallen man in his very nature being enmity to God, apart from sovereign distinguishing grace. Yet, though we see no nationwide recognition of our God, may it not be so with those of us who profess to know and love the Lord Jesus Christ. I trust we have a right concern for the welfare of those among whom we live in our nation. But may our hearts be drawn out in prayer to God that he will hear the cries of his people and still remember mercy in the midst of deserved wrath.

We would particularly have prayerful concern for those involved in caring for the sick and dying at this time, in the difficulties and dangers with which they are beset. O may the Lord have mercy upon them. May they know his upholding and preserving. There are those in our own company involved in frontline care of the sick. May we prayerfully commit them, as we seek to commit all, into the hands of our God, knowing that all things are possible with him. All is in his hand and under his control. *There* alone can we find encouragement and consolation. The days may be dark, the times distressing, restrictions pressed upon us, yet in all these things may it be our whole concern to be submissive to the will of our God. For our souls, as well as for our bodies, may we know what is expressed in those words of the apostle: "Casting all your care upon him; for he careth for you" (1 Pet. 5:7).

Here we see Micah not ignoring or unfeeling with regard to the situation he describes—far from it. But he realised there was no remedy in anything of the creature. We find him turning alone to the Lord his God. "Therefore," he says, that is, as these things are so, 'where can I go?' And where can we go in our day? To whom shall we look? Ah friends, what a mercy it is that we have a God to go to. We have one who in his word assures his believing people through his grace, that he is our Father which is in heaven who has reconciled us unto himself through the redemption that is in Christ Jesus. Moreover, he assures us that he is aware of all that concerns us. He knows all our need, even before we ask of him. Yet he still directs and encourages us in his word, to call upon his name, as did Micah. Speaking through Isaiah, the Lord says, "Look unto me, and be ye saved, all the ends of the earth: for I am God, and there is none else" (Isa. 45:22).

"Therefore will I look unto the LORD." O friend, what a mercy to be brought off and away from all trust and confidence in self or created things. The Lord alone is the one to whom we go and upon whom we seek to cast all our care, calling upon his great and holy name.

"I will wait for the God of my salvation." Precious truth! Not only is he a God to look to, but a God who is the God of our salvation. Let us wait upon him in prayer, wait upon him with praise, wait upon him in seeking to know and do his will at this time. O may he keep us close to himself. "I will wait for the God of my salvation."

Consider what is said in the context of these words in verses fourteen and fifteen. In those verses, is not the prophet looking to the Lord and the waiting upon the God of his salvation? Is not his soul going out in petitions unto the Lord? He says, "Feed thy people with thy rod, the flock of thine heritage, which dwell solitarily in the wood, in the midst of Carmel: let them feed in Bashan and Gilead, as in the days of old. According to the days of thy coming out of the land of Egypt will I shew unto him marvellous things."

"Feed thy people." Here our attention is surely directed to the great God of our salvation, God revealed in the person of our Lord Jesus Christ, the great and good shepherd of his people. I read Psalm 23 with this in mind, for the psalmist there says, "The LORD is my shepherd: I shall not want." Ah friends, I trust this morning we can come to him as the great shepherd of the sheep, as *my* shepherd. O what a precious truth is that—the Lord seal it to your soul and mine—that "the LORD is *my* shepherd; I shall not want." What gracious confidence is here manifest in the mercies of the Lord made known to the soul, as he blessedly reveals himself as *our* shepherd in the truth of the gospel.

Look at John chapter ten in which the Lord Jesus says, "I am the good shepherd: the good shepherd giveth his life for the sheep." Speaking of his own, he says, "I know my sheep, and am known of mine." "My sheep hear my voice, and I know them, and they follow me: and I give unto them eternal life; and they shall never perish, neither shall any man pluck them out of my hand." Does not that assure us of the love, the care, and the provision of the Lord for his own at all times and in all circumstances? Can anything separate us from the love of God which is in Christ Jesus our Lord? Look again at those words at the close of Romans chapter eight to which I have referred you many times. What an application they still have to us, I trust, particularly at this time. "For I am persuaded, that neither death, nor life, nor angels, nor principalities, nor powers, nor things present, nor things to come, nor height, nor depth, nor any other creature, shall be able to separate us from the love of God, which is in Christ Jesus our Lord."

The prophet here in verse fourteen looks to the God of his salvation as revealed in the person of Jesus Christ, the great and good shepherd of his sheep. He says: "Feed thy people with thy rod, the flock of thine heritage, which dwell solitarily in the wood, in the midst of Carmel: let them feed in Bashan and Gilead, as in the days of old." He speaks of the Lord's people as being a scattered people at that time. We might say that they were unable to gather together. But gathering together must surely ever be the desire of the people of God. Should we not highly prize the privilege that is afforded us to meet together for the worship of the Lord's name? At this time, when we are unable to meet, is it not brought home to us, how great has been the privilege we have been granted to be able to gather together around the word, as brethren in the Lord? How often have we lost sight of this favour. Now that the privilege is denied us, may we desire to attend on these things more diligently and prayerfully in the future, if the Lord will, concerned that he alone be honoured and our souls truly blessed in feeding together on his word.

The prophet here then speaks of the Lord's people as "the flock of thine heritage." And, though a people scattered, a people unable to gather as we do, yet what a mercy it is that as believers we are "the flock of *thine* heritage," those whom he acknowledges as his own. The Lord speaks of his people as, *"my* sheep," "the sheep of *my* pasture," those that he not only owns (blessed truth) but loves with an everlasting love. O does not the prophet declare that the Lord the Holy Spirit had appeared unto him, saying, "Yea, I have loved thee with an everlasting love: therefore with lovingkindness have I drawn thee" (Jer. 31:2). May that word speak afresh to your soul and mine this morning.

"The flock of thine heritage." O his flock are a tried people, an afflicted and distressed people as they pass through this wilderness world. "Many are the afflictions of the righteous," as the Lord testifies (Ps. 34:19). But does the care of the Lord Jesus Christ for his people ever cease? No, blessed be his great and holy name, his care for them, his love for them knows no end, it knows no change. All the circumstances we may be passing through do not alter one iota the love of the Lord to us or his care over us. May the Lord seal *that* afresh to your soul and mine.

"Feed thy people with thy rod." This is expressive of the Lord's feeding his people by his word. It can be rendered as "Feed thy people with *the rod of thy word*" And is not the word of the truth of the gospel, spiritual meat and drink to the living family of God? O is it not needful for the true spiritual welfare of our souls? O where should we be if we had not the word of God given us in holy scripture, and that word known in its blessed fulness in the person of our Lord Jesus Christ, the eternal Word? Remember,

>"The written and the incarnate Word
>In all things are the same."

Here is spiritual nourishment for the living family of God. May the Lord so own and use his word to us, not only in the preaching of it, but also in our reading of it and meditating upon it in our private devotions at this time. It must always be *the* true nourishment of our souls through the Holy Spirit ever graciously bringing us to realise our need and whole dependence on our Lord and Saviour Jesus Christ.

I particularly feel that dependence myself in conducting these services in this present time. Who is sufficient for these things? Has not the Lord spoken, and I trust he has spoken it to my own soul and may we each realise it more and more, "My grace is sufficient for thee: for my strength is made perfect in weakness"

(2 Cor. 12:9). We have nowhere else to look, none other to depend upon, as the prophet here expresses it: "Therefore I will look unto the LORD; I will wait for the God of my salvation: my God will hear me."

Micah directs his attention and ours to the Lord, the great and the good shepherd: "Feed thy people with thy rod, the flock of thine heritage, which dwell solitarily in the wood, in the midst of Carmel: let them feed in Bashan and Gilead, as in the days of old." O friends, do we not long for that time when there may be the restoration of our privilege to meet together around the word of God? Not that we place our trust in being able to meet, but how we desire to come together to realise the blessings described here, of feeding as in days past, with the gracious sense of the Lord's presence with us.

Is not this important for the church and people of God? They are described as the sheep of his pasture. Sheep do not dwell alone. Sheep dwell together in a flock. And the term, "flock of thine heritage," is expressive of the Lord's being one with his people and they one with him. Surely is not the welfare of the church wholly in the hands of our Lord Jesus Christ, our great and good shepherd? So I trust we are brought, through grace, to have a real concern for the privilege he is pleased to grant his people, of gathering around his word, as one with him and with one another. O to know the blessings of his grace for our true spiritual welfare in union and fellowship which is of the Lord, when we meet together again, subject to his will.

Friends, what a promise, what a prospect, is here set before us in verse fifteen: "According to the days of thy coming out of the land of Egypt will I shew unto him *marvellous things.*" What marvellous things did God display in Israel's coming out of the land of Egypt? Why, look at the deliverance he wrought for them that night when the angel of death passed through the land of Egypt, and all the first born died who were not under the shelter of the blood sprinkled upon the door posts and lintels! What a deliverance God wrought for Israel at that time!

See how he delivered Israel in leading them out of Egypt. Look at what took place at the Red sea. What great fear they had, being aware of the pursuing armies of the Egyptians, and conscious that they had no escape as viewed from a human stand-point. O how the Lord appeared for them! "Fear ye not, stand still, and see the salvation of the LORD, which he will shew to you to day: for the Egyptians whom ye have seen to day, ye shall see them again no more for ever. The LORD shall fight for you, and ye shall hold your peace" (Ex. 14:14). See how the Lord opened a way where there was no way, and Israel crossed the Red sea dry-shod, while their enemies perished in the waters.

"I will shew unto him marvellous things." Does not that shadow forth the greater deliverance the Lord has appointed and provided for his people? Is not this set forth in the precious truth of the gospel, in all that Jesus is and all that he has done for us in his life, sufferings, death and resurrection? O that precious blood which still speaks pardon and peace to guilty sinners! May we know the blessedness of it, its true soul-reviving, sin-pardoning, and God-glorifying power, to the praise of the glory of his name. What marvellous things the word of his grace bears witness to! He has delivered us from the curse of a broken law. He has brought in everlasting righteousness for us. He assures us of the blessings of pardon and peace and the very reality of eternal life! Yes friends, the Lord is our help; the Lord is our hope; the Lord is our salvation. And at such a time as this, let us look unto the Lord, let us wait for the God of our salvation, as did Micah. *"My God"* will hear me. O may each one of us know the same blessed realisation.

And what a God is our God! See what the prophet exclaims in verses eighteen to twenty: "Who is a God like unto thee, that pardoneth iniquity, and passeth by the transgression of the remnant of his heritage? he retaineth not his anger for ever, because he delighteth in mercy. He will turn again, he will have compassion upon us; he will subdue our iniquities; and thou wilt cast all their sins into the depths of the sea. Thou wilt perform the truth to Jacob, and the mercy to Abraham, which thou hast sworn unto our fathers from the days of old."

What more can be said? What more needs to be said? Let us look unto the Lord. Let us wait for the God of our salvation; *my* God, *our* God will hear us. He indeed is a prayer hearing and a prayer answering God. By his grace, may our trust and confidence be placed in him. Friends, the days are distressing, the times are dark, but our help is in the Lord our God. And what a God is our God! "There is none like unto the God of Jeshurun, who rideth upon the heaven in thy help, and in his excellency on the sky. The eternal God is thy refuge, and underneath are the everlasting arms" (Deut. 33:26–27). Glorious, precious truth!

"What more can he say than to you he has said,
You who unto Jesus for refuge have fled?"

I will leave the remarks there. May the Lord add his blessing. Amen.

5

I AM THE RESURRECTION AND THE LIFE

Lord's day evening 29 March 2020

"Jesus said unto her, I am the resurrection, and
the life: he that believeth in me, though he
were dead, yet shall he live: And whosoever
liveth and believeth in me shall never die.
Believest thou this?" (John 11:25–26).

One thing very evident in this account is the great love and
compassion of the Lord Jesus Christ to his own. Truly, he is our
great high priest who is not unacquainted with the feeling of our
infirmities. O how gracious is the Lord as he draws near unto his
people still, though he is now enthroned in glory. We behold him
there as the great high priest over the house of God, but he is not
a God that is afar off from his people. He is ever near to them,
manifesting his love for them, and his care over them, He does
so through the gracious ministry of the Holy Spirit who has
received of the things of the Lord Jesus Christ, and whose office
it is to show them unto us. May it be so afresh with us this
evening, as we look at what is brought before us in this chapter,
and particularly these words of our Lord Jesus Christ to Martha.

Of this family at Bethany, Mary, Martha and their brother
Lazarus, we read that the Lord loved them. What a great thing is
that! *The Lord loved them.* Yet though he loved them, we see that
sickness and even death entered into their house, with all the
sorrow that occasioned. The sisters sent to Jesus. And notice how
they expressed themselves in sending to him at that very
distressing time. They said, "Lord, behold, he whom thou lovest
is sick." They didn't say, 'he who loved thee is sick.' Without
question, I verily believe that not only did the Lord love this
family but, as recipients of the grace of God, they loved the Lord
Jesus. But his sisters said, "Lord, behold, he whom *thou* lovest is
sick." See the ground of the plea of these sisters, and surely of

the people of God still. It is neither what we are, nor what have been our returns unto the Lord. I trust, by the grace of God, we have that love to him. May it be manifest in us. O at such a time as this, how necessary it is that our love to the Lord Jesus Christ be manifest in our love to the brethren for Jesus' sake.

The sisters said, "he whom *thou* lovest is sick." Friends, that is the foundation of our hope in all our approaches to the Lord— his sovereign, saving love and grace. It is founded on what he himself is, and what he alone has done, for the redemption and salvation of his people. All is revealed in his word, and all glorifies God alone. What a firm foundation is thus laid for the faith and hope of the living family of God. As I have said so many times, our hope is not in what *we* are, not in what *we* have done, but in what *Jesus Christ* is and has done.

From the human standpoint, the Lord's dealings here might seem strange towards those whom he loved, with sickness and death entering into their house. Are we not reminded by this, that the Lord's people are not free from sickness and death? In the present situation in which we are found, we cannot claim we are any better than all those around us, or that we are any less exposed to the virus that is prevalent in the earth. In all these things we seek grace to commit ourselves wholly into the Lord's hand in submission to his holy and sovereign will.

Believers are not free from the sicknesses and infirmities to which fallen human nature is subject in this fallen world. But, as evident in this account, we know that whatever comes into the path of the people of God, is appointed of God. The Lord has a purpose in it. He will display his mercy and goodness to his own, in sustaining them in their times of trial, sickness and need, and in delivering them at his appointed time, subject to his sovereign will. All is with one great end in view: the glory of our God and the true spiritual, eternal welfare of each one of his own.

We are poor judges of what will be most profitable for us. Being what we are, we are not free from the fears to which human nature is subject, and certainly not at such a time as this. Ah, as the Lord directs Martha here, what grace we need to bring us to look wholly to the Lord Jesus Christ, with trust and confidence in him. As we were reminded in the hymn we have just sung, in all the Lord's ways and dealings with us, he is "too wise to be mistaken…too good to be unkind." I know, in one sense, it might be easy for us to say that, and even to sing that hymn. But as needy sinners, beset with what we find in our personal lives of our own weakness and utter helplessness, O may the Lord's gracious dealings bring us to trust in him and him only.

Mary and Martha did not see at this time the purpose of the Lord's dealings with them. When they sent to him, saying, "he whom thou lovest is sick," the Lord did not come and things seemed to grow worse. Lazarus died and was buried four days before the Lord Jesus put in an appearance among them. Had he forgotten them? Was he neglectful of them? No, blessed be his great and holy name. The Lord knoweth what he will do. His thoughts are not our thoughts, nor his ways our ways. As the heavens are higher than the earth so are his ways higher than our ways, and his thoughts than our thoughts. And his word assures us that he knoweth the thoughts he thinks towards his people, thoughts of peace and not of evil, to give them an expected end. That was so here with Martha and Mary, though they could not at this stage trace the Lord's dealings with them. This was unquestionably for the trying of their faith and we see how their faith was exercised.

So it is with the people of God still, and surely it is so in the situation in which we are now found. Are we not brought, I trust, to the *exercise of faith* in those things which we profess to believe? Do we really believe them? Do we indeed receive what God has revealed to us in his holy word? Is our trust and confidence in the Lord Jesus Christ alone? O friends, how active is the evil one, and how we find the workings of unbelief ever ready to question the ways and dealings of God. How faith is put to a stand, as it were, at such a time as this. And if the exercise of faith was left to ourselves, where should we be? But blessed be the Lord's name, faith is the gift of God. At times, weakness of faith may be evidenced in our response to the Lord's dealings. It was so here with Martha and Mary. But real faith which is the gift of God cannot fail.

Remember what the Lord said to Peter: "I have prayed for thee, that thy faith fail not" (Luke 22:32). *That* is our security.

The Lord began the work. He imparts the grace of living faith. He brings us to look wholly to himself and to receive out of his fulness. And,

> "The work which his goodness began,
> The arm of his strength will complete."

I trust we prove increasingly, particularly at this time, that faith *is* the gift of God, and *the exercise of our faith also* is of and from the Lord. It is wholly dependent on him. Friends, will he neglect us? Will he forsake us? Did he neglect these sisters? No. See what the Lord said when the sisters sent to him: "This sickness is not unto death, but for the glory of God, that the Son of God might be glorified thereby." O that we might thus believe that the situation in which we are presently found, must be ultimately for the glory of God. And as I have said so many times, what is for the glory of God cannot but be for the true spiritual welfare of the living family of God.

"This sickness is not unto death, but for the glory of God, that the Son of God might be glorified thereby." You say, but Lazarus died. So he did. That was not the end of God's purposes in these things. His object was to show forth the glory of the Godhead of our Lord Jesus Christ, the God-man who has complete authority and power in heaven and earth. "None can stay his hand, or say unto him, What doest thou?" (Dan. 4:35).

The Lord Jesus comes to the place where Martha met him. She says, "Lord, if thou hadst been here, my brother had not died." Jesus said, "Thy brother shall rise again." Martha acknowledges that: "I know that he shall rise again in the resurrection at the last day." What a mercy to be established in believing the truth respecting the great end of all things, even the resurrection of the dead. Assurance has been given us of this by the resurrection of our Lord and Saviour Jesus Christ. O the glorious reality of that final consummation of all things, when the Lord shall come again in power and great glory, to receive his own unto himself and to judge the world in righteousness. What a day will that be when "the dead in Christ shall rise first: Then we which are alive and remain shall be caught up together with them in the clouds, to meet the Lord in the air: and so shall we ever be with the Lord" (1 Thess. 4:16–17). Is not that a glorious prospect, a blessed hope founded upon all that God in Christ is, as revealed to us in his holy word?

But the Lord's meaning when he says to Martha, "Thy brother shall rise again," not only embraced the resurrection at the last day, but what he was about to display of his eternal power and Godhead. Look at these words of our Lord Jesus to Martha, and I trust they are brought home to you and me this evening. Jesus said, "I am the resurrection, and the life: he that believeth in me, though he were dead, yet shall he live: And whosoever liveth and believeth in me shall never die. Believest thou this?" What great and glorious things are here set before us, all founded on what Jesus says: *"I am* the resurrection and the life." This is one of the great *"I am's"* in the gospel recorded by John, which bear witness to the *Godhead* of our Lord Jesus Christ. Behold here the *man* Christ Jesus, Jesus of Nazareth. But see what he declares: *"I am."* Does not this surely direct us to the glorious truth of his Godhead? He is co-equal with the Father and the Holy Spirit, one God over all, blessed for evermore.,

Friends, does not that put the situation that faces us today into a right context? Remember, he is the same Jesus still! We look above all that affects us to our Lord Jesus Christ, the glorious, great *I am*. How that name assures us of the constancy of his love, wisdom, power and goodness towards his own. Is not all that concerns us safe in the hands of our Lord Jesus Christ? What can sin do, what can Satan do, what can even the working of unbelief in our fallen nature do, what can ungodly men do, to bring any real or lasting harm to one child of God? For God is *their* God, as revealed to them in the person of our Lord Jesus Christ.

"I am the resurrection, and the life: he that believeth in me, though he were dead, yet shall he live." How wondrous is the grace of God here set before us, in the work of regeneration in each sinner whom the Lord calls by his grace. "Though he were dead, yet shall he live." Yes, God's people were dead in trespasses and sins—alienated from him by wicked works. But these words blessedly testify to the wonders of God's saving and sovereign grace in each one of his people when they *were* dead in trespasses and sins. The same almighty power that created the world, that said (in Gen. 1:3), "Let there be light: and there was light," speaks and the dead are raised. They are brought from death in sins, into the light, life and liberty of the gospel. Is that the work of man? Is it not the work of our sovereign God, the Lord the Holy Spirit?

Friends, if we know this blessed resurrection through the Lord's mercies towards us, O what a wonder it is! What a wonder that such sinners as you and I should be brought to know the Lord Jesus Christ and believe in him unto eternal life! Surely is not this to the praise of the glory of his name? God began this good work in us. Shall not he that hath begun this good work in us, perform it until the coming of our Lord Jesus Christ? Shall he ever neglect or forsake the work of his own hands? Blessed be his great and holy name, our God, as revealed to us in the person of our Lord Jesus Christ, never fails us. He is faithful and true.

"Whosoever liveth and believeth in me shall never die. Believest thou this?" Now as I have commented in the past, the word "whosoever believeth *shall never die,*" is true of each believer. "They never die." Yes, at the appointed time the soul departs from the body to be with Christ which is far better, and the body is laid in the grave, just as Lazarus was, and it returns to the dust from whence it was taken. But it is still that which the Lord has redeemed. The dust of his people is precious in his sight. It shall never be lost sight of by him. In the day of his coming, that same body that returned to dust shall rise again. Man scoffs at this. How can these things be? O what foolishness is this! O friends, it may appear foolishness to men, but to the living family of God it is a glorious reality. We are assured of it by the unchanging word of our God, which proclaims his power to accomplish what he has promised, to the praise of the glory of his own great name.

But, "Believest thou this?" This question is particularly laid upon my mind: "Believest *thou* this?" As I have said, I trust that such a time as this, causes us to consider rightly and prayerfully the things which we profess to believe, and their application to us in a very real, practical and personal way. O in such a situation as this, we are not to take things for granted. May the Lord grant us grace to search our hearts and try our ways, to "see if there be any wicked way in me, and lead me in the way everlasting" (Ps.

139:24). May he establish us more and more upon what we profess to believe, resting and trusting wholly in the person of our Lord Jesus Christ alone.

He says to Martha, "Believest thou this?" She says, "Yea, Lord: I believe that thou art the Christ, the Son of God, which should come into the world." What a blessed statement is this of Martha! We see here one of like passions as you and me, yet a true believer in the Lord Jesus Christ, by the grace of God. And as evident in these dear women, we are brought to realise increasingly that faith is the gift of God, and we are dependent upon the gracious ministry of the Holy Spirit for the exercise of faith. Yes, when faced with the situation in our day, faith looks to the Lord, as did Martha at this time in her life, And O friends, when there is so often that faltering with us, how we have to cry, *"Lord, I believe; help thou mine unbelief"* (Mark 9:24).

How gracious is the Lord to his people! See in this chapter, the love and compassion of the Lord Jesus Christ towards his own. When he saw Mary weeping, and those weeping as well that came to comfort her, he groaned in spirit and was troubled. He asks, "Where have ye laid him?" And "Jesus wept." Ah, can we enter into the wonder of the compassion of our Lord Jesus Christ? Truly, he was a real man but no sin was ever found in him. We see here, that though he knew what he would do, he was affected when he saw death, that which is the fruit of sin. He was also aware of men's unbelief in himself.

"Jesus wept." I believe this particularly manifests his love and compassion towards his own. We have not a Saviour who is far off from us, nor have we one who is not "touched with the feeling of our infirmities" (Heb. 4:15). He truly entered into the whole human condition, sin excepted. And he is still that same loving, compassionate Saviour. O for grace to enable us truly to rest in him, to rest in his will, in the realisation of what he manifested to these sisters, that he loved them and he loves his people still. He loves them with a love so tender, so real and so full, beyond what we can ever express. All is to the praise of the glory of his name.

We come then to the grave, and a stone lay upon it. He says, "Take ye away the stone." We see the response of Martha: "Lord, by this time he stinketh: for he hath been dead four days." "Jesus saith unto her, Said I not unto thee, that, if thou wouldest believe, thou shouldest see the glory of God?" I go back to the words of our text: "Believest thou this?" Yes, Martha said she did believe that Jesus is the resurrection and the life, and that whosoever liveth and believeth in him shall never die. Yet when she comes to the grave and Jesus commanded to roll away the stone, we see the faltering of her faith. Friends, surely this underlines what I said earlier, that we have to cry again and again, "Lord, I believe; help thou mine unbelief." In the face of the realities of death, the grave and a decomposing corpse, O what grace is needed *then* to cleave to the Lord, to believe and trust in him!

We find here that Martha could not attain to this faith by her own ability. "Said I not unto thee, that, if thou wouldest believe, thou shouldest see the glory of God?" Not that what the Lord Jesus was about to do in raising Lazarus from the dead depended upon the faith of Martha. No. The Lord knew what he was about to accomplish. In effect, he is saying to Martha: 'Take thine eyes off the corpse and its decay and fix thine eyes essentially upon myself alone, the Lord Jesus Christ. Believe and trust in me as the Christ of God, and thou shalt see the greater glory of God.' And most surely she beheld that glory, as did those with her, who saw the miracle of Lazarus being raised from the dead. What an encouragement is that to us, to believe and trust in the Lord in our situation.

> "To keep our eyes on Jesus fixed,
> And there our hope to stay."

Yes, we are prone to be like Martha. She was deeply affected when the grave was opened for she was aware of that decaying corpse. How can these things be? How can that which is dead, and has been dead so long, rise again? "Said I not unto thee, that, if thou wouldest believe, thou shouldest see the glory of God?" Let us keep our eyes fixed on Jesus and stay our hope on him. Thus the Lord directs Martha to trust wholly in himself alone, and to believingly receive the word he had spoken to her. And did she not there see the greater glory of God revealed in the person of the Lord Jesus Christ?

So friends, faith beholds the power and wisdom of God, as

revealed in the person of our Lord Jesus Christ. And he that raised Lazarus from the dead is the same Jesus still! "Is any thing too hard for the LORD?" (Gen. 18:14). Cannot he uphold and keep us, as he has assured us in his word, even at such a time as this? O for grace to enable us thus to look to him, to trust in him alone, waiting upon him in all things in submission to his holy will. Yes, we know not what future days hold but we are assured that all is in the Lord's hands, the hands of "him that loved us, and washed us from our sins in his own blood" (Rev. 1:5).

We see the response to this miracle the Lord wrought. There were those that believed on him. And there were those that went their way and told the Jews what Jesus had done. This reminds us of the solemn fact that faith *is* the gift of God. People can behold such a miracle as this, and yet not believe in Jesus Christ. "The natural man receiveth not the things of the Spirit of God: for they are foolishness unto him: neither can he know them, because they are spiritually discerned" (1 Cor. 2:14). O the blessedness of those who, by the grace of God, are brought to believe and trust in Jesus Christ alone. Friends, may that be so with each one of us. And surely where it is so, we know that it is not of ourselves. All is of God and all is to his praise alone.

We see then in the events here recorded, that what redounds to the glory of God, cannot but be, in its ultimate manifestation, for the spiritual and eternal welfare of each one of his people. Yes,

> "Christ is the Keeper of his saints,
> He guards them by his power;
> Subdues their numerous complaints,
> In every gloomy hour."

I will leave the remarks there. May the Lord add his blessing. Amen.

6

THE NAME OF THE LORD IS A STRONG TOWER

Tuesday evening 31 March 2020

"The name of the Lord is a strong tower: the righteous runneth into it, and is safe" (Proverbs 18:10).

In meditating on the subject to bring before you this evening, my mind was led to the portion in Exodus that I read to you, how the Lord proclaimed his name to Moses in a very trying and distressing situation (Exod. 33&34). Israel had sinned, and sinned so grievously, and sinned so quickly after what had been displayed to them when God came down on mount Sinai and made a covenant with them. They stood to it, but how soon they broke that covenant in the matter of the golden calf. O what idolatry we see there! We have to say, "what is man." Did it not show what is in fallen man? How easily and quickly they turned aside from what had been made known to them.

Yes, they were troubling times for Moses. He stood in the breach and the Lord mercifully heard his cry and gave him that wonderful word of promise: "My presence shall go with thee, and I will give thee rest" (Ex. 33:14). But after what the Lord made known unto him there, Moses continued before the Lord: "I beseech thee, show me thy glory" (v.18). And I trust as we come around the word of God here tonight, there may be opened up to us the glory of God which Moses beheld when the Lord declared his name before him. O to behold the glory of God in its greater, fuller and more glorious manifestation in the face of our Lord and Saviour Jesus Christ! Wondrous is that name of God declared to Moses. And so it is as we consider the further glorious opening up of it, in the person of our Lord Jesus Christ. See it in the promise the Lord gave through Isaiah: "For unto us a child is born, unto us a son is given: and the government shall be upon his shoulder: and his name shall be called Wonderful, Counseller,

The mighty God, The everlasting Father, The Prince of Peace. Of the increase of his government and peace there shall be no end, upon the throne of David, and upon his kingdom, to order it, and to establish it with judgment and with justice from henceforth even for ever. The zeal of the LORD of hosts will perform this" (Is. 9:6–7).

Moses was highly favoured with that manifestation of the glory of God as the Lord declared his name before him. But greater still is the glory that is ours as set before us in the precious truth of the gospel in which we behold God revealed in the person of his only begotten and dearly beloved Son. God declared his name to Moses, "The LORD, The LORD God, merciful and gracious, longsuffering, and abundant in goodness and truth, keeping mercy for thousands, forgiving iniquity and trans-gression and sin, and that will by no means clear the guilty; visiting the iniquity of the fathers upon the children, and upon the children's children, unto the third and to the fourth generation" (Ex. 34:6–7). Well might Moses bow his head and worship. And what cause likewise do we have to bow our head and worship, as the truth of the gospel is brought home to us, by the gracious ministry of the Holy Spirit. By God-given, saving faith we are brought to behold God, as revealed in Jesus Christ, to be, "The LORD, The LORD God, merciful and gracious, longsuffering, and abundant in goodness and truth, keeping mercy for thousands, forgiving iniquity and transgression and sin."

Did the Lord say to Moses, "I will by no means clear the guilty"? Yes, God will by no means clear the guilty. They cannot be cleared, unless full satisfaction be rendered to all that divine justice demands and all the claims of God's holy law are met. God is holy, righteous, just and true. He can never forgive sin, *except* upon the ground of what he himself has appointed and provided, as accomplished in the person and finished work of the Lord Jesus Christ. Herein God is glorified in the forgiveness of sins. The wonders of his sovereign grace and goodness are fully manifested in Jesus Christ. The glory of God is revealed there.

O friends, may that glory of God, as set forth in the precious truth of the gospel, shine in our hearts, "to give the light of the knowledge of the glory of God in the face of Jesus Christ" (2 Cor.

4:6). Therein may we see the glory of God as "merciful and gracious, longsuffering, and abundant in goodness and truth, keeping mercy for thousands, forgiving iniquity and transgression and sin." Therein we see his glory, in that he himself has provided the one sacrifice for sin, whereby he justifies the ungodly, and provides a righteousness that meets all the demands of his holy law. And O, the blessings of this are made known to sinners, even the vilest and neediest of sinners, who by the grace of God are brought to cry unto the Lord for mercy.

O friends, this is the sure foundation for his people's faith and hope of salvation. Did God make a covenant with Israel at mount Sinai? How soon they broke that covenant. But before the foundation of the world, God made a covenant between the eternal Three, which is ordered in all things and sure. It is not founded upon what man can contribute, for sinners can never contribute to it. God himself has provided in that covenant all that is required for his glory in the redemption and salvation of sinners, even as many as the Lord our God shall call. And in that covenant is found all the hope and blessings of salvation for his people, for time and eternity.

But in looking this evening at this verse in Proverbs, we see what a wealth of blessed instruction is found in this book. O may the Lord the Holy Spirit increasingly open up and apply this wisdom to us by his gracious leading and teaching. But remember, where does all the teaching of the Holy Spirit direct? Yes, it exposes just what we are, and reminds us constantly that we have nothing upon which to rest in ourselves. We have to cry, as did the apostle, "O wretched man that I am! who shall deliver me from the body of this death?" (Rom. 7:24).

Ah, what a constant distress to the people of God is our fallen nature. But in this conviction of sin, the Holy Spirit always graciously leads us to the Lord and Saviour Jesus Christ. O the blessedness of that grace of our God, which brings us to the footstool of mercy, to behold our Lord Jesus Christ seated upon the throne of his grace. We then see fulfilled in him all that God revealed of his name to Moses. Yes, we see all the fulness of that name as we behold by faith our Lord Jesus Christ, risen, ascended, and seated at the right hand of the Majesty in the heavens, as the great high priest over the house of God. O friends, let us have grace, whereby we may hold fast our profession, to own and honour the Lord by coming to him alone, in all things at all times.

We have in our text, a sure refuge, a blessed place of safety in which are assured the blessings of salvation for his people, to the praise of the glory of his great and holy name. "The *name* of the LORD is a strong tower: the righteous runneth into it, and is safe."

"The name of the LORD." As we have already considered, O what an opening up there was of the greatness, glory and goodness of our God when that name was made known to Moses! He is the one and only true God. O how he has revealed of himself in his holy word! He did there to Moses. And he has done so, in the fulness of it, in the person of his only begotten and dearly beloved Son! For, "God, who at sundry times and in divers manners spake in time past unto the fathers by the prophets, hath in these last days spoken unto us by his Son, whom he hath appointed heir of all things, by whom also he made the worlds; who being the brightness of his glory, and the express image of his person, and upholding all things by the word of his power, when he had by himself purged our sins, sat down on the right hand of the Majesty on high" (Heb. 1:1–3).

What does this name of the Lord express to us? O, therein is treasured up all that his people need for time and for eternity, as poor sinners. We live in troubled times. The church of Jesus Christ has always lived in troublous times, however varied its outward circumstances. All down the generations, the people of God have proved that this is a wilderness world through which we pass. Like with Israel in the wilderness, it yields no spiritual profit whatsoever to us. Ah, do we find in the things of time, the things of this world, that which can feed the needy souls of the living family of God? Yes, we pass through this wilderness world in which are many troubles but we still have constant cause for thankfulness to our God. We are no better than Israel of old in the wilderness. But in spite of all our wanderings, our failings, he still provides graciously for us in all his providential dealings. O the goodness and the longsuffering of God!

And bear in mind, that all the providential dealings of God are to be seen in every aspect of the life of the church, of his people individually, of all men and nations, of all events in the world. Remember, God does not sit remote from his creation. He is ever present in his creation. His eye beholds all. All is not only subject to his sovereign will but is according to his divine appointments and purposes. From the human standpoint, we cannot fathom it, but blessed be God, I trust we are brought truly to believe it and find rest therein for our souls. Though we "can't his goings trace" nor understand all his ways and dealings, yet surely we are conscious, through his rich mercies towards us, that he is *our* God. And we know "he doeth according to his will in the army of heaven, and among the inhabitants of the earth: and none can stay his hand, or say unto him, What doest thou?" (Dan. 4:35). Yet in all his dealings he is "too wise to err...too good to be unkind."

"The name of the LORD is a strong tower; the righteous runneth into it, and is safe." In that name of the Lord our God, the glory of which is essentially revealed in the person of our Lord Jesus Christ, are not all the needs of his people fully met as they journey on through this wilderness world? See how the Lord provided for Israel. The manna never ceased while they were in the wilderness. It came day by day. And are not we ourselves directed, particularly in this time of trouble, to the vital importance of what the Lord spake to Israel through Moses? "Man doth not live by bread only, but by every word that proceedeth out of the mouth of the LORD doth man live" (Deut. 8:3). As believers, through his grace, is our life to be wholly preoccupied with present things? No friends, for do we not need continually the bread which is from heaven, which the Lord has graciously promised and indeed imparts? O to feed daily on the word of our God, and upon Jesus Christ as revealed therein! The Lord bless us with the grace of living faith in exercise, truly going out unto him and living upon him. Paul said, "I am crucified with Christ: nevertheless I live; yet not I, but Christ liveth in me: and the life which I now live in the flesh I live by the faith of the Son of God, who loved me, and gave himself for me" (Gal. 2:20).

As I said, we have much cause for continual thankfulness for the Lord's mercies towards us in the things of this life. But we have greater cause, not only for thankfulness, but for rejoicing as well in what God hath provided for us in all that Jesus is and has done. Present things are fading and temporary. The time is soon hastening when the place that knows us now, shall know us again no more for ever. Ah, but how great, how glorious is the hope and expectation of the child of God, in that eternal inheritance *and* in the blessed reality that even here and now, they are the Lord's and the Lord is theirs.

O was that not sweetly confirmed to Moses, when the Lord said to him, "My presence shall go with thee, and I will give thee rest"? Did that merely apply to Moses, a blessing as it was to him unquestionably? No, friends. The reality of the principle set forth to Moses, is ever promised to the church and people of God. See it confirmed in the words of our Lord Jesus Christ when his disciples were so troubled and apprehensive at the prospect of his going away. He says to them, "I will not leave you comfortless: I will come to you. Yet a little while, and the world seeth me no more; but ye see me: because I live, ye shall live also" (John 14:18–19).

"The name of the LORD is a strong tower." Yes, treasured up in the Lord our God, is all power and authority in heaven and in earth. Remember that all the things we see in the present situation are not by chance. It is not merely misfortune that has brought this virus on the nations. The hand of the Lord is in all these things. We cannot trace his goings in it, nor do we make predictions with regard to these matters either. But, as believers, we can look up and behold the Lord *our* God, whose name is revealed to us in the person of his only begotten and dearly beloved Son in the precious truth of the gospel. In him we see that all is ours and we are his. Have we then, as believers, and the church of Christ collectively, any ground to fear? Ah, as in this body, we are subject to fears, unquestionably, being what we are. But has the child of God, the believer, any ground for fear, whatever the circumstances, when we rightly consider what God has set before us in his name? "And the LORD passed by before him, and proclaimed, The LORD, The LORD God, merciful and gracious, longsuffering, and abundant in goodness and truth, keeping mercy for thousands, forgiving iniquity and transgression and sin."

Ah, in the person of his only begotten Son, God reveals his glory as a God full of grace and truth, pardoning iniquity, justifying the ungodly and bringing poor sinners into the blessings of that covenant ordered in all things and sure. And he gives them the sweet testimony of the Holy Spirit with their spirit that *he is their God.* If this God, who revealed the glory of his name to Moses and has revealed his glory in the face of Jesus Christ to us, is our God, has he not assured us that he will "our God *for ever and ever:* he will be our guide even unto death" (Ps. 48:14). Yes, as Paul wrote in his epistle to the Romans, "If God be for us, who can be against us? He that spared not his own Son, but delivered him up for us all, how shall he not with him also freely give us all things?" (Rom. 8:31–32).

"The name of the LORD is a strong tower." Yes, his name is a blessed refuge, a sure refuge for his people. As we sometimes sing:

> "A refuge for sinners the gospel makes known;
> 'Tis found in the merits of Jesus alone;
> The weary, the tempted, and burdened by sin,
> Were never exempted from entering therein."

As God provided those cities of refuge in Israel for the manslayer, so has he set before us, in the precious truth of the gospel, a sure abiding refuge for poor needy sinners in the person and finished work of the Lord Jesus Christ. And friends, what safety is therein! What assurance is given us that the law has no claim upon us. Divine justice is satisfied. Indeed, instead of its being against us, it is for us. For it has received at the hand of our Lord Jesus Christ as our blessed surety and substitute, all that it demanded, all that divine justice required, all wherein God is glorified. O friends, how great is the glory of God revealed in the redemption and salvation which is in Jesus Christ our Lord! And surely the blessedness of it to such sinners as you and me, is that it is not only full but also free.

"The name of the LORD is a strong tower: the *righteous* runneth into it, and is safe." "The righteous"? Who are these righteous? Is there anyone righteous in themselves? Left to ourselves, we are full of self-righteousness. That is not the righteousness which is referred to here. These described as *righteous,* are all sinners, sinners saved by grace, sinners brought to forsake all and to follow the Lord Jesus Christ and him alone. Blessed with the grace of living faith, they are ever declaring,

> "What was there in me that could merit esteem,
> Or give the Creator delight?
> 'Twas 'Even so, Father,' we ever must sing,
> Because it seem'd good in thy sight."

That such a sinner as I, that such a sinner as you, should obtain mercy! Indeed, be declared righteous before God! Righteous not by our own doings, but by the doings of another, even our Lord Jesus Christ! Yes, this righteousness is blessedly imputed only, but wholly, to those sinners whom the Lord calls by his grace, and to whom he reveals his pardoning love and mercy in the person and work of our Lord Jesus Christ.

And what is the effect of this in the experience of the child of God? It is as Peter wrote in his first epistle, "Unto you therefore which believe he is precious" (1 Pet. 2:7). Ah, is that so with us? Can we say this evening, truly, feelingly, that Jesus is precious to us, that he is the one we can never do without, the one on whom we are wholly dependent, especially, we would say, at such a time as this?

"The righteous runneth into it, and is safe." See in which direction the sinner always runs who is taught of God the Holy Spirit, and to whom these words have blessed application. What is the direction, the exercise we might say, of a God-given faith? It is always to the Lord Jesus Christ. He himself declares, "All that the Father giveth me shall come to me; and him that cometh to me I will in no wise cast out" (John 6:37). As I have said many a time, the reality of God-given faith is seen in a continual coming to the Lord Jesus Christ, as needy sinners, helpless in ourselves. We come dependent on him, trusting in his promise, and looking to him alone for wisdom and righteousness, for strength and for the supply of all our need.

And ah friend, one thing we are assured of is that he to whom we thus come, to whom we are brought to run as the only refuge of our souls as expressed in our text, is one that never fails. Look what he said in the words I quoted a moment ago, "I will in no wise cast out." There is another word also, and what a blessed word it is: "He is able also to save them to the uttermost that come unto God by him, seeing he ever liveth to make intercession for them" (Heb. 7:25).

"The name of the LORD is a strong tower." All that his people need, all that you and I as sinners require, as taught of God the Holy Spirit, is richly treasured up for us in Jesus Christ. What a name is given to him when Abraham saw that wondrous provision of a ram caught by its horns in a thicket, which he offered in the place of his son Isaac on mount Moriah. When Abraham named that place, he called it Jehovah Jireh, yes, "In the mount of the LORD it shall be seen," or "the LORD will provide" (Gen. 22:14). And ah, so he will, and so he does! His name is still Jehovah Jireh, Jehovah Jesus, in the fulness and glory of the revelation the Lord has given of himself in the precious truth of the gospel.

"The name of the LORD is a strong tower: the righteous runneth into it, and is safe," or, as it can be rendered, "set on high." O friends, here is the refuge for his people. Behold it, not in the things of this time's state, but in the person of Jesus Christ. Behold him there, occupying the throne of grace, full of grace and full of truth, the mighty God, the everlasting Father, the glorious Prince of Peace. And so the Lord Jesus ever will be unto his people, to the praise of his great and holy name.

"The name of the LORD is a strong tower: the righteous runneth into it, and is safe." May we know what it is, as blessedly taught of God the Holy Spirit, to trust alone in that name. As the psalmist of old said, "Trust in him at all times; ye people, pour out your heart before him: God is a refuge for us" (Ps. 62:8).

I will leave the remarks there. May the Lord add his blessing. Amen.

7

GOD WHICH RAISETH THE DEAD

Lord's day morning 5 April 2020

"For we would not, brethren, have you
ignorant of our trouble which came to us in
Asia, that we were pressed out of measure,
above strength, insomuch that we despaired
even of life: But we had the sentence of death
in ourselves, that we should not trust in
ourselves, but in God which raiseth the dead:
who delivered us from so great a death, and
doth deliver: in whom we trust that he will yet
deliver us" (2 Corinthians 1:8-10).

The apostle Paul writes this second epistle to the church at
Corinth by the inspiration of the Holy Spirit. Through the Lord's
hand upon him, he had been instrumental in the ingathering of
the brethren who formed that church. He spent eighteen months
in Corinth. Some time afterward, he wrote his first epistle, being
greatly grieved at hearing of the failings among them. He
exhorted, warned and directed them, desiring that the Lord would
have mercy on them.

He writes this second epistle in thankfulness at their right
response. The Holy Spirit had wrought in bringing them to
address the issues in which they had been so seriously wrong.
But I do not want to deal with those issues this morning. Paul,
here has cause to bless God, as do we ourselves. He says in the
third verse, "Blessed be God, even the Father of our Lord Jesus
Christ, the Father of mercies, and the God of all comfort." He
speaks of a particularly distressing situation he and his
companions experienced in Asia and testifies how the Lord was
with them and delivered them even though they had been brought
into great extremities. He speaks of the encouragement and
consolation they found in the Lord their God in those troubles.
His desire as a faithful minister of Jesus Christ is to testify to the

brethren of the greatness and goodness of the Lord our God, whatever the trials, temptations or difficulties in which the church is found. And indeed, is it not so with us at this present time? There are things that greatly trouble and distress us. One is that we are unable to gather for the public worship of the Lord's name as we are faced with the present situation in the nations of the world. I do not want to dwell unduly on those things this morning but to direct our attention, as the apostle does here, to the one in whom all our help, hope, encouragement and consolation is to be found. It is not in ourselves, nor our putting trust and confidence in men. It is to be brought through the Lord's mercies towards us to commit our way wholly into *his* hand and to trust in him alone, knowing that he, the Lord God omnipotent, reigneth. And O, set before us here is the blessed fact that this God is the God and *Father* of our Lord Jesus Christ, *and* the God and *Father* of all sinners brought by divine grace to believe and trust in Jesus alone.

When led by the Holy Spirit into these blessed truths do we not surely find that our encouragement is in looking wholly unto the Lord our God? It is not in what we see around us or in what man may predict to be the final outcome of the present trouble.

"Blessed be God, even the Father of our Lord Jesus Christ, the Father of mercies, and the God of all comfort." *"Blessed be God."* O that our hearts may be warmed, and moved as the apostle's in his addresses to the various churches. May *we* likewise exclaim, "Blessed be God, even the Father of our Lord Jesus Christ," ascribing all honour and glory unto the Lord our God, conscious that all our times are in his hand. We receive from God all that pertains to our true spiritual welfare, through the wonders of his great love manifested to us in his precious gospel and sealed to our hearts by the gracious ministry of the Holy Spirit.

"Blessed be God, even the Father of our Lord Jesus Christ, the Father of mercies, and the God of all comfort." O friends, behold all in the hands of our God and Father. Behold the blessed reality of the oneness of our Lord Jesus Christ with the Father and the Holy Spirit, one God, blessed for evermore. As the apostle experienced, and the church of Christ down the generations, so in our day, how much there is against us, but how *much, much more* there is *for us*. "If God be for us, who can be against us?" (Rom. 8:31). That is not a question of doubt as to whether God is for his people or not. No, it is a blessed testimony that as the God and Father of our Lord Jesus Christ is for us, who can be against us? Satan opposes. Unbelief raises doubts and questionings, it certainly does. And is not Satan a powerful and subtle enemy? Do not we surely see the evidence of his activity in this situation which faces us as a nation today? Friends, do not forget what Paul says in the next chapter, that we are not ignorant of Satan's devices.

We find the question readily raised, "Why are these things?" O may the Holy Spirit bring us to "the Father of mercies, and the God of all comfort," as the apostle says here. Yes, there is much that may be against us, but blessed be the Lord, there is much more that is for us, even the God of our salvation. In his hands are all things, for time and eternity, every situation in all the nations of the world. As I seek to remind you again and again, we must never lose sight of this important truth. O that we might know increasingly the encouragement and consolation of it as we go on in future days, subject to the Lord's will,

> "He holds all nature in his hand;
> That gracious hand on which I live
> Does life, and time, and death command,
> And has immortal joys to give."

"The Father of mercies, and the God of all comfort." Paul knew this consolation even in the distresses which he and the brethren with him experienced in Asia. And so he says to these Corinthians: "For we would not, brethren, have you ignorant of our trouble which came to us in Asia." He wasn't wanting to promote himself by telling them how great the trouble had been. It wasn't to inform them of the details of that situation. The details are not given us and it is vain to speculate. Where the scripture is silent let us be silent. Sufficient is told us in this verse to realise Paul had been in great trouble and that there was a purpose for that distress. It was not only to testify to the Lord's faithfulness and goodness to him and those with him. It was also to witness to the brethren to whom he wrote, that he and those with him were brought to "not trust in themselves, but in God which raiseth the dead." So the Lord doth deliver and will yet deliver his people. Do not these verses speak to us today? They blessedly set forth that the Lord did not forsake the apostle in his greatest distress. He was not without hope in his God in that situation. Shut up to God alone, did he not experience the goodness and mercy of the Lord?

"For we would not, brethren, have you ignorant of our trouble which came to us in Asia, that we were pressed out of measure, above strength, insomuch that we despaired even of life." The very words themselves surely set forth the extremity of the trouble into which they were brought, viewed from a human standpoint. Whichever way they looked, there appeared no way out whatsoever. They were brought to say, 'We had the sentence of death in ourselves. Death must surely be the end of the trouble in which we are found. What can we do? What are we to look to? What are we to rest upon?' Yet even in that situation there was a gracious purpose: "that we should not trust in ourselves, but in God which raiseth the dead." What a painful thing it is to be brought to the end of everything in self, realising our weakness and great need. But it is also a mercy if we are thereby brought to look wholly to the Lord, as did the apostle. When we rightly view things, is there help or hope for us to be found anywhere else than in the Lord our God? Whatever the circumstances of the church or child of God, even those at the present time, no change has taken place in the love of the Lord for his people.

I have reminded you many times, that his love knows no end. It knows no change. Yes, our circumstances are fluctuating and our inward exercises and feelings as well. What changes we experience! But the blessed reality is that no change has taken place in him. Of the things he has revealed to us in his word, he assures us that, "These sayings are faithful and true" (Rev. 22:6). O what a foundation is laid for us in the unchanging word of the Lord our God! Circumstances change. Indeed, we live in a day when things are very different from what they were for our forefathers. But O friends, the word of God has not changed. Through the Lord's mercies towards us, may you and I ever seek to be guided by his word and to walk in its light, looking and cleaving only to the Lord Jesus Christ as he is the God of our salvation.

But O, though the apostle was brought low, in that sense, see here how he speaks of God as "the Father of mercies, and the God of all comfort." And so with the child of God and the church of Jesus Christ, in every issue and situation. When brought to the end of everything in self, we are not brought to the end of what is treasured up in our Lord Jesus Christ. As hymn 324 which we have just sung expresses it, "The Lord will provide." Did not Abraham prove that truth when instructed of God to offer his son Isaac on a mountain to which he directed him? When they came to the place, he made an altar, laid Isaac upon it and took the knife to slay his son. But the angel of the LORD called to him out of heaven. How Abraham proved there the blessed truth that, "In the mount of the LORD it shall be seen," that is, "The LORD will provide" (Gen. 22:14).

Has the Lord provided? Blessed be his great and holy name, in the person of our Lord Jesus Christ he has provided all that meets the deepest need of his people. And friends, how great and deep is our need as sinful transgressors of God's holy law, subject to its just condemnation. If God has provided for us in the person and work of the Lord Jesus Christ, as his word of grace blessedly testifies, O what a mercy it is to be brought from trust in ourselves, to trust in God "which raiseth the dead."

Look at the situation in which each of us are found as sinners, transgressors of God's holy law. This is surely true of every one of us. We cannot claim exemption. No, "all have sinned, and come short of the glory of God" (Rom. 3:23). "There is none that doeth good, no, not one" (Rom. 3:12). Is this not true? And taught of God the Holy Spirit is it not deeply impressed upon us "that in me (that is, in my flesh,) dwelleth no good thing"? (Rom. 7:18). Yes friend, great is our need and great is the mercy to be brought from any trust in ourselves, for there is nothing that we sinners can do to meet the favour of God. Ah,

> "Could my zeal no respite know,
> Could my tears for ever flow,
> All for sin could not atone."

No zeal or tears can atone for your sins and mine. I say again, truly it is great mercy to be brought to the end of everything in self, to not trust in ourselves (painful though that be) "but in God which raiseth the dead." As I said, did not Abraham prove that God provides? And Paul testifies here that God has assuredly provided. He is "the Father of mercies, and the God of all comfort." And what a provision he has made in the person of our Lord and Saviour Jesus Christ!

He says, "we had the sentence of death in ourselves, that we should not trust in ourselves, but in God *which raiseth the dead.*" That word blessedly brings before us the sovereign power and authority of the Lord our God. *Raising the dead* is an action which truly distinguishes God. How little we consider this as believers ought to do in its application to our daily lives, certainly at such a time as this.

"God which raiseth the *dead.*" If God does this, "Is any thing too hard for the LORD?" (Gen. 18:14). As men view it, the situation is difficult and greatly distressing. But, "Is any thing too hard for the LORD?" Can all the wisdom of man, left to himself, address the issue confronting us today? Yes, we would pray for those in authority over us. We would not be unmoved over the sorrow, sickness and death that sadly prevails at this time. We would not be unconcerned over those caring for the sick and dying. May the people of God have prayerful concern for those in authority, that the Lord's hand may be upon them to guide them rightly in these things. But all the wisdom of man cannot, of itself, find a way of full deliverance from this situation. But in "God which raiseth the dead" is the encouragement and consolation of the people of God. He is "the Father of mercies, and the God of all comfort." That he is the God which raiseth the dead, sets forth his mighty power and authority. I say, is there any thing too hard for the LORD our God? We are often directed in the word of God, to the fact that he created the heavens and the earth. This is to continually remind us of the mighty power of the Lord our God. He upholds all things by the word of his power. He is a God who raiseth the dead. His word blessedly assures us that the things which are impossible with men are possible with God.

Paul goes on to say, "Who delivered us from so great a death."

I believe this not only has reference to the trouble Paul and those with him experienced in Asia. Yes, that was very distressing, as I said. It brought them to the end of everything in themselves, and to trust alone in God which raiseth the dead. But do not the words, "who delivered us from so great a death" direct us to a further deliverance which God has provided for his people? What is that *"so great a death"?* Is it not the just condemnation due to you and me, as transgressors of God's holy law? The word of God declares that "the wages of sin is death" (Rom. 6:23). This not only solemnly speaks of corporeal death but of eternal death. O your sins and mine deserve eternal death.

Friends, let us not pass lightly over these things. Surely at such a time as this, we need reminding of what we are, what we deserve, and would justly receive if God were to deal with us according to our sins. But, as Paul says here, surely we have cause to exclaim, "Blessed be God, even the Father of our Lord Jesus Christ, the Father of mercies, and the God of all comfort...who hath delivered us from so great a death." None but God who raiseth the dead could deliver from deserved eternal death. All the wisdom of man could never devise a way. All the power of which man may boast could never raise the dead. But God that raiseth the dead *hath* delivered us from so great a death.

O the wisdom and power of God manifested in the glorious gospel of his grace! Paul declares, "I am not ashamed of the gospel of Christ: for it is the power of God unto salvation to every one that believeth" (Rom. 1:16). Therein is the wisdom and power of God displayed. And surely it is the precious, believing realisation of this salvation, as taught of God the Holy Spirit, which brings us to bow before the Lord our God in wonder, love and praise.

"Delivered us from so great a death?" See how that is accomplished. The wisdom of man could never devise a deliverance. His power could never accomplish it. O the glory of God revealed in this great deliverance in the person and finished work of his only begotten and dearly beloved Son, Christ Jesus the Lord, the man Christ Jesus, Jehovah's righteous servant! What we could never do, God in Jesus Christ has most surely accomplished. The divine wisdom of God, before the foundation of the world, devised the way wherein he could be just and the justifier of him that believeth in Jesus. O the blessings that are revealed to us in the truth of the gospel and assured to us in the covenant ordered in all things and sure! Friends, we may be troubled with many things at such a time as this. But surely our greatest consolation, as brought by divine grace to believe and trust in the Lord Jesus Christ, is that he has "delivered us from so great a death."

The Lord Jesus Christ has brought in an everlasting righteousness for us. The holy law of God has nothing to say to us. It cannot condemn us. Jesus Christ has answered all that the law justly demanded of us sinners. As the surety and substitute of his people, he has paid the price demanded by divine justice. The law is magnified and made honourable. It is not against us. It fully approves the sinner who believes and trusts in Christ alone by divine grace. Divine justice is fully satisfied.

God declared concerning the Lord Jesus Christ, "This is my beloved Son, *in whom I am well pleased"* (Matt. 3:17). And that declaration was repeated several times in the new testament. As the psalmist said, "God hath spoken once; twice have I heard this" (Ps. 62:11). And friends, as sounded in your ears and mine through the Lord's mercies towards us, glorious is the truth that God the Father is well pleased with his beloved Son and with every poor sinner found in him. We are weak in ourselves. We are continually needy and destitute of all good. But O friends, as a poor sinner brought to believe in Jesus Christ, have we not all things pertaining unto life and godliness for time and for eternity?

"Hath delivered us from so great a death." Paul, even in all his troubles, tribulations and distresses, always has in view what God in Christ has done for him and what God in Christ was unto him. He ever testifies that all pertaining to his spiritual and eternal welfare, is not found in himself but is treasured up in his Lord and Saviour.

And he goes on to say of his Lord, he "doth deliver: in whom we trust that he will yet deliver us." Yes, for if God has given us all that pertains to the eternal salvation of our souls, if he has thus delivered us from so great a death as the precious gospel testifies, will he not yet deliver us? As we look back over the way the Lord has brought us in our lives, can we not surely bear testimony that he has appeared for us and delivered us by bringing us out from under our sins and follies? Has he not helped us in times of difficulty, affliction and sorrow? O have we not ever found the Lord to be a true and faithful friend? Is not his almighty arm lifted up in defence of his people, that almighty arm upon which we poor sinners are brought by his grace to lean? See how the church is described in the Song of Solomon. "Who is this that cometh up from the wilderness, *leaning upon her beloved?*" (Song of Sol. 8:5). O friends, may that be your portion and mine, increasingly realised by us, not only to be looking to our Lord Jesus Christ, but leaning upon him. One expresses it,

> "Larger communion let me prove
> With thee, blest Object of my love;
> But O for this no power have I!
> My strength is at thy feet to lie."

"He doth deliver." Friend, what assurance is found in this word! Whatever may be the issues confronting us, though the case, viewed from the human standpoint, is hopeless and we are brought to the end of all help and trust in self, yet we have one who is able to do exceeding abundantly above what we can ask or think. *"He doth deliver."* Here is no uncertainty. He that hath delivered, *doth deliver.* Having delivered us from so great a death, is there any good thing he will deny one of his own? Will he leave them to perish in their sins? No. Even though they may be brought into afflicting circumstances, even though they be brought to walk through the very shadow of death, as the psalmist says, yet even there the Lord does not forsake his people. "Yea, though I walk through the valley of the shadow of death, I will fear no evil: for thou art with me" (Psa.23:4). He delivers in life and in death. The Lord's people ever prove the mighty power and goodness, the love and mercy of the Lord, as the God who is faithful and true and who will not forsake his own.

He "doth deliver: in whom we trust that *he will yet deliver us.*" Friends, when we hear this, surely cannot we commit whatever may lie before us into the hands of our Lord, waiting upon him and for him? "We trust he will yet deliver us." He has not left us thus far. He hath not dealt with us after our sins though he might justly have done so. O how his goodness is lengthened out to us! It is as the psalmist expressed in Psalm 23: "The LORD is my shepherd; I shall not want."

The apostle goes on to say, "Ye also helping together by prayer for us, that for the gift bestowed upon us by the means of many persons thanks may be given by many on our behalf." O friends, through the Lord's mercies towards us, may we be much in prayer for one another and for ourselves, leaving all our concerns in the hands of the Lord our God. May we be found waiting upon him, by prayer and thanksgiving, in the present distressing situation. Thus the apostle wrote to the Philippians: "Be careful for nothing; but in every thing by prayer and supplication with thanksgiving let your requests be made known unto God. And the peace of God, which passeth all understanding, shall keep your hearts and minds through Christ Jesus" (Phil. 4:6).

I will leave the remarks there this morning. May the Lord add his blessing. Amen.

8

SEEING WE HAVE THIS MINISTRY

Lord's day evening 5 April 2020

"Therefore seeing we have this ministry, as
we have received mercy, we faint not" (2
Corinthians 4:1).

Among all the persecutions and afflictions the apostle Paul
suffered, was having to contend with accusations by false
brethren that he was not a true apostle of the Lord Jesus Christ.
But in writing here to the brethren at Corinth he asserts that he
surely had the marks of an apostle. They were evident in the very
gospel he had preached among them, and in the effect it had on
them by the Spirit's blessing. For through his ministry they had
been called by divine grace and brought to saving faith in the
Lord Jesus Christ. And he was assured that the work which had
been begun in them in making known the blessings of salvation
would never be left unfinished. His whole concern was always
for their spiritual and eternal welfare.

These words of our text follow on from chapter three, for he
says, *"Therefore* seeing we have this ministry, as we have
received mercy, we faint not." "Having this *ministry."* What is
the ministry to which the apostle refers? It is the ministry to
which he himself had been called of God. It is the ministration of
the spirit which he preached among them, which he had not
received from men, but by the revelation of Jesus Christ, as we
read in chapter three. This ministry sets before us the glorious
gospel of Christ. Therein, in all its fulness and freeness, is all that
pertains to the glory of God in the redemption and salvation of
sinful men and women, even as many as the Lord our God shall
call.

Paul testifies of having received *this ministry*. O friends, what
an unspeakable treasure is this ministry. Not all the wealth of this
earth can ever compare to that which is ours as brought to believe
and trust alone in Jesus Christ by divine grace. For if Jesus Christ

is ours, we have all that pertains to life and godliness for time and for eternity. As one says,

> "I'm rich to all the intents of bliss,
> If thou, O God, art mine."

O may we keep these things always in view, and know the power and truth of them in our own souls! Is not that needed at all times and particularly in the situation in which we are found in the present day? Yes, we have restrictions on us which prevent us from meeting in the public way we used to do. We trust this will not last long. Yet we know all is in the hand of our God. And as believers through divine grace, this glorious gospel ministry of the grace of God to which Paul so fully testifies here, can never be taken from us, whatever the restrictions to which we may be subjected. Satan assaults. Unbelief may raise its ugly head in questionings. The world, the flesh and the devil may combine against it. But O blessed be God, this glorious gospel of the grace of God remains unmoved and unaffected. It is still the same from generation to generation. How great and glorious it is, though not so in the eyes of the world.

Paul solemnly speaks here of those to whom this gospel was hid. What a solemn fact is the blindness upon the whole of mankind apart from divine grace. The vail is upon their hearts. They are blind to the glories of redeeming love and mercy set forth in the glorious gospel of Christ. We may well ask the question, 'Who is Jesus Christ in the eyes and estimation of the men and women of our generation?' Ask those with whom we come into daily contact, 'What think ye of Christ?' In so many respects, we fear they have no thoughts or opinions about him. If they do, it is certainly not in accordance with the revelation God has given us in his holy word. Not that we who have been brought by divine grace to believe the glorious testimony God has given of his beloved Son unto eternal life, have anything of ourselves of which to glory or boast. No. If Jesus Christ is precious to you and me, it is because of what we have received of this glorious gospel by the grace of God. It is through the sovereign operations of the Holy Spirit bringing us in true conviction as guilty needy sinners to cry unto the Lord Jesus for mercy.

O friends, what a mark of spiritual life by the work of God's

Spirit in the soul of a sinner is the being brought to cry for mercy. Do we know the living reality of it? Surely if taught of the Spirit, the continual cry will not be absent, "LORD, be merciful unto me: heal my soul; for I have sinned against thee" (Ps. 41:4). *That* is solemn confession but also a gracious petition. And those brought to cry to the Lord for mercy will never be left destitute of it. No. None that seek unto the Lord Jesus Christ shall ever be sent empty away. We sometimes sing,

> "The door of thy mercy stands open all day,
> To the poor and the needy, who knock by the way.
> No sinner shall ever be empty sent back,
> Who comes seeking mercy for Jesus's sake."

It is through his grace they are brought to cry to him for mercy, and thus we prove he giveth grace for grace. Grace brings us to cry to him for mercy in our need as a sinner, and grace imparts to us the very blessings of this glorious gospel of Christ of which Paul testifies here.

"Therefore seeing we have this ministry." Let us look a little closer at this ministry. In chapter three, he declares he was the minister, not of the letter but of the Spirit, not of the law but of the gospel. He says that the ministry of the letter was the law which God gave by Moses. Paul writes to the Romans, that "the law is holy, and the commandment holy, and just, and good" (Rom. 7:12). Unquestionably, great glory appertained to the giving of that law when God came down on Mount Sinai. The people saw that fire and God spoke to them out of the thick darkness. O what a demonstration of the power of God was there displayed. Well might the people tremble. "Moses said, I exceedingly fear and quake" (Heb. 12:21). Yes, the law delivered by God is holy, just and good. But it can never give light and life to sinful men and women. There is no hope in the law for sinners such as you and me. It demands perfect obedience of us at all times and in all things. As taught of God the Holy Spirit, we are solemnly brought to realise that there can be no hope for us by any supposed obedience of ours to that law, even though we might make many zealous efforts to keep its requirements. Why friends, we ever will come short, and surely that is borne in upon us by the teaching of the Holy Spirit.

The law declares, "the soul that sinneth, it shall die" (Ezek. 18:4). It can be satisfied with nothing less than *full* satisfaction to all its demands, and no sinner can ever render that. O the folly of those who seek acceptance with God by the law. Great was the mercy of the Lord to Paul, for at one time *he* thought he could please God by satisfying what the law demanded of him. He fully thought that if any came near to meeting its requirements he could exceed them all. But he says, "when the commandment came, sin revived, and I died" (Rom. 7:9). That is, he was brought to see the spirituality of the law by its being brought home to his conscience by the Lord, O he then saw how far short he came and that what he thought commended him to God actually brought just condemnation on him.

We have not received the ministry of the law but we do not despise the law. It has a glory pertaining to it. But the main purpose of the Lord's giving of it was that "by the law is the knowledge of sin" (Rom. 3:20). The law can never justify the ungodly, but neither can it condemn the believing soul that is justified in Jesus Christ and clothed with his righteousness. The law has nothing to say against the believer in Jesus. All that the law demands of the believer is fully satisfied in the person of our Lord Jesus Christ, sinners though they are of themselves. God the Father declares that he is well pleased with his beloved Son, and with those who by grace have been brought to believe and trust alone in Jesus.

Friend, as brought to believe and trust in Jesus Christ, you can never be brought into condemnation. His word assures us of it. "There is therefore now no condemnation to them which are in Christ Jesus, who walk not after the flesh, but after the Spirit" (Rom. 8:1). To walk after the Spirit is to be brought to look and come continually to the Lord Jesus Christ, depending on him alone. Yes, we find sin within us and without us. The daily exercise of a child of God is to mourn over the daily defilement of sin. But our defilement by sin can never bring us into condemnation. It can never alter God's purposes of love and mercy which flow to his own through the person and finished work of the Lord Jesus Christ.

Sin will indeed bring us under the chastening hand of God,

but that chastening is not in vindictive anger but in covenant love to his people. For in his ways and dealings with them, he ever seeks their true welfare and above all, the honour and glory of his great and holy name. Is not God glorified in the redemption and salvation of his people? Is he not glorified in upholding them and keeping them, and even when fallen, lifting them up again and drawing them to himself? O friend, may your concern and mine always be to seek the glory of God.

As Paul says, that which he ministered was "not of the letter, but of the spirit," not of the law but of the gospel. As I said, the law is holy, just and good. In the law, God is above us and against us. But in the glorious gospel, he is "Emmanuel...God with us" (Matt. 1:23). O see the vast difference! What wonders of grace are opened up to us here. I cannot meet the demands of the holy law, but as brought by divine grace to believe and receive the testimony God has given of his beloved Son, I find that he is not against me but for me! God declares that divine justice is well satisfied!

O friend, what a wonder is this. The great God and Saviour, our Lord Jesus Christ, never deviates in viewing his believing people clothed in his righteousness and washed in his precious blood as they journey on through this fallen world. Still the word assures us, "Ye are complete in him" (Col. 2:10). His unchanging testimony of them is, "Thou art all fair, my love; there is no spot in thee" (Song of Sol. 4:7). And the fulness of *that* will be manifest in the last great day when the Lord calls them from this earth unto himself in the hour of death. Ah, these are glorious realities!

"Therefore seeing we have this ministry." O may we always keep these precious truths in view by the Lord the Holy Spirit sealing them in our souls. As Paul goes on to testify, what light and glory shines in the gospel of the grace of God "in the face of Jesus Christ" (2 Cor. 4:6). Let us not lose sight of all these blessings I have sought to set before you. All come to us by the grace of God alone, in the wonders of his love, through the person of his only begotten and dearly beloved Son.

O how the glory of God does indeed shine "in the face of Jesus Christ." There we see a God reconciling us unto himself "through the redemption that is in Christ Jesus" (Rom. 3:24). Paul speaks later on in chapter five of this "ministry of reconciliation" of which he says "we are ambassadors for Christ" (2 Cor. 5:18–20). And in their measure so is each faithful servant of Jesus Christ. They are ambassadors for God and their whole ministry is to declare, not what man can do, but what God in Christ *has done* for them. They set forth the fulness and freeness of that salvation whereby God has reconciled poor sinners unto himself *through the redemption that is in Christ Jesus*. Remember that all is founded *in God himself,* in the outworking of his sovereign purposes of love and mercy towards his own.

O how glorious is this ministry which we have received. The ministration of the law declares *do, do, do*. The gospel of the grace of God blessedly testifies to what has been *done*. It declares a full and free salvation, full satisfaction rendered by Christ. Paul said, "we had the sentence of death in ourselves, that we should not trust in ourselves, *but in God which raiseth the dead"* (2 Cor. 1:9). Ah, what a blessing it is to trust "in God which raiseth the dead." How does God raise the dead? By what he has done for us in the person of our Lord Jesus Christ who not only "died for our sins according to the scriptures" but "rose again the third day according to the scriptures" (1 Cor. 15:3–4). O friends, what does that speak to us? It speaks of full and final victory for his church and people over all sin, over Satan, death, hell and the grave. It proclaims to us that God is well pleased for he is fully satisfied. God delights in this victory. He ever will delight in it, and delights in all who are found believing and trusting alone in our Lord and Saviour Jesus Christ, through divine grace.

And the ministry which Paul exercised was to continually preach this gospel of Christ, "Who delivered us from so great a death" (2 Cor. 1:10). He hath delivered us from death in trespasses and sins, from the curse and condemnation of God's holy law, and from the hell that would have been our deserved but dread abode. Is there then any good thing he will withhold from his people?

"He doth deliver." Do not our very lives bear testimony to the fact that he doth deliver? Surely we can trace this out in measure in our own lives? O the care of the Lord in delivering us, not only from seen dangers, but from many things of which we are totally unaware. Never lose sight of the truth that our very lives are ever subject to the love and care of the Lord Jesus Christ. His watchfulness over his people is unceasing, blessed be his holy name. Why, he speaks of them as the apple of his eye: "he that toucheth you toucheth the apple of his eye" (Zech. 2:8). Can language express more of his care over his people?

Read again Psalm 121. "I will lift up mine eyes unto the hills, from whence cometh my help. My help cometh from the LORD, that made heaven and earth…The LORD is thy keeper: the LORD is thy shade upon thy right hand." And so that psalm goes on beautifully to set his care before us. Yes friends, we face many things which are very trying and which arouse fears through our fallen nature. We do *not know* what things lie before us in future days but remember that, whatever our path, we *know* all is in the hands of our Lord Jesus Christ. And what is more, *we* are in his hands.

"Therefore seeing we have this ministry," the ministry, not of the law but of the gospel of the grace of God revealed to us in the face of Jesus Christ. Herein are the wonders of pardoning love and mercy. In the person and finished work of the Lord Jesus Christ is the full provision God has made for the pardon of sin. May the Lord seal afresh to us that our sins which are many are all forgiven. Not only are sins pardoned but righteousness is imputed so that the believer is fitted for heaven itself, as clothed in the righteousness of Jesus Christ.

In one sense, the believer is always fit for heaven. That may seem a remarkable statement, but no less is it true. The believer is always fit for heaven. Why? Because they are one with Jesus Christ, clothed in his righteousness and washed in his precious blood. Does that ever alter? Do circumstances, do the troubles of the believer, the extremities in which they may be found, alter their standing in Christ? To our feelings, they may do so. But how misleading can our feelings be. We want a feeling religion that *always* draws us to the Lord Jesus Christ, to realise his preciousness more and more. What we want to feel is what the apostle expressed when he said, "That I may know him, and the power of his resurrection, and the fellowship of his sufferings, being made conformable unto his death" (Phil. 3:10). May we know more of *that* religion of feelings, not the feelings arising from the workings of our own fallen nature.

> "Judge not the Lord by feeble sense,
> But trust him for his grace;
> Behind a frowning providence
> He hides a smiling face."

Why, as he hath made our salvation secure through the glorious gospel of Christ, then all that concerns us collectively and personally is safe in his hands.

May we know then what the apostle says here, "Therefore seeing we have this ministry, *as we have received mercy.*" Is not the very life of the child of God a continual receiving of mercy? What have we to give to God? The very life of faith is a continual coming to the Lord. Do we come with something in our hand to commend us to him? O friends, our tendency to self-righteousness is ever to think I must attain to something or some situation before I can expect the Lord to be favourable to me. O away with such legality. Away with such false thoughts for false indeed they are. As taught of the Holy Spirit, we must come and do come needy and poor. We come with nothing in our hands, simply clinging to the cross of Jesus Christ, in the blessed realisation of what he there accomplished in his life, sufferings and death for us. And as I have said, none who come looking to Jesus Christ, calling upon his name, are ever sent empty away.

"Having received mercy." Friends, we are daily receiving mercy. Are we not ever dependent on it, and indebted to it every step of life's journey? One says,

> "Without thy sweet mercy I could not live here;
> Sin soon would reduce me to utter despair."

What wonders are set forth in this glorious free mercy and redeeming love of our God.

Paul says, "as we have received mercy, *we faint not.*" What he says later in this chapter may well be our experience in measure: "We are troubled on every side, yet not distressed; we are perplexed, but not in despair" (2 Cor. 4:8). Yes, "we are troubled on every side." Are we not so? But notice what he then says: "Yet not distressed." In one sense, what is there to distress us? "If God be for us, who can be against us?" (Rom. 8:31). If Jesus is ours and our hope for eternity assured, as it is for the believer brought through grace to trust alone in him, what is there to distress us? We may be surrounded with distressing circumstances but, O friends, look up. "Say to them that are of a fearful heart, Be strong, fear not: behold, your God will come… he will come and save you" (Isa. 35:4). Behold your God coming over all the mountains of difficulty, temptation and sin. He does come, he comes as the deliverer of his people. "He hath delivered, and doth deliver: in whom we trust that he will yet deliver us" (2 Cor. 1:10).

"We are troubled on every side, yet not distressed; we are perplexed, but not in despair; persecuted, but not forsaken; cast down, but not destroyed; always bearing about in the body the dying of the Lord Jesus, that the life also of Jesus might be made manifest in our body" (2 Cor. 4:8–10). O that we might know this life of grace.

"Therefore seeing we have this ministry, as we have received mercy, we faint not." O for the grace that brings us to know the blessed rest for our souls which is found alone in the testimony of this ministry to the fulness and freeness of the mercy of God in Jesus Christ. We read in the opening chapter of the gospel as recorded by John, "The Word was made flesh, and dwelt among us, (and we beheld his glory, the glory as of the only begotten of the Father,) full of grace and truth…*For the law was given by Moses, but grace and truth came by Jesus Christ*" (John 1:14,17).

I will leave the remarks there. May the Lord add his blessing. Amen.

9

BE OF GOOD CHEER; IT IS I; BE NOT AFRAID

Tuesday evening 7 April 2020

"But straightway Jesus spake unto them, saying, Be of good cheer; it is I; be not afraid" (Matthew 14:27).

What gracious instruction and encouragement is given to the church and people of God in this account of events in the life and ministry of our Lord Jesus Christ. Through the Lord's mercies towards us may we have an ear to attend to what he speaks here. Let us not forget that these events which took place so many generations ago, still come to us as the word of God. And by the blessing of the Holy Spirit, this word is surely for the spiritual nourishing of the souls of the living family of God, to encourage them, to strengthen their faith, to confirm their hope and to draw out their hearts in love to the Lord Jesus Christ, amidst all their concerns. And surely this is so at the present time.

I would briefly notice one or two points in leading up to this text. In the opening verses of this chapter, we see the wickedness of Herod and Herodias in beheading John the Baptist. O what wickedness is there displayed! We may be sure that Herod and those involved with him did not escape the righteous judgment of God. They may not have experienced it in this life, but certainly when death came upon them they would have solemnly realised that God is not mocked. What is done to his servants is that which is done to himself and will most surely bring judgment on all who act like Herod.

But what I want to notice particularly is that we see here the sovereignty of our God in his ways with each one of his own. Humanly speaking, the end of John might appear to be very sad indeed. Yet, though beheaded in prison in such circumstances, for John it was "to be absent from the body, and to be present with the Lord" (2 Cor. 5:8). O did not this faithful servant of God hear, "Well done, thou good and faithful servant…enter thou into the joy of thy Lord" (Matt. 25:21).

There was sadness for the disciples of John. They took up his body and buried it. But notice what they did next: they "went and told Jesus" (v.12). O is not that a word to ourselves in the many issues with which we are at present confronted? Where can we go? Surely there is only one place for the people of God to go? It is not to look to self or man but to go to the Lord Jesus Christ.

"They went and told Jesus." And friends, remember we have an open way to the Lord Jesus Christ. Yes, they came to him as he was a man physically upon earth. We cannot come to him in that physical way, yet we can come to him as really and surely as did those disciples of John. True, our Lord Jesus Christ finished the work his Father gave him to do—that great and glorious work of glorifying God in the redemption and salvation of all his Father had given him. He has risen again and ascended into heaven. He is now seated "on the right hand of the throne of the Majesty in the heavens" (Heb. 8:1). Yet friends, be assured of this, we have direct access unto our Lord Jesus Christ. We do not need to go through any human mediator. We have direct access to him at the throne of his grace. See how he assures us of this in his word: "Seeing then that we have a great high priest, that is passed into the heavens, Jesus the Son of God, let us hold fast our profession" (Heb. 4:14). Yes, as sure as Jesus was here on earth, so sure is he seated on the throne of grace in the heavens as the great high priest over the house of God.

"They went and told Jesus." May we know the reality of this for ourselves. May we come boldly to the throne of grace by that new and living way which he has opened up for us. None can close that way for any poor needy sinner, any exercised child of God brought to seek to him, crying for grace and mercy to help in time of need.

Were these disciples of John disappointed when they went and told Jesus? We do not have a record of what Jesus spoke to them. But we certainly have the manifestation of his eternal power and Godhead in his wondrous mercy and compassion on that multitude in healing their sick and feeding them with those five barley loaves and two small fishes. Well does one say,

"That human heart he still retains,
Though throned in highest bliss;
And feels each tempted member's pains;
For our affliction's his."

"They went and told Jesus." Friends, may we know what it is to do the same. I say again, none will ever be sent empty away, blessed be his great and holy name.

We read that Jesus then went into a desert place, and the multitudes hearing of it, followed him and he had compassion on them in healing their sick. As I said, what a display is here given us of his eternal power and Godhead. What I always want to emphasise is that the gospel accounts of the life and ministry of our Lord Jesus Christ not only blessedly testify to us of what Jesus was but of what *he is*. These are not just ancient records. Unquestionably they are faithful records and we bless God for them. But they are the living word of God and testify of him who is indeed *the living word*. Remember that,

"The written and the incarnate Word
In all things are the same."

As the apostle writes to the Hebrews, he is "Jesus Christ the same yesterday, and to day, and for ever" (Heb. 13:8). He is full of grace, full of truth, full of compassion unto his own. Yes, he knows all that concerns us. He knows the inward feelings of our heart. As his word declares, he is "touched with the feeling of our infirmities" (Heb. 4:15). O you may feel very troubled, you may feel very much alone, but remember that as it was here with his disciples so surely is it with his people still. He not only knows about all things in our individual lives, *but all is according to his own divine appointment*. O for grace to believe it.

How the apostle's words remind us that this is not a matter of speculation. It is a *certainty* that "We *know* that all things work together for good to them that love God, to them who are the called according to his purpose" (Rom. 8:28). Unbelief questions it. Satan says, "How can that be? How can you square that text with the issues in your life or even in this account of John the Baptist?" Friends, let us not try to square these things, as it were. Let us bow our heads in worship and adoration, in the believing acknowledgement that in all the Lord's ways and dealings, he is wise, he is good, he is just and all is appointed to his glory. And as I have sought to remind you so many times, what is for the glory of God, cannot but be for the good of his people, in its ultimate manifestation. Even in the trying situation in which we are found at this present time, remember that the Lord is in these things. He is still with his people, as he was with his disciples. He is ever watching over his church. None of his own are ever outside the circle of his everlasting love to them. In his gracious purposes, his love is always manifested in his care and provision for them in all the things of this time's state, and above all, in what he has done to grant them pardon, peace and eternal life. O friends, what a rich portion belongs to the living family of God. They have a part by divine grace in our Lord Jesus Christ. He is ours and we are his. No circumstances can ever remove us from the circle of his love. Nothing can "separate us from the love of God which is in Christ Jesus our Lord" (Rom. 8:39).

Following the feeding of the five thousand, Jesus constrained his disciples to take ship and to go over to the other side, while he went up into a mountain to pray. We read in the gospels of those times the Lord Jesus spent, sometimes all night, in prayer to his heavenly Father. O what a sacred precious truth is this. The Lord Jesus Christ is the one mediator between God and men, the great high priest over the house of God, and as he prayed for his people when here on earth, so he still prays for them. We are assured that he intercedes for them, as we read: "Wherefore he is able also to save them to the uttermost that come unto God by him, seeing he ever liveth to make *intercession* for them" (Heb. 7:25).

We read that he constrained his disciples to go over to the other side. After they had gone so far over the lake they were overtaken by a threatening storm. Had Jesus made a mistake in constraining them to take ship and not to go with them? O it would be blasphemy even to think that. Our Lord makes no mistakes. He made no mistake then, and he makes no mistake in his appointments for his people today. We may not understand his dealings. We may never fully understand his purposes in them this side of the grave. But I say again that all that concerns us, as his people individually and his church collectively, is appointed by the Lord. Why, his providential ruling is over all the works of his hands in all the affairs of men and nations. And it is so in the present situation.

As concerns his people, he has not made any mistake. We are tried at this time, particularly as we cannot meet together in our accustomed manner. We are deprived of the ordinance of the Lord's house. Restrictions are upon us in our personal lives. But remember, though man is an instrument in the Lord's hand in this, yet these things come from the hand of our covenant God and Father. Ah friends, the Lord has made no mistake. He is speaking to us in these matters as much as he spoke to his disciples when here on earth.

Notice that he *constrained* them to go over. He knew what would be involved for them and, blessed be his name, he knew what he would do. Though he was alone that night on a mountain in prayer to his Father, the situation of his disciples was not unknown to him, even when they were not aware his eye was on them. Blessed be the Lord's name, it is so still. We may be full of fears and trepidation as were the disciples. Remember that many of them were experienced fishermen. They were used to those storms on the sea of Galilee but this storm was particularly troubling to them. But as I said, though they saw him not, the Lord's eye was upon them, and his eye is upon his church and people still, though we perceive him not. Job said, "Behold, I go forward, but he is not there; and backward, but I cannot perceive him: on the left hand, where he doth work, but I cannot behold him: he hideth himself on the right hand, that I cannot see him: but he knoweth the way that I take" (Job 23:8–10). Ah friends, the Lord's eye is still upon his people, his heart of love is still towards them, his promises concerning them do not fail. Even in such a storm threatening their very lives, the disciples were safe in the care of their God and Saviour. And his people are safe in every trouble today.

As I said a little earlier, we may not be able to comprehend fully why these things are appointed for us. But we may be assured that the Lord sends nothing without purpose. In all things there is the trying of faith. What an important matter that is for his people still: "If need be, ye are in heaviness through manifold temptations: that the trial of your faith, being much more precious than of gold that perisheth, though it be tried with fire, might be found unto praise and honour and glory at the appearing of Jesus Christ: whom having not seen, ye love; in whom, though now ye see him not, yet believing, ye rejoice with joy unspeakable and full of glory: receiving the end of your faith, even the salvation of your souls" (1 Pet. 1:6–9). What a promise is given us there! O may it be so blessed that we realise the Lord's mercies to us, not only in what we may be passing through at this time, but in whatever may yet be his divine appointments for us.

But we find them in a ship in the midst of the sea, tossed with waves, the winds being contrary. What a picture is here given of the church of Jesus Christ in this wilderness world, to use another metaphor. This ship is like the church, beset with troubles and difficulties on every side. And we ever find that the help of man is vain. What can we do of ourselves? O friends, what a mercy to be brought to say with Paul, "we were pressed out of measure, above strength, insomuch that we despaired even of life: *but* we had the sentence of death in ourselves, *that we should not trust in ourselves, but in God which raiseth the dead"* (2 Cor. 1:8–9). Painful as such lessons are, yet there are mercies and profit in them through the Lord's sovereign gracious dealings with his people. O what a mercy to be brought to an end of everything in self, and to realise increasingly the preciousness of our Lord and Saviour Jesus Christ, that salvation is of him. Friends, I know we can easily express such words, but did not Jonah learn that truth in the fish's belly? "Salvation," he says, "is of the LORD" (Jonah 2:9). It is in none other than the Lord. What a mercy that we shall never be disappointed by the Lord when brought by his grace to be cast wholly upon him as all our help and hope.

But I said that Jesus was fully aware of the situation of his disciples and so he is of his people still. And he comes! "Jesus went unto them." As I have repeated often just recently, "Is any thing too hard for the LORD?" (Gen. 18:14). Are the Lord's people ever brought into a situation in which the Lord does not know what he will do for them or is unable to come just where they are? What a wonder is this love and grace of our Lord Jesus Christ in that he comes, *he shall come* over all mountains of difficulty, temptation and trial. They are nothing to our Lord! It is as the one in the Song of Solomon says, "The voice of my beloved! behold, he cometh leaping upon the mountains, skipping upon the hills" (Song of Sol. 2:8). What mercy! O there are no difficulties, no troubles which can prevent the Lord from coming just where his people are. And not only is he able to come, but see his willingness, see the wonder of his love drawn out toward his own. O what compassion!

He knew his disciples were in trouble and he comes just where they are. O may we realise the blessedness of his coming and particularly at such a time as this. The Lord comes just where we are, and he speaks to us. Friends, do we not need what the Lord speaks here to his disciples to be sealed afresh to us? He comes unto them in that remarkable way—walking on the water. Yet in this very coming of the Lord to them, they mistook him. "They cried out for fear," supposing they had seen a spirit. Yes, his coming in that remarkable way filled them with fear. And how prone we are to mistake the Lord's ways and dealings with us and to think that all things are against us when in fact all is for us.

Was not that Jacob's problem when he said, "Me have ye bereaved of my children: Joseph is not, and Simeon is not, and ye will take Benjamin away: *all these things are against me...* ye shall bring down my gray hairs with sorrow to the grave"? (Gen. 42:36, 38). O how little did Jacob realise at that juncture that the Lord had been long working for him though he could not perceive it. Even in the taking away of Joseph, the Lord was working out his divine purposes for their salvation, to provide for him and his family in those seven years of famine. O what a wonder working God is our God. Truly, "the LORD hath his way in the whirlwind and in the storm, and the clouds are the dust of his feet" (Nahum 1:3). Friends, we see not, in that sense, his goings but he comes to us.

And he is coming here to his disciples, though at first unrecognised by them. How the Lord immediately addresses their fears. And in the present troublesome issues confronting us may we know the Lord coming to us and speaking afresh to our souls as he did to his disciples. Look how the Lord addresses their fears immediately. There is no delay here. "They cried out for fear," and the Lord *straightway* addresses their fears. "Straightway *Jesus spake* unto them." What words of authority are the words of our Lord, what words of grace and truth, what love and compassion is manifest, what evidence of his continual care over them!

"Straightway Jesus spake unto them." You know, here is something very personal as well. These words were addressed to his immediate disciples. The words of our Lord Jesus Christ are full of grace and truth. Who for? For all those whom his Father had given him, every one of them needy guilty sinners. And as brought by his grace to the solemn realisation of their sinful state, still the word of the Lord comes to them through the scriptures and the preaching of the blessed gospel. O how real, how precious is that! How highly prized it should be by us.

"Straightway Jesus spake unto them, saying." Notice what he says, "Be of good cheer; it is I; be not afraid." *"Be of good cheer."* It might be said, was there anything for them to be cheerful about in that situation? Yes, Jesus was coming to them, but the storm was still upon them, still threatening them. But, *"be of good cheer."* And in the midst of trouble, the Lord's living family still have much mercy for which to praise and thank the God of their salvation. They have cause for true *rejoicing*, not in their immediate circumstances, but *in the Lord their God.*

See how Paul emphasises that in writing to the Philippians. "Rejoice in the Lord alway: and again I say, Rejoice" (Phil. 4:4). Is this such a time to rejoice? Yes friend, not in our circumstances but in the Lord, the one whom I set before you tonight, "Jesus Christ the same yesterday, and to day, and for ever" (Heb. 13:8). No change has taken place in him. His love to his people is no less, blessed be his name. Why, sin, Satan, death, hell and the grave cannot alter one iota his purposes with regard to their eternal welfare and the glory of his name.

"Be of good cheer; *it is I;* be not afraid." O friends, how much is in that word, *"I."* It directs us to the person of our Lord Jesus Christ. I do not feel the disciples were necessarily alone. They had taken shipping as passengers and probably others were with them. But when Jesus, walking on the sea, came into the boat and the wind ceased, we read, "Then they that were in the ship came and worshipped him, saying, Of a truth thou art the Son of God."

"It is I." O is there any to be compared to the Lord Jesus Christ? See here displayed his eternal power and Godhead in his walking on the sea, the wind ceasing when he entered the ship and the ensuing calm. Can mere man accomplish that? Can man do anything about the situation in our day apart from the Lord's overruling in all these things? Man goes as far as he can in his wisdom, and we would pray for those in authority over us that the Lord's hand may be upon them to guide them aright. But O has man any capability of himself? No. But Jesus said, *"It is I."* O it is to him who speaks in such rich mercy that the faith and hope of the people of God, *our* faith, is to be directed.

"It is I." O friends, everything is contained in that. It was so for the disciples and it is so for his people still. He who speaks here, is none other than the Son of God, God manifest in the flesh, the sovereign Lord and creator of all things who upholds all things by the word of his power. I would emphasise *that* again and again in speaking to you. "It is I; be not afraid." See what consolation the Lord imparts to his disciples, troubled as they were, troubled even about the manner of the Lord's coming to them, as well as the situation in which they found themselves. "It is I." That speaks *everything* to us. "It is I; *be not afraid."* What peace that spoke to his disciples and speaks to his people still.

Looked at from the human standpoint, we have much to distress us at this time. We know not what the end of these things may be. But O how precious to realise that our Lord Jesus Christ, one with the Father and the Holy Spirit, God over all, *is our God.* What does the psalmist say? "This God is our God for ever and ever: he will be our guide even unto death" (Ps. 48:14).

As he comes to his disciples, he delivers Peter. Peter had said, "Lord, if it be thou, bid me come unto thee on the water." "Come," says the Lord. Peter begins to go but seeing the winds boisterous he was afraid and began to sink. O what did he cry? "Lord, save me." Jesus took his hand immediately. "O thou of little faith, wherefore didst thou doubt?" Friends, do not these things still speak to us, I trust?

"Straightway Jesus spake unto them, saying, Be of good

cheer; it is I; be not afraid." May we know the gracious application of this to us in the present situation as it concerns the cause of Jesus Christ in the earth. Friends, nations are shaken at these things, but the church of God, though in troublesome seas, shall sail calmly on. For the true church of Jesus Christ is not of man but of God. Our Lord Jesus Christ is ever with his people. And shall they not safely sail through the storms of this life and enter into their heavenly haven at last, brought home safe and sound, to the praise of the glory of his great and holy name? Glorious is the prospect for us. Blessed expectation we have even now in the Lord's promise of appearing for us and to us. "Straightway Jesus spake unto them, saying, Be of good cheer; it is I; be not afraid."

May the Lord add his blessing. Amen.

10

BEHOLD, THE LORD GOD WILL COME

Lord's day morning 12 April 2020

"O Zion, that bringest good tidings, get thee up into the high mountain; O Jerusalem, that bringest good tidings, lift up thy voice with strength; lift it up, be not afraid; say unto the cities of Judah, Behold your God! Behold, the Lord God will come with strong hand, and his arm shall rule for him: behold, his reward is with him, and his work before him. He shall feed his flock like a shepherd: he shall gather the lambs with his arm, and carry them in his bosom, and shall gently lead those that are with young" (Isaiah 40:9-11).

What glorious words of truth and grace are set before us in this chapter. They direct our whole attention, not to man, but to the one true God, the triune God, Father, Son and Holy Spirit, as revealed in our Lord Jesus Christ. Viewing our present situation in the light of this chapter, I trust we may increasingly realise what cause we have for thankfulness and praise unto the Lord our God. For he here testifies of himself as the one with all authority and power. He points to all the works of his hands in the whole of creation, nature, providence and grace. All proclaims the glory of his name and all is for the true welfare of his church, even every one of his believing people. They have been gathered to him by his grace. For surely it is entirely of the fulness and freeness of his grace that any of us have been brought to believe and trust in the Lord Jesus Christ alone.

Is not the most vital matter for each one of us at all times, to not be found destitute of the everlasting salvation of our souls? As we are sinners, what is the foundation of our salvation? Through the riches of grace, it is in the wonder of that great love wherewith the Lord has loved his people, bringing us as guilty, needy sinners to Jesus Christ. Throughout the word of God, the Holy Spirit always directs every poor, guilty sinner to the Lord Jesus alone. The Spirit brings them to cry to him for mercy and reveals to them where that mercy is found: "Behold the Lamb of God, which taketh away the sin of the world" (John 1:29).

What words of gracious consolation are found in the opening verses of this chapter. See the Lord's gracious purpose in appointing prophets and apostles and his servants today, to go forth declaring the good news of the gospel of salvation. This salvation is full and free. It does not come according to man's deserts but out of the wonder of the love of God revealed in Jesus Christ. What a commission is here given to the true servants of Jesus Christ: "Comfort ye, comfort ye my people." O for grace to be kept faithful in bearing witness to what the Lord sets before us in the opening verses, and the whole of this chapter.

It is as the apostle himself declared to be the sum and substance of all his ministry: "I determined not to know any thing among you, save Jesus Christ, and him crucified" (1 Cor. 2:2). Even in the present troubles, can anything less than what the Lord speaks here by the prophet, bring true consolation and lasting peace to your soul and mine, through the witness of the Holy Spirit with our spirit? "Comfort ye, comfort ye my people, saith your God. Speak ye comfortably to Jerusalem, and cry unto her, that her warfare is accomplished, that her iniquity is pardoned: for she hath received of the Lord's hand double for all her sins."

O friends, what wondrous grace, what glorious truth is here set before us! Here we see the very foundation of our salvation, not in anything we can do, but in what God in Christ *has done* as revealed to us in the precious truth of the gospel. In that gospel, the Lord declares he has once for ever put away the sins of his people and brought in everlasting righteousness for them. Full satisfaction has been made in the sufferings, death and glorious resurrection of our Lord Jesus Christ. *These are not cunningly devised fables*. Satan and unbelief will ever seek to assault these truths but, blessed be God, they can never be undermined. How full, how free is the rich consolation and peace that ever flows from them. May our souls be grounded and established in the believing receiving of this testimony God has given us in the person of his only begotten and dearly beloved Son. To him our whole attention in this passage is directed. This is the glorious good tidings proclaimed in this ninth verse!

See how the verses preceding our text show that salvation is not in what man can do. "The voice said, Cry. And he said, What shall I cry? All flesh is grass, and all the goodliness thereof is as the flower of the field: The grass withereth, the flower fadeth: because the spirit of the LORD bloweth upon it: surely the people is grass. The grass withereth, the flower fadeth: but the word of our God shall stand for ever." What a description is that of the utterly helpless state of fallen men and women, poor creatures perishing under the curse which the holy law of God righteously and solemnly declares upon all transgressors. What a mercy to be taught by God the Holy Spirit to know our helplessness, our truly lost condition as sinners. Is there anything we can bring forth to meet the requirements of the righteous God who demands perfect obedience to his holy law? As these things are brought home to our conscience do we not have to cry out, 'O how utterly hopeless is our condition and ever must be so'? Well may we ask, 'Is there no hope, is there no help for us ruined, guilty, needy sinners?'

O friends, to such poor sinners are these good tidings declared, not in a corner, but openly, clearly, fully and loudly. For we are shown God himself coming forth in the person of his only begotten and dearly beloved Son. O the wonder of it! The very God against whom we have sinned has himself made a way wherein he can be just and the justifier of every sinner brought by his grace to believe and trust alone in the Lord Jesus Christ.

In verse three, we read, "The voice of him that crieth in the wilderness, Prepare ye the way of the LORD, make straight in the desert a highway for our God." This obviously directs us to John the Baptist, the forerunner of our Lord Jesus Christ. He was the last, yet the greatest of all the old testament prophets. All before him bore witness of the coming Saviour, according to the light they were given by the Holy Spirit. O how they rejoiced in certain anticipation of the coming of our Lord Jesus Christ. But John comes forth, not foretelling his coming, but testifying that he hath come, Jesus of Nazareth, the Son of God. What wonders are here set before us concerning the ministry of John the Baptist. He called the people to repentance and confession of their sins. He testified as did as the apostles after him, that there is salvation in none other than Jesus, the Lamb of God. "There is none other name under heaven given among men, whereby we must be saved" (Acts 4:12).

Verse four says, "Every valley shall be exalted, and every mountain and hill shall be made low: and the crooked shall be made straight, and the rough places plain." And what but divine power and wisdom can appoint and accomplish the mighty things of which we read further in this chapter? Are not the greatness, glory and goodness of our God set before us? "O Zion, that bringest good tidings, get thee up into the high mountain; O Jerusalem, that bringest good tidings, lift up thy voice with strength; lift it up, be not afraid; say unto the cities of Judah, Behold your God!" And friends, what is our concern in our gathering for the worship of our God this morning? I trust it is that the eyes of our spiritual understanding may be opened to behold the Lord in a very real and personal way by the sovereign operations of the Holy Spirit.

"Behold your God!" O how the greatness and glory of our God is here set before us. Undoubtedly, we are troubled by many things, particularly in the present situation. There are implications for our own lives and fears engendered by the sickness and death so prevalent in the world today. These things are solemn and searching. I trust that, through the Lord's mercies, they bring us to the feet of the Lord Jesus Christ. By his grace may we cast all our care upon him. For stamped upon all set forth in this chapter and indeed throughout all scripture is, yes, the *greatness* but also the *goodness* of our God as revealed to us in our Lord Jesus Christ. He is not a God afar off from us but a God near to us. Behold the wonder of his love in the person of Jesus Christ, full of grace and truth. See his care and kindness towards his own, wrought out for them in the life, sufferings, death and resurrection of Jesus, our great high priest. And in these words before us, see Jesus as the great and good shepherd who laid down his life for his sheep. O I say, do not these things speak to us of the greatness but also the goodness of our God?

See this brought out further in this fortieth chapter. Surely here is truth to which we should never be afraid or ashamed to bear witness in our generation. The Lord our God is the one and only true God who rules in heaven and earth amongst all the inhabitants of the world. Friends, look at our present situation in the light of the prophet's description here of the Lord our God. O is there any to be compared to him, any like unto him? No, there is none beside him. O his greatness and goodness is seen here in the person of our Lord Jesus Christ, the glorious King in Zion, the great high priest over the house of God, the good shepherd declared in our text! Here we read of his love and care over his people. Absolute assurance is given that they are safe in his hands, that none can possibly pluck them out of his hands, whatever the outward circumstances.

Remember that all things are appointed and ordered of God. It is blessedly true that if our soul is found in Jesus hands, "our souls can ne'er be lost." One says,

> "What harm can ever reach my soul
> Beneath my Father's eye?"

These are great and good tidings that we are to declare. He says, "O Zion, that bringest good tidings." These tidings are to be declared continually to his church through the ministry of his word in the gatherings of his people. And the Lord's blessing will rest upon them, to the praise of his name. "Say unto the cities of Judah, Behold your God!"

> "To keep our eyes on Jesus fixed,
> And there our hope to stay,
> The Lord will make his goodness pass
> Before us in the way."

"Behold your God." Where do we behold God? Alone in the person of Jesus Christ, as set before us in his holy word. See what we read this morning in the fifty-third chapter of this prophecy of Isaiah. Therein we gloriously behold the Lord our God. We behold our Lord Jesus Christ, he who suffered and died for us and rose again. Likewise we see the Lord Jesus in the verses before us: "Behold, the Lord GOD will come with strong hand, and his arm shall rule for him: behold, his reward is with him, and his work before him." "Behold, the Lord GOD *will come.*"

He of whom the prophet speaks *hath come*—our Lord Jesus Christ. John the Baptist bore testimony of it when they asked him, "Who art thou?" He said, "I am not the Christ...I am the voice of one crying in the wilderness, Make straight the way of the Lord, as said the prophet Esaias." "He that sent me to baptize with water, the same said unto me, Upon whom thou shalt see the Spirit descending, and remaining on him, the same is he which baptizeth with the Holy Ghost. And I saw, and bare record that this is the Son of God" (John 1).

John never pointed to himself and no true servant of Jesus Christ ever points to themselves. They direct all to him of whom Isaiah spoke and who has now come. John declared the Lord had come into their very midst. And this is the testimony of the true church of Jesus Christ all down the generations. We direct to him alone who has come, who has accomplished the work his Father gave him to do, who has risen from the dead and gloriously ascended "into heaven itself, now to appear in the presence of God for us" (Heb. 9:24).

"Behold your God!" Behold him in the glorious reality of the incarnation of our Lord Jesus Christ. O friends, the wonders revealed to us in the glorious truth of the gospel! Who would ever have thought the Lord God would come in the way and manner that he did? He came not with great pomp, authority or power but as that little babe laid in a manger at Bethlehem. He came as the man Christ Jesus, seen in his ministry during those years here upon earth. O behold there the true servant of God. "Behold my servant" (Isa. 42:1) he who in obedience to the will of his heavenly Father, when "found in fashion as a man...humbled himself, and became obedient unto death, even the death of the cross" (Phil. 2:8). "Behold your God...the Lord GOD will come." Blessed be his name, he hath come, "come with strong hand, and his arm shall rule for him."

See in the gospels what Jesus has done. Behold "the *man* Christ Jesus" (1 Tim. 2:5). What mighty works were wrought by him in his perfect obedience to the holy law of God to bring in everlasting righteousness for us. Could any but he that is "mighty to save" (Isa. 63:1) ever accomplish the full, perfect obedience required by the holy law of God? That which we could never accomplish, he himself has gloriously wrought out. How painstakingly he wrought out that righteousness in every aspect of his life. In thought, word and deed we see his perfect obedience to the holy law of God. He, the holy One of God, needed it not for himself. He did it all for sinners such as you and me. And it is through that righteousness of our Lord Jesus Christ alone that God justifies us, ungodly as we are. Nothing else will do. "All flesh is grass, and all the goodliness thereof is as the flower of the field: the grass withereth, the flower fadeth." And so it does. What is all the supposed righteousness of man, all our supposed obedience?

I trust we desire to be obedient to the will of our God, through the work of God's grace in our souls bringing us to believe and trust in Jesus Christ,. We desire to know and do his will as we journey on through life, in utter dependence always upon himself. But does our obedience, though the fruit of his grace, comprise the righteousness upon which we can found the salvation of our souls? No. That is a very sandy foundation indeed. The only foundation for the salvation of your soul and mine is the righteousness of Jesus Christ imputed to us, received by faith which is the gift of God. It is always a case of *receiving* the riches of divine grace and mercy made known to us in the person and work of the Lord Jesus Christ. Faith *brings* nothing to God. It *receives* all from God and rejoices in that. Is there any ground for rejoicing for such a sinner as you and me in anything less than what God in Christ has wrought out for us? O can I find joy, can I find peace, even in the best obedience of my hands? I am brought again and again to realise that sin is mixed with all I do. My best, my most holy thing, is not without sin. No, I cannot find rest there, nor I trust will you ever be left to seek to find rest there. Seek it only where it is to be found, where God makes known the blessings of it, in the person of his only begotten Son, in the finished work of our Lord Jesus Christ.

"Behold, the Lord GOD will come." God has come, come in the person of Jesus Christ, Jesus of Nazareth. Yes, come "with strong hand, and his arm shall rule for him." Friends, nothing but the mighty power of God could ever accomplish what Jesus Christ has accomplished for us. And remember, he has accomplished it in the *man* Christ Jesus. *He* has satisfied the demands of God's holy law and justice. See the strong hand of our Saviour in that fifty-third chapter of this prophecy. Could any one less than he that is "mighty to save" ever endure what divine justice demanded when the Father made to meet upon him the iniquities of us all—all whom the Father had given him? Can we even begin to contemplate what that involved for our Lord Jesus Christ? Your sins and mine are so many that we cannot even begin to calculate the number of them. And if one sin deserves eternal death, and Jesus Christ suffered for all the sins of all whom his Father had given him, O how great was the load that was laid upon him! Yet he bore it all away. O the strong hand of our God, his arm ruling for him. It may appear to be in weakness that he suffered and died upon the cross. Yet what almighty power was displayed in his sufferings at the hand of man and enduring the wrath of God against the sins and transgressions of his people. See how he comes off victorious! O is there any more glorious truth! The wondrous opening verses of this chapter are founded upon that great cry of the Lord Jesus Christ from the cross: *"It is finished!"* (John 19:30). Therein is salvation in all its fulness and freeness for sinners such as you and me. "It is finished!" O may we ever sound abroad the word *"finished,"* full satisfaction rendered through the substitution of our Lord Jesus Christ.

"Behold, his reward is with him, and his work before him." What is his reward? "He shall see of the travail of his soul, and shall be satisfied: by his knowledge shall my righteous servant justify many; for he shall bear their iniquities" (Isa. 53:11).

"Behold, the Lord GOD will come." And, blessed be his name, he has come. And friends, he is *still* coming. He comes in the word of his grace. He comes in the operations of the Holy Spirit in the lives and hearts of his people still. O may we know the blessed reality of *that* coming of our Lord Jesus Christ to us, particularly in the situation in which we are found, the restrictions under which we find ourselves. From the human standpoint how irksome are these things to us. We pray for grace to submit to the Lord's will and for patience to wait for and upon the Lord. What is the encouragement and consolation for the

Lord's people even at such a time as this: "Behold, the Lord GOD will come." And he does come. He comes in his word. He comes in the promises of his word and the blessed application of them afresh to our souls this morning. He comes with the testimony, 'I am thy God, thy Saviour and thine all.'

See what we read in the latter part of this chapter. And how we need the truth of it brought home to us continually. The question is asked, "Why sayest thou, O Jacob, and speakest, O Israel, My way is hid from the LORD, and my judgment is passed over from my God?" (v.27). Friends, do we ask, "Hath God forgotten to be gracious?…will he be favourable no more?" (Ps. 77:7–9). We know the subtle workings of our own fallen nature. Unbelief is rooted therein. We find it raising its ugly head. It seems to question the ways, works and dealings of our God with us and with his church. Ah, "Hast thou not known? hast thou not heard, that the everlasting God, the LORD, the Creator of the ends of the earth, fainteth not, neither is weary? there is no searching of his understanding. He giveth power to the faint; and to them that have no might he increaseth strength Even the youths shall faint and be weary, and the young men shall utterly fall: But they that wait upon the LORD shall renew their strength; they shall mount up with wings as eagles; they shall run, and not be weary; and they shall walk, and not faint" (vs. 28–31).

I will leave the remarks there this morning. May the Lord add his blessing. Amen.

11

THE GOOD, GREAT AND CHIEF SHEPHERD

Lord's day evening 12 April 2020

"I am the good shepherd: the good shepherd giveth his life for the sheep" (John 10:11).

This morning the word to us was "Behold your God!…Behold, the Lord GOD will come" (Isa. 40:9–10). And he has come, in the person of our Lord Jesus Christ who accomplished the glorious work his Father gave him to do in the redemption and salvation of his people. Isaiah goes on to declare, "He shall feed his flock like a *shepherd:* he shall gather the lambs with his arm, and carry them in his bosom, and shall gently lead those that are with young." Great is the love of God in the provision he has made for his people in *the* shepherd, the Lord Jesus Christ. He fully atoned for all their sins and brought in everlasting righteousness for them. Do not those words of Isaiah assure us of God's continuing kindness and care for his own? And does not this evening's text fully set forth our Lord Jesus Christ as the good shepherd that giveth his life for the sheep?

Can it be thought for one moment that he will ever neglect, let alone forsake, one of his own, one that his Father gave him, one for whom he laid down his life, one for whom he is risen again and entered into heaven to appear in the presence of God for them? That embraces the entire church of Jesus Christ, every sinner that the Lord has brought by divine grace from death in trespasses and sins, into the light, life and liberty of the gospel. O how great is the wonder and blessedness of this deliverance when experienced by us personally! We are brought to know we are sinners. We are brought to realise that we are utterly lost and ruined in the fall and by our own transgressions. But the blessings of our salvation are also revealed to us. We are delivered from the guilt of our sins and the curse of God's holy law. All is fully removed from us by our Lord Jesus Christ. He died for us, rose again and ever liveth for us.

He is the Lord who spoke to the apostle John on the Isle of Patmos saying, "Fear not" (Rev. 1:17). O friends, may that truth be ever impressed deeply on our souls. May we be enabled to live and walk in the light and comfort of it. For surely, when we rightly view things, what ground is there for fear when he says, "Fear not; I am the first and the last: I am he that liveth, and was dead; and, behold, I am alive for evermore, Amen; and have the keys of hell and of death" (Rev. 1:17–18). What ground is there for fear when we hear Jesus declaring himself in our text to be the *good* shepherd that giveth his life for the sheep? And he is the *great* shepherd as Paul writes in his concluding words to the Hebrews. "Now the God of peace, that brought again from the dead our Lord Jesus, that *great* shepherd of the sheep, through the blood of the everlasting covenant" (Heb. 13:20). And Peter testifies of our Lord Jesus Christ as the *chief* shepherd, when he exhorts the elders to faithfulness in the work to which they had been called: "And when the *chief* Shepherd shall appear, ye shall receive a crown of glory that fadeth not away" (1 Pet. 5:4).

I want to speak to you tonight of Jesus as the *good* shepherd, the *great* shepherd and the *chief* shepherd. Firstly, I would just refer again to those words in Isaiah: "He shall feed his flock like a shepherd." I say again, how that expresses the love and care of the Lord for his own! To feed them is to provide for them. The Lord Jesus ever emphasises they are his own, whom his Father has given him, whom he has purchased with a great price, and whom he calls by his grace at the appointed time by the sovereign work of the Holy Spirit. He not only identifies himself *with* them, he assures us that they are *his,* and he is *theirs* in an indissoluble union. Ownership of sheep by the shepherd is very expressive. But a shepherd may own his sheep yet he may part with them, he may sell them. O no such thing applies to our Lord Jesus Christ. He is the good shepherd of those whom his Father has given him. The promises of the word of God are very precious and blessed to his own. All are sure and certain. Not one can fail. They are yea and amen in Jesus Christ, who is the very fulfilment of them all. They are from and through our Lord Jesus Christ, that great, good and chief shepherd of his flock.

Jesus says, *"I am* the good shepherd." See the emphasis here. The Lord refers to himself a number of times using those words, *"I am."* How much is in those two words! They express to us that he truly is God manifest in the flesh. Can any but God, speak of themselves as "I am." It was on this point that the scribes and Pharisees, the religious leaders of that day, were so incensed against him. They said, "Thou, being a man, makest thyself God" (v.33). They accused him of blasphemy because the expression "I am," in the fullest understanding of it, belongs to God alone. They did not mistake what he was saying, but sadly, solemnly, they hated it and persecuted him for it. They wholly rejected it. And that is ever the attitude of fallen, sinful men and women apart from sovereign, divine grace. O how great is the mercy if your eyes and mine have been opened to behold Jesus Christ as our God, the great I AM. Friends, how that surely speaks afresh to your soul and mine tonight!

"I AM," says the Lord. And is there anything too hard for the Lord our God? Are the problems which concern us at this present time too hard for our Lord Jesus Christ? Is he now unable to uphold those whom he loves, unable to keep them, provide for them and deliver them from all the dangers that threaten them? No, blessed be his name. As the present situation unfolds, we increasingly see how helpless man is, even those in authority over us. Yes, we would pray for them. In a sense, we sympathize with them. How weighty is the responsibility laid on them to know what to do in all the matters affecting the welfare of this nation. How helpless is man. Sadly, they do not recognize it, so as to turn from themselves to the only source where true help and deliverance can come, even from the very God whom they deny and reject. Solemn truth! Yet should not the believing church of Jesus Christ still seek to cry unto the Lord that for his name's sake, amidst all these things, it may please him to have mercy? Ah friends, our hope and help is in the Lord alone. O may we cease from man whose breath is in his nostrils, and trust alone in him who changes not.

As I have said, Jesus speaks of himself as "I am." In the

parable at the beginning of this chapter, he says *"I am* the door." What does this statement blessedly set forth? It is that there is only one way of access to God, one way of acceptance by the Father, one way into the true church. It is through the person of Jesus Christ. There is no other way. He says, "I am the *door"* and "he that entereth not by the *door* into the sheepfold, but climbeth up some other way, the same is a thief and a robber." He says, "I am the *door* of the sheep. All that ever came before me are thieves and robbers." What a solemn truth is set before us there. All who do not come with the doctrine of our Lord Jesus Christ are not of God. In effect, they are thieves and robbers. The apostle John in his second epistle warns of those who bring not the "doctrine of Christ," God manifest in the flesh. And he says, "receive him not into your house, neither bid him God speed: for he that biddeth him God speed is partaker of his evil deeds" (1 John 10–11). O how we need the grace of true discernment to bring all things to the touchstone of God's holy word.

"I am the door," says the Lord Jesus Christ. There is but one way of access to God for sinners. And O friends, remember that the way to the Father *is for sinners*. Yes, "the vilest sinner out of hell who lives to feel his need" will never be turned away when brought to come to the Father in the way he has appointed in Jesus Christ. God gives them blessed faith to flee to the Lord Jesus Christ to hide them. Needy, exercised, burdened soul, O do your sins testify against you? Does Satan say there is no hope for you in God? What presumption it would be for you even to seek to cry to the Lord in your condition? Are you urged to try to do something to better yourself before you seek to come to the Lord Jesus? Remember that Satan is a liar and it is the very working of unbelief to suggest those things.

The word of God assures us that the only manner in which we can come to the Father is through Jesus Christ as sinners, ruined, wretched, poor and needy, with *nothing* in our hand. Why friend, to bring something in our hand is to set up a barrier in the way. Coming to the Father, through Jesus Christ, with a sense of our ruin and guilt as a sinner,

> "No sinner shall ever be empty sent back,
> Who comes seeking mercy for Jesus's sake."

That blessed door of access and acceptance is ever open, but it is open for guilty, needy sinners, brought to know their solemn state by the Holy Spirit.

> "Venture on him, venture wholly;
> Let no other trust intrude:
> None but Jesus,
> Can do helpless sinners good."

That is the testimony of his word. O friends, it is still true that our Lord Jesus Christ, the great shepherd of the sheep, "receiveth sinners, and eateth with them" (Luke 15:2). Man may despise him but nothing can ever overturn this blessed truth, as proved in the experience of each sinner taught of the Holy Spirit.

"I am the good shepherd; the good shepherd giveth his life for the sheep." This then expresses his love and care for his sheep. And he says, "I know my sheep, and am known of mine." Is that not a precious truth? *"I know my sheep."* The Lord knows every sheep, the weak in faith as well as the strong in faith, however far off they may be. He has known them from before the foundation of the world. He says, "I have graven thee upon the palms of my hands; thy walls are continually before me" (Isa. 49:16). They are never out of his sight even though they may often feel to be far off. But whatever they may feel, they are never outside the circle of the love of God in Jesus Christ.

"I know my sheep, and *am known of mine."* O how glorious is the wonder that the Lord knows his sheep, and every one of them is brought *to know him.* They are brought to realise their need of him. Friends, do we realise our need tonight? Have we ever been brought to realise our need of the Lord Jesus Christ? But we are not only brought to realise our need of him. We are brought to know the wonder of his mercy towards us. We are brought to realise that none but Jesus can do us helpless sinners any good. And we find him to be "the chiefest among ten thousand...altogether lovely" (Song of Sol. 5:10,16).

"I know my sheep, and am known of mine." O how precious in the sight of the Lord is each one of his own! And how precious is the Lord, the great shepherd of the sheep, to each one brought to know themselves as sinners and to know him and what he has done for them. O may our hearts be more drawn out in love to the Lord Jesus Christ, love flowing out of that great love wherewith he loved us (Eph. 2:4), even before we loved him, blessed be his holy name.

"I am the good shepherd: the good shepherd giveth his life for the sheep." "The *good* shepherd." He speaks of the hireling that fleeth when the wolf cometh, when danger threatens the sheep. But O the good shepherd! How indebted the sheep are to him, how dependent upon him. It is he who cares for them, does everything for them, provides for all their earthly needs as they journey on through this fallen world and, above all, for their spiritual, eternal welfare. O he leads his people into rich pastures in the word of his grace. What gracious provision is made for them in the person and finished work of our Lord Jesus Christ. What alone brings true peace to your troubled soul and mine? Wherein do we find true refreshing for our souls amid all the trials, difficulties and temptations to which we are exposed? Is it not as, according to his promise, we are led by the Holy Spirit into the precious things of Jesus Christ set before us in the word? O what blessings flow from him!

"I am the good shepherd: the good shepherd giveth his life for the sheep." O what he has done for them! "Giveth *his life* for the sheep." Does this not direct us to the very realities of Gethsemane and Calvary? What great things are set before us here! Who has given his life for the sheep? Consider who the shepherd is? God manifest in the flesh! Consider for whom he gave his life? Wretched, ruined, hell-deserving sinners! O what love is this! Can we say it arises from anything in us? No. Blessed be the Lord's great and holy name, he has loved us so as to lay down his life for us? But is there anything in us to induce him to do so? Why friends, search as we may every moment of our lives, we can never find anything in ourselves to induce the Lord to be favourable to us, let alone lay down his life for us! But as the good shepherd, he giveth his life for the sheep. And how willingly he gave,

> "How willing was Jesus to die,
> That we wretched sinners might live!
> The life they could not take away,
> How ready was Jesus to give!"

Ah, remember that all the blessings of salvation you and I receive as sinners, flow out of the *gift* of God in Jesus Christ to us. Nothing is earned, nothing deserved, nothing of our best works, our best duties performed, even done in faith by the outworking of the grace of God in our lives. None of these things are taken into account in the manifestation of the love of God in Jesus Christ toward us. No. All is founded on the free grace of God revealed to us in the precious truth of the gospel.

"The good shepherd giveth his life for the sheep." How willingly he laid down his life. And he further says here, "No man taketh it from me, but I lay it down of myself. I have power to lay it down, and I have power to take it again. This commandment have I received of my Father." Behold the solemn sufferings of our Lord and Saviour in Gethsemane and at Calvary. He did not die as a result of the cruelty he received at the hands of man. He did not die as a result of the wounds he suffered. He died willingly, *giving* his life a ransom for many. In the Levitical offerings and sacrifices, it had to be a willingly given sacrifice and had to be without blemish. How that shadowed forth the person of our Lord Jesus Christ, who offered himself as a willing sacrifice without blemish. In him was no sin but he was made sin for us. Can you and I comprehend the wonder that "the LORD hath laid on him the iniquity of us all"? (Isa. 53:6). "God hath made him to be sin for us, who knew no sin; that we might be made the righteousness of God in him" (2 Cor. 5:21). Wonders of grace to him belong! O may we ever show forth the praises of our God and Saviour, exclaiming "Unto him that loved us, and washed us from our sins in his own blood, and hath made us kings and priests unto God and his Father; to him be glory and dominion for ever and ever" (Rev. 1:5–6). "The good shepherd giveth his life for the sheep," and has thereby laid the foundation of our faith and hope and the blessings of salvation.

And our Lord Jesus Christ is referred to as the *great* shepherd of the sheep. This also surely directs us to what he accomplished in Gethsemane and at Calvary and to his rising again from the dead "the third day according to the scriptures" (1 Cor. 15:4). Yes, the great shepherd has risen again, thereby proclaiming the blessed truth that he has overcome sin, Satan, death, hell and the grave for his people. Their victory is sure, their salvation is certain, to the praise of the glory of his name. Not only has he died for us but he rose again as the ever living one, the *great* shepherd. And as the great, the ever living shepherd, we are assured that his love and care are constant over all that concerns each one of his people, from day to day, even from *moment to moment*. O no shepherd cares for his flock as the Lord Jesus Christ cares and provides for his own.

You look at a flock of sheep. As one said, they do not worry their woolly heads where their next meal is coming from, or even what their future days may hold for them. No. The sheep is entirely reliant on the shepherd. All is left to the shepherd. Friends, may we learn to do likewise through the Lord's mercies toward us. Leave all to the shepherd. Rely upon him alone. He is faithful to what he has promised. Has he failed us yet? No, blessed be his name. Nor will he fail us, whatever may yet lie before us. We cannot predict the future. No man can. It is vain for us to speculate what may lie before us, not only in the weeks and months ahead, but even in the next few days. But our great shepherd knows. All is in his hands. As the great shepherd, he reigns over heaven and earth, and among all the inhabitants of the earth, and "none can stay his hand, or say unto him, What doest thou?" (Dan. 4:35). Such is the great shepherd of the sheep and blessed are those who are the sheep of his pasture. O are we not surely safe in his hand? Will he not provide for us, keep us and preserve us unto his everlasting kingdom?

Also, Jesus is set before us as the *chief* shepherd. Peter, exhorting the church elders to be faithful in the ministry appointed them, says, "When the chief shepherd shall appear, ye shall receive a crown of righteousness that fadeth not away" (1 Pet. 5:4). *"When the chief shepherd shall appear."* He that is the good shepherd, the great shepherd will most surely come again as the *chief* shepherd "the second time without sin unto salvation" (Heb. 9:28). We considered this morning that the "Lord GOD will come." And he has come in the person of our Lord Jesus Christ in his incarnation. He still comes by the ministry of the Holy Spirit to his church and people. *And he is coming again.* What a glorious prospect lies before the church and people of God. Sickness and death are all around us and we are all thus exposed. Indeed, the day may be fast hastening (we know not how soon) when we shall be called from this time state into eternity. O the blessedness if we are found in Jesus Christ as the sheep of his pasture. See how the psalmist could say, "The LORD is my shepherd; I shall not want" (Ps. 23:1). Notice that the Lord *is* my shepherd and "I *shall* not want," not 'I *may* not want.' No. "I *shall* not." See how emphatic is the word of our God in sealing home his promises to his people.

"Yea, though I walk through the valley of the shadow of death, I will fear no evil: for thou art with me" (Ps. 23:4). Has the Lord ever forsaken one of his own? O can we not go forward confidently, not in ourselves for we daily realise our weakness sinfulness and need, but confident in the love of our Lord Jesus Christ? May we go forward confidently, knowing that as the *good* shepherd, Jesus has given himself for us, as the *great* shepherd he loves and cares for his people to the end, and as the *chief* shepherd he is coming again to receive us unto himself. As he says, "that where I am, there ye may be also" (John 14:3). O the blessedness of the church and people of God as found in the hands of our Lord Jesus Christ! He himself declares, "My sheep hear my voice, and I know them, and they follow me: and I give unto them eternal life; and they shall never perish, neither shall any man pluck them out of my hand. My Father, which gave them me, is greater than all; and no man is able to pluck them out of my Father's hand. I and my Father are one" (John 10:27–30). Can more be said? Does more need to be said? We sometimes sing,

"What more can he say than to you he has said,
You who unto Jesus for refuge have fled?"

Ah friends, no more needs to be said to assure us of the reality of these things which are found and centred in the person of our Lord Jesus Christ, the *good* shepherd, the *great* shepherd and the *chief* shepherd. Through the riches of divine grace may we daily live in the blessed believing realisation that "The Lord is *my* shepherd; I shall not want."

I will leave the remarks there. May the Lord add his blessing. Amen.

12

BELIEVE YE THAT I AM ABLE TO DO THIS?

Tuesday evening 14 April 2020

"And when Jesus departed thence, two blind men followed him, crying, and saying, Thou Son of David, have mercy on us. And when he was come into the house, the blind men came to him: and Jesus saith unto them, Believe ye that I am able to do this? They said unto him, Yea, Lord. Then touched he their eyes, saying, According to your faith be it unto you. And their eyes were opened; and Jesus straitly charged them, saying, See that no man know it. But they, when they were departed, spread abroad his fame in all that country" (Matthew 9:27-31).

O how this chapter, and all the gospel records of the life and ministry of our Lord Jesus Christ, bear witness to what a great Saviour is ours, how wonderful he is, how wondrous in working! "Is any thing too hard for the LORD?" (Gen. 18:14). The prophecy of the glorious person in Isaiah chapter nine is surely fulfilled in Jesus, the God-man who lived, suffered, died, rose again and ascended into heaven to appear in the presence of God for us. And, brought to believe in him, what a source of encouragement and consolation it is for us to know that *he is the same Jesus still.*

Isaiah prophesied that "unto us a child is born, unto us a Son is given, and the government shall be upon his shoulder" (Isa. 9:6). And does not all authority and power belong to our Lord Jesus Christ as he is the great and glorious head of the church? Has not the Father given all things into his hand? What rich encouragement and consolation is that to the church of God, to every poor needy sinner brought to believe and trust in the Lord

Jesus Christ! Yes, the government *is* upon his shoulder. The word of God tells us that all the authorities we see on earth are appointed and used of him to fulfil his purposes. Ultimately, all shall redound to the glory of his name. Let us never lose sight of that. The one thing the Lord ever has in view, in all his ways and dealings with men and nations, is the glory of his name. But O, wondrous truth, glorious grace, *bound up* with that is the true spiritual and eternal welfare of all whom he hath loved with an everlasting love. He has redeemed them by the precious blood of Christ. In his appointed time he calls them by his grace. And in *every* step of their life's journey, his constant care, kindness and mercy are lengthened out towards them.

As I said, do we not see the prophecy of Isaiah gloriously realised in the chapter before us? "The government *shall* be upon his shoulder: and his name *shall* be called Wonderful, Counseller, The mighty God, The everlasting Father, The Prince of Peace." *"His name shall be called wonderful."* Friends, what a *wonderful* Saviour we have, one mighty to save, the *wonder* of whose love is manifest in his kindness and care for every needy sinner he calls by his grace.

Last Lord's day we considered our Lord Jesus Christ as the *great, good* and *chief* Shepherd, foretold in the spirit of prophecy, as the one who "shall feed his flock like a shepherd: he shall gather the lambs with his arm, and carry them in his bosom, and shall gently lead those that are with young" (Isa. 40:11). Do not we see that gracious ministry, that wonderful Saviour, that great Shepherd of the sheep in his dealings, when he was on earth, with sinful men and women in all their needs? How many and varied were those needs! Look at the sicknesses and infirmities brought to him, all beyond the ability of man with all his ingenuity to resolve. We do not despise for one moment what God has provided providentially for our bodily health in medicines and surgical skills to minister to the sick in our day. We have much for which to be thankful to the Lord. But in their right use we must always be dependent on him. For ultimately, healing is not by what man can do, even the most skilful of physicians. It comes from the hand of the Lord alone, our wonderful God and Saviour.

As we read here, Jesus is set before us as the great and good physician. He healed all manner of sicknesses and diseases amongst the people. There was not one issue he was unable or unwilling to deal with. In them all, he manifested the wonder of his power, goodness and mercy to the afflicted. And blessed be his great and holy name, our Lord Jesus Christ is still a wonderful Saviour, a great physician who heals all manner of bodily sicknesses. But what is far more important, he is the *only* physician of sin-sick, hell-deserving sinners. He alone can deliver transgressors from the curse and condemnation of God's holy law. And are we not all transgressors of God's holy law? Are we not sinners vile and base? Friends, to many that might sound a very hard saying, but it is solemnly true. O what a mercy to realise the truth of it by the teaching of the Holy Spirit.

We see here demonstrated that the Lord not only healed bodily diseases. See what a wonderful Saviour our Lord Jesus was in the glory of his grace to that paralysed man. He said, "Son, be of good cheer; thy sins be forgiven thee." The scribes and Pharisees did not misunderstand the implication of what he said. They did not express it openly but the Lord knew their thoughts. What a solemn fact that the Lord not only looks on our outward appearance but he looks on our heart. He knows our thoughts afar off. He knew what they were thinking and what their attitude was towards him. They were thinking 'This man blasphemeth, for it is God's prerogative alone to forgive sin. Who is this man who is saying, thy sins be forgiven thee?" But though *they* were offended at him, *we* see here in "this man." our wonderful Saviour, the mighty God, the everlasting Father. And blessed be his name, this man receives sinners and eats with them as we see in this chapter.

After calling Matthew from the receipt of custom, we read that many publicans and sinners were taking a meal with Jesus in the house. The Pharisees asked the disciples, "Why eateth your master with publicans and sinners?" But our Lord Jesus Christ says, "I am not come to call the righteous, but sinners to repentance." Ah, this man receives sinners. He forgives sins, he forgives sins fully, he forgives sins freely. Those of us who trust that by divine grace we know the blessedness of the forgiveness of our sins, receive that forgiveness freely and fully.

But friends, how dearly was it purchased, as we read on Lord's day evening of our Lord Jesus Christ as the good shepherd who "giveth his life for the sheep" (John 10:11). *There* was the price that was paid. "Forasmuch as ye know that ye were not redeemed with corruptible things, as silver and gold, from your vain conversation received by tradition from your fathers; but with the precious blood of Christ, as of a lamb without blemish and without spot" (1 Pet. 1:18–19). Should you try to calculate the vast value of the precious blood of the Lord Jesus Christ, you will find you cannot even begin to do so. All the wealth of the world could not begin to match that value. O the wonder and reality of that blood—he laid down his life for the sheep.

In this chapter, we see how the Lord, our wonderful Saviour, displayed his power in forgiving sins, raising the dead, healing the sick, giving sight to the blind and casting out devils. But my desire in bringing these things before you this evening, is to stress that this account surely has application to the issues that confront us at this particular time in our day. I cannot emphasise enough, that he is the same Jesus still. O do not think that the Lord is remote from the circumstances in which we are found today, or that his hand is not in all these things. He appoints them. He overrules them. And he will surely bring to pass his purposes in them. We do not know the Lord's ultimate purposes in the present situation. But may we who have been brought by divine grace to believe and trust in the Lord Jesus, seek continually to commit into his hands all that concerns us at this present time. Through his enabling grace, may we wait upon him in the believing expectation that he hears the cries of his people.

Friends, we can be assured that the Lord has not forgotten his own. He will never neglect one of them. All that concerns his people is safe in his hands. We are under the care and guidance of our Lord Jesus Christ. Remember what I brought before you on Lord's day concerning the Lord Jesus Christ as the great and good shepherd of the sheep. David said in Psalm 23: "The LORD is my shepherd." And in the events described in this chapter, we behold the goodness and mercy of our Lord Jesus Christ as the great shepherd of the sheep. We see those who came to Jesus. Jairus went to him, knowing his daughter was dead, but believing that if Jesus laid his hand upon her, she would live. The woman with the issue of blood: "If I may but touch his garment, I shall be whole." These two blind men crying, "Thou Son of David, have mercy on us."

Do we not see in all these cases that the Lord giveth *grace for grace?* (John 1:16). I am certain that where a sinner is brought to cry unto the Lord for mercy, that cry is not the result of the working of fallen human nature. Even where there is grievous sickness which may well be unto death, a true cry for mercy does not arise from the natural working of our fallen nature. It is of his grace alone that there is a cry unto him or indeed any saving response to his word.

Look at Matthew sitting at the receipt of custom. There was no cry from him for mercy, but what an immediate effect the word of the Lord had on him! "Follow me." "And he left all, rose up, and followed him" (Luke 5:27). See there *"grace for grace,"* grace manifest in the power of the Lord on Matthew, grace bringing him to follow Jesus in response to those words, "Follow me." Likewise with that woman with the issue of blood. What brought her to know that if she but touched the hem of his garment she would be perfectly whole? Did not grace bring her there? Is it not grace alone that brings a sinner to seek unto Jesus, as he is Lord? And if grace thus brings a sinner to cry unto the Lord, can that sinner be sent empty away? Will they not obtain what they have been brought to seek for, by the grace of God? They *shall* obtain it, blessed be the Lord. He giveth grace for grace.

These two blind men cried, "Thou Son of David, have mercy on us." How did they know he was the Son of David? No doubt they had heard what he had done, for the fame of him went abroad. But many heard, many saw the miracles that he wrought, but did not cry like these two blind men, "Thou *Son of David*, have mercy on us." Using that term, "thou Son of David" showed that they believed he was the promised Messiah. I do not say how deep was their understanding of that truth, but the essence of it was manifest in them. Who but the Spirit of God could give a sinner grace to behold Jesus as the Son of David, and to cry to him for mercy?

"And when he was come into the house, the blind men came to him: and Jesus saith unto them, Believe ye that I am able to do this?" Friends, what a word is that to these two blind men: *"Believe ye that I am able to do this?"* Consider what they sought of the Lord? They were blind. What implications that had for them in those days. Being blind, they no doubt were beggars. Their situation was very distressing, unquestionably. When the Lord asked them, "Believe ye I am able to do this?" had this ever been done before, that the blind should literally receive their sight? They answered, "Yea, Lord." O friends, he giveth grace for grace. Brought to cry unto him for mercy, they are blessed with the faith which is the gift of God. And see how real and personal this was to them. They truly did believe that Jesus is the Christ, the Son of God. Their answer, "Yea, Lord" to his question, "Believe ye I am able to do this?" gave to the Lord the glory which is due to him. It was the acknowledgement and confession that he is the Christ, the Son of God, co-equal with the Father and the Holy Spirit, God over all.

O friends, do not lightly pass over the wonders of grace here opened up to us. The same wonders are manifest in each sinner brought to cry to the Lord for mercy and to believe and trust in him by God-given faith. They receive out of the fulness that is in Christ Jesus. I do not say that such are without their fears or questionings. Though the people of God, blessed with a God-given faith, we cannot say we are always in the full confidence of that faith. Oftentimes it is weak. But it is blessed certain truth that he will never forsake the work of his grace, despite its being assaulted by the workings of sin and Satan, and the questions that arise in us. Yes, we may be brought very low but, blessed be his great and holy name, we can never be cast out of the hands of our Lord Jesus Christ.

What I particularly want to emphasis tonight is this question, *"Believe ye that I am able to do this?"* Look at it concerning the need of these two blind men. Look at it concerning the issues in our own lives. *"Believe ye that I am able to do this?"* O does not this set before us a vitally important point? The *reality* of God-given faith is to truly believe that Jesus is the Christ, the Son of God, and that there is nothing too hard for the Lord. Here was an issue which was impossible for men, but nothing is impossible for the Lord our God. Our Lord Jesus Christ is one that is mighty to save, one that is a wonderful Saviour.

"Believe ye that I am able to do this?" O for grace that brings us to the footstool of mercy. 'Yea, Lord, we believe thou art able to do this, able to save such a sinner as I am, to save me even unto the uttermost. Why? Because thou hast said it.' So the hymnwriter expresses it:

> "What Christ has said must be fulfilled;
> On this firm rock, believers build;"
> (and what a firm rock it is upon which believers build)
> "His word shall stand, his truth prevail,
> And not one jot or tittle fail."

What glorifies God in the life and experience of a sinner taught by the Holy Spirit? It is a poor sinner being brought to believe the testimony that God has given of his only begotten Son. Yes, we are weak, we are beset with fears on every hand, we are conscious of our own weakness, sinfulness and need. "Believe ye that I am able to do this?" Do we believe that he is "able also to save them to the uttermost that come unto God by him" (Heb. 7:25). Ah, may your response and mine *not* be questioning. 'Well Lord, I am not really sure about it; I would be more confident if I could see something in myself to encourage me.' No friend, the teaching of the Holy Spirit brings the sinner in all his helplessness to receive the testimony God has given of his Son, as able to save to the uttermost *all* that come unto God by him.

"Believe ye that I am able to do this?" "Yea, Lord." See his response. "Then touched he their eyes, saying, According to your faith be it unto you. And their eyes were opened." *"According to your faith."* As with every believer, their faith was the gift of God, but it is *our faith* as given to us. And in the exercise of that faith in every aspect of our spiritual lives, are we not wholly dependent upon and indebted to the Lord? This does not bring praise to men—far from it. All praise is due to the Lord alone.

"And their eyes were opened; and Jesus straitly charged them, saying, See that no man know it." Sadly, we know they did not obey the Lord. In one sense we can understand it. Were they not so filled with wonder and joy for receiving their sight, that they could not keep it in? But "Jesus straitly charged them, saying, See that no man know it." There was a purpose in this. Our wondrous Saviour, the mighty God, the everlasting Father, the Prince of Peace, did not come to this earth to be acclaimed by men. We see rather that he came to be "despised and rejected of men; a man of sorrows, and acquainted with grief" Isa. 53:3). There is much instruction for the church of God in the word of the Lord to these men. O friends, we are not to follow *our* will, but to give all honour to our Lord Jesus and seek to do *his* will. We see how he humbled himself when on this earth. Yet the scripture sets before us that God has now "given him a name which is above every name, that at the name of Jesus every knee should bow...and every tongue confess that Jesus is Lord" (Phil. 2:8–11).

O friends, the reality of God-given faith is that we are brought to "believe that Jesus is the Christ, the Son of God; and that believing ye might have life through his name" (John 20:31). And as the Lord thus reveals himself to his people in saving mercy, are we not to seek by his grace "to show forth the praises of him who hath called us out of darkness into his marvellous light"? (1Pet. 2:9).

"Believe ye that I am able to do this?" Friends, view every situation, whatever it may be, in the light of the testimony here given of our Lord Jesus Christ. Is he able? Will unbelief question it? Ah, let unbelief question it, let the devil seek to dispute it, we are assured that he *is* able. "Believe ye that I am able to do this?" O may your response and mine ever be, by the Lord's gracious enabling, 'Yes Lord, we believe that thou art the Christ the Son of God.' And thus, through his grace, "believing, ye might have life through his name" (John 20:31).

"Believe ye that I am able to do this?" O may our eyes and hearts always be up unto the Lord. What the prophets declared we see wonderfully fulfilled in the life and ministry of our Lord Jesus Christ upon earth. And as we see him now risen, ascended and glorified at the right hand of the Majesty in the heavens, he is that *same* Jesus still. Still "mighty to save" (Isa. 63:1). Still able "to save them to the uttermost that come unto God by him."

May the Lord add his blessing. Amen.

13

THERE IS NONE LIKE UNTO THE GOD OF JESHURUN

Lord's day morning 19 April 2020

"There is none like unto the God of Jeshurun, who rideth upon the heaven in thy help, and in his excellency on the sky. The eternal God is thy refuge, and underneath are the everlasting arms: and he shall thrust out the enemy from before thee; and shall say, Destroy them. Israel then shall dwell in safety alone: the fountain of Jacob shall be upon a land of corn and wine; also his heavens shall drop down dew. Happy art thou, O Israel: who is like unto thee, O people saved by the Lord, the shield of thy help, and who is the sword of thy excellency! and thine enemies shall be found liars unto thee; and thou shalt tread upon their high places" (Deuteronomy 33:26-29).

We have recorded in this chapter "the blessing, wherewith Moses the man of God blessed the children of Israel before his death" (v.1). For forty years Moses had led the people on that wilderness journey from Egypt down to the borders of the land of Canaan. O what grace had been manifest in this man of God, as the hand of God had been upon him, had upheld, kept, preserved and provided for him all those years. As he comes now to the age of one hundred and twenty it is said that "his eye was not dim, nor his natural force abated" (Deut. 34:7).

In this blessing, Moses speaks unquestionably in the spirit of prophecy regarding the twelve tribes of Israel and their future possession of Canaan. Indeed, following his death, they were shortly to enter the land under the leadership of Joshua. This was what God had promised to Abraham, Isaac and Jacob many years before. O what a testimony this is to the unchanging faithfulness of our God, that what he has promised he will most surely perform, to the praise of the glory of his name.

As I have mentioned to you many times, what is for his praise and glory, cannot but be for the true good, the spiritual and eternal welfare, of every one of his own. He has loved them with an everlasting love and in his appointed time calls them by his grace. He has redeemed them to himself through the person and finished work of the Lord Jesus Christ. He has brought them into the blessings of the covenant ordered in all things and sure, made between the eternal Three from before the foundation of the world.

Coming to these last verses of the blessing of Moses, O how he seeks to honour and bless the God of Israel, the one and only true God, Father, Son and Holy Spirit. What he testifies of the Lord our God not only had respect to Israel of old but has *now* to the true spiritual Israel of God. This is his church, his people, a remnant in the earth, his beloved, the subjects of his continual care, kindness and provision. He has saved them with an everlasting salvation and will most surely bring every one of them by saving grace and mercy unto himself. At his appointed time they shall enter the glorious inheritance provided for them, not by any merit in them, but through the wonder of the great love wherewith the Lord has loved his people even when they "were dead in trespasses and sins" (Eph. 2:1). All is of his sovereign love and free mercy through the person and work of our Lord and Saviour Jesus Christ.

Moses says in this twenty-sixth verse, *"There is none like unto the God of Jeshurun,* who rideth upon the heaven in thy help, and in his excellency on the sky." Yes, there in none like unto the Lord our God. He himself declares, "Is there a God beside me? yea, there is no God; I know not any" (Isa. 44:8). "There be gods many, and lords many" (1 Cor. 8:5) which men set up for themselves, which can neither hear, nor see, nor be of any help whatsoever. And, "They that make them are like unto them: so is every one that trusteth in them" (Ps. 115:8). But he who is the one and only true God, the God and Father of our Lord Jesus Christ, is described here as the God of Jeshurun. O the blessedness if we, through the witness of the Holy Spirit with our spirit, can look up with Moses to the one true God, assured that "this God is our God for ever and ever: he will be our guide even unto death" (Ps. 48:14).

O is not this true, rich encouragement and consolation for us in the circumstances in which we are found? Indeed, have not the church and people of God encouragement at all times, through the unchanging love and faithfulness of our God? Here it is said that there is none like unto him! He is supreme in power, perfect in wisdom. All his ways and dealings are wise, just and good in the affairs of men and nations. We see the hand of God, ruling, overruling and bringing to pass what is for his own glory and the good of his people, according to his divine purposes. Never lose sight of the fact that, central to all the Lord's dealings, is the manifestation of the glory of his grace in the redemption and salvation of every one whom he hath loved and chosen. He has given them to our Lord Jesus Christ, the glorious mediator of the covenant of grace, through whom every grace and favour comes, in all fulness and freeness, to such sinners as you and me.

"There is none like unto *the God of Jeshurun.* " What does the name Jeshurun express? It is only found three times in the scriptures—twice in the chapter I have read this morning. The name Jeshurun encompasses the true Israel of God, a people the Lord has loved and chosen and brought into the blessings of a covenant relationship with himself. It denotes a people who have been brought to see what God had spoken to them. That was true of Israel. God made that covenant with them at Sinai, of which Moses was the mediator.

What a display was given to them of the glory, power and divine majesty of God as he appeared to them on Sinai. What things were made known to them through his servant Moses in all the appointments for the worship and service of God in the Levitical order, and for their walk before him! For they were a people whom the Lord had chosen and separated from among all the nations of the earth to be unto him a peculiar people. They were a people whose *sole* purpose was to serve him in their day and generation. They were to bear witness that he is the one and only true God. As he said of them by the prophet Isaiah, "ye are my witnesses, saith the Lord, that I am God" (Isa. 43:12).

Yes, God made a covenant with them at Sinai, "which my covenant they brake" (Jer. 31:32). Yet God's faithfulness to what he had promised did not fail. We know that what was shadowed forth in that Levitical dispensation had its glorious fulfilment in what is described as the new covenant promised by the Lord through his servant Jeremiah. It is quoted by Paul in his epistle to the Hebrews. "I will make a new covenant with the house of Israel and with the house of Judah: not according to the covenant that I made with their fathers in the day when I took them by the hand to lead them out of the land of Egypt; because they continued not in my covenant...this is the covenant that I will make with the house of Israel...I will put my laws into their mind, and write them in their hearts...for I will be merciful to their unrighteousness, and their sins and their iniquities will I remember no more" (Jer. 31:31–34; Heb. 8:8–12).

Yes, Moses was an honoured servant of God. The word declares that there was no prophet like unto Moses, "whom the LORD knew face to face" (Deut. 34:10). Moses was the mediator of the covenant God made with them at Sinai. But, as Paul shows in his second epistle to the Corinthians chapter three, the glory of *that* covenant is *eclipsed* by the glory of the new covenant of which our Lord Jesus Christ is the mediator! In the old covenant there was the remembrance of "sins once a year" (Lev. 16:34). But in the new covenant, God declares "their sins and their iniquities *will I remember no more.*"

When we read "There is none like unto the God of Jeshurun," we behold God, not only in the covenant of Sinai, but in the covenant of grace revealed to us in the glorious gospel. This centres in the person of our Lord and Saviour Jesus Christ. This is the *new,* the greater covenant, by which the old covenant of Sinai is done away because it has been completely fulfilled by our Lord Jesus Christ for his people, his Jeshurun. Yes, he is still the God of Jeshurun. *There is none like unto him!* They are the people whom he calls by grace into a blessed relationship with himself. They are his one true church. They are but a remnant in the earth in our day, as they have been all down the generations.

O friends, how blessed are these people, whose God is described here as the God of Jeshurun! Yes, they are a tried people, often distressed, not only by outward circumstances, but by the daily defilement of sin in their own hearts and lives. Do we not often have much cause for the humbling of ourselves under the mighty hand of our God, in confession and sorrow for our sins? But see what a foundation is laid for the faith and hope of the living family of God. Though weak in ourselves, helpless in the face of many issues we daily experience, and certainly at this present time, yet behold this glorious truth that "There is none like unto the God of Jeshurun." One thing is sure. The God and Father of our Lord Jesus Christ is the only true God. And he is the God and Father of all he hath loved, chosen and called by his grace. And from this blessed relationship we draw all our help and hope at this present time.

Ah, "There is none like unto the God of Jeshurun." And it is very evident from our text that the Lord our God does not forsake his people, neither is he indifferent to their situation and concerns. In his dealings with Israel of old, was not his eye ever upon them even though, sadly and solemnly, they were a rebellious people? How often they forgot him. How often they murmured and complained with blessings in their hands. Yet see his faithfulness to his promises. The manna came daily. They drank the water which flowed out of the rock that followed them. God was faithful to a people who were so often rebellious and forgetful of him.

Among them was a remnant according to the election of grace, brought to receive his promise and look forward to its fulfilment in the coming of our Lord Jesus Christ. They knew the blessedness of the pardon of their sins and acceptance with God through the promised Saviour, not by their own worth or doings.

I trust, through the Lord's mercies towards us, we desire to be obedient to his revealed will and to walk before him in all humbleness of mind and lowliness of spirit. But how conscious we are of how short we come. As it was with Israel of old, so it is with the people of God still. The Lord's favour towards us is not founded on what *we* are, what *we* have done, or what *we* do even by the gracious enabling of the Lord the Holy Spirit. His favour is founded wholly upon what *Jesus is and has done for us*. O look not for any favour from the Lord our God which is not founded on the fulness and wonder of his saving grace and mercy revealed to us in the person of Jesus Christ *alone*. What a sure foundation is that!

You know, if the Lord's favour towards us was founded on our obedience to his will as a people he has called by his grace, would not that be a very shaky foundation? Where is there one of his people who can say that they do not offend? Does not the child of God have to confess daily how far short they come? Is not our daily cry, "LORD, be merciful unto me: heal my soul; for I have sinned against thee" (Ps. 41:4)? May we know daily what it is to bow low at the Saviour's feet, humbled under the sense of his great goodness and our utter undeserving of the least of his mercies.

O friends, our encouragement and consolation is not drawn from what *we are* but what *Jesus Christ is*. O in all the changing scenes of life and the circumstances in which we are found at this present time, the Lord Jesus is the same. As it is declared of him here, "There is none like unto the God of Jeshurun," the people whom he has loved, chosen, and brought into a covenant relationship with himself.

He "rideth upon the heaven in their help, and in his excellency on the sky." Does not that express his divine sovereignty, his almighty power and the reality of his love, not in word only but in deed and in truth? *"He rideth upon the heaven in thy help."* That is, does he not surmount all difficulties and dangers confronting his church? To address every need and distress of his people, he rideth upon the *heaven* in their help. There are *no* restrictions with our God, no distresses in which he is unable or unwilling to help, blessed be his great and holy name. Is there any power or authority *above* the one who is the God of Jeshurun, the one and only true God? No. And as the psalmist said, "this God is our God for ever and ever: he will be our guide even unto death."

"He rideth upon the heaven in thy help." O friends, what encouragement is then given us in all things and at all times to look to him only, to trust in him alone. Should we not fully commit our way and all our concerns into his hands and wait on him even in our present trying circumstances? Are we not each affected in not being able to meet in the gatherings of the Lord's people, a privilege granted us all our lives thus far? Is it not our prayerful desire that the Lord, subject to his will, may hasten the time when we can meet together once more in the fellowship of his people, knowing his presence with us in the means of grace? Yes friends, may our eyes and hearts be up unto the Lord who "rides upon the heaven in our help and in his excellency upon the sky."

How precious also is the consideration that the Lord not only knows all things but he knows what is best for us. O for grace to wait upon him, to cry to him in such a situation as this, that if it is his sovereign will, his hand may be withdrawn and he deliver from this scourge abroad in the earth. The purpose of this visitation is known alone to the Lord. But let us not overlook the importance of the prayers of his people in their crying unto him. You know, the Lord does hear and answer the cries of his people, though not always in the way we might think or may have desired. But certainly, no cries of the Lord's people go unheeded by him. He will answer in his own good time and way.

Remember what we read of Elijah. He "was a man subject to like passions as we are" (Jas. 5:17). Friends, take that in—*a man of like passions* as we are! Yet "He prayed earnestly that it might not rain: and it rained not on the earth by the space of three years and six months. And he prayed again, and the heaven gave rain, and the earth brought forth her fruit." "The effectual fervent prayer of a righteous man availeth much" (v.16). If one man prevailed to the manifestation of the Lord's mercies and goodness, can then the Lord's people cry unto him in vain?

"There is none like unto the God of Jeshurun." He is a prayer-hearing, prayer-answering God, who "is able to do exceeding abundantly above all that we ask or think" (Eph. 3:20). Let us then be found among those that call upon the name of the Lord in the exercise of a God-given faith, trusting him, waiting upon him and for him.

"He rideth upon the heaven in thy help, and in his excellency on the sky. The eternal God is thy refuge, and underneath are the everlasting arms." O friends, what words of encouragement and consolation are here. *"The eternal God is thy refuge."* Notice that it doesn't just say what God *does* for his people but what he *is in himself* for his people. The eternal God, Father, Son and Holy Spirit, is the refuge of his people and this is assured to us in the precious truth of the gospel. One says,

"A refuge for sinners the gospel makes known;
'Tis found in the merits of Jesus alone."

Yes, in all that the Lord Jesus Christ is as God manifest in the flesh, and in all that he has done, a sure foundation is laid for the faith, hope and salvation of his living family, to the praise of the glory of his name. Yes, a mighty, sure refuge is our God. "The eternal God is thy refuge." O, may not one of us be strangers to the living reality of this. We are in this wilderness world, beset within and all around by things that trouble us. Where would we be if we had not the precious truth of the gospel assured to us in our text: "The eternal God is thy refuge"?

O friends, here is the only place to which you and I can flee. Does not the word of his grace blessedly bear witness to it? Indeed, at all times and in all situations, do we not hear the voice of our Lord, the voice of the Beloved saying, "Come unto me, all ye that labour and are heavy laden, and I will give you rest" (Matt. 11:28)? O what words of grace and truth our Lord Jesus spake, the eternal God manifest in the flesh, he "who rideth upon the heaven in thy help, and in his excellency on the sky."

Yes, "The eternal God is thy refuge, *and underneath are the everlasting arms."* Those arms are ever there to uphold and keep his people amidst all the dangers that beset and threaten them. And even though brought into trying distressing circumstances we are assured that not only is the eye of the Lord upon us, but the arms of everlasting love and mercy are underneath us. And, blessed be the Lord's great and holy name, not one of his people shall ever fall out of those arms. As we considered recently, does not the Lord Jesus Christ testify of this when he said, speaking of himself, "I am the good shepherd, and know my sheep, and am known of mine...My sheep hear my voice, and I know them, and they follow me: and I give unto them eternal life; and they shall never perish, neither shall any man pluck them out of my hand.

My Father, which gave them me, is greater than all; and no man is able to pluck them out of my Father's hand. I and my Father are one" (John 10:11, 27–30)

"The eternal God is thy refuge." View it, friends, in the light of the glorious truth of the gospel. O what consolation flows from the gospel to us poor, guilty sinners, in all our weakness, sinfulness and need and in all that may beset us in our day. O what a mercy that in the person of our Lord Jesus Christ we have a sure refuge for our souls, a true friend that loveth at all times, a brother born for adversity. We have every encouragement to come, commit and cast all our care upon him! The word says, "he careth for you" (1 Pet. 5:7) And does not what is set before us here assure us of this?

As Moses goes on to say, "Israel then shall dwell in safety alone: the fountain of Jacob shall be upon a land of corn and wine; also his heavens shall drop down dew." Again we see what full and glorious provision is made for his sinful people in the precious truth of the gospel. Israel was abundantly provided for throughout all their wilderness journey and in their entrance into the land of Canaan. So is the Lord the refuge of his people and the provider for them in all that pertains to them in time and for eternity. As Paul could assure the brethren at Philippi: "My God shall supply all your need according to his riches in glory by Christ Jesus" (Phil. 4:19). And those riches in glory by Christ Jesus never diminish for the blessing of his people. They are still full, still free to every poor needy sinner, who by his grace is brought to believe and trust in him alone, to the glory of the Lord's name.

"Happy art thou, O Israel." Why, we might ask, how can this be? Oftentimes the Lord's people are tried, burdened, exercised, troubled, beset with things within and without? Happy? Ah, surely none but those who have been brought to know and love the Lord Jesus Christ in sincerity and truth can be spoken of as a happy people. They are a people brought by divine grace to know rest for their souls, not in what they have done but in what Jesus Christ is and done for them. *There* we can rejoice in the Lord in thankfulness and praise to our God.

"Happy art thou, O Israel: who is like unto thee, *O people saved by the LORD.*" Ah, from thence alone our happiness arises. What cause we ever have for thankfulness and praise to the God of our salvation! Again I say, salvation is by what *he* has done and what he ever *is* to his people in time and all eternity.

"The shield of thy help, and who is the sword of thy excellency! and thine enemies shall be found liars unto thee; and thou shalt tread upon their high places." What an assurance is given us here that we shall be, indeed we are "more than conquerors through him that loved us" (Rom. 8:37). We may be passing through trying times but remember that all is in his hand, all is under the control of him who is the Lord our God. Wait upon him and for him, calling on his great and holy name. Seek in all things to be brought into submission to his holy and sovereign will and to rest in him as the God of our salvation. Friends, he has not failed us yet and he never will fail us, blessed be his great and holy name. He is "the same yesterday, and to day, and for ever" (Heb. 13:8). May the Lord the Holy Spirit seal these things afresh to our souls. "There is none like unto the God of Jeshurun, who rideth upon the heaven in thy help, and in his excellency on the sky. The eternal God is thy refuge, and underneath are the everlasting arms." Blessed be his great and holy name.

I will leave the remarks there. May the Lord add his blessing. Amen.

14

I PRAY FOR THEM: I PRAY NOT FOR THE WORLD

Lord's day evening, 19 April 2020

"I pray for them: I pray not for the world, but
for them which thou hast given me; for they
are thine" (John 17:9).

Although I have read this verse by way of a text, I want to
comment this evening on what is set before us throughout this
great high priestly prayer of our Lord Jesus Christ. And may the
Lord the Holy Spirit be pleased to take these things of Jesus, the
wonders of grace set before us, and show them unto us. May we
know their power and blessedness in our souls, as those that have
a part in him, he being ours and we his, in the indissoluble
covenant.

This morning we considered the blessing of Israel by Moses,
that great man of God, who was so owned and used of God in his
day. His ministry was unique in that all he communicated to the
children of Israel, he received from God speaking to him *"face
to face"* (Exod. 33:11). It was not by visions or in dreams. And
he was a faithful servant, through the grace of God upon him. As
Paul testifies in his epistle to the Hebrews: "Moses verily was
faithful in all his house, as a servant, for a testimony of those
things which were to be spoken after; but Christ as a son over his
own house; whose house are we, if we hold fast the confidence
and the rejoicing of the hope firm unto the end" (Heb. 3:5–6).
The word declares "there arose not a prophet since in Israel like
unto Moses, whom the LORD knew face to face" (Deut. 34:10).
Yet Moses himself testified, "The LORD thy God will raise up
unto thee a Prophet from the midst of thee, of thy brethren, like
unto me; *unto him ye shall hearken"* (Deut. 18:15). And that
prophet greater than Moses is unquestionably our Lord and
Saviour Jesus Christ.

As he came to the end of his life, Moses blessed the children of Israel. By the Spirit of God, he prophesied of what the children of Israel would surely experience and enjoy when they entered into possession of the land God had promised Abraham, Isaac and Jacob. Israel broke the covenant God made with them at Sinai in which he said he was a husband unto them. Yet we see his longsuffering and faithfulness in still bringing the posterity of Abraham into possession of that land. Also, there was made known to Moses on Sinai all the appointments of the Levitical order in that covenant of which Moses was the mediator. And this Levitical dispensation set forth great things which were to come. Indeed, our Lord Jesus himself testified, Moses "wrote of me" (John 5:46). O how all that was made known to Moses in the Levitical dispensation shadowed forth the greater glory which is manifest to us in the glorious truth of the gospel. For Jesus Christ is the sum and substance of all the shadows of the Levitical order. All is fulfilled in his person and in his glorious, finished work by which he has once forever put away the sins of his people.

O the blessedness that you and I, as sinners brought by divine grace to trust in the Lord Jesus Christ, are assured by his word that in the *new* covenant he will remember our sins and iniquities no more. O the wonder of that—to believe that our sins are for ever put away, full satisfaction having been rendered for them in the finished work of our Lord and Saviour Jesus Christ! Does not his word testify, "There is therefore now no condemnation to them which are *in Christ Jesus*" (Rom. 8:1). Our Lord Jesus speaks particularly in this chapter before us of the real union and oneness with him through the wonders of redeeming love and mercy. All flows out of the fulness of grace that is in him and streams to us from our triune God, Father, Son and Holy Spirit.

O what great and glorious things are these! Yes, there is much that troubles us, particularly at this present time in the restrictions upon us. We know how irksome these things are. Yet friends, in all the issues in our lives, have we not something surely for which to be thankful unto the Lord? Have we not continual cause for rejoicing and for praising the Lord our God? Remember that in all his dealings with us he is good, just and kind, as much as when he denies us things of this time-state, as when he imparts to us his daily benefits. We have cause to give him thanks for *all* things.

But over and above all, have we not ground for rejoicing that Jesus is ours and we are his? See what is opened up to us in this verse I have read: "I pray for them: I pray not for the world." Great is the mercy if, by the gracious inditing of the Holy Spirit, we are found instant at the throne of grace, pouring out our hearts before the Lord. Yet how often imperfect are our prayers. It is a mercy of the Lord, that with all the imperfections of his people's prayers, yet his ear is still open to their cry and he will answer as consistent with his holy mind and will. And we may be assured that in his answers to the cries of his people, he is wise and good.

But the point I want to make is this. Jesus said, "I pray for them: I pray not for the world." Is it not a great and glorious thing that we have a part and interest in the intercessory prayer of our Lord Jesus Christ? O the wonder of this: *"I pray for them."* Who are these for whom he prays? They are those whom his Father has given him even from before the foundation of the world. He says, "thine they were, and thou gavest them me." O what deep things of electing, sovereign distinguishing grace are blessedly set forth here! Can words fully express the height, depth, length and breadth of the wonder of the love of God revealed in Jesus Christ? He loved his people with an everlasting love. He chose them even before the foundation of the world. In the "everlasting covenant, ordered in all things and sure," (2 Sam. 23:5) he provided everything needful for his glory in the eternal salvation of everyone for whom the Lord Jesus here prays. For he laid down his life for these for whom he prayed. He "redeemed us from the curse of the law, being made a curse for us"! (Gal. 3:13).

"I pray for them." This morning we considered Moses, the man of God, the mediator of the covenant God made with Israel at Sinai. Here we behold our Lord Jesus Christ as the mediator of what is described as that better covenant, established upon better promises. Look at chapter eight of Paul's epistle to the Hebrews. He says of our Lord Jesus Christ, the man Christ Jesus, "But now hath he obtained a more excellent ministry, by how much also he is the mediator of a better covenant, which was established upon better promises. For if that first covenant had been faultless, then should no place have been sought for the second. For finding fault with them, he saith, Behold, the days come, saith the Lord, when I will make a new covenant with the house of Israel and with the house of Judah: not according to the covenant that I made with their fathers in the day when I took them by the hand to lead them out of the land of Egypt; because they continued not in my covenant, and I regarded them not, saith the Lord. For this is the covenant that I will make with the house of Israel after those days, saith the Lord; I will put my laws into their mind, and write them in their hearts: and I will be to them a God, and they shall be to me a people: and they shall not teach every man his neighbour, and every man his brother, saying, Know the Lord: for all shall know me, from the least to the greatest. For I will be merciful to their unrighteousness, and their sins and their iniquities will I remember no more. In that he saith, A new covenant, he hath made the first old. Now that which decayeth and waxeth old is ready to vanish away" (Heb. 8:13). And so it has. The old covenant has vanished away.

Now set before us is the *new* covenant of which our Lord Jesus Christ is the glorious mediator and the great high priest, "after the order of Melchisedec" (Heb. 7). There is a mystery surrounding this person Melchisedec who met Abraham returning from the slaughter of the kings and blessed him. But Paul applies this "order of Mechisedec" to the Lord Jesus Christ as being "a priest for ever," a "King of righteousness," and a "King of peace." The apostle says that all those descriptions are only fully seen in the person of our Lord Jesus Christ. Moses was described as *"king* in Jeshurun" (Deut. 33:5). But here we behold our Lord Jesus Christ as *the* priest and *the* king upon his throne! The great and glorious head of the church is revealed to us in the word, as prophet, priest and king.

And in this prayer of our Lord Jesus Christ we behold him as the great high priest over the house of God. He prayed for his disciples. He prayed for his people. And he ever lives to make intercession for us. And we are assured that because he ever lives to make intercession for us, "he is able also to save them to the uttermost that come unto God by him" (Heb. 7:25).

Moses blessed the children of Israel before he went up mount Nebo to die. Our Lord Jesus Christ, before his death, prays for his people. And does not his prayer set forth great, precious, blessed things? His prayer is not merely petition. "Father, *I will.*" O see that all the blessings set forth in this prayer of our Lord Jesus Christ are founded upon the *shalls* and *wills* of our Jehovah Jesus, not on any worth or merit in those who receive the blessings. They are founded wholly on what he declares of himself. "Father, I have finished the work which thou gavest me to do."

Moses blessed the people. So does our Lord Jesus Christ before his death. Moses died, was buried and entered into the joy of his Lord. Jesus was slain for us but rose again the third day and entered into heaven itself. There we behold him as the eternal priest upon the throne of his grace, ever living to make intercession and able to save unto the uttermost all that come unto God by him.

Friends, these are not cunningly devised fables. They are glorious realities. When the Lord says here, "I pray for them: I pray not for the world, but for them which thou hast given me," O what a favoured people these are! They are blessed indeed. They must be blessed. Moses blessed the children of Israel. Here are a people, the *Lord's people,* ever in the world as a remnant according to the election of grace. This is the true church, the living family of God, comprised of every sinner the Lord calls by his grace and brings from death in trespasses and sins, into the light, life and liberty of the gospel. As needy sinners they are brought to flee for refuge to the hope set before them in the person and finished work of the Lord Jesus Christ. They are brought to believe in him by the sovereign operations of the Lord the Holy Spirit. O what a blessed people they are! The Lord speaks of them as "my people" (2 Cor. 6:16), those whom the Father "hast given me" (John 17:9). As I have reminded you again and again, they are ever the subjects of his constant love and care. Last Lord's day evening, we considered our Lord Jesus Christ as the great shepherd, the good shepherd and the chief shepherd—all expressive of his love, care and provision for his people.

As he prays for his people here, what a solemn word is this. "I pray for them, *I pray not for the world.*" How solemn. As one well said, "poor world" for whom the Lord Jesus prayed not. Let us bow before the sovereign will of our God. Man is ever ready to question God's divine sovereignty in his electing love and predestinating grace. But these are great and glorious truths and, as taught of God the Holy Spirit, do we not glory in the blessed truth that our God is sovereign in all his ways and dealings? "He doeth according to his will in the army of heaven, and among the inhabitants of the earth: and none can stay his hand, or say unto him, What doest thou?" (Dan. 4:35). And we are assured that in all God's manifestations of his sovereignty, he is wise, good and just. How that is surely seen in the wonders of his grace and mercy, revealed to us in the precious truth of the gospel. For friends, what hope or expectation can you and I have, but in the riches of redeeming love and mercy given to us in the precious person and work of our Lord and Saviour Jesus Christ?

Jesus here prays, "Father, I will that they also, whom thou hast given me, be with me where I am" (v.24). See how he prays with authority: *"I will."* Not that his will and the will of his Father are contradictory. Far from it! All that the Lord Jesus prayed for was in full conformity to the will of his heavenly Father. Remember that our Lord Jesus Christ and his Father and the Holy Spirit are one, one God over all, blessed for evermore. He prays here as the God-man, the one mediator between God and men, the man Christ Jesus. O is not the person of our Lord Jesus Christ a blessed reality!

Moses prayed for the people as the mediator between God and men in the covenant made with them at Sinai. Here we behold our Lord Jesus Christ as the mediator of the *new* covenant. Is not all that pertains to the glory of God, the welfare of his people, your welfare and mine, poor sinners brought to believe and trust in Jesus Christ, *safe in his hands?* Does he not carry on the work which is for the true welfare of his church and people, the ingathering of them, the bringing of them safely home unto himself? As he prayed here, "Father, I will that they also, whom thou hast given me, be with me where I am; that they may behold my glory, which thou hast given me: for thou lovedst me before the foundation of the world." Friends, can this prayer of our Lord Jesus Christ fall to the ground? Blessed be the Lord's name, no it cannot. Neither sin, Satan, nor hell itself can ever undermine anything for which our Lord Jesus Christ prays. For all is founded on the sure and certain foundation of the unchanging love and faithfulness of our God, and his power to accomplish all he hath promised and appointed, to the praise of the glory of his own great and holy name.

As I have said, Moses blessed the people before his death. Here our Lord Jesus Christ prays for his own. I repeat again, he is the *one* mediator between God and men. "These words spake Jesus, and lifted up his eyes to heaven, and said, Father, the hour is come; glorify thy Son, that thy Son also may glorify thee…I have glorified thee on the earth: I have finished the work which thou gavest me to do. And now, O Father, glorify thou me with thine own self with the glory which I had with thee before the world was." See what his prayer is founded on: "I have finished the work which thou gavest me to do." O what that work involved! O what it cost our Lord Jesus Christ to redeem his people from the curse of a broken law being himself made a curse for them! Read again the record in the gospels of the life, ministry, sufferings and death of our Lord Jesus Christ.

"I have finished the work." O what a great work which none but our Lord Jesus Christ could ever accomplish. Blessed be his name, he did accomplish it. He went round the whole circumference of the law. He fulfilled every minute detail of it. He brought in everlasting righteousness. He offered one great sacrifice for sin, the just for the unjust. The Lord made to meet on him the iniquity of all his people. He fully satisfied for them, so that the Lord declares, "Their sins and iniquities will I remember no more" (Heb. 8:12). No, because full satisfaction has been given for them by the substitution of Jesus himself in the place of his people. O friends, may this precious truth be sealed to your soul and mine—Christ in your place, Christ in my place, delivering us from the curse of a broken law, he being made a curse for us that we might be made the righteousness of God in him.

Jesus goes on to say, "As thou hast given him power over all flesh, that he should give eternal life to as many as thou hast given him." See the authority and power of our Lord Jesus Christ! Moses, as I said, was a great man of God. He blessed the people

PRAY

before his death. He was owned and used of God in his day and generation. Behold here our Lord Jesus Christ, to whom all authority and power is given in heaven and in earth. Did he not assure his disciples when he directed them to go forward preaching and teaching the glorious truths of the gospel, that "All power is given unto me in heaven and in earth"? (Matt. 28:18). Did he not assure them of the promised coming and abiding of the Lord the Holy Spirit upon them?

"I pray for them," yes, for these the Father had given him and to whom the Lord Jesus gives eternal life. And what is that eternal life? "This is life eternal, *that they might know thee* the only true God, and Jesus Christ, whom thou hast sent." Not merely to know *about* him but to know him as brought by the sovereign operations of the Holy Spirit, from death in trespasses and sins, into the light, life and liberty of the gospel. They are made partakers of the new nature, "being born again, not of corruptible seed, but of incorruptible, by the word of God, which liveth and abideth for ever" (1 Pet. 1:23). They are made partakers of the new nature, that is, "partakers of the divine nature" (2 Pet. 1:4).

O, the wonder of this! Such is the blessedness of these for whom the Lord prays that, yes, they are still in this frail, sinful body, yet they possess a new nature, that "new man" of grace. And consequently they find a continual conflict within between the flesh and the spirit born of God, for "these are contrary the one to the other" (Gal. 5:17). O friends, assurance is given that grace shall "reign through righteousness unto eternal life by Jesus Christ our Lord" (Rom. 5:21).

The Lord goes on to pray, "I have given unto them the words which thou gavest me; and they have received them, and have known surely that I came out from thee, and they have believed that thou didst send me. I pray for them: I pray not for the world, but for them which thou hast given me; for they are thine. And all mine are thine, and thine are mine; and I am glorified in them. And now I am no more in the world, but these are in the world, and I come to thee. Holy Father, keep through thine own name those whom thou hast given me, that they may be one, as we are." The Lord does not pray that they should be taken out of the world but that his Father would keep them from the evil. He says, "keep through thine own name those that thou hast given me."

Ah friends, our true welfare as we journey on through life is entirely dependent on the Lord's unchanging mercies and sustaining grace. He alone keeps us. He alone preserves us in the love and fear of his name. His grace enables us to persevere unto the heavenly kingdom he hath promised. O how most certainly we are wholly dependent on the Lord every step of life's journey. Have we not to cry continually as the Lord instructed his disciples, "Lead us not into temptation, but deliver us from evil"? (Matt. 6:13). Yes, we continually need the upholding, sustaining grace of our God. The Lord promises this to us. *He prays for it.* We have the assurance he will impart it to us, to the praise of his name.

"Holy Father, keep through thine own name those whom thou hast given me, that they may be one, as we are." See the reality of the oneness, the union of the Lord's people, yes, with one another, but essentially with our Lord Jesus Christ and the Father. O friends, what glorious things these words open up to us! Every true believer, through the riches of divine grace, is brought into union and fellowship with God through the person of our Lord Jesus Christ! He and we one! All that Jesus is, so are we! All that he has accomplished is ours in all the fulness and freeness of it! See how John in his first epistle, blessedly sets this before us. He says, "Herein is our love made perfect, that we may have boldness in the day of judgment: *because as he is, so are we* in this world" (1 John 4:17). O wonders of grace here set before us!

"Sanctify them through thy truth: thy word is truth." What does the Lord mean by this? Well, are not the Lord's people a sanctified people? Let us rightly understand what is meant when the Lord speaks of his people being sanctified. As believers, washed from all their sins in the precious blood of Jesus Christ and justified in his righteousness, they are sanctified, that is, set apart by God for himself. They are made holy through the comeliness that he has put upon them. The believer's true sanctification, their holiness, is as found in Jesus Christ, as righteous as he is righteous, as holy as he is holy.

"Sanctify them through thy truth: thy word is truth." This

does not mean they are made *more* holy. It is that they be brought into more conformity to the revealed will of God in his holy word. This is manifest in their lives by increasing devotion and commitment to their Lord and Saviour and the welfare of his cause in their generation. It is expressed in the words of the apostle Peter, "that ye should shew forth the praises of him who hath called you out of darkness into his marvellous light" (1 Pet. 2:9). Should we not thus manifest whose we are and whom we serve, by increasing, deeper devotion to the Lord Jesus Christ and his holy word?

The Lord Jesus himself says, "I sanctify *myself.*" That does not mean he made himself *more* holy. That can never be so. He is ever the Holy One of God. Its meaning is manifest in the life and ministry of our Lord Jesus Christ. He was *wholly devoted* to the will of his heavenly Father and gloriously fulfilled *that will* in his life, sufferings, death and resurrection.

"I pray for them: I pray not for the world, but for them which thou hast given me." O the wonderful blessings in this prayer of our Lord. Did Moses bless the children of Israel? O what glorious blessings are in this prayer of our great High Priest, the glorious King in Zion, King of righteousness, King of peace— righteousness and peace still flowing from him to sinners, to the praise of the glory of his name! And he goes on to say, "Father, I will that they also, whom thou hast given me, be with me where I am; that they may behold my glory, which thou hast given me: for thou lovedst me before the foundation of the world."

I have but touched on a few things in this seventeenth chapter of John this evening. May we be enabled to meditate further upon it. May the Lord the Holy Spirit enlighten our understanding and give us a deeper appreciation and assurance of the wonders of redeeming love and mercy in all that Jesus is and all that he has done for us. Friends, when we view what confronts us in our day, and the situations in which we may be found as we journey on through life, cannot we say, in the light of this prayer, what Paul writes to the Corinthians? "Our light affliction, which is but for a moment, worketh for us a far more exceeding and eternal weight of glory; while we look not at the things which are seen, but at the things which are not seen: for the things which are seen are temporal," all passing away, "but the things which are not seen are eternal" (2 Cor.4:17–18). And these things for which Jesus prays here, *are* spiritual, eternal realities. O may we be more and more grounded and established in the believing receiving of all that the Lord bears witness to us here in his holy word.

But I will leave the remarks there this evening. May the Lord add his blessing. Amen.

15

GET THEE TO ZAREPHATH WHICH BELONGETH TO ZIDON

Tuesday evening 21 April 2020

"And the word of the Lord came unto him, saying, Arise, get thee to Zarephath, which belongeth to Zidon, and dwell there: behold, I have commanded a widow woman there to sustain thee" (1 Kings 17:8-9).

Although I have read these verses by way of a text, I want to bring before you the whole context in which they are found, as the Lord is pleased to help me. In this account, is there not much gracious instruction and encouragement for the Lord's people in the most trying times in which they may be found, individually and collectively? One thing we are assured of, as was so evident in the Lord's dealings with Elijah and this widow at Zarephath, *all* circumstances are of God and ultimately for his glory. This is true of all his ways and dealings among the nations of the earth, especially and essentially as they concern his church and people.

I surely do not have to remind you again of what is ever set before us in the word. That which redounds to the glory of God cannot but be for the good of his chosen. That is evident in the Lord's gracious dealings with them in providence. What a glorious truth is this! Our God *is* the God of providence. Every situation, life's minutest circumstance, is not only subject to his eye but is appointed of him. Blessed be the Lord's name, he knows what he is doing, he knows the purpose of it. We might not always see it. The path in which we may be called to walk at present may seem very strange and mysterious to us. Yet, without question, if through divine grace we are the Lord's, it is the path of his appointment for us. And what's more, have we not the assurance that he is with us in that path? And as he is with us, he will surely supply all our needs, not only in material matters, but also upholding us in the ways of his grace. O how we need keeping, keeping from ourselves particularly, keeping from the wiles of the enemy, and deliverance from the sinful staggerings of the unbelief rooted in our fallen nature.

O friends, what assurance we are given of the constancy of the Lord's care of his own in all their circumstances. What a foundation is laid for the assurance of the believer! Blessed be his great and holy name, he has redeemed our souls from the curse of a broken law. In the person and work of the Lord Jesus Christ he has provided all that pertains to the eternal welfare of our never-dying souls. We have the hope and expectation of eternal life though Jesus Christ our Lord. How rich, how glorious is this treasure! It can never be taken away, never be sullied with sin. What the Lord has given he will never take away. That which is done cannot be undone. O how sure a foundation is laid for the faith and hope of the living family of God! If he hath done so much for us (and who can even begin to comprehend how much the Lord has done for us?), if he has done so much for his own glory and the eternal salvation of our souls, is there any good thing he will deny us? Does he not declare: "The LORD will give grace and glory: no good thing will he withhold from them that walk uprightly"? (Ps. 84:11). And what is it to walk uprightly? It is as we see here with Elijah and this woman of Zarephath— needy sinners walking in belief and trust in the Lord Jesus Christ and him alone. It is summed up in those words of the apostle John when he says, "This is his commandment, That we should believe on the name of his Son Jesus Christ, and love one another, as he gave us commandment" (1 John 3:23). *That* is to walk uprightly. O friends, may we walk accordingly by grace.

Let us look then, as helped, at a few of the things brought before us in this portion of the word of God I have read to you this evening. I know we are familiar with the account of Elijah and this widow woman and the wonders of God manifested in their situation. It speaks to us still. He is the same God today as he was in the days of Elijah. All the revelation God has given us in his holy word, centres in the person of his only begotten and dearly beloved Son. One once said of the ancient Roman empire that all roads lead to Rome. We can unquestionably say of the blessed scriptures of truth, the old testament as well as the new, that all leads to the Lord Jesus Christ alone. Thus, on the road to Emmaus, the Lord Jesus opened up to those two disciples "in *all* the scriptures the things concerning himself" (Luke 24:27). Patriarchs and prophets bore witness, throughout the whole of the old testament dispensation, to him that was to come. And the apostles testified of the wonders of grace gloriously manifested in the coming, the incarnation of our Lord Jesus Christ. All directs to him. May your soul and mine ever be increasingly directed and led by divine teaching into the believing receiving of the testimony God has given us of his dearly beloved Son. Remember, "He that believeth on the Son hath everlasting life: and he that believeth not the Son shall not see life; but the wrath of God abideth on him" (John 3:36). Solemn truth, but a blessed reality, if by divine grace we have a part in the Lord Jesus Christ. In every situation, is it not our concern that the Holy Spirit bear witness to *our part* in Christ? As one cries in the word, "Say unto my soul, I am thy salvation" (Ps. 35:3).

So, looking at what is brought before us in this chapter, we are introduced, first of all, to Elijah. This man of God, this prophet of God, appears suddenly upon the page of holy scripture. We are only told where he came from—Elijah the Tishbite of the inhabitants of Gilead. Nothing else is told us of his ancestry. And it is needless to enquire. Where scripture is silent, let us be silent. One thing we are assured of. Here is a man raised up of God and used of God in his generation. Later in history, we are told that John the Baptist came in the spirit and power of Elijah as an immediate forerunner of our Lord and Saviour Jesus Christ. And we behold Elijah with Moses on the mount of transfiguration when the glory of the Lord Jesus Christ was manifested to his disciples and that voice from heaven was heard, "This is my beloved Son, in whom I am well pleased; hear ye him" (Matt. 17:5; Luke 9:30).

See here the God-given faith manifest in the boldness of Elijah as he went in before Ahab and said, "As the LORD God of Israel liveth, before whom I stand, there shall not be dew nor rain these years, but according to my word." What a grievous famine followed upon the land for three years and six months, as the judgment of God on an idolatrous and a sinful people. Ahab was a wicked king and his wife Jezebel a very wicked woman who promoted the worship of Baal in Israel. Four hundred prophets of Baal were eventually slain by Elijah as recorded in the following chapter. How he feared he was the only prophet of God left. At such times, when the judgment of God is upon the earth and all seems so dark and distressing, we may fear like Elijah, 'I am the only one left.' But here is a word of the Lord to Elijah, and to the people of God still. He has a remnant in the earth, seven thousand that he had reserved to himself, that had not bowed the knee to Baal nor kissed him. And see God manifesting the wonders of his grace in the hearts and lives of sinners, so unlooked for, so unexpected, as in the case of this widow of Zarephath.

But Elijah makes that solemn declaration to Ahab. And so it was. The word of the Lord never falls to the ground. God does not threaten that which he will not ultimately bring to pass. This famine in Israel and the nations round about as well, was God's voice speaking in that day. And friends, is not the voice of the Lord still speaking in our own day, in the virus that is upon our nation and the nations of the world? How it proclaims the solemn fact that man, with all his boasted authority, power and wisdom, is helpless. How quickly can the situation change as it has done in our day. We would acknowledge the hand of God in this and would fall before him in acknowledgement that, in all his ways and dealings, he is righteous. And is not his *wisdom* perfect? The Lord knows what he is doing. O let us not overlook the blessed fact that in the midst of all these things the Lord still has a remnant according to the election of grace. And the welfare, indeed the eternal welfare, of that remnant is central to all the Lord's dealings with men and nations, to the praise of the glory of his name. And surely, as the voice of the Lord is speaking to us today, O may we cry unto him that he would open the ears of men and women in our generation to hear what God the Lord speaks and be brought in true repentance before him.

Friends, we know not the purpose of God in these things. What we do know is that the Lord provides for and keeps his own people as he did Elijah in those dark, distressing days. Is not this seen through all the generations in his dealings with his people?

Not that the Lord's people are necessarily exempt from the evils prevalent in the society in which they live. Elijah himself was not exempt from the effects of that famine. But we see how graciously the Lord provided for him. And the Lord's people are not necessarily exempt from the situation in our own nation at this time. But O friends, what is the encouragement and consolation of the Lord's people? We have a sure refuge in the Lord our God, one mighty to save, one who holds all nature in his hand, having all authority and power in heaven and earth. He is the great and glorious head of the church. To him we are directed. To him we can come and pour out our hearts before him, committing our way and all our concerns into his hands.

In the person of our Lord Jesus Christ, what a merciful and faithful high priest we have! He assures us he is not unaffected but touched with the feeling of our infirmities. "He was in all points tempted like as we are, yet without sin" (Heb. 4:15) and "in that he himself hath suffered being tempted, he is able to succour them that are tempted" (Heb. 2:18). Friends, how gracious are the Lord's dealings with us. In the most trying, darkest times, has he utterly left us to ourselves? The way indeed may be dark, but his word still remains. O for grace to be enabled to believe and trust him. We see here with Elijah and this widow of Zarephath, that what the Lord has said is the ground of faith for the living family of God. Faith believes and trusts his word, and receives out of the fulness that is in Christ Jesus. It receives what God has spoken. There it finds its resting place, in the sure hope and expectation that what God has said he most surely will perform.

Was not *that* the reality of the faith of Abraham and of this widow of Zarephath who, though a Gentile, was a true daughter of Abraham? She could not claim to be of the commonwealth of Israel. She was a Zidonian, as was that most wicked woman Jezebel, the daughter of the king of Zidon. Ah see the manifestation of the sovereign distinguishing grace of God in this widow, a true daughter of Abraham. How can I say that? She believed God as evidenced in what she did. It was no small thing that she did what Elijah requested of her. He came to Zarephath and found this woman as the Lord had directed him. "The word of the LORD came unto him, saying, Arise, get thee to Zarephath…behold, I have commanded a widow woman there to sustain thee." You know, humanly speaking, the prospects for Elijah did not seem very promising. Go to Zarephath, to that heathen nation and a widow woman there to sustain him? But Elijah believed God. Elijah obeyed God. He previously went and dwelt at Cherith as the Lord directed him. How wonderfully the Lord provided for him there, ravens bringing him bread and flesh morning and evening.

Why friends, we see that every creature, even those ravens, are all in the hand of God. "He doeth according to his will in the army of heaven, and among the inhabitants of the earth: and none can stay his hand, or say unto him, What doest thou?" (Dan. 4:35). Is there anything our Lord is not able to use and overrule for his glory and the good of his people? Though we may not see how things can be, yet be assured of this, the Lord sees, and "is able to do exceeding abundantly above all that we ask or think" (Eph. 3:20).

Elijah could well have resided at Cherith for up to twelve months. He drank of the brook. The time came when the brook dried up. Ah, what a trying of faith was that to Elijah. For though we see God-given faith in Elijah and this widow of Zarephath, yet faith is tried. The Lord *will* try it. For what purpose? Why, to manifest the very *reality* of faith, that it is not of man but of the operations of the Lord the Holy Spirit. And the end of the trial is for his honour and glory and the true spiritual welfare of his people.

Elijah's faith was tried. That brook did not dry up all of a sudden, but gradually, because of no rain in the land. The water in the brook became less and less. The day came when there was no water at all. I know this has been pointed out before, but notice that Elijah did not move until the Lord directed him to move. Human reason would say, 'Look, Elijah, the water is drying up. The time must come when you must move. Surely should you not begin to make preparations to do something about it?' Elijah waited until the word of the Lord came to him. And blessed be the Lord's name, in his dealings with his people, as here with Elijah, he "never is before his time, and never is behind."

The word of the Lord came at the very time when it was needed.

And we see how gracious is the Lord to his servant when he directs him to go to Zarephath: "I have commanded a widow woman there to sustain thee." He goes. Where there is God-given faith one thing that will be evident is obedience to the word of the Lord. O, may that grace be more abundantly seen in us. Not only that we hear the word of the Lord but that we are brought to believe and heed it. As James says, "Be ye doers of the word, and not hearers only" (Jas. 1:22). The grace of living faith gives heed to what God has spoken and walks in the way the Lord directs. Though it may seem strange and mysterious to us, we find that it is the right way. As it was with Israel of old, "He led them forth by the right way, that they might go to a city of habitation" (Ps. 107:7). It was not the most direct way, not the way they would have chosen, but it was the right way, the way wherein the Lord manifested his greatness and goodness to his own.

Elijah arises and goes to Zarephath. See how the Lord directs and how his providence is seen in all these things. He arrives at the very time this widow is gathering a few sticks to cook a last meal for herself and her son. As I said a little earlier, the prospect did not seem very rosy. Elijah meets this widow woman. Does he find she has any great provision to meet his need? All she has is a handful of meal in a barrel and a little oil in a cruse. Why, she was about to make her last meal. She had no further provision. Once that was gone they must starve to death. Such is the situation Elijah finds when he comes here. Yet see the word of the Lord! "He called to her, and said, Fetch me, I pray thee, a little water in a vessel, that I may drink. And as she was going to fetch it, he called to her, and said, Bring me, I pray thee, a morsel of bread in thine hand. And she said, As the Lord thy God liveth, I have not a cake, but an handful of meal in a barrel, and a little oil in a cruse: and, behold, I am gathering two sticks, that I may go in and dress it for me and my son, that we may eat it, and die. And Elijah said unto her, Fear not; go and do as thou hast said: but make me thereof a little cake first, and bring it unto me, and after make for thee and for thy son."

What a request Elijah makes to this widow woman! She was preparing her last meal. He says to her, 'Yes, go and bake that cake, but make me a little cake first.' O friends, as I said earlier, see here a true daughter of Abraham in this widow woman, even though of a Gentile nation with no claim to physical descent from the Israel of God. We see one in whom the Lord was manifesting a work of sovereign grace. O how wondrous are the ways of God—so different to what man would have thought or planned. Surely would not the Lord have sent Elijah to a place where there was abundance of food? No, he is sent to a widow in Zarephath as poor and destitute as he was, apart from a little meal and oil.

Friends, how wondrous are the ways of God. Remember what Jesus said of this woman when he preached the first time in the synagogue at Nazareth. He testified concerning the words he read out of the prophecy of Isaiah, "This day is this scripture fulfilled in your ears" (Luke 4:21). They wondered at the gracious words that proceeded out of his mouth. "They said, Is not this Joseph's son?" as they thought him to be. But then the Lord began to speak of divine sovereignty, the wonders of his grace manifest even to those of Gentile nations like this widow woman of Zarephath. He said that many widows were in Israel in the days of Elijah, but he was only sent to Zarephath. Many lepers were in Israel in the days of Elisha, but only Naaman the Syrian was cleansed. O how this stirred up the enmity of their hearts against him. And so it ever will, sadly and solemnly, in the natural man, particularly the natural *religious* man. Nothing is so hateful as the doctrine of divine sovereignty and divine grace, as manifest in the freeness and fulness of it, to those wholly undeserving. That God should favour one of a Gentile nation above all the widows in Israel! Why, how offended they were. Let man be offended as he is, we bless God for the reality of his sovereign, saving grace wherever it is manifest. Friends, I trust with ourselves we have continual cause to thank God for sovereign grace. We have to come to that place again and again:

> "Why me, why me, O blessed God
> Why such a wretch as me?
> Who must forever lie in hell,
> Were not salvation free."

But see the faith of this woman as a true daughter of Abraham. Against all human reasoning and hope, she goes and makes a cake and gives it to Elijah, when afterward she had nothing left herself! She and her son must starve, having no possibility of any provision as viewed from a human standpoint. Ah, here is the faith of Abraham, "Who against hope believed in hope, that he might become the father of many nations" (Rom. 4:18). Remember that the true children of Abraham are not those who can claim natural descent from him, but those "who also walk in the steps of that faith of our father Abraham, which he had being yet uncircumcised" (Rom. 4:12). This is the reality of the life of God in the soul of a poor sinner brought from death in trespasses and sins into the liberty of the gospel. They believe and trust in Jesus Christ alone for all their salvation for time and eternity.

See again how, against all the human reasoning, she brings this cake to Elijah. It might be thought, was it not unkind of Elijah to request her last meal for himself, that he should have it and she have nothing? He might have said, 'let us share it between us.' No, 'go and bake a cake and bring it to me first. Afterwards make for thee and thy son.' What is brought before us here? *"Fear not...*For thus saith the LORD God of Israel, The barrel of meal shall not waste, neither shall the cruse of oil fail, until the day that the Lord sendeth rain upon the earth." And that woman believed in God. She trusted in him through the word Elijah spoke to her. So she acted and so she prevailed. What blessings she and he and her house experienced as they lived many days. For the barrel of meal never wasted nor did the cruse of oil fail until the Lord sent rain on the earth. Does not this speak to us? Whatever the time and situation, is not God still able to provide for his people, still able to keep them and to manifest his goodness and his mercy towards them, blessed be his great and holy name?

But this was not the end of the trial of faith for this woman and for Elijah himself. It came to pass after these things that her son sickened and died. We see the reaction of this dear woman. O how distressed she was! O is this the end for which Elijah had come, to call her sins to remembrance, as she thought, and her son be taken from her? We do not find Elijah reasoning with her. He knew the distress that she was in. Friends, remember all things are in the hand of the Lord. Elijah takes the child up into the loft where he dwelt and prayed unto the Lord. What wonders are here manifest. Had it ever been heard until the days of Elijah that one should be raised from the dead?

You know, here in this account of the life and ministry of Elijah, are we not directed wholly to the Lord Jesus Christ? See how God sovereignly wrought in that day. He heard the cry, the prayer of that widow and of Elijah himself. He raised the child to life. What a manifestation of the work of his grace at such a time of distress, darkness and evil! Yet these things surely direct us to our Lord Jesus Christ. We can say that we find a greater than Elijah in the person of our Lord Jesus Christ. See it in the Lord's ministry when he was here upon earth. See how he provided for his own, for needy sinners, not only in meeting their physical needs and sicknesses and such like, even in raising the dead. O the greater wonder manifest to us in the truth of the gospel, that he, through the eternal Spirit, offered *himself* without spot, the just for the unjust, to bring us to God! He himself, in his own body upon the tree, has suffered for us, has once for ever put away our sins by the sacrifice of himself and brought in everlasting righteousness for us.

I mentioned in my earlier remarks this evening, that if God has done the greatest thing of all for us, as set before us in the precious truth of the gospel, where is there any good thing that he will withhold from his people? As Paul sums it up in his epistle to the Romans: "He that spared not his own Son, but delivered him up for us all, how shall he not with him also freely give us all things?" (Rom. 8:32). Blessed be the Lord's name, the God of Elijah lives.

In this widow of Zarephath we see a true daughter of Abraham. We see the wonders of sovereign distinguishing grace and mercy manifest to her. And this speaks to us still. As I said, the God of Elijah lives. Our Lord Jesus Christ is "the same yesterday, and to day and for ever" (Heb. 13:8). O for grace which brings us in all trying, distressing times to believe God, to trust in him only and wholly. As the Lord spoke by his servant Jehoshaphat, "Believe in the LORD your God, so shall ye be established; believe his prophets, so shall ye prosper" (2 Chron. 20:20).

May the Lord add his blessing. Amen.

16

WHY ART THOU CAST DOWN, O MY SOUL?

Lord's day morning 26 April 2020

"Why art thou cast down, O my soul? and why
art thou disquieted within me? hope thou in
God: for I shall yet praise him, who is the
health of my countenance, and my God"
(Psalm 42:11).

I have read these two portions of the word of God to you this
morning, Psalm 42 and 1 Kings 19. In the account of Elijah, we
find him fleeing for his life at the threat of that wicked woman
Jezebel. We see the obvious distress of this man of God, through
the circumstances that had unfolded. No doubt they were so
different to what he may have expected after the display of divine
power and glory on mount Carmel. The fire descended from
heaven and not only consumed the sacrifice but the stones of the
altar. It licked up the water that was in the trench round about it.
The people cried, "The LORD, he is the God; the LORD, he is the
God." And then there was the great rain after those three and a
half years of severe drought and famine. As Elijah viewed the
situation little seemed to have changed. Ahab was the same.
Jezebel was still manifesting her spite and enmity, not only
against the prophet, but against the one and only true God. It
would appear that the judgments God had brought on the nation,
and his mercy in sending rain upon the earth to end that famine,
had little effect upon the people generally. And Elijah, fleeing
into the wilderness and lying under that juniper tree, says, "I am
not better than my fathers." It appeared that no deliverance had
been wrought.

We find that David experienced the same distress as the
prophet, though the circumstances were very different. It is
generally considered that the background to the psalm was when
he had to flee from Jerusalem because of the insurrection of

Absalom. How troubled was the man of God by many things at that time. What added to his distress and fears was the news that even one of his most trusted advisers, Ahithophel, had turned against him. And David was also greatly troubled by being deprived of the favour of meeting in the tabernacle in which God dwelt and was worshipped in those days. For the Lord had said by Moses: "there I will meet with thee, and I will commune with thee from above the mercy seat, from between the two cherubims which are upon the ark of the testimony" (Exod. 25:22). David highly prized those things but now felt himself deprived of them. And he was not only troubled by all these outward circumstances but also by what worked in his own soul at that time, especially in respect to the favours he now felt denied to him.

Now looking at those things in the light of the teaching of the word of God, let us not forget that "whatsoever things were written aforetime were written for our learning, that we through patience and comfort of the scriptures might have hope" (Rom. 15:4). Unto us, individually and collectively, may the Lord bless his word of instruction concerning his dealings with Elijah and David. The Lord's gracious dealings are still seen with his people, as they have been down all the generations. As manifested to David and Elijah, whatever the outward circumstances, yet one thing of which we are assured is that the Lord is the same—he changes not. Yes, his judgments were abroad in the earth but O his mercy towards his people, his care and kindness over them, was not altered by the outward circumstances in which they were found. True, there was the trying of their faith. They found how active was the enemy of souls in seeking to raise discouragements and doubt with regard to the issues they faced. Yet did they not prove what the apostle Paul expressed in the very trying path the Lord had appointed for him in the gospel ministry? "We are troubled on every side, yet not distressed; we are perplexed, but not in despair; persecuted, but not forsaken; cast down, but not destroyed" (2 Cor. 4:8–9). And it is still so for the people of God today. As we look at these things this morning, O may the Lord speak to us and grant us the encouragement and consolation he made known to his servants Elijah and David.

First of all then, let us look a little closer at the situation of Elijah, this man of God. In chapter eighteen we see the display which Elijah witnessed of the power and majesty of God upon mount Carmel. There was also the prayer of Elijah for the rain which ended the three and a half years of drought and famine. O what displays of the power and goodness of God! Yet, as I mentioned a few moments ago, it did not seem to Elijah to have had any significant effect on Ahab or Jezebel or upon the people. Surely this speaks to us that neither judgments nor mercies can ever sway the hearts of sinful men and women unto the one and only true God. The judgments of God poured out on Israel and on the earth today, display his power. They testify that "the Lord, he is the God," whether men will hear or whether they will forebear, and that they certainly cannot escape the judgment of God. But it makes no saving change of itself in the hearts and lives of sinful men and women. Do not expect the judgments of God poured out upon the earth, to have a saving effect in any way on the hearts and lives of men and women.

> "Judgments nor mercies ne'er can sway
> Their roving feet to wisdom's way."

Saving change is the work of God's sovereign grace alone.

But there was something Elijah did not perceive at that time. Did he say, "I, even I only, am left; and they seek my life, to take it away"? Had the work of God's grace altogether ceased in Israel? The Lord informs him, "I have left me seven thousand in Israel, all the knees which have not bowed unto Baal, and every mouth which hath not kissed him." O, in the darkest and most distressing times, the work of God's grace still goes forward in the ingathering of his elect. In our day, it may appear to us that very few truly manifest any concern to worship the one and only true God in spirit and truth. But let us not forget that the Lord has his elect, a remnant in the earth, and will do so until he comes the second time in power and great glory. The work of God's grace is still going forward in those towards whom he has purposes of grace and mercy. Is not that surely our encouragement, as the church and people of God, that the Lord has not forgotten nor forsaken the work of his grace? The power and unction of the

Holy Spirit is no less today than in all past generations. O to realise more of its blessed reality.

See how the Lord comes to Elijah. O how gracious is the Lord, how kind in his care over his distressed, distraught servant, wearied and cast down as our text expresses it. The Lord sends an angel to provide a meal for him as he slept under the juniper tree. You know, one of the Lord's kindnesses to him was that he granted him rest, indeed sleep. He provided for him at the brook Cherith in sending ravens to feed him with bread and flesh, morning and evening. He provided for him in the house of the widow at Zarephath. The barrel of meal wasted not, the cruse of oil did not fail. And the Lord here provides for him in sending an angel to prepare a meal for him such that he went in the strength of that meat forty days and forty nights to mount Horeb. O friends, what is our God not able to do? See here his kindness and care over his servant. And is the Lord's love for his own any less today? Are we not still encouraged to cast all our care upon him? "He careth for you" (1 Pet. 5:7) is still the precious word God gives to his people, tried and distressed as they may be, as was Elijah.

He comes then to mount Horeb and the Lord asks him, "What doest thou here, Elijah?" Ah, what a question is that! I do not believe the Lord comes to him in condemnation. We might put the Lord's question to his servant in this way: 'Why so troubled, why so distressed, child of God? Why so anxious about the issues and situation in which you are found?' The psalmist puts the same question to his own soul, "Why art thou cast down, O my soul? and why art thou disquieted in me?" Why so troubled, thou child of God? Our circumstances are very trying. Indeed, you may be conscious of *the working of sin* in your heart and life. Do not *these things* trouble you? Unquestionably, they do. But why so troubled, why so distressed? Ah yes we say, there is a cause for it. 'O Lord, thou seest the situation in which I am found in my outward circumstances but also in myself personally as well. My sin lies heavy upon me, the defilement of it upon my conscience. Can I not but be distressed and troubled with these things?'

See how the Lord deals with his servant Elijah. There is gracious instruction for us in it. The Lord bids him go out and stand upon the mount before the Lord. And the Lord passed by. There was a wind that rent the mountains, an earthquake and then a fire. But each time it is said that the Lord was not in those things—the wind, the earthquake or the fire. O what a display was given of the divine power, majesty and greatness of the Lord our God, but the Lord was not in them in the sense of his dealings with his servant. But after those things, there was a still small voice. O friend, what a contrast, what a difference. See how the Lord does not speak in judgment to his own people. Remember, the Lord's judgments against his people as guilty sinners and transgressors of his holy law have been dealt with in the sufferings and death of our Lord and Saviour Jesus Christ. O can judgment ever come upon a true believer? No. God has laid all his iniquities on Jesus. True, the Lord's chastening hand may be upon them, his faithful loving rebuke realised. It is very needful. But the Lord's dealings with his people are never in vindictive anger or judgment against them. For all the wrath of God against all the sins and transgressions of his people truly fell upon our Lord Jesus Christ when he suffered and died. One says,

> "My soul looks back to see
> The burdens thou didst bear
> When hanging on the accursed tree
> And *knows* … (O may the Lord the Holy Spirit seal it
> to your soul and mine)
> And *knows* her guilt was there."

Ah friends, in our daily defilement by sin, O may the grace of God ever enable us not to look to our own doings but to what Jesus Christ has done for us. *That* can never be moved. *That* is the foundation for the faith and hope of the living family of God. *That* draws out our souls in love to him who hath loved us and washed us from our sins in his own blood. All circumstances, outward and inward, do not alter the glorious reality of what the gospel makes known by "a still small voice." What is this still small voice and what does it speak? Ah, is it not the Lord the Holy Spirit bearing witness by his sovereign operations to the wonders of the redeeming love and mercy of our Lord and Saviour Jesus Christ?

What Elijah saw in the wind, the earthquake and the fire, we might express as the thunderings of God's holy law against all sin, and his just condemnation of hardened and impenitent sinners. But O, the Lord does not come to his people in judgment but in mercy. He still comes, revealing the precious truth of the gospel to his people by the teaching of the Holy Spirit, amid all our circumstances and concerns even at this time. O the glory and blessedness of the gospel of the grace of God! May we increasingly know the mercies of the Lord towards us, the rich consolation that comes through all the Lord Jesus *has done* for us, and all he *now is* to us at the right hand of the Majesty on high.

Remember, "we have not an high priest which cannot be touched with the feeling of our infirmities; but was in all points tempted like as we are, yet without sin" (Heb. 4:15). So it was with his servant Elijah when the Lord spoke to him. The Lord "knoweth our frame; he remembereth that we are dust" (Ps. 103:14). O his kindness and care! Does he grant the request of Elijah: "O LORD, take away my life; for I am not better than my fathers"? No. The Lord's word to him is, "Go, return on thy way to the wilderness of Damascus." The Lord still had a work for him to do. And indeed, the Lord still owned and used him until he was taken up into heaven, translated that he should not see death as Enoch had been before him. O, the wonders of God's dealings with his own! How great and glorious is the Lord our God, how great are his mercies to his people!

Likewise, here with David as well, "Why art thou cast down, O my soul? and why art thou disquieted in me?" This may well be our case. What a mercy it is to be brought rightly to face these things, to own them and to pour out our hearts before the Lord. Are there things that thus trouble and cast us down at this present time? Where shall we go, what shall we do in these situations? Friends, there is one place only to go. The psalmist says again, "Trust in him at all times; ye people, pour out your heart before him: God is a refuge for us" (Ps. 62:8). O that never changes!

"Why art thou cast down, O my soul? and why art thou disquieted in me?" Is there an answer? Blessed be the Lord's name, there is. *"Hope thou in God."* What a word is that for the church and people of God still! "Hope thou in God." This hope is not as men so often express it. They hope this, that or the other, very uncertain as to whether the things which they hope for will be finally realised. As it concerns the Lord's people, their hope in God is not founded upon any uncertainty but upon the oath and promises of God himself as revealed to us in the precious truth of the gospel. We should never forget that the foundation which is laid in Jesus Christ our Lord is firm, stable and sure. Nothing can undermine it. Nothing can overthrow it! It is as sure and certain as the one and only true God himself. The Lord has given his word and oath to it. "Hope thou in God." O the reality of that hope in the experience of the child of God!

The Lord declares three things that abide: "faith, hope, charity" (1 Cor. 13:13). True, the greatest of these is charity (or love) but where one is, there the others will also be: faith, hope and love. These are realities in the sovereign work of the Holy Spirit in his people. These are poor sinners brought to believe and trust alone in the Lord our God, and in what he has revealed in his holy word of what Christ has done for us, not what we can do ourselves. Faith looks alone to God himself. Faith receives the fulness that is in Christ Jesus our Lord. Faith rests upon the word he has spoken.

Where faith is, there is also hope. O by the Lord's mercies towards us, may we know the blessed reality of this faith and hope. "Hope thou in God." By the outpouring of his grace and mercy, may we be brought to trust alone in the Lord, to commit all things wholly into his hands, and to rest in his holy, sovereign will. "Hope thou in God." This is a hope which "maketh not ashamed; because the love of God is shed abroad in our hearts by the Holy Ghost which is given unto us" (Rom. 5:5).

Did not David prove that so? "Why art thou cast down, O my soul? and why art thou disquieted within me? hope thou in God." Why? "For I shall yet praise him, who is the health of my countenance, and my God." *"For I shall yet praise him."* O see what cause for thankfulness there is in the prospect this hope opens before us. As the Lord has been our help, as he has manifested his saving mercies towards us, so we may be assured that what he has been unto his people so he will always be. His mercies to his own do not lessen as the days and years unfold or in whatever circumstances they may be found. As his word declares, the Lord's mercy to his people "endureth for ever" (Ps. 136).

"For I shall yet praise him." See what a prospect is here set before us. See the hope and expectation of the church and people of God. What ground is it founded upon? It is on what he has revealed of himself. The precious truth of the gospel is the foundation for all the thankfulness and praise of the living family of God. The gospel of his grace is the truth that abideth forever, blessed be his name. "I shall yet praise him, who is the health of my countenance, and my God."

Look at that word, "the health of my countenance." The margin expresses it: *"his presence is salvation."* Friends, is not that so for us: *"his presence is salvation."* Have we not the assurance of the abiding presence of the Lord with his own? See how the Lord comforted his disciples before he went forth to Gethsemane and Calvary. Troubled they were at the prospect of his going away from them, apprehensive of the events that were soon to unfold, though not fully realising what was involved. Yes, their hearts were troubled. What was the Lord's word to them? "His presence is salvation." That is, "I will not leave you comfortless: *I will come to you.* Yet a little while, and the world seeth me no more; but ye see me: because I live, ye shall live also" (John 14:18–19). O his presence *is* salvation. See this unfolded in all the gospel makes known of the fulness and freeness of the redeeming love and mercy which comes to us through the person and finished work of our Lord and Saviour Jesus Christ.

And the psalmist goes on to say, "who is the health of my countenance, *and my God."* Friends, is there not everything bound up in that word, *"and my God."* In the face of all the issues that confront us at present, may divine grace bring us to believingly realise that the one true God who spoke to Elijah and revealed himself to David, is the God and Father of our Lord Jesus Christ, and of every poor sinner brought to believe and trust in him. My God, my Father which is in heaven. O the blessedness of that relationship. All is ours, as poor sinners brought to trust in Jesus Christ alone.

"And my God." I say again, everything is founded in what God has revealed of himself as the one and only true God. His divine majesty was seen by Elijah and the wonders of his saving grace and mercy made known to both Elijah and David. He is *my* God, revealed unto me in the person of Jesus Christ, "the same yesterday, and to day, and for ever" (Heb. 13:8).

I will leave the remarks there. The Lord add his blessing. Amen.

17

BEHOLD MY SERVANT

Lord's day morning 26 April 2020

"That it might be fulfilled which was spoken by Esaias the prophet, saying, Behold my servant, whom I have chosen; my beloved, in whom my soul is well pleased: I will put my spirit upon him, and he shall shew judgment to the Gentiles. He shall not strive, nor cry; neither shall any man hear his voice in the streets. A bruised reed shall he not break, and smoking flax shall he not quench, till he send forth judgment unto victory. And in his name shall the Gentiles trust" (Matthew 12:17-21).

When we consider this quotation by Matthew out of the prophecy of Isaiah, O what a testimony we see is given by prophets and apostles to the person of our Lord and Saviour Jesus Christ. See how all the scriptures ever direct us to this one glorious person, God manifest in the flesh. The whole ministry of the Holy Spirit by his work of grace in the hearts and lives of his people is always to *direct* us and *bring* us, as needy sinners to one who alone is able to save to the uttermost.

Surely friends, are we not, I trust, increasingly brought to realise there is salvation for us in none other? "There is none other name under heaven given among men, whereby we must be saved" (Acts 4:12). Is not this the most important matter that concerns us personally? Whatever the outward circumstances that confront us at this time, surely the most important thing for us as needy guilty sinners, is to know the Lord Jesus Christ, to flee to him for refuge, to trust in him alone. What a mercy to be brought to realise this as graciously taught of God the Holy Spirit. The scriptures testify that if Jesus is thus ours, and we are his, we are in an indissoluble covenant, ordered in all things and sure. Is not this the greatest of all things? Is not this the only thing in which we have unceasing cause to give thanks and praise to our God—knowing the joy of the Lord in pardoning love and saving mercy? O in our present situation, may our souls be led increasingly into a deeper appreciation and believing realisation of this glorious salvation. Only in the person of the Lord Jesus Christ, as set before us in our text, do we find true rest for our souls amidst whatever may trouble us within and without. Our attention is *wholly* directed to behold the Lord Jesus Christ, full of grace and truth. We see here the power of his healing mercy extended to all that came, or were brought to him, in need of healing. However difficult their case, our Lord Jesus Christ was able to heal all. How he manifested his care and compassion to sinners! And, blessed be his name, he is the same Jesus still.

We cannot emphasis this enough. What cause we have to continually give thanks to God for the faithful records in the gospels of Matthew, Mark, Luke and John of the person and ministry of our Lord Jesus Christ when here on earth. We are assured of the glorious reality of these things. Unbelief may question as it does. Ungodly men in the religious world may pour scorn upon the accounts given us. "Let God be true, but every man a liar" (Rom. 3:4).

For the church and people of God there is ever cause to bless and praise him for the faithful record given us, not only in the gospels but in the whole of his word. It *is* the word of the Lord. Not only is it a true account handed down the generations, but we are assured that all scripture has been given *by inspiration of God*. (2 Tim. 3:16). Through it, we have been brought to know his mercies towards us, his power and truth in our own souls. How is it any one of us has been brought to believe the record God has given of his only begotten Son? Does this arise from the natural working of our fallen nature? Certainly not!

As we see in this chapter we have read this evening, what more powerful demonstration than his words and great works could have been given of the person of our Lord Jesus Christ? Behold his powerful ministry here on earth. Did that of itself bring sinful men, even the religious world of his day, to accept him, to believe in him, to acknowledge him as the Son of God? No, such is the blindness and hardness of men's hearts. In the religious world of that time they professed to know God and to be fully acquainted with the scriptures of the old testament which bore witness to him who was to come. They had the very evidence before their eyes of the fulfilment of what all the prophets had spoken. Yet they received him not. And not only that, we see again and again their bitter enmity against him. Why had the Scribes and Pharisees such enmity against the Lord Jesus Christ? They had no just complaint against him. He went about always doing good. In him was no sin. They could bring no fault against him though they tried again and again to do so. What stirred up their enmity was the testimony he gave as Jehovah's righteous servant who had come to do the will of his Father. In his ministry, he set forth the glory of God in the redemption and salvation of sinners, that it was not of their works but solely by the sovereign, distinguishing grace of God. O how that stirred up the enmity of their hearts as it does still in self-righteous, ungodly men and women even down to our day. And friends, *so are we*, apart from the distinguishing grace and mercy of God.

As some of us, I trust, can bear witness, how great is the work of God which brings such sinners as ourselves to receive the testimony God has given of his beloved Son, and to believe on him to eternal life. All is by the sovereign operations of God the Holy Spirit. Great were the works of our Lord Jesus Christ here on earth, in healing all manner of sickness and disease among the people, opening the eyes of the blind, raising the dead. Great and glorious *are* his works! But is it not a greater work that he should manifest his grace in the hearts of sinners, bringing them from death in trespasses and sins, into the life and liberty of the gospel? Nothing less than *divine* power can accomplish this. Nothing less than the wonder of the love of God as revealed in Jesus Christ our Lord can accomplish it. All is to the praise of the glory of our Triune God.

This sovereign power of God in salvation is clearly set before us here in what God the Father declared of his Son Jesus, by the prophet, generations before the coming of Christ. "Behold my servant, whom I have chosen; my beloved, in whom my soul is well pleased: I will put my spirit upon him, and he shall shew judgment to the Gentiles." *"Behold my servant."* O friends, see from whence flows all that pertains to the glory of God in the redemption and salvation of sinful men and women such as you and me. Its origin is in God himself. Never forget that it does not arise from the earth. The salvation that the gospel makes known comes down to us from heaven. The divine power and wisdom of God, the wonder of his grace and love, is revealed to us in the person of our Lord and Saviour Jesus Christ alone.

"Behold *my servant.*" O what wonders of grace are brought before us in this word. See that the blessings of salvation arise from God himself according to his eternal purposes. Here we see what divine wisdom has appointed and provided. Here our attention is directed to the very God against whom we have sinned. He alone has provided the means whereby he can "be just, and the justifier of him which believeth in Jesus" (Rom. 3:26). Herein his glory is fully manifested and will be so to all the ages of eternity, to the praise of his great name.

Who is this servant? Why, he is God the Father's only begotten and dearly beloved Son. He describes him thus: "Whom I have chosen; my beloved, in whom my soul is well pleased." Ah friends, can we even begin to comprehend the height, depth, length and breath of the love of God as revealed in Jesus Christ our Lord? In him he has provided all things for his glory in the salvation of sinners whom he has loved and chosen from before the foundation of the world. And in his appointed time he calls them by his grace, having redeemed them by the precious atoning blood of Christ. This servant of Jehovah is Jesus Christ, God manifest in the flesh, his only begotten and dearly beloved Son, co-equal with the Father and the Holy Spirit, one God over all, blessed for evermore. O the wonder of the grace of God revealed in the person of Jesus Christ! He, co-equal with the Father and the Holy Spirit, is found in fashion as a man and became obedient unto death, even the death of the cross. Well might the question be raised, why such wonders as here set before us? The Lord Jesus Christ, begotten of the Father, came willingly to this earth as a man, saying, "I delight to do thy will, O my God: yea, thy law is within my heart" (Ps. 40:8).

Friends, words can never adequately express the wonder, fulness and freeness of redeeming love and mercy. Jesus,

Jehovah's righteous servant, came forth delighting to do the will of his heavenly Father. We see him perfectly obedient in every aspect of his life and ministry. Though opposed by religious, ungodly men and by Satan himself, and enduring such contradiction of sinners against himself, yet nothing moved him one iota from fulfilling the work his Father had given him. And he did all, not just as it were out of duty, but *out of love to his heavenly Father*. Do not lose sight of that important point. Yes, the Lord Jesus Christ, in all he did for the salvation of his people, did so in love for them, but above all, he did so in love to his heavenly Father. "I delight to do thy will, O my God." O do we not have cause to increasingly give thanks unto the Lord for this? All that our Lord Jesus Christ wrought for our salvation, the fulness and freeness of the love of God manifested therein, all redounds to the glory of God alone.

Are not these things beyond our finite minds to fully comprehend? Why friends, it will require eternity itself to realise the wonder of the fulness of redeeming love and mercy set before us in the gospel. And as we see in our text, all centres in our Lord Jesus Christ. *"Behold my servant."* What do these words mean to you and me? You remember when John the Baptist saw Jesus coming to him, he cried, "Behold the Lamb of God, which taketh away the sin of the world" (John 1:29). Might not then the question be asked, What is Jesus Christ to you and me? Let us examine that rightly here this evening. What is Jesus Christ to us? What application do these words have to us? What do they mean to us? I trust we among those brought to behold this "servant" so as to say of him:

> "The one thing needful, dearest Lord
> Is to be one with thee."

And, as taught of the Holy Spirit, according to the measure of grace made known unto us, I trust we can honestly say before the Lord, "He is the chiefest among ten thousand…Yea, he is altogether lovely" (Song of Sol. 5:10,16).

Peter says, "Unto you which believe he is precious" (1 Pet. 2:7). Friends, is that so with us? It means he is the one whom we increasingly realise we cannot do without. There is none to compare with our Lord Jesus Christ. O to know the blessedness of what he says to us, as eternally one with him, "I have loved thee with an everlasting love: therefore with lovingkindness have I drawn thee" (Jer. 31:3). O Holy Spirit, seal it afresh to our souls tonight.

"Behold my servant, whom I have chosen; my beloved, in whom my soul is well pleased: I will put my spirit upon him, and he shall shew judgment to the Gentiles." Yes, as our Lord Jesus Christ came forth as Jehovah's righteous servant, there is none like unto him. This text was true of no servant of God, except the Lord Jesus. Behold the perfect man in whom was no sin, who in thought, word and deed was always perfectly obedient to the will of his heavenly Father. We cannot even begin to comprehend the wonder and blessedness of this. Though despised and rejected of men, yet approved of God the Father. And poor sinners are blessed of the Spirit to know his pardoning voice, his healing touch, his deliverance from the curse of a broken law, the forgiveness of their sins, and the sure hope of eternal life. O truly, cannot they bear testimony to this declaration, *"behold my servant,"* as they behold him whom God has set forth as his salvation to the ends of the earth? Cannot they say, 'In him is all my hope and help for time and eternity; none other than the Lord Jesus Christ *can* and, blessed be his great and holy name, *has* met the deepest needs of my soul'? That is true of every believer.

Do not overlook the blessed fact that the Lord Jesus, set before us as Jehovah's righteous servant, most surely accomplished what he came forth to do. Did he not himself declare, "I have finished the work which thou gavest me to do"? (John 17:4). Therein is everything which brings down the blessings of salvation upon us poor sinners brought to trust alone in him. There is nothing yet to be done. All has been done by Christ alone. He has given full satisfaction, perfect obedience, to the law's demands. He has brought in everlasting righteousness which is imputed to every sinner brought to flee to him for refuge. Yes, truly he is the sure refuge of his people in all their concerns.

"He shall bring forth judgment to the Gentiles." There is no *doubt,* no *if,* no *but* or *peradventure* to this. By Isaiah, the Lord says of Jesus Christ, his righteous servant, *"He shall not fail"* (Isa. 42:4). And blessed be his name, he has not failed. He has fully accomplished the work which his Father gave him to do. Have we not the assurance of this, in that God raised him from the dead the third day according to the scriptures? We behold him now, the ever living one, glorious at the right hand of the Majesty in the heavens. But though there, he is not one remote from us— far from it. Though there, he is ever present with his people. We are assured of his presence with us in the gracious ministry and indwelling of the Lord the Holy Spirit, the Spirit of our Lord and Saviour Jesus Christ. And as he ministered to needy sinners when here upon earth, so he ministers to his people still.

Look at what is said of him. "He shall not strive, nor cry; neither shall any man hear his voice in the streets." When our Lord Jesus Christ was here on earth, he did not seek honour from men. He did not seek to be acclaimed by the multitude, nor seek to stir up rebellion against the Roman authorities. He sought honour alone from God his Father. See how, as Jehovah's righteous servant, he went about fulfilling the work his Father gave him to do, never distracted or diverted from it, all in perfect loving obedience to the will of his heavenly Father. As I said a little earlier, all the life and ministry of our Lord Jesus Christ showed forth the wondrous reality of that great love wherewith he loved his people even when they were dead in trespasses and sins. That love was surely manifest in his perfect obedience to his Father: "I delight to do thy will, O my God: yea, thy law is within my heart."

See how our Lord Jesus is set before us as well: "A bruised reed shall he not break, and smoking flax shall he not quench, till he send forth judgment unto victory." As I said, though he is glorified at the right hand of the Majesty in the heavens, yet he is ever present with his people. He will not break the bruised reed nor quench the smoking flax! How this blessedly opens up to us, the love and compassion of his heart to his own people. How kind he is. He condescends to our low estate. He comes to his people just where they are. He comes by the ministry of the Lord the Holy Spirit.

O in these present times may we know gracious refreshing from his presence. He draws near to us in the ministry of his word. He speaks to our hearts, tried, fearful and troubled as we often are with many things. Yes, he comes to us. Surely, I trust, we are not strangers to his coming to us and saying, "Be of good cheer: it is I; be not afraid" (Matt. 14:27); "I am with thee" (Gen. 28:15); "I will never leave thee, nor forsake thee" (Heb. 13:5)? Friends. these are not empty words, far from it. They open up to us the love of our Lord Jesus Christ, his kindness and care over his needy people, weak and fearful as they are, yet still upheld and kept by his almighty hand. Though they are subject to the workings of sin within and the assaults of Satan and oppressed with outward circumstances, yet be assured of this, *all* their concerns are in the care of Jesus, our Lord and Saviour. As I said recently, no shepherd ever cared for his sheep as the Lord Jesus cares for his own. We are never outside the circle of his love, blessed be his name.

"A bruised reed shall he not break, and smoking flax shall he not quench," Does that not express great weakness and feebleness? It is almost as if life is extinguished. But O, what reviving and refreshing there is from the gracious presence of the Lord. What effect his word can and does have!

Remember what we considered this morning, how the Lord came to Elijah, distressed as was that man of God, by the situation in which he found himself. "What doest thou here, Elijah?" I do not believe they were words of particular reproof to his servant. The Lord spoke to him by that "still small voice," and so he does to his people still. What is that still small voice? It is the voice of love and mercy which speaks forth from Calvary. It comes to us in the gospel by the gracious ministry of the Spirit making known the love, grace and mercy of the Lord in all its fulness and freeness, to the hearts of his people.

What can bring peace to the troubled hearts of his children? What can speak true consolation to them? Is it not as Jesus is pleased to draw near, revealing himself to them as he does not unto the world, revealing himself to them by his own word and his blessing upon it? Cannot *one* word, does not *one* word from the Lord make all the difference? We may feel to be in a situation like David—our soul cast down within us. But the word of the Lord comes, "Fear not, for I am with thee" (Gen. 26:24). Though cast down, as Paul says, yet not forsaken, blessed be the Lord's great name. May the Holy Spirit lead our souls more and more into the believing realisation of this consolation.

"He shall shew judgment to the Gentiles…till he send forth judgment unto victory" Friends, how blessedly this speaks to us. Yes, though the situation is trying and difficult, yet we are assured that the victory is sure unto his people. There is deliverance, for the Lord "is able also to save them to the uttermost that come unto God by him, seeing he ever liveth to make intercession for them" (Heb. 7:25). Yes, by the Lord alone is the salvation of his people. Victory over sin, Satan, death, hell and the grave is assured for us, because Jesus died for us and rose again and is now entered into his glory. O may our souls be grounded, established in the believing realisation of these truths.

"And in his name shall the *Gentiles* trust." What a word was that, even when our Lord Jesus was here on earth. One thing that greatly offended the Jews was the Lord's teaching that his mercy was not only to the Jews but to the Gentiles as well. He "came not to call the righteous, but sinners to repentance," sinners not only from the Jews but from the Gentiles also, blessed be the Lord! (Matt. 9:13). *"In his name* shall the Gentiles trust." What word is that to sinners such as you and me! *"In his name,"* that name which is above every name, that name the preciousness of which we are brought to realise more and more as taught of the Holy Spirit. And his word declares that as brought to trust in his name, we shall *never* be confounded. By the rich mercies of the Lord towards us, may our whole attention be increasingly drawn in these troubled times to Jesus alone, Jehovah's righteous servant who accomplished the work his Father gave him to do. Behold him now at the right hand of the Majesty in the heavens. Well does the word therefore testify, "Strengthen ye the weak hands, and confirm the feeble knees. Say to them that are of a fearful heart, Be strong, fear not: behold, your God will come…" (Isa. 35:3–4). And he *does* come. He comes with the blessings of salvation, to the praise of the glory of his great and holy name. And no sinner that is brought through his grace to believe and trust in him shall ever be confounded.

I leave the remarks there. The Lord add his blessing. Amen.

18

THIS GOD IS OUR GOD FOR EVER AND EVER

Lord's day morning, 3 May 2020

"For this God is our God for ever and ever: he
will be our guide even unto death" (Psalm
48:14 but all the psalm).

Truly, this is a psalm imparting instruction, and drawing out the souls of the living family of God, in praise and thanksgiving unto the God of our salvation. In it, we are assured of the glorious truth of the Lord's relationship to his own people, manifested in his lovingkindness to his true church which rests on one foundation, even Jesus Christ the Lord. The psalmist celebrates the greatness, goodness and glory of God displayed to his people of old. The Lord had made known himself to them in all the ordering of the worship and service of his name, first of all in the tabernacle and then in the temple Solomon built in Jerusalem upon mount Zion.

But this morning I want to direct our attention, as this psalm surely does, to the wonders of the Lord's sovereign and saving grace to his *one true* church. For this grace, the psalmist expresses praise in verse one: "Great is the LORD, and greatly to be praised in the city of our God, in the mountain of his holiness." O the wonder that this God is the one and only true God who inhabiteth eternity, whose name is holy, and whom the heaven of heavens cannot contain! The question is asked by Solomon, "Will God in very deed dwell with men on the earth?" (2 Chron. 6:18). He will, and let us not forget that the dwelling-place of God with men upon earth is in the person of our Lord Jesus Christ. In him dwells the one true church, the true spiritual Zion, the true Jerusalem. The psalmist praises the glory of God manifest in Zion, his people of old. But consider what he says in the light of new covenant mercies now revealed to us in the glorious truth of the gospel. See there the full revelation of the glory of God manifested in his sovereign grace and mercy in the outworking of his divine appointments and purposes, as he gathers the people whom he hath loved and chosen from before the foundation of the world! See how he brings them into the blessings of that covenant ordered in all things and sure. See the oneness of the church and people of God as found in Jesus Christ, he in them and they in him. This indeed constitutes the true church of Jesus Christ, a people gathered out of every nation, kindred, tribe, and tongue from under heaven.

See the blessed consummation of these things set before us in the book of the Revelation. They are the redeemed of the Lord before the throne of God on high. And that is the distinguishing mark of these who are gathered—they are the redeemed of the Lord. Ah, read the seventh chapter of that book. John beheld a number which no man could number of every nation, kindred, tribe and tongue from under heaven. He was asked, "What are these…and whence came they?" "These are they which came out of great tribulation, and have washed their robes, and made them white in the blood of the Lamb. Therefore are they before the throne of God."

O friends, what a glorious prospect is surely before the church and people of God. We hear of one and another of the people of God whom the Lord calls to himself. We sorrow that they are taken from this time state, for we miss their company. We are thankful for the work God had wrought for and in them, and by them, making them a blessing in their day and generation. But friends, we glory that they have entered into the very presence of the Lord. What a glorious prospect is that which awaits every believer through the riches of divine grace. "Absent from the body…present with the Lord" (2 Cor. 5:8). Paul had a great desire "to depart, and to be with Christ; which is far better" (Phil. 1:23). But notice that Paul desired in all things to be submissive to the will of God.

Yes, the people of God have that glorious prospect before them. And in their anticipation of it, what encouragement and consolation is known by the inward witness of the Holy Spirit that Jesus Christ is ours and we are his. Yet let us not overlook this important point as we journey on in this wilderness world—

what should be our chief concern? It is to seek to serve the Lord in our day, to wait upon him, to bear testimony unto him, as we are encouraged in this psalm. As it is said in verse thirteen, "tell it to the generation following." Surely should not that ever be the concern of the living family of God, those who profess to know and love the Lord Jesus Christ in sincerity and truth? Should not their concern ever be to bear witness in their life and in the ministry to which they are called, to him that loved them and washed them from their sins in his own blood? Surely they should not be afraid or ashamed to bear witness to whose they are and whom they serve, the only true God, the sovereign ruler of heaven and earth who has revealed himself to us in the person of our Lord and Saviour Jesus Christ?

As I have said, the greatness, glory and goodness of the Lord our God, set before us by the psalmist, is revealed essentially in Jesus Christ. There is no access and acceptance with God, apart from the sovereign operations of the Holy Spirit bringing us to believe and trust in Jesus. God is only revealed, in the wonders of his sovereign, saving grace to sinners, in the person of Jesus Christ. Jesus is the only way. Out of Christ, God is a consuming fire. O friends, how solemn is that word. Out of Christ, how can any sinner stand before a holy, righteous and just God? Why friends, the holy law of God condemns us. Divine justice demands our condemnation. We sinners have nothing of our own to look to or plead. O the wonders of God's grace! Troubled, burdened and exercised soul, you that feel the great weight of your sins upon you and are brought to cry unto the Lord for mercy, Satan is so active in suggesting there is no hope for you in God. 'How can you expect a holy God to look upon you, being what you are and where you are?' Well friends, let me tell you that *whatever you are,* whatever you have done, however great your sins may be, however heavy the burden of your sin that presses you down, let me emphasis this precious truth—*there is hope, hope in God.* Be assured that there is salvation in none other, but in our Lord and Saviour Jesus Christ, as the gospel makes known. As one has said,

> "The vilest sinner out of hell,
> Who lives to feel his need,

Is welcome to a Throne of Grace,
The Saviour's blood to plead."

O friend, when sins press heavy upon you, behold the glorious reality that "the blood of Jesus Christ his Son cleanseth us from all sin" (1 John 1:7). O may the Lord the Holy Spirit open this truth to you afresh this morning. Is not this what the church, the believing people of God, should ever bear testimony to in their generation? Should we not ever be witnessing to the truth that there is salvation for sinners? Remember that it is for sinners that Jesus Christ came into this world. Was not that declared by the angel to Joseph at the time of Christ's birth? "Thou shalt call his name JESUS: for he shall save his people from their sins" (Matt. 1:21). Is not that the greatest and most glorious wonder set forth in the precious truth of the gospel? Where should the ministry of the word and the faithful witness of the church and people of God direct sinners? To one place only. To one glorious person who is able "to save to the uttermost all that come unto God by him" (Heb. 7:25). Does not the glorious truth of the gospel bear witness to this? O hear the Saviour's voice. May it come afresh to us this morning by the unction of the Holy Spirit, "Come unto me, all ye that labour and are heavy laden, and I will give you rest" (Matt. 11:28).

You say, where is *that* to be found in this psalm? It is very much to be found in this psalm. For the glory of the true church of Jesus Christ, the mount Zion, the heavenly Jerusalem as described here, is not found in what she is in herself. What is she, what is this "daughter of Judah"? What is she in herself, but a sinner born in sin and shapen in iniquity and defiled throughout with sin. The psalmist's word in another place is verily true, "There is none that doeth good, no, not one" (Ps. 14:3). The apostle Paul testified to this in Romans chapter three. He was brought to deeply realize the solemn truth of it for himself. Yes, "all have sinned, and come short of the glory of God." Not one is exempt. O friends, the glory of Zion, the church of Jesus Christ, is that they are sinners *saved by grace!* And how is the glory of his grace manifest to sinful men and women in his church? It is by what God has provided in the person and work of his Son, who has once for ever put away our sins and has brought in everlasting righteousness for us. God thus *justifies the ungodly*.

As I have said, the glory of Zion, the church of Jesus Christ, is in the manifestation of the wonders of his sovereign, saving grace to sinners. Thereby he has brought them believingly into the bonds of his everlasting covenant, the wonderful reality of union and fellowship with the Lord and Saviour Jesus Christ. And so the psalmist says, "Beautiful for situation, the joy of the whole earth, is mount Zion, on the sides of the north, the city of the great King." What is here spoken has application to Zion, the *true* church of Jesus Christ. It sets forth the glory of the church as found in Jesus Christ "who is made unto us wisdom, and righteousness, and sanctification, and redemption" (1 Cor. 1:30). This alone is the glory of Zion, of every poor sinner taught of God the Holy Spirit. How glorious is the church in the eyes of our triune God. Yes, in herself she is defiled but as found in Jesus Christ she is the undefiled. O the glory and blessedness of the true church of Jesus Christ and every believer through the riches of divine grace!

We referred earlier to that great company of the redeemed before the throne, as recorded in the book of the Revelation, of whom it is said, "These are they which came out of great tribulation, and have washed their robes, and made them white in the blood of the Lamb" (Rev. 7:14). *That* is the glorious covering of the people of God. *That* is where needy sinners are found all glorious in the eyes of our triune God. It is as they are clothed in the righteousness of Jesus Christ and washed from all their sins in his precious blood. What is the testimony concerning them which proceeds from the very throne of God and comes to us through the person and finished work of our Lord Jesus Christ? "Thou art all fair, my love; there is no spot in thee" (Song of Sol. 4:7). "These were redeemed from among men" by the Lord (Rev.14:4). These have been brought into the bonds of the everlasting covenant. They are blessed as being the sons and daughters of God, heirs of God and joints heirs with Christ Jesus.

Friends, what can compare with this, whatever may be attained unto in the things of this present time state? Men set their affection on things here on earth. O how diligently they seek after

riches and honour and power among men. But what is all that a
sinner may attain to in this life, compared with the wonders of
redeeming love and mercy? For thereby we are brought into the
bonds of the everlasting covenant, as members of the true church
of Jesus Christ which he has loved and redeemed by his precious
blood. And we are assured here that the Lord has provided for his
people all things that pertain to their true welfare for *time* and
eternity, for *body* and *soul*. Sure provision is made in the person
of our Lord Jesus Christ for every one of his believing people.

Remember this, do not look on what you are in yourself, or
what is found in your own life, in judging the Lord's mercies and
favours towards you. As I have said many a time, the people of
God, poor sinners as they are in themselves, are never outside the
circle of the love of God in Jesus Christ their Lord. We are so
prone to judge the attitude of the Lord toward us according what
we find and feel in ourselves. But do we, and will we, ever find
anything in ourselves to give us any ground for encouragement
or consolation? No! For surely what imperfections, frailties and
infirmities are sadly found with us. Is there anything in us we can
rest upon? Do we see anything in ourselves for which God should
be favourable to us?

The only blessed foundation for the faith and hope of the
living family of God, the only ground of encouragement is not in
what we are. We do seek grace to serve the Lord in our generation
and to know more, through his grace, of closer fellowship and
communion with him. But O friends, the ground of encouragement is not in what we are or have done, but in what *Jesus Christ
is,* as revealed to us. Ever remember the precious truth that he
will ever be the *friend of sinners*. What a statement is that! The
Lord the Holy Spirit bring it home afresh to your soul and mine
this morning. We sometimes sing,

"What a friend we have in Jesus."

Yes, he is a *friend that loveth at all times*, a *brother* that is born
for adversity. That is surely brought before us in the spirit of this
psalm in which the greatness and glory of God is revealed
towards his church and people in their being *his* habitation, the
very creation of his hands. Look at what is said of the city of the
great King, her palaces, the lovingkindness of God in his temple,

the joy of the daughters of Zion, the towers and bulwarks of her salvation. How great and glorious are the works of God and we ever desire to bear testimony unto him in them. We see his glorious works in creation, indeed in nature as we see it even now this springtime. The earth begins to bud and bring forth. The flowers and fruits begin to appear. The seasons return. O is not this work of God's hands still seen in our day and generation? Does he not fulfil his promise: "While the earth remaineth, seedtime and harvest, and cold and heat, and summer and winter, and day and night shall not cease"? (Gen. 8:22). Is he not faithful to his word? We see the seasons come and go, night and day likewise. The greatness and glory of his work is seen in his providential dealings, especially in every detail of the lives of his people. All is of God in the outworking of his purposes for his people amid all the affairs of men and nations. Is there anything that comes to pass which is not according to what God has appointed for the glory of his name and the true profit of his one true church? See this in his dealings with the kings and nations around Zion in this psalm.

O to be brought above all, to behold the wonderful works of God in his sovereign grace and mercy to sinners, as set forth in the gospel and made known in the hearts and lives of each whom he calls by grace. O friends, what a mighty, glorious work of God it is that you and I are brought to not only know what we are and where we are as sinners, but also to believe and trust in Jesus Christ alone. He brings us to look away from everything in self, that Jesus Christ may truly be *all and in all* unto us.

How this wondrous work of grace is set before us in this psalm! Zion is the church of Jesus Christ, the whole of the elect of God, every individual member of that church! Each believer has a part in that true church, the city of our God. As described by the apostle, each is a member of the body of Jesus Christ, of which he is the head. O what a unity is in that body, and what blessedness in that union! It is as described in another psalm: "Behold, how good and how pleasant it is for brethren to dwell together in unity!" (Ps. 133:1). There *is* a true unity of the church and people of God. As found in Jesus Christ the church is *one*.

O friends, may we know increasingly that blessed unity

among the companies of the Lord's people. For though the church here on earth is *one*, one complete whole as found in Jesus, its manifestation on earth is in the local companies of the Lord's people, sinners called by grace and brought into fellowship with one another.

What solemn implications does this have for us that profess to be members of the church of Jesus Christ. Are we not to walk together in the local church in the bonds of love and union in our Lord, prayerfully seeking to dwell together as brethren in "the unity of the Spirit in the bond of peace"? (Eph. 4:3). Are we not to have a right care and concern for one another? Are we not to witness to our generation whose we are and whom we serve. Yes, there are things that trouble, being what we are, still possessing a fallen nature. O friends, what grace we need to walk together as brethren in the Lord. O for grace to know more of what it is to drink into the spirit of our Lord Jesus Christ.

Remember the occasion when there had been contention among his disciples as to who should be the greatest. The Lord took a little child and set him in the midst and said, "Whosoever shall not receive the kingdom of God as a little child shall in no wise enter therein" (Luke 18:17). O friends, how prone we are to the pride of our fallen nature. O may the Lord deliver us from all that is of sin and self. May he cause us to realize more of the greatness and glory of our Lord Jesus Christ and how he has provided for us who are believers through grace, as brethren together in him, though sinners every one of us. Can one of us claim we have no sin? No. We have to come daily in confession of our sins before the Lord. Yet, through the rich mercy of our God, we are assured of this: "My little children, these things write I unto you, that ye sin not. And if any man sin, we have an advocate with the Father, Jesus Christ the righteous: and he is the propitiation for our sins: and not for ours only, but also for the sins of the whole world," the sins of the whole elect of God (1 John 2:1–2).

Here then in this psalm we see the glory of the church of God as built on the one foundation of Jesus Christ, as one with him and partaker of all that the gospel testifies of the sovereign grace and mercy of God in the blessings of redemption and salvation.

And look at what the psalmist says: "God is known in her palaces for a refuge." Cannot we bear witness to this, that God is our refuge and strength at all times, in all situations? He says as well, "Walk about Zion, and go round about her: tell the towers thereof. Mark ye well her bulwarks, consider her palaces; that ye may tell it to the generation following." This is what God in Jesus Christ has provided for his people. Truly, our whole salvation is of the Lord. We are held, kept and provided for by our God. See how his promises, rooted as they are in his unchanging love and faithfulness, do not vary like the outward circumstances of our lives.

See how the psalmist concludes: "For this God," as revealed in Jesus Christ to every sinner called by grace, *"is our God."* O friends, the vital importance of this word *"our."* Is it not in this that our consolation is found? This God, the one and only true God, the sovereign ruler of heaven and earth, God as revealed in the person of Jesus Christ, full of grace, full of truth—*this* God is *our* God? It is as we read this morning in Isaiah's prophecy, chapter 25: "O LORD, thou art *my* God." O friends, is it not a blessed reality that "this God is *our* God"? Each sinner taught of God the Holy Spirit can come in here: 'he is my God, my Father—O blissful name.' May we know more and more of this blessed relationship, by the witness of the Holy Spirit with our spirit.

But "this God is our God," *my* God and that "for ever and ever," not just for a time, not just for a season, not just when things are trying and difficult in our lives, but *"for ever and ever."* How this embraces all that pertains to the people of God, in time and to all eternity as well. For God never ceases to be the God of his people, the God and Father of our Lord Jesus Christ, who loved us and called us by his grace and who redeemed us from all iniquity, through the glorious work of his beloved Son.

"This God is our God for ever and ever: *he will be our guide* even unto death." Ah, what a sure guide we have here! We are reminded again—to whom shall we look? Where shall we go with all that concerns us in our personal lives? O may we not be left to lean to our own understanding. May we be looking and coming continually to him who is the sure guide and guard of his people.

For surely if the Lord is our guide (and he *is* the guide and guard of his people), not one can ultimately go astray, not one can ever be lost. No, for Jesus is the one that saves to the uttermost.

"He will be our guide *even unto death.*" Here we are indeed reminded of the solemn fact and reality of death, particularly at this time when we see many passing into eternity, many, we fear, with no hope whatsoever. O friends, the solemn fact of eternity:

"Eternity, tremendous sound!
To guilty souls a dreadful wound;
But O, if Christ and heaven be mine,
How sweet the accents, how divine!"

"He will be our guide even unto death." You know, as it concerns the child of God, death is not the end. In a very real sense the believer never dies. As Jesus himself testifies, the death of the believer is a passing from this time state, into the fulness of that eternal life that is theirs in Jesus Christ our Lord. It is said in that chapter we read in Isaiah: "He will swallow up death in victory" (Isa. 25:8). Ah friends, the glorious reality of that for the people of God, the true church of Jesus Christ: He has swallowed up death in victory.

"He will be our guide even unto death." And even there, in the hour and article of death, the assurance is given us: "I am with thee saith the LORD," "I will never leave thee, nor forsake thee." (Jer. 1:19; Heb. 13:5). O the unchanging love and faithfulness of our God, that "this God is our God for ever and ever: he will be our guide even unto death." I will just repeat once more, *"even unto death,"* O what a glorious prospect awaits us! We think of our dear brother Don (Fortner) being taken from us. The last book he wrote was, "Going home." And surely has he not entered into the full realization of those things he endeavoured to set forth in his ministry? The sum and substance of it was ever *preaching Jesus Christ*. Could he not say, and should it not be so with each true servant of Jesus Christ, "I determined not to know any thing among you, save Jesus Christ, and him crucified" (1 Cor. 2:2).

I leave the remarks there. May the Lord add his blessing. Amen.

19

YE ARE COME UNTO MOUNT ZION

Lord's day evening 3 May 2020

"For ye are not come unto the mount that might be touched, and that burned with fire, nor unto blackness, and darkness, and tempest, And the sound of a trumpet, and the voice of words; which voice they that heard intreated that the word should not be spoken to them any more: (For they could not endure that which was commanded, And if so much as a beast touch the mountain, it shall be stoned, or thrust through with a dart: And so terrible was the sight, that Moses said, I exceedingly fear and quake:) But ye are come unto mount Sion, and unto the city of the living God, the heavenly Jerusalem, and to an innumerable company of angels. To the general assembly and church of the firstborn, which are written in heaven, and to God the Judge of all, and to the spirits of just men made perfect, And to Jesus the mediator of the new covenant, and to the blood of sprinkling, that speaketh better things than that of Abel" (Hebrews 12:18-24).

We turn to the word of God this evening and Hebrews chapter twelve, verses eighteen to twenty-four. As we do so, may we know the Lord's mercies towards us and with joy draw water out of these wells of salvation—the fulness and freeness of grace in our Lord Jesus, the wonder of his abiding love and faithfulness to his people at all times in every situation. May our one concern be that the Lord's name alone has all the glory.

In considering, as helped, these verses I have read by way of a text, how important to do so in the light of the context in which they are found. We go back first of all to the close of chapter ten. Remember how the apostle is here ministering to his brethren after the flesh, sinners who had been called by grace. The path in which they had been brought to follow the Lord Jesus Christ was no easy path. As Jews brought to turn away from Moses to receive the glorious truth of the gospel, they found much opposition from their fellow-countrymen. As a result, many of them were much discouraged and cast down by the difficulties. And has it not always been so for the church of God, for each one of the Lord's people? As the Lord calls them by his grace, they find, as they journey on through this wilderness world, that it *is* indeed a wilderness to them. They are brought to realise that here "have we no continuing city" (Heb. 13:14). A mercy that it is so! But I am sure you know how much these things affect our human nature. How often, in the face of the difficult situations in which we are found, there is a cry of our souls to the Lord. And, experiencing how hard and difficult is the path we are called to walk, how prone we are at such times to murmuring and complaining, even with mercies in our hands.

The apostle's whole concern is to instruct, encourage and exhort the people of God in their pilgrimage. And that encouragement is entirely founded on the treasures God has revealed to us in the person and finished work of the Lord Jesus Christ. What a blessed testimony is given to him in this epistle, him in whom by the grace of God we are brought to believe, even our Lord Jesus Christ who died for us and rose again. He is the ever living one, who is now at the right hand of the Majesty in the heavens, there to appear in the presence of God for us. His word assures us that he is *full* of grace and truth. As I have repeated many times, his love to his people knows no change and no end. Whatever the discouraging circumstances in which we may be found, they do not alter the Lord's purposes of love and mercy towards us.

Yes, there is the trying of our faith—and that is very needful. As Paul reminds us here, are we not ever in need of the Lord's gracious dealings with us, even his chastening hand upon us, reminding us of what we are and where we are of ourselves?

What would be the consequences if left entirely to ourselves? We are brought to realise that we are wholly dependent on the Lord in the fulness and freeness of his grace. We have to be delivered again and again from our tendency to look to self and created things, and be brought, as the apostle here directs us by the Holy Spirit, to look to the Lord Jesus Christ alone,

At the close of the tenth chapter we read this: "Now the just shall live by faith: but if any man draw back, my soul shall have no pleasure in him. But we are not of them who draw back unto perdition; but of them that believe to the saving of the soul." Examples are given us in chapter eleven of God's grace manifest in the faith and lives of old testament believers. Was the world in which they lived, the path in which they were called to walk, vastly different from that of the church of Jesus Christ today? No. Our Lord Jesus declared, "In the world ye shall have tribulation: but be of good cheer; I have overcome the world" (John 16:33).

The reality of the life of faith brought before us in that chapter is seen in the fruit of the work of grace in the lives of those men and women. Truly their testimony to us is that they trusted in the Lord. And what a work of grace is that which brings a sinner such as you and me to believe and trust alone in the Lord Jesus Christ. This is not the work of our own fallen nature. It is not what man can impart to us. It is the rich gift of God, for faith "is the gift of God" (Eph. 2:8), flowing out of the fulness of grace which is in Christ Jesus our Lord. "They trusted in thee, and were not confounded" (Ps. 22:5). Very difficult and distressing was the path they were called to walk, but one thing they still testify to us is that the Lord did not fail them, the Lord was with them. They knew his sustaining grace and mercy. They were brought safely to their desired haven. As the psalmist puts it, "He led them forth by the right way, that they might go to a city of habitation" (Ps. 107:7). And not one of them failed to reach that heavenly inheritance. Confessing themselves to be strangers and pilgrims on the earth, they "looked for a city which hath foundations, whose builder and maker is God" It was true of them and of every believer throughout the new testament dispensation that "they overcame him [Satan] by the blood of the Lamb, and by the word of their testimony" (Rev. 12:11). As I have said, in that long record of those men and women of God, we see the work of divine grace in their lives in that they believed in God, they trusted in him and were not confounded.

Coming to this twelfth chapter the apostle says, "Wherefore seeing we also are compassed about with so great a cloud of witnesses, let us lay aside every weight, and the sin which doth so easily beset us, and let us run with patience the race that is set before us, Looking unto Jesus the author and finisher of our faith." Keep in mind those two important points: "let us run with patience the race that is set before us" and "looking unto Jesus the author and the finisher of our faith." This, and what follows in this chapter, is of great importance for the people of God. What grace do we need, as the apostle said, to "Cast not away therefore your confidence, which hath great recompence of reward" (Heb. 10:35). What need of patience, of persevering, of going forward in the face of all the difficulties and temptations which may well beset us. Truly, we cannot endure in our own strength, but only in "looking unto Jesus." The apostle's whole emphasis is to direct us to this glorious truth: "Looking unto Jesus the author and finisher of our faith; who for the joy that was set before him endured the cross, despising the shame, and is set down at the right hand of the throne of God. For consider him that endured such contradiction of sinners against himself, lest ye be wearied and faint in your minds." Yes, weary, heavy laden, needy child of God, O may grace enable you to lift up your eyes to behold our Lord Jesus Christ as set before us here, not only as an example of one that patiently endured but as the one who fulfilled the work his Father gave him to do. He was never discouraged nor did he fail in that work. His one aim in every aspect of his life was to do the will of his heavenly Father. He delighted in that will and in the joy that was set before him. O friends, the wonder and blessedness that in all that was involved for Jesus in his life, his sufferings and sorrows to save his people, yet what *delight* he had in the will of his Father. What love he had to his heavenly Father and to all whom his Father had given him. His love never wavered and so it is still, for he is the same Jesus "yesterday, and to day and for ever" (Heb. 13:8).

We see then the example of our Lord Jesus Christ, but we also see the emphasis on what he has done for his people. And it is from this that all encouragement and consolation arises. "Who for the joy that was set before him endured the cross, despising the shame, and is set down at the right hand of the throne of God." What does that blessedly open up to us? In the life, sufferings and death of our Lord Jesus Christ, he overcame sin, Satan, death, hell and the grave. This is beautifully brought before us in Isaiah chapter 53. O may the Holy Spirit open it up more and more to your soul and mine. "All we like sheep have gone astray; we have turned every one to his own way; and the LORD hath laid on him the iniquity of us all." And what can Jesus declare? "I have finished the work which thou gavest me to do" (John 17:4).

There are two wonderful words which declare the relationship of the Lord Jesus Christ with those his Father gave him and what he has done for them—*substitution* and *satisfaction*. Yes, our Lord Jesus Christ stood as the *substitute* in the room, place and stead of all his Father had given him. Friends, it comes to the personal application of it—Christ in your place, Christ in my place. "He hath made him to be sin for us, who knew no sin; that we might be made the righteousness of God in him" (2 Cor. 5:21). *There* is the reality of *substitution*.

Also, there is *satisfaction*. All that divine justice demanded has been fully satisfied. "The LORD is well pleased for his righteousness' sake; he will magnify the law, and make it honourable" (Isa. 42:21). Instead of the law being *against* us, it is *for* all those that are found by grace, through faith, in Jesus Christ. The law has nothing to say to them. Divine justice has no demands upon them, as found in him. All the law's demands, all the requirements of divine justice have been fully satisfied by our Lord Jesus. And this is the blessed ground of encouragement for the people of God even in the most trying paths in which they may be found.

"Looking unto Jesus the author and finisher of our faith; who for the joy that was set before him endured the cross, despising the shame, and is set down at the right hand of the throne of God. For consider him that endured such contradiction of sinners against himself, lest ye be wearied and faint in your minds." Can we not sum it up in the words of that hymn,

> "His way was much rougher and darker than mine;
> Did Christ, my Lord, suffer, and shall I repine?"

Remember also, we are told here that all the Lord's dealings with his people are the outworking of his love to them, yes, even in the deepest trying of their faith. The Lord's chastening hand upon them is never in vindictive anger. No. For as found in Jesus Christ, all divine wrath against them as sinners was poured out upon him. He rendered full satisfaction. All the Lord's dealings are in covenant love. Friends, we need his loving chastening. What proneness there is with us, as one said,

> "Prone to wander, Lord, I feel it;
> Prone to leave the God I love;
> Here's my heart, Lord, take and seal it;
> Seal it from thy courts above!"

As I said earlier, there is much gracious needful instruction in the Lord's dealings with his people. Thereby he brings us to realise our whole dependence on the Lord Jesus in all things. He weans us from self and the things of this present time state, to set our affections more upon those things which are above, where Christ sitteth on the right hand of God" (Col. 3:1).

> "To keep our eyes on Jesus fixed,
> And there our hope to stay,
> The Lord will make his goodness pass
> Before us in the way."

Let us never lose sight of the truth that the design of God in all his dealings with his people is, above all, for his glory and for their true spiritual welfare. We may consider the path in which we are called to walk very trying and difficult. And Satan is ever ready to suggest that the hand of the Lord is gone out against you, in dealing with you now as your sins deserve. O friends, what a liar is Satan. Is not the purpose of the Lord's dealings with his people, as it says here? "Now no chastening for the present seemeth to be joyous, but grievous: nevertheless afterward it yieldeth the peaceable fruit of righteousness unto them which are exercised thereby. Wherefore lift up the hands which hang down, and the feeble knees; And make straight paths for your feet, lest that which is lame be turned out of the way; but let it rather be healed" What a word of gracious exhortation is that for the people of God! O may we daily seek grace to walk in true, loving, filial fear of our Lord Jesus Christ, and particularly as he goes on to say, "Follow peace with all men, and holiness, without which no man shall see the Lord."

"Follow peace with all." You notice that the word *men* is in italics. It was inserted by our translators. The context in this chapter is the people of God. And this word surely refers to *their* relationships with one another as *brethren* brought into the bonds of union and fellowship in the gospel church of our Lord Jesus Christ. "Follow peace with all." O may the Lord grant us grace so to do.

It goes on to say, "and holiness, without which no man shall see the Lord." Has not that statement often been a trouble to the people of God? Looking at ourselves, where is that holiness? O surely, there is so much found in me and with me in my life which seems so contrary to *holiness.* How can I attain to it? Does this merely apply to my outward walk and conversation? (Yes, let us seek by the Lord's grace, to walk humbly and uprightly before our God in all relationships with our brethren in the church and before the world as well). But what is this holiness without which no man shall see the Lord? I believe it is in "Looking unto Jesus the author and finisher of our faith." *That* is following after holiness. It is "to keep our eyes on Jesus fixed," to seek to follow on to know the Lord as those that have been brought through grace to believe and trust in him only. This is what the apostle directs us to in that "cloud of witnesses" and the exhortations he gives through the ministry of the Holy Spirit. The holiness of believers is as we are found in Jesus Christ, "who of God is made unto us wisdom, and righteousness, and *sanctification...*" (1 Cor. 1:30). Our holiness is *not* in what we are in ourselves, *not* in what we attain to by the outworking of the grace of God in our daily lives, but in what is ours as found in Jesus Christ. And to *"follow holiness"* is to be looking unto Jesus, the author and finisher of our faith. All that pertains to the blessings of our salvation is not founded on what we are, not what we can do, but what Jesus Christ has done for us. I cannot repeat that enough. As believers, your holiness and mine, wherewith we can be accepted before God, is as we are found in Jesus Christ. It is as we are washed in his precious blood and clothed in his righteousness—his perfect obedience to the will of God in satisfying all the demands of his holy law on our behalf.

O friends, what glorious things the gospel opens up to us in what Jesus is made to his people! I am nothing but sin in myself but as a believer, through grace in Jesus Christ, I have everything in him! By him I can approach, as a poor sinner, unto God and be accepted by him through Christ's person and finished work. Blessed be the Lord's great and holy name!

The apostle continues, "Looking diligently lest any man fail of the grace of God; lest any root of bitterness springing up trouble you, and thereby many be defiled." See here the exhortation and warning of the apostle to the people of God. "Looking diligently lest any man fail of the grace of God," that is, *any man turns away from Jesus Christ*. Friends, how real is that temptation when things are trying and difficult for us. Remember when our Lord Jesus was here on earth, teaching the multitude those deep, hidden and glorious things regarding himself, he said to them, "Except ye eat the flesh of the Son of man, and drink his blood, ye have no life in you" (John 6:53). Many were offended and said, "This is an hard saying; who can hear it?" And sadly, many are still offended at the glorious truth of sovereign, free, electing grace. Many turned away from him and followed him no more. He says to his disciples, "Will ye also go away?" Ah, what a question is that for you and me this evening. "Will ye also go away," being so discouraged and disheartened by the difficulties of the way? Why, says one,

"Depart from thee?—'tis death—'tis more;
'Tis endless ruin, deep despair!"

We are also here reminded to have prayerful concern for one another's spiritual welfare, and to exhort and encourage one another in the way the Lord has called us to walk as brethren in him. "Looking diligently lest any man fail of the grace of God; lest any root of bitterness springing up trouble you, and thereby many be defiled." Friends, I say what grace we need for the outworking of this in our daily lives, in our relationships and fellowship with one another.

He sets before us the example of Esau. He says, "Lest there be any fornicator, or profane person, as Esau, who for one morsel of meat sold his birthright." What did Esau despise? It was the blessing of the firstborn. How readily he sold it to Jacob. We know Jacob, in those actions, was a supplanter and a deceiver but subsequently we see in him the working of divine grace. The point is that Esau had no time for what God had promised to Abraham and Isaac—the blessing in which was all that pertained to the glory of God in the salvation of sinful men and women by him who was to come, even our Lord and Saviour Jesus Christ. We can put it this way. Ultimately, Esau had no time for Jesus Christ. And, sadly and solemnly, that is not only the attitude of the world generally, but is even manifest within the professed Christian church in our day—*no time for Jesus Christ*. Yes, his name may be used but is there really and truly the believing and trusting alone in him? We are here told that Esau afterwards sought a blessing of his father, but it was not so much for the spiritual blessing promised to Abraham, but for the material possessions of his father. He sought with tears a blessing from his father, but see what Isaac, by the grace of God, said concerning Jacob: I "have blessed him, yea, and he shall be blessed" (Gen. 27:33). Despite the deceit of Jacob and his mother, we see the outworking of sovereign discriminating grace even in God's providential dealings. "Jacob have I loved, but Esau have I hated" (Rom. 9:13). What a warning is here given to the people of God, to "follow peace with all men, and holiness, without which no man shall see the Lord."

Friends, see the further encouragement given us here as the apostle goes on to say, "For ye are not come unto the mount that might be touched, and that burned with fire, nor unto blackness, and darkness, and tempest." This sets before us that the living family of God have been delivered by divine grace from all the demands of God's holy and righteous law promulgated on mount Sinai. How fearful and solemn it was! Moses himself said, "I exceedingly fear and quake." Paul says ye are not come to the law, not to Sinai. O the wonders of grace which bring us to Zion.

The point I would emphasis is the testimony here given that believers, brought through the grace of God to put their trust alone in the Lord Jesus Christ, are delivered from the law by the body of Christ. It has no more to do with us. It can never bring us into condemnation. We are delivered by the *substitution* and *satisfaction* wrought for us by Jesus Christ.

You know, the holiness "without which no man shall see the Lord" is never to be found at Sinai, never to be found by our seeking to be obedient to what the law demands of us. O may we daily seek grace to be obedient to the revealed will of God given us in holy scripture, to walk in the fear and love of our Lord and Saviour. But ever remember that the holiness without which no man shall see the Lord, is never to be found at Sinai. What is the tendency of fallen human nature when any conviction grips the conscience? To what does it turn? So much of what goes under the name of religion today is merely the religion of the natural man, a religion of works, always looking to something they think they must do to obtain favour of the Lord. And friends, that proneness is still found with us, even as believers through grace,

"To wait on self, or something base,
Instead of trusting sovereign grace!"

But here we are assured that as believers we do not come to Sinai. It is not to that mount but to Calvary we are brought. O the wonder and blessedness of this! What does the holy law of God speak from Sinai? Condemnation. It could do nothing other to sinners. It is holy, just and good—there is no denying that. But it has no salvation for sinners such as you and me. In the law, God is above us and against us. His holy law demands perfect obedience in every aspect of our life. But one thing is sure. *That* obedience can never be rendered by us sinners. As transgressors of the law how can we meet the debt we owe to a holy God? But we are not come to Sinai. The demands of God's holy law against the believer have been fully met in the person of our Lord Jesus Christ.

O friends, what encouragement is here given us always to look only to the Lord Jesus and "follow on to know the Lord" (Hos. 6:3). "Ye are not come unto the mount that might be touched, and that burned with fire, nor unto blackness." No. "Ye are come unto mount Sion." O, what a glorious mountain is this! Here we see God revealed in Jesus Christ. Here we see the relationship of our triune God to all who are brought into the blessings of the covenant ordered in all things and sure. Here we see the true church of Jesus Christ as described in Psalm 48 which we considered this morning. O what a glorious mount this is! Pardon, peace and eternal life are here assured to every sinner brought by grace to cry to the Lord Jesus for mercy and to trust in him alone, whatever their need. This speaks not only of what shall be, but what is *even now* the portion of the living family of God.

He says, "Ye are come unto mount Sion, and unto the city of the living God, the heavenly Jerusalem, and to an innumerable company of angels." Ye are come to where God dwells with his people. God came down on earth in giving the law. But in the blessings of which believers are here assured, God has come *down* in the person of his Son, Jesus Christ. And Jesus is now ascended into heaven, there to appear in the presence of God for us. And in our union with Jesus, he brings *us up* into fellowship with God. O the wondrous love and mercy of the Lord Jesus to us. We are his people. We are the city, the dwelling-place, of the living God, the heavenly Jerusalem!

True, this word directs us to the glorious inheritance which God has appointed for his people. But the entering into the blessings of this inheritance, the assurance of our soul's personal interest in it, is as we are brought by divine grace to believe and trust in Jesus Christ *now*. O to keep our eyes fixed on Jesus, following after the holiness which he has provided for us, with a true sense of our deep indebtedness to him, having his love shed abroad in our hearts by the Holy Spirit.

"To an innumerable company of angels." Paul, in chapter one of this epistle, says of angels, "Are they not all ministering spirits, sent forth to minister for them who shall be heirs of salvation?" How little we comprehend what we owe to God for the ministry of angels. "The angel of the LORD encampeth round about them that fear him, and delivereth them" (Ps. 34:7). Look at Psalm 48 again. See how the Lord watches over his people. Are not all things in his hand and under his control? "God is known in her palaces for a refuge…We have thought of thy lovingkindness, O God, in the midst of thy temple." And included in that lovingkindness to his own is his provision for them of the ministry of an "innumerable company of angels."

"To the general assembly and church of the firstborn, which are *written in heaven."* Every poor sinner brought through divine grace to believe and trust in the Jesus Christ, has been brought into the general assembly and church of the firstborn. When the disciples returned from preaching in the places where Jesus had sent them, they said, "Lord, even the devils are subject unto us through thy name." But he replied, "Rejoice not, that the spirits are subject unto you; but rather rejoice, because your names are *written in heaven"* (Luke10:20). And so it is expressed here. Their names are *written in heaven*. That is blessedly true of every sinner who by grace has been brought to trust in the Lord Jesus Christ alone.

"And to God the Judge of all." Is there not deep, precious consolation that God is the Judge of all? He knows all things in our present path. As sinners saved by grace, we have access and standing before him. He knows and judges all. Upon his judgment which he has revealed to us in his holy word, we can implicitly rely. Never lose sight of the important and precious truth that God is the Judge of all. "And to the spirits of just men made perfect." Is that something yet to be realised in the fulness of it? Why friends, it is a *present* blessing for every poor sinner brought by divine grace to believe and trust in Jesus Christ. "God the Judge of all" approves of them. He fully acquits them. What is his testimony concerning his people? "Who shall lay any thing to the charge of God's elect? It is God that justifieth. Who is he that condemneth? It is Christ that died, yea rather, that is risen again, who is even at the right hand of God, who also maketh intercession for us" (Rom. 8:33–34). See how the testimony of God himself is not against us, but for us as we are found in Jesus Christ our Lord!

"And to Jesus the mediator of the new covenant, and to the blood of sprinkling, that speaketh better things than that of Abel." O how precious is that name of our Lord Jesus Christ, the mediator of the new covenant. He that ever undertakes the cause of his people. And as he assures us in his word, are not all whom his Father has given him, safe in his hands? Does he not keep them? Does he not intercede for them before his Father's throne? Has he not loved them with a love that knows no end, no change, blessed be his great and holy name?

"The blood of sprinkling, that speaketh better things than that of Abel," yes, that precious atoning blood of the Lord Jesus Christ. At the present time, we are not able to partake of the Lord's Supper on this first Sunday. O friends, how important is that ordinance of the Lord's house, not merely to attend on it but because of what it speaks to us? Though not able to partake of it this evening, may our souls know what is set forth in it. The Lord Jesus himself has declared, "Take, eat: this is my body, which is broken for you: this do in remembrance of me" (1 Cor. 11:24). "This is my blood of the new testament, which is shed for many for the remission of sins" (Matt. 26:28). What pardon, peace and eternal life comes to us though the precious atoning blood of the Lord Jesus Christ, assuring us that all that the law demanded has been met, all that divine justice required, *satisfied*. God is not now above and against us as he is in the law. God is now for us in the glorious person of our Lord Jesus Christ, who is "Emmanuel ...God with us" (Matt. 1:23). "Ye are come to the blood of sprinkling, that speaketh better things than that of Abel." Abel's blood cried for justice. The blood of Jesus Christ,

"Speaks peace as loud from every vein."

"Follow peace with all men, and holiness, without which no man shall see the Lord." Friends, what encouragement is here given us so to do. Whatever situation we may be in this evening, may we still be going forward, "Looking unto Jesus the author and finisher of our faith," in complete dependence and trust in him, through his enabling grace.

The apostle goes on to say, "See that ye refuse not him that speaketh." O that our ears may ever be opened to hear, not what man says, not what unbelief says, but what our God and Saviour speaks. And does he not still speak peace to his people, to the praise of the glory of his name? May that word to Jacob speak afresh to your soul and mine this evening: "Behold, I am with thee, and will keep thee in all places whither thou goest, and will bring thee again into this land; for I will not leave thee, until I have done that which I have spoken to thee of" (Gen. 28:15).

But I will leave the remarks there. May the Lord add his blessing to his own word. Amen.

20

IF ANY OF YOU LACK WISDOM, LET HIM ASK OF GOD … IN FAITH

Tuesday evening 5 May 2020

"If any of you lack wisdom, let him ask of God, that giveth to all men liberally, and upbraideth not; and it shall be given him. But let him ask in faith, nothing wavering. For he that wavereth is like a wave of the sea driven with the wind and tossed. For let not that man think that he shall receive any thing of the Lord. A double minded man is unstable in all his ways" (James 1:5–8).

In turning to this epistle of James this evening, my mind was particularly directed to what we find in the sixth verse, "let him ask in faith, nothing wavering." But in considering that statement we must not lose sight of all that the apostle James sets before us in this epistle under the gracious inspiration of the Holy Spirit. We see it is addressed "to the twelve tribes which are scattered abroad." To them he sends "greeting." Now if we rightly consider this in the light of the word of God, his reference to the twelve tribes embraces, not only Jew, but Gentile, indeed the true spiritual Israel of God.

See how James again and again addresses those to whom he writes as *"brethren," "my brethren," "my beloved brethren."* Here we see what should surely prevail among the people of God, even the true sense of union, of fellowship together in Christ Jesus their Lord, through the riches of grace. For is not the true church one in Christ, and he one with them? O may our souls be exercised to be led more fully into the believing realisation of our *oneness* with our Lord and Saviour Jesus Christ, and our union with one another in him. Surely this is the only ground for encouragement for the living family of God. The Holy Spirit brings us to see what is ours through divine grace. He applies to us all that Jesus is and has done in the wonders of "his great love wherewith he loved us" (Eph. 2:4).

James addresses the *brethren*. I say again, what a mercy to know for ourselves the bonds of covenant union and fellowship with the Lord and with one another. Truly this is of God. It is not of man. In that union, believers taught of the Spirit find that which strengthens their faith and encourages them as they journey on through life. For our expectation of all that the Lord has promised is founded on the unchanging love and faithfulness of our covenant God.

James says, "My brethren, count it all joy when ye fall into divers temptations; knowing this, that the trying of your faith worketh patience." We see that all the apostles of our Lord Jesus Christ bear witness with James to the same important things. Peter expresses it in this way: "If need be, ye are in heaviness through manifold temptations: that the trial of your faith, being much more precious than of gold that perisheth, though it be tried with fire, might be found unto praise and honour and glory at the appearing of Jesus Christ" (1 Pet. 1:6–7). Our Lord Jesus Christ himself taught the same things to his disciples before they went out to Gethsemane. "These things I have spoken unto you, that in me ye might have peace. In the world ye shall have tribulation: but be of good cheer; I have overcome the world" (John 16:33).

What is spoken here of *temptations,* refers to the trying things in the path of the Lord's people, collectively and individually. In the way wherein the Lord leads and teaches his people, there is invariably the trying of their faith. Is there one child of God who does not experience the trials that arise from the working of sin rooted in our fallen nature and from our external circumstances? But see the important point to which we are directed by James: "Knowing this, that the trying of your faith worketh patience." *"Knowing this."* That is, important instruction is here being given to us. There is a purpose in these things. They are not according to mere chance. Far from it. These trials, difficulties and temptations to which the church of God is subject, journeying on through this wilderness world, do not originate from man. They come by the appointment of the Lord our God, our loving, heavenly Father who is too wise to err and too good to be unkind. We cannot always fathom the reasons for the Lord's dealings with us. The important thing is that grace be given us to own his hand and fall before him as did Job.

O what a trial was Job subject to! The reason behind it is disclosed in the opening chapters of that book. The evil one was very active in the troubles brought on Job, yet all was under the *control* of the Lord his God. But see what Job says in acknowledging the hand of God in those things. "Naked came I out of my mother's womb, and naked shall I return thither: the LORD gave, and the LORD hath taken away; blessed be the name of the LORD" (Job 1:21). Ah friends, what grace! And do not *we* need this grace continually? O may we seek the Lord for grace to help us in all our times of need in the tribulations, trials and temptations that may be in our lives? O may we be kept in the constant realisation of our need to depend on him. We are directed by James to look to the Lord alone, to fall before him, to seek gracious submission to his holy will, to desire that our ear may be opened to hear what he says to us in these things. For these trials and temptations do have a speaking voice. O may we hear the voice of the Lord speaking to us in this epistle.

He says, "Knowing this, that the trying of your faith *worketh patience.*" There is a purpose in it, which the Lord will bring to pass to the praise of the glory of his name and for the spiritual good of each one of his people, however severely tried and tempted. Paul reminds us of this when he says, "There hath no temptation taken you but such as is common to man: but God is faithful, who will not suffer you to be tempted above that ye are able; but will with the temptation also make a way to escape, that ye may be able to bear it" (2 Cor. 10:13).

"Knowing this." May we seek grace to behold the hand of the Lord in all we are passing through at this time as unable to gather together for the worship of his name because of the pestilence in the earth. Is not the Lord's voice to be heard and his hand seen in these things? O for grace to ever draw us to our Lord Jesus Christ in this situation, kept low at his feet, seeking his face in submission to his will. "Knowing this, that the trying of your faith worketh patience," patience in the sense of being brought to true heartfelt submission to the Lord's will, not submission because we can do no other. You know, one of the most precious places to be brought in every time of trial and need, is to say, "not my will, but thine, be done" (Luke 22:42). O that is no easy thing, knowing what we are of ourselves. Our fallen human nature does not take to that very readily. Far from it. Behold it in the person of our Lord Jesus Christ. O may we often know what it is to visit that place called Gethsemane. There we behold our Lord, he who did no sin, made sin for us, "that we might be made the right-eousness of God in him" (2 Cor. 5:21). See what he experienced in Gethsemane's garden, as he received that cup which his Father had given him and begins to drink it to the very dregs. And we see the end thereof in his sufferings and death on the cross at Calvary. Jesus prayed, "O my Father, if it be possible, let this cup pass from me: nevertheless not as I will, but as thou wilt" (Matt. 26:39). O may we truly know fellowship with our Lord and Saviour Jesus Christ. Surely it is true that,

> "His way was much rougher and darker than mine,
> Did Christ my Lord suffer, and shall I repine."

James says, "Knowing this." What a mercy that the Lord is pleased to disclose this to us. He does not necessarily disclose to us the *why* and *wherefore* of things he may bring into our path, but he does disclose to us that his purpose in these things is not for evil but for good. Thus he assured the remnant carried into captivity in Babylon: "I know the thoughts that I think toward you, saith the LORD, thoughts of peace, and not of evil, to give you an expected end" (Jer. 29:11). And are not those always the thoughts of the Lord to his people, as founded on his unchanging love and faithfulness? O may we be given grace to keep us low at the Saviour's feet in true confession and godly sorrow for our sins, crying unto him as needy sinners for his mercy and grace to help in every time of need.

"Knowing this, that the trying of your faith worketh patience." This patience is not only in being brought through grace into submission to his will, but also in enduring, in persevering and going forward in the face of all the difficulties and discourage-ments we may meet. See how Paul wrote to the Hebrews to encourage them and strengthen their faith. "Wherefore lift up the hands which hang down, and the feeble knees" (Heb. 12:12). His words are for our encouragement. How easily we become disheartened because of issues in our path. How active is Satan with lying suggestions that 'the Lord has forsaken you; he will be gracious no more; see what you have been brought to now; is there not cause for this?' We do indeed have to humble ourselves before the Lord and say, 'Yes, surely if thou dealt with us as our sins deserve, then this trouble is only a part of what we deserve; we deserve far more than this.' But friend, remember the Lord does not deal with his people as their sins and iniquities deserve. He cannot, he will not so deal with them, for he has dealt with their sins in the person of our Lord Jesus Christ. Jesus paid the full price for the redemption and salvation of his people. The Lord's dealings with his people are not in punishment for their sins. No! His dealings manifest his love for them. In his faithfulness, his concern is for their true spiritual welfare as they journey on through this life.

"Knowing this, that the trying of your faith worketh patience," patience in enduring and persevering. O friends, how we are directed here to seek for the fulness of grace treasured up in Christ Jesus our Lord. In the latter part of this epistle, James says, "Ye have heard of the patience of Job." What was the patience of Job? See, under all the pressures on that dear man of God, the tragedies in his life, everything taken from him, reduced from riches to poverty, physically afflicted, yet we find Job still *persevering*. Amid the many things in Job's life, one thing is evident: by the grace of God, his faith did not fail. More than once we hear him express his faith and trust in the Lord his God. He says, "I know that my redeemer liveth, and that he shall stand at the latter day upon the earth; and though after my skin worms destroy this body, yet in my flesh shall I see God: whom I shall see for myself, and mine eyes shall behold, and not another" (Job 19:25–27). And again, "Though he slay me, yet will I trust in him" (Job 13:15). We see the trying of Job's faith. We see the patience of Job, his perseverance by the grace of God, still looking and cleaving to the Lord, even with "no sweet enjoyments blessed." All outward things seemed against him. He also felt the Lord had hidden his face from him. He lamented that he could not find God even though he sought him. But he did not depart from his God. His faith did not fail. And in all the trials of the Lord's people as recorded in holy scripture, we see their faith did not fail.

Look at the case of Simon Peter. O how he grievously sinned in denying his Lord after the warning Jesus had given him. Peter sadly fell, but his faith failed not, because it was not founded upon his ability to keep himself, but upon the grace and mercy of his Lord and Saviour. As Jesus said, "I have prayed for thee, that thy faith fail not" (Luke 22:32). So it was with Job, and so it is with each believer. They "are kept by the power of God through faith unto salvation ready to be revealed in the last time" (1 Pet. 1:5).

James goes on to say, "But let patience have her perfect work, that ye may be perfect and entire, wanting nothing." Friends, may we be brought in true submission to the Lord's will to still go forward in the way of his appointments, persevering in the face of all the difficulties and discouragements that may beset us. But is not this beyond what we are able to accomplish by the supposed abilities of our fallen nature? "Let patience have her perfect work, that ye may be perfect and entire wanting nothing!" How can that be outworked in the life and experience of the child of God?

"If any of you lack wisdom." Does not this express what I trust we are brought increasingly to realise? 'I am poor, I am needy; yes Lord, I lack wisdom to know what to do. Even if I did know, I lack wisdom to know how to do it. I cannot rely on anything in myself.' See where we are directed in all that may confront us in our personal lives and the cause of Jesus Christ. Our text surely tells us that the people of God are not to look to self in all their needs, nor to any creature. They are not to depend on an arm of flesh. These cannot ultimately help. To one place, to one person only, are we are directed. "If any of you lack wisdom, *let him ask of God*, that giveth to all men liberally, and upbraideth not; and it shall be given him." Do we find such a lack with us in many aspects of our spiritual lives? Ah, "Let him ask of God." O what precious truth is brought before us here. Remember, the throne of grace is open still, and the Lord our God occupies that throne. O is not a fulness of grace treasured up in him?

Our text expresses how the Lord is not only ever ready to hear us but ever ready to impart the wisdom needed by his people in the hour of temptation and trial. "He giveth to all men *liberally, and upbraideth* not." O friends, there is no niggardliness in our Lord Jesus Christ. Why, he is "able to do exceeding abundantly above all that we ask or think" (Eph. 3:20). Paul could write to the Philippians, "My God shall supply all your need according to his riches in glory by Christ Jesus" (Phil. 4:19). The Lord is ever ready and willing to manifest himself thus to his poor, needy and often desolate people. In all their need, he is ever ready to minister to them out of the fulness of his grace, not according to their deserts but "according to his own purpose and grace, which was "given us in Christ Jesus before the world began" (1 Tim. 1:9).

Look at the ministry of our Lord Jesus when here on earth. Was he ever reluctant to address the needs of those drawn to seek unto him, to call upon his name? No, he was always ready to hear. And so it is still. His ear is ever open to the cries of his people. His arm is not shortened that he cannot help them and deliver them.

"If any of you lack wisdom, let him ask of God, that giveth to all men liberally, and upbraideth not; and it *shall* be given him." Notice how blessedly positive these statements are. It is not, he *may* do, or you can rely upon him to help *if you* do certain things. No, it is all of grace. And it is in the *fulness* of grace. He "giveth to all men *liberally*, and *upbraideth not."* What a wonderful thing that the Lord *upbraideth* not! Unbelief is ready to say, 'How can you expect God to hear your cry or to address your needs? Maybe if you had behaved better in the past, but look at all those things you have done. Will they not be held against you?' Friends, that is *never* how the Lord deals with his people, blessed be his holy name.

Yes, he *chastens* them, but ever in covenant love, *never* in punishment for their sins. All is in concern for their true spiritual welfare. True, it is for the humbling of them. And what grace we need to bring us to humble ourselves under the mighty hand of God. But as I have ever emphasised, his dealings with his people always flow from his covenant love. His mercies are lengthened out towards them. All proceeds, not upon the ground of their deserts, but from what he is in himself and has provided in the person and finished work of the Lord Jesus Christ. Does he delight, as the word assures us he does, in his only begotten and dearly beloved Son, our Lord Jesus Christ? As he delights in him, is well pleased with him, so does he delight in every poor sinner brought through grace to cry unto him in Jesus' name.

"Let him ask of God, that giveth to all men liberally, and upbraideth not; and it shall be given him. *But let him ask in faith.*" This is the point particularly laid upon my mind: *let him ask in faith*. Now we might ask the question, what is faith? Indeed, faith is the gift of God. The reality of it is seen in all the old testament believers in that they believed God and trusted in him. What was their faith founded upon? The word and promise that God had spoken to them and the faithfulness of God to fulfil all that he had spoken.

Now I want to direct our thoughts to this: "Let him ask in faith." What is the great object of faith? Where does faith which is the gift of God, always lead the soul? *It is to Jesus Christ.* Remember that there is no way of access to God for us, no acceptable coming before him even in prayer, *unless we come in the name of our Lord and Saviour Jesus Christ.*

"Let him ask in faith." What is prominent here is not our personal believing and trusting in itself, but it is *him* in whom we are brought to believe and trust, even Jesus. He himself said, "If ye shall ask any thing in my name, I will do it" (John 14:14). In all true seeking, what grace we need to be brought to come to God at the throne of grace, *in the name of our Lord Jesus Christ*, looking only and wholly to him. We are not to depend in the slightest upon what we are or what we have done. In those things there is no ground of acceptance with God for us. We must come solely on the ground of what the Lord Jesus Christ is and has done.

In the epistle to the Hebrews we read, *"without faith* it is impossible to please him: for he that cometh to God must believe that he is, and that he is a rewarder of them that diligently seek him" (Heb. 11:6). As I have said, the faith of all the old testament believers mentioned in that eleventh chapter was evidenced by their trust in God. They rested on his faithfulness to the word he had spoken to them. And that word comes to us still. It sets before us the only way of acceptance by God—that we poor sinners be brought to trust in the person and finished work of our Lord Jesus Christ alone.

"But let him ask in faith, nothing wavering." O we are not to look to one thing or another but are to keep our eyes wholly fixed on Jesus Christ. "Let thine eyes look right on, and let thine eyelids look straight before thee" (Prov. 4:25). In all our approaches to God, in prayer, preaching and meditating on his word, there must be the looking alone to Jesus. He himself declared, "I am the way, the truth, and the life: no man cometh unto the Father, but by me" (John 14:6). That is true in every aspect of the spiritual life of the living family of God. It is true in all that pertains to the blessings of salvation. It is true for all the encouragement and consolation of our souls, and for the supply of all our needs as we journey on through life. All comes to us through Jesus Christ alone. *There* we are to look for all things. All is to be sought on the ground of what God has appointed in the person and finished work of our Lord Jesus Christ.

Friends, the mark of the faith which is the gift of God is that it believes the record God has given of his only begotten and dearly beloved Son. God is well pleased with none other than his beloved Son. And O, the blessing for poor sinners brought by grace to trust in Jesus is that the Father is well-pleased *with them* as they are found in his Son, believing and trusting in him.

"Let him ask in faith, nothing wavering. For he that wavereth is like a wave of the sea driven with the wind and tossed. For let not that man think that he shall receive any thing of the Lord." No. Friends, expect nothing from the Lord but that which comes to us through the fulness of his grace in Jesus Christ alone, and is received by us in the exercise of faith which worketh by love.

"Let him ask in faith, nothing wavering." Have we not the witness of the word of God that if we ask anything in his name, he hears us? See how this is enjoined again and again in the ministry of the apostles. We are to come, seeking unto the Lord *for that which he himself has promised*, and waiting upon him for the realisation of it according to his sovereign will and good pleasure. *That* is the reality of God-given faith. It is as we come in times of trial, difficulty, temptation and need, indeed whatever the situation, to seek the Lord solely on the ground of those things he has promised in his holy word through what Jesus is and has done. It is coming to the Lord, looking wholly to Jesus Christ, in the believing expectation that he will hear us, according to his own will and good pleasure.

I come back to what I said earlier. What a mercy it is to be brought and kept low at the Saviour's feet. 'Here am I, Lord; deal with me as seems good in thy sight.' O there is no better place for a child of God, a needy sinner, to be found than low at the footstool of divine mercy. And what encouragement is given us to be ever found looking unto "Jesus, the author and finisher of our faith" (Heb. 12:2). Paul directs us in that same epistle to the Hebrews, to ever come to Jesus as he is the great high priest over the house of God, the one who "is able also to save them to the uttermost that come unto God by him" (Heb. 7:25). Coming to him at the throne of grace, we come to one who knows all the issues and situations that concern us far better than we know them ourselves. So often we do not know our way, as it were. We often have no real understanding of the issues confronting us. We know not what future days hold. But, O friends, he to whom we come knows all things, from beginning to end. He knows what his purposes are and how he will fulfil them in mercy for his people. O how blessed it is to be found, through the rich mercy of the Lord, in the hand of our God and Saviour. How blessed to realise the truth spoken by Peter: "kept by the power of God through faith unto salvation ready to be revealed in the last time" (1 Pet. 1:5). That is, kept coming to the throne of grace.

"Let him ask in faith," the faith which brings us to look alone to Jesus, to come to him continually, daily seeking mercy and grace to help in every time of need. O how we need his grace in all the concerns of our personal lives and in our witness as believers joined together as a local church. Our text expresses how wholly dependent we are upon the Lord and how indebted we are to him.

"If any of you lack wisdom, let him ask of God, that giveth to all men liberally, and upbraideth not; and it shall be given him. But let him ask in faith, nothing wavering." O, as one says,

> "To keep our eyes on Jesus fixed,
> And there our hope to stay,
> The Lord will make his goodness pass
> Before us in the way."

I will leave the remarks there. May the Lord add his blessing. Amen.

21

IN THE LORD HAVE I
RIGHTEOUSNESS AND STRENGTH

Lord's day morning 10 May 2020

"I have sworn by myself, the word is gone out
of my mouth in righteousness, and shall not
return, That unto me every knee shall bow,
every tongue shall swear. Surely, shall one
say, in the Lord have I righteousness and
strength: even to him shall men come; and all
that are incensed against him shall be
ashamed. In the Lord shall all the seed of
Israel be justified, and shall glory" (Isaiah
45:23-25).

How there is set before us in this chapter the greatness and
omnipotence of the Lord our God, that he knows all things from
the beginning to the end! All events in all the nations of the earth
and in all the individual lives of men and women, have been
appointed by him according to his sovereign will and good
pleasure. Certainly, this is a glorious truth for the people of God.
It is a sure resting-place for them to realise that *all* their concerns
are in the hand of the Lord their God. May the Holy Spirit seal it
afresh unto us! We need continual reminding that,

"My life's minutest circumstance
Is subject to his eye."

How great is the mercy that the sovereign ruler over all things
in heaven and earth, is *our* God, *our* Saviour, *our* all, as revealed
to us in the precious truth of the gospel by the sovereign teaching
of the Holy Spirit. Amid all the changing scenes of life, in the
issues that confront us in our personal lives and in society, the
sickness and death abroad in the earth, yet the Lord God is the
refuge of our souls! O by his grace may we be enabled to commit
ourselves and all our concerns into his hands. What a blessed
resting-place that is for the child of God, tried, troubled, and

exercised by the anxieties, cares and fears that so often prevail against him. The Lord our God alone is our sure refuge, our blessed resting-place, our rock, our salvation.

See the wonder of his love fully revealed and flowing to us in the precious gospel of our Lord and Saviour Jesus Christ. His love to his people is not in word only, but in deed and in truth. Jesus himself testified that "God so loved the world, that he gave his only begotten Son, that whosoever believeth in him should not perish, but have everlasting life" (John 3:16). That embraces all the elect of God throughout the whole world whether Jew, Gentile, bond, free, male or female—all to whom the Lord has purposes of sovereign, saving grace. By the Holy Spirit, each is brought as a needy, guilty sinner to cry to the Lord for mercy. Does any troubled soul before the Lord this morning say, 'Can these things apply to such a sinner as I am? Does not what I find in my heart and life speak against any idea that the Lord should love such a sinner as I am?' O friend, do not forget the purpose for which Jesus Christ came into this world. Why did he humble himself and become obedient to the death of the cross? It was to save his people from their sins. It is for sinners that the Lord came. It is to sinners that the love of God in Christ is revealed by the Holy Spirit. Your sins, my sins, however great, many and vile, are no hindrance, no barrier to the manifestation of the love of God in Jesus Christ. The hymnwriter states it wonderfully:

> "The vilest sinner out of hell,
> Who lives to feel his need,
> Is welcome to a Throne of Grace,
> The Saviour's blood to plead."

Satan ever seeks to keep us away from Jesus Christ and one of his devices is to impress upon us our own vile state, so that we cannot think God will look favourably on us. But what does our Saviour say? "I came not to call the righteous, but sinners to repentance" (Mark 2:17). The Lord is afar off from self-righteous persons who think they have something of their own to commend themselves to him. But the sinner brought by grace to cry with the publican, "God, be merciful to me a sinner," is not sent empty away (Luke 18:13).

In making those few opening remarks, we might ask what

have they to do with this chapter? Well, here we see the omnipotence of our God in his dealings in all the affairs of men, but essentially as they concern his church. He says, "Ask me of things to come concerning my sons" (Isa. 45:11). We are so limited in our knowledge and appreciation even of things *present*, let alone things *to come*. What a mercy it is that though we know not the future, nor would we enquire curiously into it, yet we know him who holds the future in his hand and appoints all things from the day of our birth to the day of our death. Blessed be the Lord's name! May we rest in the truth that every circumstance in our lives is appointed of God and all must be to his glory and for the spiritual, eternal welfare of every one of his own. His faithful love is unchanging.

See the opening verses: "Thus saith the LORD to his anointed, to Cyrus, whose right hand I have holden, to subdue nations before him; and I will loose the loins of kings, to open before him the two leaved gates; and the gates shall not be shut." Cyrus was the general of the armies of the Medes and Persians. The Lord speaks here of events to be unfolded probably two hundred years after these words were spoken by Isaiah. His appointed time would come to deliver the children of Israel out of their seventy years' captivity in Babylon. Who would ever have thought that such a great nation, such a mighty power as the Chaldeans, such a strongly fortified city as Babylon, should fall *in one night* before the armies of the Medes and Persians under Cyrus? Belshazzar was partying securely as he thought in his palace, not solemnly realising that in a few hours all would be brought crashing down upon him. Then the hand wrote upon the wall of his palace: "Thou art weighed in the balances, and art found wanting...Thy kingdom is divided, and given to the Medes and Persians" (Dan. 5:27). This interpretation of the writing by Daniel was fulfilled that very night. Belshazzar, the king of the Chaldeans, was slain by Darius, the ruler of the Medes and Persians. Cyrus, the general of his armies, later became the king.

This chapter clearly teaches us that what God declares will most surely come to pass. "Is there any thing too hard for the LORD?" (Gen. 18:14). Shall Babylon be shut up secure in its defences, impregnable as was thought, capable of withstanding twenty years of siege? Surely it is impossible that such defences be breached in one night? But God had spoken of Cyrus that he would "open before him the two leaved gates; and the gates shall not be shut; I will go before thee, and make the crooked places straight: I will break in pieces the gates of brass, and cut in sunder the bars of iron" (v.1–2). He delivered Babylon into his hand as Isaiah predicted. Cyrus knew not God, yet God used him in accomplishing his divine appointments. Central to all the Lord's purposes was his chosen people. And as that was so with Israel of old, how much more so is it with regard to his church now. Central to all God's dealings with men and nations, are his chosen people, the subjects of his grace and mercy, the one true church of our Lord Jesus Christ.

Is not this the greatest of mercies that such sinners as you and me should be found in that one blessed church of Jesus Christ? Is it not the greatest wonder that we should have union with him as members of his mystical body, he being the glorious head? What wonders of sovereign grace are revealed to us in that great love wherewith the Lord has loved his people when we were dead in trespasses and sins! *All* that concerns them for time and eternity is appointed of God. His great love is made known by his personal dealings with them, to the praise of the glory of his name.

But it is not so much with Cyrus that I want to deal this morning, but to come to what the Lord declares in the verses I have read by way of a text. Leading up to it, we read: "Assemble yourselves and come; draw near together, ye that are escaped of the nations: they have no knowledge that set up the wood of their graven image, and pray unto a god that cannot save. Tell ye, and bring them near; yea, let them take counsel together: who hath declared this from ancient time? who hath told it from that time? have not I the LORD? and there is *no God else beside me*; a just God and a Saviour; *there is none beside me."*

See the constant emphasis in the word of God: *there is none beside him.* The apostles, at the beginning of their ministry following Pentecost, declared the same glorious truth: "There is none other name under heaven given among men, whereby we must be saved" (Acts 4:12). There is none other name than the one that God has revealed to us in the precious truth of the gospel, even *Jesus*, our Lord and Saviour. He says here, "Look unto me, and be ye saved, all the ends of the earth: for I am God, and *there is none else.*" Our whole attention is here directed to God revealed in the person of Jesus Christ. Friends, never lose sight of the vitally important fact that for you and me as sinners there is no acceptance with God except through the person and work of our Lord Jesus Christ, by grace, through faith in his name. There alone is God revealed as merciful and gracious, abundant in goodness and truth, forgiving iniquity, transgression and sin. There alone can he "be just, and the justifier of him that believeth in Jesus" (Rom. 3:26). Salvation for sinners such as you and me is a *work of God*. He here declares, "Look unto me, and *be ye saved.*" Salvation rests on a sure foundation. There are no *ifs, buts* or *peradventures*. *"Be ye saved*, all the ends of the earth."

Does not that surely speak to sinners? I trust it speaks to your soul and mine. We may feel to be afar off. And are we not *far off* as sinners in relation to the one true God? And it is in this realisation of our *far-off* state as sinners that this word of the Lord comes in the power of the Holy Spirit. He says to sinners *in their sins:* "I am God, and there is none else." *That* is where salvation is founded. As I ever seek to emphasise, it is not in what the sinner can do, utterly helpless, ruined, lost and undone as he is in himself. Salvation is in what God has done and what he makes known in the riches of his grace to sinful men and women, bringing them from death in trespasses and sins, into the life, light and liberty of the gospel. To him is all the glory.

"I have sworn by myself, the word is gone out of my mouth in righteousness, and shall not return, That unto me every knee shall bow, every tongue shall swear." See the solemn testimony here given. God has *sworn*. That is a solemn oath and there is no countermanding what God thus declares. "I have sworn *by myself.*" There is no greater authority and power than the Lord our God. What he has declared will most surely come to pass. "I have sworn by myself, the word is gone out of my mouth in righteousness, and shall not return, *That unto me every knee shall bow, every tongue shall swear.*" This will most surely be accomplished, either in righteous judgment on sinners who live and die in their sins, or in the wonders of sovereign, saving grace to sinners whom our God shall call.

Let us look at this in the light of the glorious testimony given in Paul's epistle to the Philippians chapter 2 verses 1 to 11 which I read this morning. O the wondrous fact of the incarnation of our Lord Jesus Christ, that he, the eternal Son of God, should be "found in fashion as a man" and be obedient unto the death of the cross. For what purpose? To "save his people from their sins" (Matt. 1:21) by fulfilling all appointed him by his heavenly Father. All was for the glory of God in the salvation of sinful men and women in a way in which he is just and yet the justifier of the sinner brought by grace to trust alone in Jesus Christ.

Paul says of Jesus, "And being found in fashion as a man, he humbled himself, and became obedient unto death, even the death of the cross. Wherefore God also hath highly exalted him, and given him a name which is above every name: *That at the name of Jesus every knee should bow, of things in heaven, and things in earth, and things under the earth; and that every tongue should confess that Jesus Christ is Lord, to the glory of God the Father.*" And what God has sworn by a solemn oath he will most surely perform in the exaltation of his only begotten and dearly beloved Son. Jesus himself declared, "All power is given unto me in heaven and in earth" (Matt. 28:18). *All* must and will bow before him, acknowledging that he is indeed the One set before us in the word. "Every knee shall bow...every tongue shall confess" even if it be in the solemn realisation of the righteous judgment of God upon them. The book of the Revelation states that when the Lord comes, they shall cry "to the mountains and rocks, Fall on us, and hide us from the face of him that sitteth on the throne, and from the wrath of the Lamb" (Rev. 6:16). Yes, every knee shall bow, every tongue shall confess that he is what the scriptures reveal him to be. O friends, what a solemn thing it is to be brought to bow the knee before him in righteous judgment. Be assured that none can escape the righteous judgment of God.

But O the wonders of God's grace that there is a people who justly deserve his eternal wrath upon them as wretched, ruined sinners, but to whom the Lord will reveal himself in sovereign grace and mercy! They are made willing in the day of his power. His grace is manifest in the heart and life of every sinner to whom he reveals himself in pardoning love and mercy. Are not *they* brought to bow the knee before him, to own him as their Lord and Saviour, to confess with the mouth that in him is all their help, hope and salvation? What a wonderful manifestation of grace to be brought as a sinner to the feet of Jesus to own him as Lord of all, as *"My* Lord and *my* God" (John 20:28). O to be brought there by the Holy Spirit's mighty work! And this is not through fear of wrath, justly though we deserve the wrath of God. It is by the revelation of his pardoning love and mercy to the sinner. Nothing else bows the hard stubborn heart of a sinner, nothing brings us to the feet of the Lord Jesus Christ in godly sorrow and repentance over our sins. It is our being granted to see that *he* fulfilled in his righteous life and sin-atoning death all that God's holy law justly demands of *us*. One rightly says,

> "Law and terrors do but harden,
> All the while they work alone;
> But a sense of blood-bought pardon
> Soon dissolves a heart of stone."

Friends, nothing else can do it. O the mercies of the Lord towards his people! And surely will they not be drawn by the love of Jesus Christ revealed to us in his word? Will not that word be precious to us? Will it not be our concern to be guided by it, to walk in the light of it? As the living family of God, how we must confess how far short we come. How we must humble ourselves before the Lord. Yes, the right desire is with us, but O how often we find ourselves at a loss to perform, through the working of our fallen sinful nature. But let us not overlook the important truth that though we have nothing in ourselves, yet as brought by divine grace to believe and trust in Jesus Christ we have everything in him. In bowing before the Lord Jesus and seeking in our lives to know and do his will, there is the continual realisation that we are altogether dependent upon his grace.

This is why our Lord Jesus Christ is set before as the great high priest over the house of God. We see all things are in his hand, all is under his control *and* the fulness of grace is treasured up in him. *And* that grace is freely made known to poor sinners.

When one of his own is brought to seek to him (and we have to come daily seeking mercy and grace to help in time of need), has the Lord ever yet said to such a one, to "the seed of Jacob, Seek ye me in vain"? (Isa. 45:19). Is any poor sinner who is brought to cry unto the Lord, ever sent empty away? No, blessed be his great and holy name.

Every knee shall bow, every tongue shall own and confess that Jesus is Lord. Friends, do we know the reality of that in our own lives, in all that concerns us personally and collectively, as people who profess to know and love him? Our concern should surely be to *know* but also to *do* the will of God in our day. And even at such a time as this, should not our concern be what the Lord Jesus sets before us in his holy word, more than what men say to us? Should we not seek to follow *him* and to own that he is Lord, to the glory of God the Father?

Isaiah goes on to say, "Surely, shall one say, in the LORD have I righteousness and strength: even to him shall men come; and all that are incensed against him shall be ashamed." See the blessedness of being brought through divine grace to the feet of the Lord Jesus Christ, owning him as Lord of all. What accompanies this? "Surely, shall one say, *in the LORD* have I righteousness and strength." See how all that pertains to our material, spiritual and eternal welfare is not in our own resources but is treasured up in our God and Saviour. Are we brought to say that? Is our testimony that all our hope is fixed alone upon Jesus Christ? As one puts it in that verse,

> "My hope is built on nothing less
> Than Jesus' blood and righteousness;
> I dare not trust the sweetest frame,
> But wholly lean on Jesus' name.
> On Christ the solid rock I stand;
> All other ground is sinking sand."

Friends, is that your testimony? Are we brought to say, 'In the Lord is *my* righteousness and strength?' Certainly, we have no righteousness of our own, nothing to commend us to God. Is that not painfully, increasingly realised by us, as God the Holy Spirit teaches us our sinfulness and nothingness in ourselves? Are we not brought to realise that our salvation is *not* founded on what we have done or can do? It is in what Jesus Christ has done for us, that is, *his righteousness* wrought out by perfect obedience to the will of his Father, not for himself but for us as our surety and substitute, to the glory of our triune God.

"In the LORD have I righteousness and *strength.*" We are here assured that all our help is found in the Lord. "In the LORD shall all the seed of Israel be justified, and shall glory." What does Paul say to the Corinthians is the only ground for their glorying as taught of the Holy Spirit? "But of him are ye in Christ Jesus, who of God is made unto us wisdom, and righteousness, and sanctification, and redemption: that, according as it is written, *He that glorieth, let him glory in the Lord"* (1 Cor. 1:30–31). Ah friends, do we desire to glory in anything else? Everything else is fading. It will bring us under the judgment of God. Our glory as a poor sinner is not in what we can do but in what Jesus Christ has done for us. And what is the fruit and effect of that grace? It is looking only to Jesus, trusting alone in him, depending on him, coming daily with the felt need of him in every aspect of our lives for time and eternity. "In the LORD shall all the seed of Israel be justified, and shall glory."

But I will leave the remarks there this morning. May the Lord add his blessing. Amen.

22

OUR SAVIOUR JESUS CHRIST...HATH ABOLISHED DEATH

Lord's day evening, 10 May 2020

"Be not thou therefore ashamed of the testimony of our Lord, nor of me his prisoner: but be thou partaker of the afflictions of the gospel according to the power of God; who hath saved us, and called us with an holy calling, not according to our works, but according to his own purpose and grace, which was given us in Christ Jesus before the world began, but is now made manifest by the appearing of our Saviour Jesus Christ, who hath abolished death, and hath brought life and immortality to light through the gospel" (2 Timothy 1:8-10).

The apostle here writes from imprisonment in Rome to "his son Timothy." What gracious instruction and encouragement he gives, not only to this young servant of Jesus Christ, but to all the people of God down the generations. O how we ever need the Holy Spirit to lead us into the grace of our Lord Jesus Christ set before us in all the apostolic writings, indeed to heed *all* set before us in the word of God. Unquestionably *it is* the word of God and *all* is faithful and true. Therein has he revealed himself.

The apostle draws our attention to the blessings of redeeming love and mercy which flow to the people of God through his dealings with them. O what a body of divinity is in these three verses of our text! Herein we see the very fundamentals of the faith "once delivered unto the saints" (Jude 1:3). Here we see the blessed assurance that the salvation of sinful men and women such as you and me, is *all* of grace. *All* is of God alone, according to his divine appointments from before the foundation of the world. *All* parts of salvation are by God alone. *All* is to the glory of his name alone.

O what a foundation is laid here for the faith and hope of the living family of God, sinners taught of God the Holy Spirit and brought through almighty grace to receive the testimony God has given of his only begotten Son. Our hope is not on our doings, but on what God in Christ has done for us. There's no other hope for us sinners except in the gospel directing us alone to the Lord and Saviour Jesus Christ. To him alone all honour belongs for the salvation of sinful men and woman. Not one iota of the glory of salvation belongs to man. May the Lord alone be given all the glory. By his grace may we ever be found low at the Saviour's feet, ever seeking to give him all the honour and glory for our salvation.

O may our souls ever be led into the truly precious consolation in our text. It speaks pardon and peace to guilty sinners, assuring us of what God in Christ has done. This is the gospel! Here are not cunningly devised fables, but glorious realities. May we know increasingly the sanctifying influence of this gospel in our lives, drawing us to our Lord Jesus Christ, to hear his voice and to seek to follow and serve him in our generation. May it be our chief concern to heed what he has spoken to us in holy scripture. He is the great head of the church. He is king in Zion. To him we owe all the blessings of salvation. There may be things we owe to men in this time-state, but our first, chief and whole loyalty should be to what our Lord Jesus Christ says in his word. We are not to be guided by what man says. As the Lord spoke by his servant Isaiah, "To the law and to the testimony: if they speak not according to this word, it is because there is no light in them" (Isa. 8:20). The word itself directs us to search the scriptures to determine whether the things we hear are according to the mind and will of God. Let us be guided by the word of our God.

Paul here encourages Timothy. "Be not thou therefore ashamed of the testimony of our Lord, nor of me his prisoner: but be thou partaker of the afflictions of the gospel according to the power of God." Yes, it was a very trying, suffering path the apostle was called to walk as a faithful servant of Jesus Christ. But in the face of all he could testify, "I am not ashamed of the gospel of Christ" (Rom. 1:16). I am sure the Holy Spirit brings us to realise *we* have much to be ashamed of. Often how cold and fickle is our love to the Lord Jesus and how little diligence we give to his worship and service. Yes, we have much to be ashamed of ourselves. But O how great is the mercy that Paul could say, "I am not ashamed of the gospel of Christ." The world is ashamed of Jesus Christ. There's no desire or concern for him. It wholly rejects him, as we see in this generation. But though the world rejects him let not us who profess to know and love the Lord Jesus Christ be ashamed of him.

"Be not thou therefore ashamed of the testimony of our Lord, nor of me his prisoner." Are we not here exhorted to increasingly manifest love to the Lord, not in word only, but in deed and in truth, believing and trusting in him, committing our concerns into his hand, *and* loving the brethren for Jesus' sake? How important that we be prayerfully concerned to walk out in our lives, love to the Lord *and love to the brethren*, in all the trying times we are called to pass through, even at this time. We have much to be thankful for, having many material benefits, but I trust we are concerned at being unable to meet for the worship of God at present. This is vitally important for the church's welfare and the prosperity of the gospel. We manifest true loving allegiance to our Lord and Saviour Jesus Christ, by seeking to know and do his will as set before us in his word, and to attend upon his appointed ordinances. There is a blessing in them, as we are exercised with concern for the glory of God, the welfare of the church, and the spiritual profit of our never-dying souls. I know the Lord can maintain his people whatever the circumstances in which they are found. But O friends, let us not despise what the Lord clearly directs us to in his word, the "not forsaking the assembling of ourselves together, as the manner of some is; but exhorting one another: and so much the more, as ye see the day approaching" (Heb. 10:25). We would heed what men say, but always in subjection to what the Lord requires of us as believers, even obedience to his holy mind and will as given us in the scriptures.

"Be thou partaker of the afflictions of the gospel according to *the power of God.*" O the blessedness of this! The power of God is not God *against* us, but God *for* us. Indeed, it is God *with* us. "Emmanuel…God with us" (Matt. 1:23). *There* is all our help and strength. Though we are feeble in ourselves may we know the blessedness of being strong in the grace which God gives through his beloved Son. *His* almighty arm upholds his church. We are assured here that he can and does deliver his people from all distresses.

See in our text what this *power* of God has accomplished: "Who *hath saved us*, and *called us* with an holy calling." Does not that display the mighty power of God? "Saved us"! O could anything less than the mighty power of God, put forth in the person and finished work of Christ, save us? Paul declared, "I am not ashamed of the gospel of Christ: for it is the power of God unto salvation to every one that believeth" (Rom. 1:16). Yes, the gospel is nothing less than *almighty power* displayed in the person of the man Christ Jesus. In what men look on as weakness we see the mighty power of God displayed. Jesus was crucified, despised and rejected of men. But the mighty power of God was displayed in the perfect manhood of Christ, *God manifest in the flesh.*

O friends what wonders of the power and grace of God are set before us here. He hath saved us in a way in which he alone is glorified and the deep needs of guilty sinners satisfied. For them, Jesus fulfilled the demands of God's holy law. He suffered the claims of divine justice. He delivered them from condemnation. He brought in everlasting righteousness wherewith God justifies the ungodly. Is not this glorious truth ever set before us in the word, as it was in our text this morning? "In the LORD shall all the seed of Israel be justified, and shall glory" (Isa. 45:25). That is just what Paul is saying here of all the true spiritual Israel, all sinners saved by grace who glory alone in what the Lord Jesus has done for them. *"In the LORD,"* for it is the Lord's work, the mighty power of God that has saved us. As oft as we know the guilt and defilement of sin, may we turn our eyes in faith to Calvary, to behold him who suffered on the cross, crucified in apparent weakness but displaying the mighty power of God. O friends, what a great work was wrought in the life, sufferings and death of our Lord Jesus Christ, a work which none but God manifest in the flesh could ever have accomplished!

"Who *hath* saved us." I emphasise that it doesn't say, who *will* save us. We are assured here that salvation is an accomplished fact. He *hath* saved every sinner brought through divine grace to trust in Jesus Christ. He paid the great price for their sins when he died. Divine justice demands no more. It was fully satisfied with what it received at the hand of our Lord Jesus Christ as the surety of his people. All that comes to us, all the blessings of pardon, peace and the assurance of eternal life, are through what Christ the God-man has done. Is not that the blessed theme of the glorious gospel of grace? It does not say to sinners what they must do, but declares what God in Christ *has done.* Our text tells us that God *"hath saved us."* How precious are those words! How consoling to the tried exercised family of God! Friend, look away from all that is in self. Look to what God has done. *There* is the foundation for your faith. *There* are blessings of salvation for you. *There* eternal life is ours, not by what we have done or can do, but by what Jesus Christ has done for us. *He has saved us!* See this blessed truth in what Paul writes to the church at Rome: "There is therefore *now* no condemnation to them which are in Christ Jesus" (Rom. 8:1).

"Who hath saved us, and called us with an holy calling." *"An holy calling."* Yes, this salvation is made known to us by the sovereign work of the Holy Spirit in *calling us.* Is not this a great work of our God—the calling of his people as sinners dead in trespasses and sins? It is the same almighty voice that spoke to Lazarus dead in the tomb as he was, "Lazarus, come forth." He came forth. See there the mighty power of God in raising the dead! And that same wondrous miracle is still wrought today when the Lord manifests his grace in calling a sinner from death in trespasses and sins. And that call is not merely in the sense of inviting them or encouraging them to do something for them- selves. How can the sinner dead in trespasses and sins do anything for himself? He has no desire to do anything for himself, for the dead know not anything. It is a certain fact that the sinner dead in trespasses and sins has no spiritual desires, no concern whatsoever about the needs of his guilty soul, and no regard for that salvation which is all of grace. No, it is a work of God "who hath called us with an holy calling." And how does God the Holy

Spirit *call* his people? By applying his word in the scriptures to the souls of guilty sinners. It is a *mighty* call! It is declared: "Thy people shall be willing in the day of thy power" (Ps. 110:3). Yes, the soul is made willing. By nature we are not willing, indeed we are enmity against God with no desire for him. But when the Lord speaks, not "in word only, but also in power, and in the Holy Ghost" (1 Thess. 1:5), O what a great work is then accomplished! It brings a soul from death in trespasses and sins, into the light and liberty of the gospel.

And it is "an *holy* calling." Remember what he has called us from and what he has called us to, when he calls us into the fellowship of his Son Jesus Christ our Lord. How vast is the change from darkness to light, from death to life. And *that* is what the Lord's calling does for his people. And I take *holy calling* to mean there is nothing whatsoever in it of the creature. If there is anything of ours required in it, would it not mar it? Could it be an *holy* calling if something in it is required of us? No, all the blessings of salvation *come to us fully and freely,* as blessed with the grace of living faith. The reality of God-given faith is always in the receiving of what the Lord makes known to us in the gospel. It is that which is *received*, which we are brought to embrace, to lay hold upon, through the Lord's mercies to us. It is looking and cleaving to the Lord Jesus Christ only, realising that "none but Jesus" can do us as guilty sinners any real or lasting good.

"Called us with an holy calling, *not according to our works.*" Does not that sound the death-knell to all supposed human ability? Most certainly it does! "Not according to our works." They do not even begin to enter into it. True, they are the fruit of the life of God given to his people when regenerated. But our works have nothing to do with our acceptance by God. O let us not even think that *after* the Lord has called us by his grace, we are accepted by him because of anything we do in obedience to his word. Obedience to his word is important to show our love and thankfulness to him for his salvation. But our obedience is never the basis of our salvation and acceptance by him. *That* is wholly upon what Jesus Christ is and has done. Let nothing of man, before or even after calling, be part of the *foundation* of our hope. As David said, "Although my house be not so with God; yet *he hath made with me* an everlasting covenant, ordered in all things, and sure: for this is all my salvation" (2 Sam. 23:5). David did not look to what he had been able to do. He was a great king over Israel, a mighty warrior used of his God in his day, but not without his faults and failings as every child of God. David's whole hope of salvation was founded entirely on what God had done for him.

"Given us in Christ Jesus *before the world began.*" What a glorious truth is electing, predestinating grace, the Lord's love to his people "before the world began," arising solely in his sovereign will and good pleasure. They were chosen of the Lord and given to Christ, "before the world began." And can that will of God ever be frustrated? Blessed be his name, the proof that he has saved them is that *he calls them* by his grace in his appointed time. In that call is manifested the eternal love and good pleasure of the Lord towards them, sinners as they are, yet a people saved with an everlasting salvation. As the Lord himself declares, "Yea, I have loved thee with an everlasting love: therefore with loving-kindness have I drawn thee" (Jer. 31:3).

"*Given* us in Christ Jesus before the world began." The emphasis is always on God's *giving.* The whole truth of the gospel testifies of God's great gifts *given* to us in Christ Jesus even before the world began. Is there any merit in the sinner God calls by his grace which causes God to call them and save them with an everlasting salvation? No. This ever lays the sinner low and exalts a precious Christ. All is of God. To him alone be all the praise and glory.

The apostle says, *"But is now made manifest by the appearing of our Saviour Jesus Christ."* How this sets before us the glorious coming and incarnation of our Lord Jesus Christ. The gospel assures us that *he has come.* And we are brought by divine grace to believe that he has come. Is not this our trust and confidence? John declared, "And many other signs truly did Jesus...which are not written in this book: but these are written, that ye might believe that Jesus is the Christ, the Son of God; and that believing ye might have life through his name" (John 20:30–31). See the assurance given us that Jesus *has* come, he *has* accomplished all the gospel makes known. Salvation is "now made manifest by the *appearing* of our Saviour Jesus Christ." These are not hidden things. No. They are things revealed and set before us in the precious truth of the gospel of the grace of our God.

And see what was accomplished by the appearing of our Lord Jesus Christ. *"He hath abolished death."* What a word is that! Is not this something that should be published abroad, north, south, east and west? *Abolished death!* What a tremendous statement, but gloriously true! But you say, are not all appointed of God to death in this fallen world? Yes. Even for the Lord's people, the day is fast hastening when all must pass through the dark valley of the shadow of death. But here is the encouragement and comfort for the living family of God, sinners brought to trust in Jesus Christ. He has *abolished death* for them. How? Paul says, "There is therefore now no condemnation to them which are in Christ Jesus…for the law of the Spirit of life in Christ Jesus hath made me free from the law of sin and death" (Rom. 8:1–2). He has delivered us from the *death* we are subject to as transgressors of God's holy law. As believers, trusting in the Lord Jesus Christ we are no longer in bondage to condemnation. We are delivered, never to be brought into bondage again. May this ever be a living reality with us.

"He hath abolished death." He has "destroyed him that had the power of death, that is, the devil" (Heb. 2:14). Is not Satan a fallen foe, defeated by what our Lord Jesus Christ accomplished upon the cross at Calvary? Jesus said, "Now shall the prince of this world be cast out," and he was (John 12:31). He has no power or authority in the kingdom of our Lord and Saviour Jesus Christ. Yes, "as a roaring lion, he walketh about, seeking whom he may devour" (1 Pet. 5:8). But though the Lord's people, as they journey on through life, are subject to the assaults of the enemy, he cannot prevail over them. Jesus, through death, has destroyed him that had the power of death, that is, the devil; and has delivered them "who through fear of death were all their lifetime subject to bondage" (Heb. 2:14–15). O does not this address the fears of the people of God with respect to the time of death? I know human nature shrinks from it but if Jesus is ours it is blessed! Paul could say that to be absent from the body, is to be

present with the Lord (2 Cor. 5:8). We know not the circumstances of our own death, but we know that all things are in the
hand of the Lord. And how gracious and merciful he is to his
people at all times, in all situations!

"He hath abolished death," because sin and guilt, the sting of
death, have been removed. Paul testifies of this in the fifteenth
chapter of his first epistle to the Corinthians where he speaks of
the glorious resurrection of our Lord Jesus Christ and of all his
people in him. He says, "Then shall be brought to pass the saying
that is written, Death is swallowed up in victory. O death, where
is thy sting? O grave, where is thy victory? The sting of death is
sin; and the strength of sin is the law. But thanks be to God, which
giveth us the victory through our Lord Jesus Christ. Therefore,
my beloved brethren, be ye stedfast, unmoveable, always
abounding in the work of the Lord, forasmuch as ye know that
your labour is not in vain in the Lord" (1 Cor. 15:54–58).

"Abolished death." That is, not one of his people shall ever
come into condemnation, whatever may be found in their lives
after his calling them by grace. Not one of the Lord's people can
ever claim they are without sin. Failings, indeed grievous sins at
times, are found in their lives. Look at the people of God in holy
scripture. See David's adultery and murder. He brought on
himself the chastening hand of his God. What a painful path he
then had to walk, yet nothing could bring him into condemnation.
For the Lord hath abolished death, that is, the second death.
"Blessed and holy is he that hath part in the first resurrection: on
such the second death hath no power" (Rev. 20:6). The first
resurrection I take to be the work of God's grace in regeneration,
in bringing from death in trespasses and sins into the life of the
gospel. Having part in that resurrection, the second death hath no
power over us.

He "hath abolished death, and hath brought *life and
immortality to light* through the gospel." O what glorious light
shines in the precious truth of the gospel of the grace of God.
There is life. The Lord Jesus himself declared, "I am come that
they might have *life,* and that they might have it more
abundantly" (John 10:10). As needy sinners brought by grace to
trust alone in the Lord Jesus Christ, he *is* our life. In him we *live.*

That is true of our physical life. And our spiritual and *eternal* life is in all that Jesus is unto us. He hath "brought life and immortality to light." We are poor sinful mortals having an *immortal* soul. *Every* soul continues to exist after death. Those who die in their sins will suffer God's just condemnation in hell for ever. Solemn truth. But the believer has an immortal life which is revealed to us in the blessed gospel. If Jesus lives, so must his people live in him to all eternity. O glorious reality!

Remember what Jesus said to Martha at the death of Lazarus (John 11): "Then said Martha unto Jesus, Lord, if thou hadst been here, my brother had not died." "Thy brother shall rise again." "I know that he shall rise again in the resurrection at the last day." "I am the resurrection, and the life…whosoever liveth and believeth in me shall never die. Believest thou this?" O what a glorious truth. In a sense, the believer never dies. Immortality, eternal life is ours. It is assured to us in Jesus Christ. Unless the Lord comes first, we shall pass through the valley of the shadow of death. But even there the Lord assures us, "I am with thee." The psalmist could rest in that blessed truth, "Yea, though I walk through the valley of the shadow of death, I will fear no evil: for thou art with me" (Ps. 23:4).

Does not this encourage and comfort the living family of God, amidst their many real fears? We are subject to the same things to which fallen men are subject in this fallen world, even the present fear throughout society because of the virus from which many have died. We do not dismiss this concern for one moment. But what has the believer to fear? If Jesus Christ is ours, if we are brought through divine grace to believe and trust in him, cannot we commit ourselves entirely into his hands?

As Paul says, "I know whom I have believed, and *am persuaded* that he is able to keep that which I have committed unto him against that day" (2 Tim. 1:12). O may we know the same blessed persuasion. The word testifies that our Lord Jesus Christ *faileth not,* and the soul brought to trust in him shall never be brought into condemnation. While Jesus lives, they can't be lost, and the word assures us that he lives for ever and ever. May then our souls be increasingly drawn in true faith and love, "Unto him that loved us, and washed us from our sins in his own blood" (Rev. 1:5), to him that brought us from death in sins into the glorious liberty of the gospel. To him be all the praise.

I will leave the remarks there. May the Lord add his blessing. Amen.

23

FEAR NOT, LITTLE FLOCK

Tuesday evening 12 May 2020

"Fear not, little flock; for it is your Father's good pleasure to give you the kingdom" (Luke 12:32).

Though at this time there was an innumerable multitude of people "insomuch that they trode one upon another," yet the ministry of our Lord Jesus Christ on this occasion was primarily addressed to his disciples. And surely it embraces all his true disciples who, through the grace of God, have been brought from death in trespasses and sins into the light, life and liberty of the gospel. O what a great thing it is to be a disciple, a true follower of the Lord Jesus! Such have been brought by divine grace and the teaching of the Holy Spirit to the feet of Christ. Their ears have been opened to hear what the Lord will speak to them. They have been subdued by sovereign grace and made willing in the day of his power. Such a one delights and rejoices to hear the voice of the good shepherd. He has the witness of the Holy Spirit so that he is able to say with the psalmist, "The LORD is my shepherd." And surely, as we are enabled by grace to realise personally that he is our shepherd, then we can confidently say, "I shall not want." No. I shall not want any good thing. The Lord has graciously promised it. And that promise is founded on his unchanging love and faithfulness.

What I would have afresh for us this night, is to hear for ourselves the voice of the good shepherd speaking to us, addressing our fears, those things which so often trouble and distress the people of God. Being what we are of ourselves (and we do not make any excuse) are we not very much aware of the workings of our fallen and carnal nature? How so often the wretched unbelief rooted therein seeks to draw us away from trust and confidence in the Lord Jesus Christ alone. 'O Lord, deliver us from questionings and doubts.' May that always be your cry and mine. 'Lord, deliver me from myself, my most sinful self and my righteous self.'

One thing I am sure we are increasingly brought to realise is that we cannot keep ourselves. O how dependent we are. What a mercy it is to realise how wholly dependent we are upon the Lord. Our fallen nature does not relish that. No. But, as taught of God the Holy Spirit, what a blessed place to be found and kept as a needy sinner at the feet of the Lord Jesus Christ, looking to him alone, having nothing in ourselves. What a painful experience to the flesh is having nothing in self, but what is defiled with sin throughout, yet having all things in Jesus Christ. O the blessedness of this! Jesus made everything, as he most surely is, to his people! All that we need is richly treasured up in him, and as we are assured here, is freely given to us as well. Freely given! Is not that a blessed reality!

You know, every mercy we receive, every manifestation of the kindness and care of the Lord our God towards us, any realisation by the testimony of the Holy Spirit of his pardoning love and mercy to us, all comes freely flowing out of the fulness of the grace which is in Christ Jesus our Lord. For it comes to us from our Triune God who has loved his people with an everlasting love and, in his appointed time, calls by his grace. We may well say, "what hast thou that thou didst not receive?" (1 Cor. 4:7). And, for all we have received, is there not cause continually for thanksgiving and praise unto the Lord? For surely it never comes to us for any worthiness of ours. If he were to deal with us as we deserve, where should we be? Hell must be our just and deserved abode. But the Lord, through the redemption wrought out by his beloved Son, has most surely delivered his people from the just condemnation in hell that their sins deserve.

So then, as I was saying, the Lord here primarily addresses his disciples. We cannot go over everything he taught in what we read this evening. There is obviously a connection between the words of our text and verse twenty-two. "And he said unto his disciples, Therefore I say unto you, Take no thought for your life, what ye shall eat; neither for the body, what ye shall put on. The life is more than meat, and the body is more than raiment." This was in response to one that said, "Master, speak to my brother, that he divide the inheritance with me." The Lord warns his disciples against covetousness. He tells the parable of that rich man, whose trust and delight were altogether in his riches, and to whom those solemn words were spoken: "Thou fool, this night thy soul shall be required of thee: then whose shall those things be?" Are we not there reminded of how wholly dependent we are upon the Lord? Friends, what a mercy that our times, our very lives, are in the Lord's hand. Indeed, all that concerns our true welfare, materially and spiritually, is in the hands of our Lord and Saviour. And what loving hands they are!

And so the Lord speaks to us here. He says, "Take no thought." He warns against what we are so prone to, even care and over-anxiety for material things and the circumstances in which we are found. O how troubling they are so often and weigh heavy on us. See how the Lord addresses the cares of his people. He reminds us of himself as the one and only true God, the Creator of the heavens and the earth, who provides for the birds of the air and clothes the grass of the field. He says, "Are not five sparrows sold for two farthings, and not one of them is forgotten before God?" Consider the little sparrow, such an insignificant little bird, yet we are assured that God so cares for the sparrows that not one of them falls to the ground without your Father's leave. He even goes further than that. He says, "even the very hairs of your head are all numbered." O how that surely sets before us, if we might put it this way, the intense reality of the care and love of the Lord for his own. Does he so condescend in manifesting his care and love to his people as to provide for their every care, even in what might be considered the most insignificant matter? Yes, he does, blessed be his great and holy name.

O how little we comprehend the greatness of the love of our Lord Jesus Christ! We see it gloriously displayed in what he has wrought out for the redemption and salvation of his people. Surely the greatness of that love of God is evident in that he gave his only begotten Son. For what purpose? To save his people from their sins. He hath not withheld his only begotten Son to be their *substitute*. Divine justice demanded of him and received full *satisfaction* for all the sins of those his Father had given him, every sinner loved and chosen of God from before the foundation of the world. As his love is manifest in that great and glorious work, see also that love evident in his tender care and watchfulness over his own. So he warns them against over-anxiety and care.

But also, we see what the encouragement bound up in the warning, is founded upon. "Your heavenly Father knoweth that ye have need of all these things." See there the relationship of the Lord our God with each sinner he calls by grace and brings into the bonds of that eternally secure covenant. Therein God is revealed as our covenant God and Father, who loved us and chose us in Christ and redeemed us by his grace. O the glorious reality of that relationship!

Remember what the Lord Jesus spoke to Mary Magdalene concerning those whom his Father had given him. "Go to my brethren, and say unto them" (John 20:17). O friends, may that message from our risen Lord himself come afresh in all its blessedness to your soul and mine. "Go to my brethren, and say unto them, I ascend unto my Father, and your Father; and to my God, and your God." Blessed be his name, he did not disown them even though they had failed that night when they forsook him and fled, and Peter grievously denied him. Ah, he did not disown them and he *never* will disown one of his own, not even though they be so fearful, even failures, as his people so often are. If he dealt with us in these things as we deserve, we might surely say he cannot do any other than disown us. No, friends, remember this, the Lord seal it afresh unto us, that where sin abounds grace does much more abound. And can one of us say we are without the sad working of sin in our hearts and lives? But O the fulness and freeness of the grace of our God. That does not give us encouragement to sin. Far from it. But should it not bring us to the Saviour's feet, our selves abhorring, our sins confessing, yet adoring the wonder of his love and mercy still made known to the neediest of sinners? All is to the glory of his name.

But see then the encouragement he gives in these words to his disciples and to his people still. "Your heavenly Father knoweth that ye have need of all these things." "For all these things do the nations of the world seek after." Yes, is not that the predominant concern with men and women in this fallen world? "What shall we eat? or, What shall we drink? or, Wherewithal shall we be clothed?" (Matt. 6:31). They are always striving after the things of this present time state. Yet, though divine providence abundantly provides, they are never satisfied. That is ever the attitude of fallen human nature—never satisfied. It is as we read in the Proverbs: "The horseleach hath two daughters, crying, Give, give" (Prov. 30:15). That is sadly evident in the nations of the world. They seek after those things wherein is no real, lasting and full satisfaction, things which can never do the soul of a sinner any real, lasting good. No, they are broken fountains indeed, which sadly deceive all who put their trust in them.

Yet he says, "your Father knoweth ye have need of these things." Cannot we then leave all in his hand? Has he failed yet? Will he fail? No. His word assures us, "But rather seek ye the kingdom of God; and all these things shall be added unto you." See that the Lord ever directs us, not downward but upward, not merely seeking the things of this time state but seeking those things which are above. O that it may be so with us. Remember what the Lord spoke to Baruch in the prophecy of Jeremiah. Baruch was greatly distressed because, being involved with Jeremiah and subject to all the threats of the king against Jeremiah and himself, all his earthly prospects had been blighted. "Seekest thou great things for thyself? seek them not" (Jer. 45:5). And see how the Lord gave Baruch the assurance that he would be with him and deliver him. His life would be given to him for a prey. Even though the enemy would come, as the Chaldeans did upon Jerusalem, yet he would be spared, and the Lord's hand would be upon him for good. So friends, it speaks to us: seek not great things for thyself but seek those real things, those spiritual, eternal realities. O to love the Lord Jesus Christ in sincerity and truth, to be followers of him as dear children, to drink more deeply out of the wells of salvation by the blessed leading of the Holy Spirit. "But rather seek ye the kingdom of God; and all these things shall be added unto you." And our text goes on to say: "Fear not, little flock; for it is your Father's good pleasure to give you the kingdom." What we are encouraged to seek, we are here assured that it is the Father's good pleasure to give to his people, described here as a little flock.

Let us first of all, in looking at this verse, attend to those opening words: "Fear not." O friends, how precious are these words as they fall from the lips of our Lord Jesus Christ! Why, they express the very love of his heart towards his own. What a mercy his word assures us that "he knoweth our frame; he remembereth that we are dust" (Ps. 103:14). He knoweth those very things that distress us, the anxieties that press upon us. O tried, exercised, troubled child of God, "Fear not." Not because there is nothing to fear or because you are not exercised by those things. It would be a sad thing if we are not truly exercised about what troubles us and are not brought to cry to the Lord for his mercy, help and deliverance. But how this word comes in here as cold waters to a thirsty soul. "Fear not." Fear not, troubled child of God. Upon what is this "fear not" founded? It is on the blessed fact that "Your *Father* knoweth that ye have need of these things." How graciously he hath provided for you. As we sing:

"He that has made my heaven secure

Will here all good provide."

You may be fretful in the things of this life but what are they in comparison with what the Lord here assures us he has appointed and gives. Why, he gives a kingdom, as it is said here, "Fear not, little flock; for it is your Father's good pleasure to give you the *kingdom,"* the kingdom of his grace here and of glory hereafter, with all that is bound up in that gift.

"Fear not, little flock." What words of endearment are these of our Lord to his own! "Little flock." See how they express the deep love of his heart to them. O how precious in the sight of the Lord are his people, how dear they are to him. His word assures us that he counts them as his jewels. He loved them with an everlasting love even before the foundation of the world. And can there be any diminishing of that love? Here he comes again unto you, tried, exercised disciples of the Lord, fearful though you often may well be. "Fear not...your Father knoweth." Blessed be his name, he assures us that he is ever ready to attend to the needs of his people. He assures us that he gives us far more than we can ever begin to think. As we read in another place, he is "able to do exceeding abundantly above all that we ask or think" (Eph. 3:20). What a mercy to be a praying people by his grace. O that we may be instant in prayer, seeking the promised help of the Holy Spirit to indite prayer in our hearts to bring to the Lord *all* that concerns us—our material needs, our spiritual welfare, the glory of his name and the welfare of his cause in the earth at this present time. May there be concern among us to pray one for another, for his name's sake. And may we not only know the mercy of being brought to be a praying people, but also to be a people who receive out of his fulness. For we are assured the Lord will surely hear prayer he has indited, blessed be his name.

"Little flock." Yes, the church upon earth is only a remnant, but a blessed remnant, a people loved of the Lord, his little flock, ever the subject of the loving care of the great and good shepherd, our Lord Jesus Christ. But though a little flock, a remnant on the earth, we are assured that the people of God will ultimately be seen to be a redeemed company which no man can number. O how great and glorious is the wonder of the grace of our God, revealed in the redemption and salvation of all whom he has loved and chosen, all whom he has called out of every nation, kingdom, tribe and tongue from under heaven. O the blessedness of being found one with them, now and to all eternity. Is not this all of grace? Do we make any contribution towards it? No. We are utterly and deeply indebted to the Lord. To him alone all the praise is due.

"Fear not, little flock." You know, the eastern shepherd was very different to the shepherd in our country today. The eastern shepherd led out his flock in the morning and brought them back to the fold at night. He was with them all day, leading them to pastures and water and protecting them. See what an example is given us in David, the youngest of Jesse's sons. Samuel was directed of the Lord to anoint one of Jesse's sons to be king over Israel. All the sons of Jesse passed before him and Samuel naturally looked on the outward appearance. When he came to the end, he asked whether he had any more sons. Jesse said, 'yes, the youngest who keepeth the sheep.' David is sent for, a shepherd lad who cared for the sheep. "Arise, anoint him: for this is he" (1 Sam. 16:12). The point I make is that we see David, a shepherd lad who, as he cared for his father's flocks, was with them all the while. Remember when he came to that confrontation with Goliath, he said, "Thy servant kept his father's sheep, and there came a lion, and a bear, and took a lamb out of the flock...Thy servant slew both the lion and the bear...The Lord that delivered me out of the paw of the lion, and out of the paw of the bear, he will deliver me out of the hand of this Philistine" (1 Sam 17:36).

And the Lord's little flock, to whom he says, "Fear not," is ever the subject of his care and watchfulness. He is always with them. Is that not blessedly made known in his word? "I am with thee...I am thy God" (Isa. 41:10). Can the welfare of our body and soul be in better hands than those of our great and good shepherd, he that gave his life for us and now liveth at the right hand of the Majesty in the heavens! As he has loved his people, has died for them and risen again, he surely will never leave them nor forsake them. O this is the point I want to emphasise. "Fear not, little flock; for it is your Father's good pleasure to give you the kingdom." As a little flock, as the people of God, the sheep of his pasture, subject to his love and care, will there be any good thing he will withhold from them? Yes, they shall know his chastening hand, for oftentimes are they prone to wander.

"Prone to wander, Lord, I feel it;
Prone to leave the God I love;
Here's my heart, Lord, take and seal it;
Seal it from thy courts above!"

They are prone to wander but the Lord will not leave these wandering ones. He goes after them until he finds them and brings them again unto himself. Blessed be his name!

The Lord says, "it is your Father's good pleasure to give you the kingdom." Are we troubled and careful about earthly things? O the Lord here promises a kingdom. He assures us of it. He delights to gives it. "It is your Father's *good pleasure* to give you the kingdom." He does not give only a part of that kingdom. He gives us all that kingdom embraces. All is ours as a believer through grace in the Lord Jesus Christ and *one* with him.

Let us notice what the Lord said to Nicodemus. "Except a man be born again, he cannot see the kingdom of God." What is this kingdom of God? Why, it is the rule, the reign of his grace in the hearts and lives of his people. It is the very work of our God. It is the one true church, Zion, of which the Lord Jesus Christ is the glorious king and blessed head. It embraces the whole of the elect of God. "To give you the kingdom," the kingdom of his grace here, the kingdom of glory hereafter. To our God be all the glory!

Let me remind you that as Paul could say of himself as a Roman citizen, believers are the citizens "of no mean city." No. They are the citizens of an everlasting kingdom. And, as citizens of that country, we are strangers and pilgrims here upon earth. We are but passing through. Is there not, I trust, the daily reminder to us that "here have we no continuing city, but we seek one to come" (Heb. 13:14). We have the assurance that we are the citizens of that kingdom of which the Lord Jesus Christ himself declared: "My kingdom is not of this world: if my kingdom were of this world, then would my servants fight…but now is my kingdom not from hence" (John 18:36). No, Jesus reigns over the glorious kingdom of our God and Saviour. O may the living reality of his reign be known in your heart and mine and manifest in our lives as brought in true submission to the Lord's sovereign will. May it be our delight to serve him in our generation. True, we come far short. Are we not daily conscious of that? We would mourn over it before the Lord. 'O Lord, work in me to will and to do of thy good pleasure. Draw me closer to thyself. Give me more of a single eye for thy glory, to know and do thy will in my day and generation.'

Friends, may that be so with us. Yes, we live in this nation of which we form a part. We would be subject to those in authority, as far as that goes. But when they seek to intervene in what pertains to the kingdom of our Lord Jesus, then we have to say, as did the apostles: "Whether it be right in the sight of God to hearken unto you more than unto God, judge ye…We ought to obey God rather than men" (Acts 5:29). If they require of us that which is contrary to the word of our God, then we have to say that we will obey God rather than man. May the Lord grant us his grace and its application in all that concerns us, particularly at this time.

"Fear not, little flock; for it is your Father's good pleasure to give you the kingdom." This is not only a prospect, but a glorious reality! Let us just read again that passage in this chapter: "And he spake a parable unto them, saying, The ground of a certain rich man brought forth plentifully: And he thought within himself, saying, What shall I do, because I have no room where to bestow my fruits? And he said, This will I do: I will pull down my barns, and build greater; and there will I bestow all my fruits and my goods. And I will say to my soul, Soul, thou hast much goods laid up for many years; take thine ease, eat, drink, and be merry. But God said unto him, Thou fool, this night thy soul shall be required of thee: then whose shall those things be, which thou hast provided? So is he that layeth up treasure for himself, and is not rich toward God." O friends, how rich towards God is a believing soul. As a poor sinner brought to believe and trust alone in Jesus Christ, all that Jesus is and has, is theirs. What a kingdom which can *never* decay! It is eternal because all that pertains to it, the blessings of sovereign saving grace manifested to his people, rise out of the *everlasting love* of God. All centres, not in what the sinner can do, but in what God in Jesus Christ has done to give them everlasting salvation, everlasting life, to the praise of the glory of our God.

But I will leave the remarks there. May the Lord add his blessing. Amen.

24

THE EYE OF THE LORD IS UPON
THEM THAT FEAR HIM

Lord's day evening 17 May 2020

"Behold, the eye of the Lord is upon them that
fear him, upon them that hope in his mercy;
to deliver their soul from death, and to keep
them alive in famine" (Psalm 33:18-19).

In addressing our text, I will be referring to the words we considered this morning[1] out of Paul's epistle to the Romans chapter five, the second verse. Referring to our Lord Jesus Christ, he says "By whom also we have access by faith into this grace wherein we stand, and rejoice in hope of the glory of God." O the fulness and blessedness in that statement expressing the grace of God in his purposes of mercy for his own, as set before us in the gospel. For in the gospel is all that pertains to the glory of God, and the eternal welfare of each one he calls by grace. For them he had purposes of love and mercy even from before the foundation of the world. It is through the grace of God that we are brought to know the blessed position of "being justified by faith, we have peace with God through our Lord Jesus Christ" (Rom. 5:1). God has assuredly accomplished all his purposes for us through the person and work of the Lord Jesus Christ.

We further read in the epistle to the Romans, "He that spared not his own Son, but delivered him up for us all" (Rom. 8:32). Do not those words express the wondrous gospel truth of the grace and love of God as revealed in Jesus Christ? He "spared not his own Son," as his Son stood in the place of all whom his Father had given him, wretched, ruined sinners such as you and me. And through the wonders of that grace, believers "are justified from all things, from which ye could not be justified by the law of Moses" (Acts 13:39). All is founded on the offering

---

[1] The morning service is not available as it was not recorded.

and sacrifice of our Lord Jesus Christ, the Holy One of God, God manifest in the flesh. Yes, I know we are familiar with these things. I repeat them again and again to you. O friends, is there any other subject really worth speaking of again and again? What a fulness is here. We have surely to be thankful for all the Lord has made known to us, but in comparison with that which is to be known, O how little we know.

Yet how blessed is the poor sinner brought by divine grace to believe and trust in the Lord Jesus Christ alone. What a good work of God is that. "He which hath begun a good work in you" (Phil. 1:6). It is by a work of God's grace that we are brought to the Lord Jesus, humbled under the mighty hand of God with the conscious sense of our wretchedness and ruin as a sinner. Yet by that same wondrous grace, we are raised up to know the blessedness of the pardon of our sins. We have acceptance with God through the person, work, sufferings and death of our Lord Jesus Christ and through the righteousness he wrought out, wherein God *"justifieth the ungodly"* (Rom. 4:5). What a word is that! Friends, I trust we are brought to bless God for it. If it were not true, would there be any hope for such sinners as you and me? Do we not have to acknowledge the solemn fact that we are *ungodly?* So I am of myself and, solemnly, must ever be so apart from rich, sovereign, distinguishing grace.

O the wonders of that grace of God by which he is glorified in the eternal welfare of every one of his own! As I said a moment ago, he "spared not his own Son, but delivered him up for us all." That is a blessed, glorious fact for each sinner brought to believe and trust in Jesus Christ. It can never be undone. It lies as the very foundation of the faith and hope of the living family of God as taught of God the Holy Spirit. He spared not his own Son. He delivered him up for us all. Is not this the grace in which, through faith, we stand? I repeat again that, as sinners we have no other standing but in the person and work of our Lord Jesus Christ. May the Holy Spirit bring this grace afresh to our souls this evening. If he spared not his own Son, is there any good thing he will deny those to whom he has purposes of love and mercy? Will he not with him, "also freely give us all things?" That is the very grace to which we have access, through faith. And in that grace is the hope and expectation of the living family of God.

So let us now consider this precious psalm I read before you and may the Holy Spirit lead us into its theme: "Rejoice in the LORD, O ye righteous: for praise is comely for the upright." Paul says the same in writing to the Philippians: "Rejoice in the Lord alway: and again I say, Rejoice" (Phil. 4:4). And is there not ever cause for rejoicing in the Lord by all taught of the Spirit their ruin through sin, and their salvation solely by what Jesus Christ has done for them? Is there no cause of rejoicing in this? Friends, most surely there is cause for rejoicing in thankfulness to the God of our salvation as we journey on through life. O the wonder of it, that he should manifest his saving mercies to such sinners as you and me! Will not that be our constant theme when brought into the full realisation of the wonders of his love in the eternal inheritance appointed for his own, as the scriptures assure us? Is not that the very theme of the rejoicing of all the redeemed before the throne? They ascribe all honour and glory to him who loved them and washed them from their sins in his own blood. There they shall sing the blessed song of Moses and the Lamb, the song that testifies of sovereign, free, saving grace and mercy to sinners, to the praise of the glory of our God. We do not *begin* to learn that blessed hymn of praise when taken from this world to heaven "where he unveils his lovely face." We begin to know it *now* by the blessed teaching of the Holy Spirit. Surely it should ever be our desire to sing that song *now* as sinners saved by grace.

"Rejoice in the LORD, O ye righteous." Ah indeed, is not every sinner saved by grace *righteous,* not by anything they have done, but by what Jesus Christ has done for them? See this in the opening words of Psalm thirty-two. "Blessed is he whose transgression is forgiven, whose sin is covered. Blessed is the man unto whom the LORD imputeth not iniquity, and in whose spirit there is no guile." Ah, *there* is the righteousness by which God justifies the ungodly. "Being justified by faith, we have peace with God through our Lord Jesus Christ" (Rom. 5:1). It is not our believing that justifies us. It is the object of faith revealed in God's word. It is his provision of his beloved Son. It is what Christ has accomplished. God justifies the ungodly, wholly upon the ground of what we believe as taught of the Holy Spirit. Faith only finds rest, and blessed rest it is, in all that Jesus is and has done. As Paul writes to the Hebrews, this is the rest that remains to the people of God. And it *ever remains.* It can never be overthrown, never taken away. Blessed is the soul that truly enters into the rest that is found alone in our Lord Jesus Christ and in what he accomplished in his life, sufferings, death and resurrection. That alone answers all the demands of God's holy law for each poor sinner brought by divine grace to believe and trust in Jesus Christ. That alone glorifies God. What alone brings peace to your troubled conscience and mine is the precious blood of Jesus Christ, "the blood of sprinkling, that speaketh better things than that of Abel" (Heb. 12:24). One says, "Oft as sins, my soul, assail thee." Do we not find *sins defiling and assailing us* a sad fact?

> "Oft as sins, my soul, assail thee,
> Turn thy eyes to Jesus' blood;
> Nothing short of this can heal thee,
> Seal thy peace, or do thee good."

True peace with God is found alone in our Lord Jesus Christ, in his precious blood shed upon the cross at Calvary. Still it speaks! Did Abel's blood speak? God declared its voice cried unto him against the wickedness of Cain. O friends, the precious blood of Jesus Christ speaketh "better things than that of Abel." For it speaks the assurance of sins forgiven, of access to God and acceptance by him for us poor sinners. I say it again, we are justified alone by what Jesus has wrought out for us.

What a testimony is given us in this psalm of the grace into which "we have access by faith" as the apostle says. We see here the wonder of the Lord's watchful care over his own. "Praise is comely" for them, that is, "for the upright." The psalmist goes on to show that the Lord's people should continually praise, bless and thank him for what we receive through his rich mercies towards us, and supremely for what he is in himself. He reveals *himself* in his holy word. "By the word of the LORD were the heavens made; and all the host of them by the breath of his mouth. He gathereth the waters of the sea together as an heap: he layeth up the depth in storehouses. Let all the earth fear the

LORD: let all the inhabitants of the world stand in awe of him. For he spake, and it was done; he commanded, and it stood fast. The LORD bringeth the counsel of the heathen to nought: he maketh the devices of the people of none effect. The counsel of the Lord standeth for ever, the thoughts of his heart to all generations." In the things set before us here, O what ground we have for thankfulness and praise unto our God in that he *is* God. And all that his word sets forth of himself is truth. The psalm is summed up, in a sense, in those words I often quote:

"He holds all nature in his hand;
That gracious hand on which I live."

Friends, see all things in the hand and under the control of our God. I know it is easy to say these things. But O, may we realise increasingly, by the rich mercies of the Lord towards us, the entering into this grace wherein we stand, and the rejoicing in hope of the glory of God. See how God's glory is set before us in this psalm in what it reveals of himself. As he said to Abraham, *"I am the Almighty God;* walk before me, and be thou perfect" (Gen. 17:1). O for grace enabling us to walk not only before, but *with* the Lord our God, in the conscious believing realisation that he is God and has all things in his hand and under his control.

Look at this in the light of the present circumstances in which we are found. Many are the fears we have. Many apprehensions so often crowd in upon us. Ah friend, when thus bowed down under present things, whatever may be found in our path, O for grace to enable us to enter "into this grace wherein we stand." What a firm foundation is laid in this grace." What assurance is given us, as those whom the Lord has reconciled and brought to himself. How real is that peace of which Paul wrote to the Romans: "being justified by faith, we have *peace* with God through our Lord Jesus Christ." That peace is in the fact that God has reconciled us to himself "through the redemption that is in Christ Jesus" (Rom. 3:24). If that is ours, O in what grace do we stand! We have the assurance that Jesus is ours and we are his and all our concerns and times are in his hand. And this truth is laid down in the very words of our text this evening.

See how the text is prefaced. *"Behold."* O tried exercised child of God, *behold* here is something not only to look to but, by the Lord enabling us, to believingly *lay hold upon.* Here we are assured of the consolation for the living family of God in the trials we are passing through as we journey on through life, even in our situation at this present time. *Behold* the person by whom "we have access by faith into this grace wherein we stand, and rejoice in hope of the glory of God." All comes to us in and through the person and doings of our Lord and Saviour Jesus Christ. In him this *grace* is richly treasured up for us, for life and godliness, for time and eternity.

"Behold, the eye of the LORD is upon them that fear him, upon them that hope in his mercy." The word, *behold,* calls our attention to what is spoken. O the Lord grant us grace to truly heed these things. *What is the Lord saying to us?* May it come afresh to your soul and mine at this time, by the anointing of the Holy Spirit. "The eye of the LORD is upon them that *fear* him, upon them that hope in his mercy." What is this fear? It is not a slavish fear, not being frightened of God. These are poor sinners to whom God reveals himself in love and mercy. In this there is nothing for them to be afraid. Yes, as sinners, if we have to stand upon what we are and have done, then we have just cause to be afraid of God. For as transgressors of his holy law, he is against us and above us and we have just cause to be afraid. But as reconciled to God through the redemption that is in Christ Jesus, and as freely justified by God who justifieth the ungodly through the grace of Christ, there is no ground for a poor sinner to fear. There is everything to encourage them.

The fear of which the psalmist speaks is not being afraid of God, but being brought to believe and *trust* in the Lord Jesus Christ alone. This is the fear of God which is often referred to in the holy scriptures. I say again, it is not a slavish fear. It is a filial fear wrought in us by the fulness of mercy and love in Christ Jesus being made known to us, and we granted grace to trust in him. And surely, in the scriptures we have every ground to trust in the Lord alone.

O what a testimony is given to us in the word of God, of the men and women in past generations, sinners saved by grace, and the situations they passed through. What is their testimony to us today? "They trusted in thee, and were not confounded" (Ps. 22:5). What great difficulties they often faced, even imposs-ibilities! So it is still for the church and people of God. Viewed from the human standpoint, what impossibilities face us which are beyond our ability, and any others to deal with. Yet, as it concerns the people of God, is there anything impossible with him?

Just to illustrate this a little further, remember how the Lord came to Jeremiah shut up in the prison, and instructed him to buy a field from his nephew who came to ask him to purchase it. Jeremiah did so in obedience to the word of the Lord. Yet humanly speaking, what prospect was there of his ever enjoying that purchase? Why, it seemed most foolish to buy land when the armies of the Chaldeans were besieging the city. And Jeremiah knew the time was at hand when Jerusalem would be conquered and destroyed, and the people carried into captivity for seventy years in Babylon. How foolish to buy land. But Jeremiah, in trust and confidence in his God, lays the matter before the Lord. 'Lord, you told me to buy the land but how will I take possession of it. It is impossible?' "Then came the word of the LORD unto Jeremiah, saying, Behold, I am the LORD, the God of all flesh: is there any thing too hard for me?" (Jer. 32:27). Ah friends, I trust that speaks to you and me afresh this evening: "I am the LORD, the God of all flesh: is there any thing too hard for me?"

It is the same Lord that speaks to us in our text: "Behold, the eye of the LORD is upon them that fear him." What do we understand by the eye of the Lord? It is his watchfulness and care over his own. As a poor sinner brought through grace to believe and trust in the Lord Jesus Christ, the child of God is never outside the circle of his love and care. Never does a shepherd care for his sheep as the Lord cares for his own. Night and day, even hour by hour, are not all the Lord's people continually the subjects of his care? O may we realise this more and more. I know we readily say our times are in his hand, but how little are we truly conscious of the gracious reality that,

> "My life's minutest circumstance,
>   Is subject to his eye."

If the Lord's eye is thus upon us, if we are the subjects of his love and care,

> "What harm can ever reach my soul
> Beneath my Father's eye?"

Have we not the assurance then that the Lord will ever provide for us? That is not to say we shall not be subject to trials, difficulties, sicknesses and dangers. Indeed, how little we comprehend what dangers we are preserved from, not only in things seen but in many things unseen. "The angel of the LORD encampeth round about them that fear him, and delivereth them" (Ps. 34:7). As I said on other occasions, how little we are aware of how much we owe to the ministry of angels. Remember all is in the hand of our God in the outworking of his purposes of love and mercy towards his own.

"The eye of the LORD is upon them that fear him, upon them that *hope* in his mercy." As Paul writes to the Romans, we "rejoice in *hope* of the glory of God" (Rom. 5:2). This hope of the believer is not some uncertain thing. Men speak of hope as something we look forward to, uncertain that it will ever come to pass. We hope things will be better but they may not be so. But the hope of a child of God maketh not ashamed. It is not some uncertain thing. It is founded upon the oath and promise of our God himself. What God has promised to his living family, is the ground of our hope and it can never fail. Has he indeed justified us by faith? Is that a gracious reality? Then how sure is the hope of the poor sinner brought to trust in Jesus Christ. It cannot fail to come to a glorious fulfilment as the Lord has promised in his holy word.

"Them that hope in *his mercy.*" Hope in the mercy of God is hope in his grace and favour made known to us as undeserving sinners. His mercy is given to us in the person of Jesus Christ. He *is* the mercy promised. He is the ground of hope for all the living family of God as taught by the Holy Spirit. O the fulness and freeness of the mercy of God revealed in our Lord and Saviour Jesus Christ! May we ever behold the substance of this sure mercy of God in Jesus Christ.

See what the apostle declares of this assured mercy. "I know whom I have believed, and am persuaded that he is able to keep that which I have committed unto him against that day" (2 Tim. 1:12). What a blessed testimony of God-given faith by one who truly hoped in the mercy of God in Jesus Christ! He *is* the mercy promised. And all we receive from the hand of our God, his care, kindness, love in all his provisions for us for time and to all eternity is surely treasured up in our Lord Jesus Christ alone. I come back to what I said earlier. "He that spared not his own Son, but delivered him up for us all, how shall he not with him also freely give us all things?"

Our text goes on to say, "to deliver their soul from death, and to keep them alive in famine." See the practical outworking of this mercy in the experience of each sinner brought by the Spirit to hope in the mercy of God centred wholly in Jesus Christ. Cannot we safely leave all our welfare, for time and eternity, in his hands?

"To deliver their soul from death, and to keep them alive in famine." Indeed he has delivered our soul from death, as poor sinners brought to trust in Jesus Christ. For God has justified us. He justifies the ungodly. Has he not delivered us "from so great a death," as Paul could speak of it? (2 Cor. 1:10). Yes, he has. It is as one says,

> "Our sins deserve eternal death,
> But Jesus died for me."

O may that precious truth, *"but Jesus died for me"* come afresh to us at this time. "Who delivered us from so great a death, and doth deliver: in whom we trust that he will yet deliver us." Our trust and confidence is in Jesus. It is not founded on what we are or can do, but on what he has done for us. *That* can never fail.

"To keep them alive in famine." O what gracious provision the Lord makes for his people in trying circumstances. His love faileth not. David could say, "I have been young, and now am old; yet have I not seen the righteous forsaken, nor his seed begging bread" (Ps. 37:25). And you will never see the righteous forsaken. For a sinner brought to believe and trust in Jesus Christ, he "of God is made unto us wisdom, and righteousness, and sanctification, and redemption" (1 Cor. 1:30). You will never see the righteous forsaken nor his seed begging bread in the sense of the rich provision God hath made for us in all that Jesus Christ is and has done. Is not the Lord Jesus the living bread to his people? Are not their souls fed by his word? For therein Jesus, the bread of life, is revealed to them and they are brought to realise more and more the wonders of his saving grace and mercy.

The psalmist goes on to say, "Our soul waiteth for the Lord: he is our help and our shield." Is that where we are found this evening? O how wondrously watched over and kept are the people of God, believing and receiving these things by the teaching of the Holy Spirit. "For our heart shall rejoice in him, because we have trusted in his holy name. Let thy mercy, O Lord, be upon us, according as we hope in thee."

I will leave the remarks there. The Lord add his blessing. Amen.

25

NOT FORSAKING THE ASSEMBLING OF OURSELVES TOGETHER

Tuesday evening 19 May 2020

"Let us hold fast the profession of our faith without wavering; (for he is faithful that promised;) And let us consider one another to provoke unto love and to good works: Not forsaking the assembling of ourselves together, as the manner of some is; but exhorting one another: and so much the more, as ye see the day approaching" (Hebrews 10:23-25).

The opening chapter of the book of Revelation records how the Lord Jesus Christ appeared to his servant John, exiled on the lonely isle of Patmos. John says, "I was in the Spirit on the Lord's day." What a sight he had of the glory of our Lord Jesus, the great head of the church, "God blessed for ever" (Rom. 9:5), who has all authority and power in heaven and earth over all the affairs of men. Particularly shown to John was the blessed relationship of Jesus Christ with his one true church. As John beheld the Lord Jesus in the midst of those seven golden candlesticks, he was told that they represented the seven churches of Asia. Further he was told that the stars in the Lord's right hand were the angels of those churches, that is, his ministers to them. Now John was given a message by the Lord to each church ending with the words: *"He that hath an ear, let him hear what the Spirit saith unto the churches."* Now those messages have application to the church and people of God in every generation. And likewise, are not the words before us this evening the words of our Lord Jesus Christ still speaking to his church and people through the ministry of the Holy Spirit?

As we look at this subject before us, may we know the Lord's mercies giving us an ear to hear "what the Spirit saith unto the churches." True, the Lord is speaking here through his servant Paul to the brethren among the Jews in all the circumstances in which they were found. But it is not in regard to them that I particularly want to draw our attention. I desire that its application may be realised by us personally and as a company of the Lord's people in his mercy to us. For what constitutes the church of Jesus Christ on earth? Is it not men and women brought to believe and trust alone in the Lord Jesus Christ, and through his grace joining together in church fellowship? Is it not their being baptised in his name, and their knowing the great privilege of meeting together to worship him? Do they not attend upon the ordinances of his house as directed particularly in these words this evening?

In looking at matters further as the Lord may help me, we see the emphasis placed in this twenty-third verse on the words, *"Let us hold fast the profession of our faith without wavering."* See how all that follows is grounded and centred in the glorious revelation God has given us of the person of the Lord Jesus Christ in the gospel. "Our faith," *the faith,* is this glorious revelation, and the emphasis is on our holding fast to the profession of it. See how objective it is as we are directed to all God makes known in the glorious truth of the gospel. And friends, it *is* a glorious gospel, is it not? It is the gospel of salvation in the fulness and freeness of it to ruined, guilty, hell-deserving sinners, and all to the praise of the glory of our God. And that salvation has not been accomplished by the doings of the sinners who are the recipients of it, but by the great and glorious Saviour, our Lord Jesus Christ.

Here then in this chapter is particularly set before us the reality of *the* faith once delivered to the saints, the faith of which our Lord Jesus Christ is the sum and substance. Here is revealed to us what God in Christ has done for us. Yes, those things were shadowed forth in the Levitical dispensation, all the ordinances of which pointed to Jesus Christ. He fulfilled *all,* in his incarnation, life, sufferings, death and glorious resurrection.

The incarnation of our Lord Jesus Christ was of God alone, his human nature being formed in the womb of the virgin Mary by the overshadowing of the Holy Spirit. This is surely the greatest of wonders that God, the Creator of all things, should be manifested in the flesh as a babe laid in a manger at Bethlehem! What a wonder is this, beyond our ability to comprehend fully! But where we cannot comprehend, faith believes and bows in worship and adoration of the Lord our God for such wonders of grace manifest in the redemption and salvation of *sinful* men and women such as we are. Was not that the great purpose of the coming of our Lord Jesus Christ into this world? As was said before his birth by the angel to Joseph: "Thou shalt call his name JESUS: for he shall save his people from their sins" (Matt. 1:21). And, blessed be his great and holy name, that which was spoken of him has most surely been accomplished.

We are assured of it in this chapter where we read, "Sacrifice and offering thou wouldest not, but a body hast thou prepared me: in burnt offerings and sacrifices for sin thou hast had no pleasure. *Then said I."* O behold here our Lord Jesus Christ! Hear the voice of our Saviour speaking to his Father. And that voice still speaks to his church and people. "Lo, I come (in the volume of the book it is written of me,) to do thy will, O God. Above when he said, Sacrifice and offering and burnt offerings and offering for sin thou wouldest not, neither hadst pleasure therein; which are offered by the law; then said he, Lo, I come to do thy will, O God. He taketh away the first, that he may establish the second. By the which will we are sanctified through the offering of the body of Jesus Christ once for all. And every priest standeth daily ministering and offering oftentimes the same sacrifices, which can never take away sins: but this man, after he had offered one sacrifice for sins for ever, sat down on the right hand of God."

This glorious man, our Lord and Saviour Jesus Christ, offered *one* sacrifice for sins. What was that *one* sacrifice? It was the offering of himself, through the eternal Spirit, without spot to God (Heb. 9:14). He did so as one who perfectly, willingly fulfilled all that was required to satisfy the just demands of God's holy law against all the transgressors his Father had given him. Here is the glorious gospel of the grace of God. It speaks to us, as I have said so often, not of what is to be done by us but what has been accomplished by our Lord Jesus Christ. As taught by the gracious, wondrous ministry of God the Holy Spirit, are we not brought to look to Jesus who has accomplished our redemption and salvation, providing everlasting righteousness for us? Are not we ruined sinners blessed with God's gift of living faith to receive this salvation?

See how it is expressed by the apostle: "Whereof the Holy Ghost also is a witness to us: for after that he had said before, This is the covenant that I will make with them after those days, saith the Lord, I will put my laws into their hearts, and in their minds will I write them; *and their sins and iniquities will I remember no more.*" What a wondrous truth is that! Who says this? It is God himself who declares that he is fully satisfied with the one offering and sacrifice of his only begotten Son. He will never bring into condemnation those who are the recipients of the blessings of pardoning love and mercy through what Jesus Christ has wrought out for them. Friends, this is the standing of every believer through the riches of grace, the weak as well as the strong. Whatever may be the case and outward situation of every child of God, their standing before him is upon a sure foundation. It is not founded on their worth, their merits or what they have done but what Jesus Christ has done for them. By the teaching of the Holy Spirit, O may our eyes always be fixed on Jesus Christ.

You know, how beautifully simple, in one sense, is the glorious truth of the gospel in its application to each sinner taught of the Spirit. It is: "Christ is all, and in all" (Col. 3:11). What profound things! But what blessed simplicity also. The wonder of the saving grace and mercy of God to me a sinner is in this: "Christ is all and in all" to me. What more do I need? Is not everything a poor sinner needs found in this? If Jesus Christ is ours, then all is ours, in time and for eternity, to the praise of the glory of his great and holy name.

Paul goes on to say, "Now where remission of these is, there is *no more offering* for sin." For each sinner blessed by sovereign saving grace, there is no other offering required for their sins. Past, present and future, have been fully atoned for, once for ever, in the offering and sacrifice of our Lord Jesus Christ. O how that speaks to us still: "the blood of Jesus Christ his Son cleanseth us from all sin" (1 John 1:7). These are the realities of the faith once delivered unto the saints, the faith of which Paul says, "Let us hold fast the profession of our faith without wavering."

He goes on to say, "Having therefore, *brethren.*" See what a blessed and glorious privilege, divine grace bestows on sinners whom the Lord calls by grace and brings into true fellowship with himself. For remember, the Lord Jesus Christ and his people are *one* in an indissoluble union. And the blessings of that union are ever set before us in the precious word of God.

He says, "Having therefore, brethren, *boldness to enter into the holiest by the blood of Jesus.*" O what glorious things are set before us! You and I, as sinners brought by divine grace to believe and trust alone in the Lord Jesus Christ, have right of access even into the holiest, that is, into the very presence of God, there to be accepted by him! Friends, are not these great things? Is not this the reality of that faith "once delivered unto the saints"? (Jude 3). O may our souls be led more and more by the blessed teaching of the Holy Spirit into the believing realisation of these glorious truths, with wonder, love and praise unto the Lord our God.

He says, "By a new and living way, which he hath consecrated for us, through the veil, that is to say, his flesh." Yes, a new and living way and, blessed be the Lord's name, it is a way ever new and never to be closed up. It is a way, lined as it were, with the precious blood of Jesus Christ. I repeat again, it is only in the sacrifice of our Lord Jesus Christ that God is well pleased. And only on account of that one offering are sinners, called by grace, accepted by him.

"By a new and living way, which he hath consecrated for us, through the veil, that is to say, his flesh; and having an high priest over the house of God." See not only what Jesus has done for us, but what he is and ever will be to his people as a great high priest. All our coming to the Lord our God, all our access unto him, is through the person of our Lord Jesus Christ, that great high priest. And remember, he is the ever living One, ever living to make intercession for all that come unto God by him. Did he not comfort the apostle John with those words, "Fear not; I am the first and the last: I am he that liveth, and was dead; and, behold,

I am alive for evermore, Amen; and have the keys of hell and of death" (Rev. 1:17–18). What a blessed *"fear not."* And that still speaks to the people of God. "Fear not." Why? Because Jesus lives. He is the same today. He has all authority and power in heaven and earth. What's more, he is our great high priest. And as Paul says here "having an high priest over the house of God...Let us hold fast the profession of our faith without wavering."

The apostle continues, "And having an high priest over the house of God; let us draw near with a true heart in full assurance of faith, having our hearts sprinkled from an evil conscience, and our bodies washed with pure water." *"Full assurance of faith."* That is, the full assurance of the faith once delivered to the saints that these things are faithful and true. O what a wonder! As Peter says, "We have not followed cunningly devised fables" (2 Pet. 1:16). These are living realities revealed unto us in the truth of the gospel. They are sure and certain. This is still the word of God to *us*. O may the Lord bless us increasingly with the grace of living faith, in the believing receiving and cleaving to these things, as we are exhorted here. "Let us hold fast the profession of our faith without wavering." Ah, "He that hath an ear, let him hear what the Spirit saith unto the churches." Here is the word of the Lord unto *us*. O friends, may we daily seek grace to cleave fast to the Lord Jesus Christ, looking to him only and wholly, in all things that concern us for time and for eternity. May we indeed know, through his grace, true trust and confidence in him.

How often we find the working of unbelief rooted in our fallen nature. O what questions arise. When called to walk in trying paths how often we do not behold these truths as we should. They seem so dim and far off. And what's more, our soul's personal interest in them is questioned by the enemy of souls. Ah friends, we are subject to these changes. What cause we have to grieve over them and to come before God acknowledging our sinful weakness, crying unto him, "O LORD, I am oppressed; undertake for me," "Lord, I believe; help thou mine unbelief" (Isa. 38:14; Mark 9:24).

Paul says here, "let us draw near with a true heart in full assurance of faith." Whatever the enemy may say or do, whatever may confront us from within or without, *one thing alters not,* blessed be his great and holy name. It is the assurance we are given here that the things revealed to us in the gospel are faithful and true. Here the soul can find a sure anchor. O may we know the blessing of it by the teaching of the Holy Spirit. He says later in this epistle, "let us lay aside every weight, and the sin which doth so easily beset us, and let us run with patience the race that is set before us, *looking unto Jesus the author and finisher of our faith"* (Heb. 12:1–2). And again Paul declares, "God, willing more abundantly to shew unto the heirs of promise the immutability of his counsel, confirmed it by an oath: that by two immutable things, in which it was impossible for God to lie, we might have a strong consolation, who have fled for refuge to lay hold upon the hope set before us: which hope we have as an anchor of the soul, both sure and stedfast, and which entereth into that within the veil; whither the forerunner is for us entered, even Jesus, made an high priest for ever after the order of Melchisedec" (Heb. 6:20).

The point I am making is that our assurance is founded on the word of God himself. "In hope of eternal life, which God, *that cannot lie,* promised before the world began" (Titus 1:2). As we are reminded here, "he is faithful that promised." What assurance is given us that *the faith* once delivered to the saints is assuredly true, that is, what God has revealed in Jesus Christ of saving grace and mercy. And it is to this that the soul taught of God the Holy Spirit looks. In this it finds its rest and enjoys that peace with God which passeth all understanding. O may our souls be grounded and established more and more in the realisation of these things.

"Let us hold fast the profession of our faith without wavering," Is this what we profess? As brethren, I trust we ever desire to bear witness that we have been brought by grace to believe in the Lord Jesus Christ, who of God, is made unto us everything that pertains to the blessings of salvation. Do we not profess to believe the testimony God has given of his only begotten, beloved Son? "Let us hold fast the profession of our faith." Put it this way, what do we profess? Do we profess these things? Do we truly believe what is here set before us in the word? Friends, let us ever daily seek grace to hold fast to these things and not be moved away from the hope of the gospel. We meet with many hindrances in our path. O what stumbling blocks seem to be put in the way. Unbelief raises its ugly head as well. But let us ever be kept close to the Lord Jesus, looking to him in spite of all we find in self or outward circumstances. "Let us hold fast the profession of our faith without wavering," not being moved away from the blessed hope of the gospel, *"and so much the more, as ye see the day approaching."*

There is a day approaching when the Lord shall come the second time in power and great glory. It is the day of judgment which the word of God solemnly sets before us. We know not when that day will be, but we are assured it certainly will come. O to be found as those "looking for that blessed hope, and the glorious appearing of the great God and our Saviour Jesus Christ" (Titus 2:13). As our Lord Jesus Christ warns us in his word, may we be found ready and prepared when he shall come, or when he shall call for us. "Be ye also ready: for in such an hour as ye think not the Son of man cometh" (Matt. 24:44).

"Let us hold fast the profession of our faith without wavering; *(for he is faithful that promised.)"* Underlining all brought before in these verses is the faithfulness of God to what he has promised. Here we are reminded that the Lord our God is one on whom we may implicitly rely. As I have said already, he changeth not. He is faithful and true. Has he ever gone back on his word? Has one of his promises ever come to nothing? Has anyone who has been brought to trust in him and rest on his word of promise, professed finally that God has disappointed them by failing them in the hour they most needed his help? No. They may be tempted to fear that might be so, but blessed be the Lord's name, he is far better to us than our fears, far better then our deserts, far better than all that Satan may suggest to the contrary. "He is faithful that promised," and,

> "A faithful and unchanging God,
>   Lays the foundation of my hope,
>   In oaths, and promises, and blood."

As we go on in our text, we see that it has particular application to us. And as I said, "He that hath an ear, let him hear what the Spirit saith unto the churches." For the Holy Spirit still speaks here to his church and to us personally. O for grace to be given us to heed these things. "And let us consider one another to provoke unto love and to good works." Ah friends, should it not be our increasing concern to consider one another, preferring others before ourselves. O to enter more deeply into the true spirit of our Lord Jesus Christ. Remember the commandment the Lord gave his disciples in that upper room shortly before he went forth to Gethsemane and Calvary: "A new commandment I give unto you, That ye love one another; as I have loved you, that ye also love one another" (John 13:34). O, is not that word of the Lord as authoritative to us today as it has been to the church down the generations? How we need grace to fall under it and seek grace of the Lord to walk in the light of it in our relationships with one another as brethren in the Lord. May we prefer others before ourselves and seek one another's real good, not only in material things but in spiritual welfare as well. Are we not directed and encouraged to watch over one another? "Bear ye one another's burdens, and so fulfil the law of Christ" (Gal. 6:2). The Lord grant us grace so to do. Speaking for oneself, how I find I come so far short in this. O how much of self still cleaves to us. O may the Lord deliver us from self.

"To provoke unto love and to good works." What are these good works? Well, see before us the example of our Lord Jesus Christ. May we be humble followers of the Lamb. May we love one another as he has loved us. May we walk before him and with him, seeking his honour and glory. May we seek to know and do his will in all our relationships with one another as brethren in the Lord and as a church of Jesus Christ, as we journey on through life. O may each one of us be rightly concerned to know increasingly that flowing together to the goodness and mercy of the Lord made known to us. How this is described in that beautiful psalm: "Behold, how good and how pleasant it is for brethren to dwell together in unity!" (Ps. 133:1). Friends, that has application to each one of us in our attitudes and our concerns for one another. Not one of us has ground to look judgmentally at another. No, let us look at ourselves in this. "Behold, how good and how pleasant it is for brethren to dwell together in unity! It is like the precious ointment upon the head, that ran down upon the beard, even Aaron's beard: that went down to the skirts of his garments...for there the Lord commanded the blessing, even life for evermore."

And so we are to exhort one another unto love and good works. And the apostle goes on to give an exhortation which is as much the word of the Lord to us today as it has always been to the church of Jesus Christ. What has always distinguished the true church of Jesus Christ down the generations? It is the local congregations, their gatherings together for the worship of the Lord their God, and that *publicly* as well. He says here, "Not forsaking the assembling of ourselves together, as the manner of some is; but exhorting one another: and so much the more, as ye see the day approaching."

Now obviously this has very practical implications for us at this time, personally and as a church collectively. And I want at this juncture to read one or two things that I have come across recently which relate to the importance of assembling together with one another in the church of Jesus Christ. For it is the commandment of the Lord to us, designed for the welfare of the church under the Lord's blessing and above all for the glory of his name. It is also a witness to the world in which we live.

Firstly, "Each local congregation of believers is a house and temple of the living God. No material building is a house and temple of God; but the gathering, the assembling of the saints in the name of Christ to worship him is! When redeemed sinners gather in Christ's name, God the Holy Spirit makes the assembly his house. Such an assembly is 'an habitation of God through the Spirit.' God reveals his glory, gives out his law, makes known his will, bestows his blessing and instructs his people in his temple, his church. It is in this place that God speaks to men by the Spirit through his word.

In all ages the people of God have been known and identified by their public gatherings for worship. Wherever God has a people in this world, he has had a congregation to worship him. Sheep are always found in flocks. The only sheep that are alone are either lost or sick. And God's elect are sheep. No matter how few, they always gather together in public worship. In the public assembly they bare public, united testimony to the world of their Saviour's grace and glory. As an assembled body of believers they strengthen, cheer, comfort, encourage, edify, and help one another by prayer, praise and preaching of the word."

Secondly, "Our Saviour has promised that wherever his people gather in his name, he will be with them. To gather in Christ's name is to gather by faith in his name, for the honour of his name and to worship in his name. If only two or three gather to worship the Son of God, he will meet them. The old man, Simeon, found God's salvation, the Lord Jesus Christ, in the temple, the appointed place of public worship; and if we would see Christ we must come with his saints when they gather in the place of public worship."

Now I believe that is essentially what we are directed to in these words, "not forsaking the assembling of ourselves together, as the manner of some is." This is as vitally important to us in our day as it has been for the church down the generations. Now I know, as I said a moment ago, this has a very practical implication for us at this particular time. I know that over recent weeks we have been subject to the requirements of the government not to meet together for the worship of the Lord's name. Now we have suffered that over these weeks, but I feel there comes a time when we must begin to look very closely at this matter as it particularly concerns us here as a church and people. I know we are directed in the word to obey those in authority over us, but friends, this can put us in a dilemma that the church of Jesus Christ has faced many times down the generations. Authorities may require and demand one thing, but the word of God requires another. It is so with us. The government says we should not meet. The word of God says we should meet together. The Lord has promised to be with and bless his people when they meet. So it comes to this point, who do we have to believe and how do we act in this matter? How did the apostles act when confronted with a similar dilemma? I know you may say the circumstances are very different. In one sense they are, but the principle remains. They said, "We ought to obey God rather than men" (Acts 5:29). And though they were commanded not to meet or even speak in his name, they immediately went away and continued to meet and preach. Look at Daniel and the three Hebrew children in the old testament.

The point I am making is how this principle respects us at this particular time. I know we have honoured what the government required over us these weeks. The time is now coming when we must look at this matter more closely. What does the Lord require of us? What is his word to us? His word is here in our subject this evening. "He that hath an ear, let him hear what the Spirit saith unto the churches." What then is the practical application of this to us here at this time? Well, what I am saying is this: in the next two weeks there will be a decision made on the opening of the chapel here and the resuming of our public worship, hopefully early next month, God willing. Now I know there may well be differences among us over this matter. What I am saying is that each one must be free to make their own decision as they see it, led of the Lord, with regard to the situation as it concerns them personally. And we must accept one another's decision in this matter. Friends, I leave it with you and with the Lord with regard to going forward in this matter. What I am saying is that, subject to the Lord's will and wholly in dependence upon the Lord, within the next two weeks we will make a decision when the chapel be opened and those that are able to come are free to do so and no criticism whatsoever will be made of the decision you make in your personal consideration of the matter. We are to accept one another's position in these things. I trust we may find a union and fellowship together. All I can say is, see how we are here directed by the word of God. And surely we must be so directed as his people and not by what man says. We acknowledge human authority in all secular matters but what saith the Lord to us in our text this evening?

"Let us hold fast the profession of our faith without wavering; (for he is faithful that promised.)" Yes, we have a faithful, loving God upon whom we can wholly depend. All our life, all our concerns, are in his hand. And this matter in which we are found is no different. The dangers that may threaten by this virus are in the hand of our God and we are in his hand as well. Shall we not rest there by his enabling grace?

"Consider one another to provoke unto love and to good

works: not forsaking the assembling of ourselves together, as the manner of some is; but exhorting one another: and so much the more, as ye see the day approaching." That day approaching! The day is fast hasting with some of us when the Lord shall call us. And there is that day when he will come in power and great glory.

I will leave the remarks there tonight. I leave it with the Lord. May his blessing attend his word. Amen.

26

THROUGH DEATH HE MIGHT DESTROY HIM THAT HAD THE POWER OF DEATH

Lord's day morning 24 May 2020

"Forasmuch then as the children are partakers of flesh and blood, he also himself likewise took part of the same; that through death he might destroy him that had the power of death, that is, the devil; And deliver them who through fear of death were all their lifetime subject to bondage" (Hebrews 2:14-15).

What a glorious testimony the apostle bears in the opening verses of this epistle to the person of our Lord and Saviour Jesus Christ as the head over all things to the church. "God, who at sundry times and in divers manners spake in time past unto the fathers by the prophets, hath in these last days spoken unto us *by his Son.*" Though Paul was writing to the Hebrews, this epistle speaks to the people of God still. Without question, all holy scripture is the word of the Lord to his church and his people individually. May we know its personal application at this time and throughout our lives as taught of God the Holy Spirit. See the foundation laid for our encouragement in that the Lord *still speaks to us by his word* and that "he hath in these last days spoken unto us *by his Son*, whom he hath appointed heir of all things, by whom also he made the worlds; who being the brightness of his glory, and the express image of his person, and upholding all things by the word of his power, when he had by himself purged our sins, sat down on the right hand of the Majesty on high."

Those truths concerning Christ are gloriously set before us throughout this epistle. O what words of grace! Surely the Holy Spirit ever directs us to Jesus Christ alone and brings us to trust in him at all times, even at this present time. Fears prevail around us. And there is the working in our own spirit of the sin which so easily besets us. There are fears in personal matters which press heavily upon us. But the apostle points us to our Lord Jesus Christ. He assures that all things and all our times are in the hands of him who is "a merciful and faithful high priest in things pertaining to God." We are assured he ministers to his people as the great head of the church. He is the glorious *King* in Zion, the great *High Priest* over the house of God, the great *Prophet* to the church. O what a mercy if our ears are open to hear what the Lord says to us.

Our text assures us of the great love of the Lord Jesus to his own, even though he is so high, glorious and lifted up. He has been so from all eternity, as the eternal Son of God, one with the Father and the Holy Spirit, one God over all. O friends, what wonders are set before us here. "Forasmuch then as the children are partakers of flesh and blood, he also himself likewise took part of the same." What grace, what love is here manifest! He, co-equal with the Father and the Holy Spirit, is found in fashion as a man! Is there a greater wonder set before us in the scriptures, especially when they assure us that this was appointed for the glory of God in the redemption of such sinners as you and me? Remember what the angel of the Lord declared to Joseph, "Thou shalt call his name JESUS: for he shall save his people from their sins" (Matt. 1:21). O what a glorious name is that! His name shall be called Jesus to express the truth that he is the *one* Saviour of his people. As sinners, they have no part in obtaining salvation. They are merely recipients of the riches of God's grace and mercy. All the blessings of salvation for sinful men and women whom the Father has given to his Son, come freely and fully through Jesus. All is to the praise of the glory of *his* name. All is for the spiritual, eternal welfare of every poor, needy, guilty, hell-deserving sinner to whom these things are made known by the Lord the Holy Spirit.

"Forasmuch then as the *children* are partakers of flesh and blood." Who are these children? They are those whom the Father has loved, chosen and given to his only begotten and dearly beloved Son before the foundation of the world. Jesus himself declares, "Behold I and the children which God hath given me." Jesus came forth for their salvation and in his life, sufferings, death and glorious resurrection fulfilled all that was demanded for their redemption. These are they to whom the blessings of salvation are made known by the sovereign operations of the Holy Spirit.

What a mercy, what a wonder, that salvation is in the hands of him "for whom are all things and by whom are all things." And "it became him... in bringing many sons unto glory, to make the captain of their salvation perfect through sufferings." The purpose of all this was to bring many sons to glory. Is not that set forth in the great high priestly prayer of our Lord Jesus Christ in John seventeen? "Father, I will that they also, whom thou hast given me, be with me where I am; that they may behold my glory, which thou hast given me: for thou lovedst me before the foundation of the world" (John 17:24). Friends, these are glorious realities which can never fail to be fully realised in the eternal welfare of each one to whom this salvation is made known by the Holy Spirit. For it is by the inward witness of the Spirit we are brought to truly know the blessedness of being sons and daughters of God, heirs of God and joint heirs with Christ Jesus. By the Spirit we are brought to cry "Abba, Father" (Rom. 8:15). O the blessed wonder of it! Can this world give us anything greater or more glorious? A sinner, wholly deserving the wrath of God as a transgressor of his holy law, yet blessed as one whom God hath reconciled to himself by the redemption in Christ Jesus! One who has the witness of the Holy Spirit that God has loved them, chosen them and called them by his grace! One brought into the blessings of that eternal covenant in which they are God's sons and daughters, joint heirs as one with Christ Jesus!

And remember, this union is an *eternal* union. Nothing can undermine its blessedness.

> "One with Jesus,
>   By eternal union one."

Neither sin, Satan nor all the believer may pass through in this life can destroy this union. Yes, the felt enjoyment of it in our personal experience can at times be sadly disturbed by many questionings as to whether we know anything savingly of the truth that is in Christ Jesus. How active is Satan in seeking to undermine the believer's confidence in the things they have received by the Holy Spirit's blessed application of the word to them. O friends, what is the foundation of the faith and hope of the people of God? It is not in what we feel though we want to have right feelings. The foundation is what God has spoken to us in the holy scriptures concerning his unchanging love and faithfulness. What he has promised he will most surely fulfil. Faith looks not to self but to the Lord Jesus Christ alone. It finds consolation only in the word and promise of our faithful God. "God is not a man, that he should lie; neither the son of man, that he should repent: hath he said, and shall he not do it? or hath he spoken, and shall he not make it good?" (Num. 23:19).

"Forasmuch then as the children are partakers of flesh and blood, he also himself likewise took part of the same." Wonder above wonders that God should be found manifest in the flesh! That the eternal Son of God should take into union with his divine nature, human nature, the flesh and blood of those his Father gave him! And this union of the divine and human natures in the person of our Lord Jesus Christ is *eternal*. It is never to be severed. We see him born of Mary, laid as a babe in a manger at Bethlehem, growing in wisdom and stature as a real man. We see his life, ministry, sufferings and death in the records of the gospel. And the same glorious God-man has entered heaven itself to reign in the presence of God for us.

See also, in the verses following our text, the wonder of the love of the Lord Jesus Christ as the great high priest of his people: "Wherefore in all things it behoved him to be made like unto his brethren, that he might be a merciful and faithful high priest in things pertaining to God, to make reconciliation for the sins of the people. For in that he himself hath suffered being tempted, he is able to succour them that are tempted." Is not that a word of encouragement for you and me today? The Lord knows all things that concern us, and he is able to succour us in all the fears engendered by our trials, temptations, weakness, sinfulness and need. Not only is he able but O the loving willingness of the Lord Jesus Christ! See how he condescends to his own. Blessed be his great and holy name, his people are not left entirely to their own devices. If that were so, where would we be? What are we to look to and rely upon? We have one that is well described as "a friend [that] loveth at all times, and a brother is born for adversity" (Prov. 17:17).

The main thought I want to bring before you this morning is at the end of our text: "that through death he might destroy him that had the power of death, that is, the devil; and deliver them who through fear of death were all their lifetime subject to bondage." Now what a solemn subject is death, the scourge of the human race. Friends, does not human nature recoil from the very thought of death? There is little speaking about death. Sadly and solemnly, we know what fears are engendered by the deaths resulting from the virus abroad in the earth at present. And I say that death is a very solemn subject indeed. What I would emphasis is that *it is appointed unto all men once to die*. It is an appointment not one of us can escape. Young or old. the day is coming when the place that knows us now shall know us again no more for ever. So this is not just to be viewed in a passing way. It is a solemn fact. Sadly, many may be carried off by death at this present time. We would rightly sympathise with those that thus suffer the loss of loved ones. But friends, let us come to ourselves. How solemnly true is what the wise woman of Tekoah said to David: "we must needs die, and are as water spilt on the ground, which cannot be gathered up again" (2 Sam. 14:14). No man can escape the solemn appointment. Death is the *certain* consequence of our sin.

But that woman also said to David, "Yet doth [God] devise means, that his banished be not expelled from him." See how those means are gloriously set before us in our text. "Forasmuch then as the children are partakers of flesh and blood, he also himself likewise took part of the same; that through death he might destroy him that had the power of death, that is, the devil; and deliver them who through fear of death were all their lifetime subject to bondage." Yes, the very God against whom we have sinned *has* appointed glorious means! "The wages of sin is death; but the gift of God is eternal life through Jesus Christ our Lord" (Rom. 6:23).

The question might be asked how is it that the devil has "the power of death"? Was it not in the deceiving of our first parents that "sin entered into the world and death by sin; and so death passed upon all men, for that all have sinned"? (Rom. 5:12). Thus Adam and Eve came under the curse and condemnation of the holy law of God. And did not the devil obtain the power over all the human race to hold them in bondage to sin and death? Most certainly that is so. Is not this bondage in sin solemnly manifest? Is there one upon earth of whom it can be said they have no sin? The word tells us that "There is none that doeth good, no, not one...all have sinned, and come short of the glory of God" (Rom. 3:12,23). So then all are under the curse and subject to death. That not only means the separation of soul and body. It means *eternal* death. And such it must ever be apart from sovereign, distinguishing grace and God's provision of our Lord Jesus Christ who through death destroyed him that had the power of death. What a powerful influence does death have on the human race. I said we do not like to speak of these things. We put the day of our death far from us. How little does it enter our thoughts amidst our daily activities. Yet we are solemnly reminded, we know not "what a day may bring forth" (Prov. 27:1), not even an hour. O the Lord prepare us for his will! Friends, how vitally important that we be brought to know him who alone delivers from the power of death and from the *fear* of death as well. See how this is accomplished. See the means God devised to deliver his people from the power the devil obtained by deceiving our first parents to bring them into bondage to sin and death. No power of man can save us from death. But as I have already said, the God against whom we have sinned has accomplished deliverance by his only begotten and dearly beloved Son, our Lord Jesus Christ.

Ah friends, death is a powerful thing. No man can deliver himself from it. But there is something more powerful than death. You may say, what is that? What is *more powerful* than the power of death over fallen men and women, *even* over the bodies of the Lord's people laid in the grave until the resurrection of the dead? What power is greater than death? *It is the love of God revealed in Christ Jesus our Lord*. It is only through the love of God that the blessings of salvation flow to sinners to deliver them from

death, from *eternal* death, the due desert of their sins and transgressions. And we are here told God himself has accomplished
this deliverance *"through death."* See the cost! Yes, salvation
comes full and free to sinners to whom this blessing is made
known by sovereign grace. But great was the price paid! O what
a wonder this is! The eternal God took human nature, sin
excepted, into union with his divine nature. For what purpose?
That by death he himself, in his sacred person, should suffer the
just deserts of the law-breakers his Father had given him. He
endured what they justly deserved, to deliver them from the curse
and condemnation of God's law and to bring them pardon, peace
and everlasting life. He, who is life itself, experienced death!
Divinity cannot die but God manifest in the flesh, the Lord Jesus
Christ, truly laid down his life. He said, "I lay down my life for
the sheep...I lay down my life...that I might take it again...this
commandment have I received of my Father" (John 10:15,17,18).
Yes, no man took his life from him.

> "How willing was Jesus to die?
> That we wretched sinners might live
> The life they could not take away
> How willing was Jesus to give?"

Ah friends, eternal praises be to our triune God, as revealed
in the person of Jesus Christ, for all that he is and has done. "That
through death he might destroy him that had the power of death,
that is, the devil; and deliver them who through fear of death were
all their lifetime subject to bondage."

As I said a moment ago, death is the scourge of the human
race. O what fears it engenders. But see the assurance given to
every poor sinner brought by divine grace to believe and trust
alone in the Lord Jesus Christ. If we are brought to solemnly
realise our sin and guilt, and brought to cry to the Lord for mercy,
he will surely hear that cry. Does the Lord Jesus ever send one
empty away who is brought as a sinner to his feet? You know, in
the midst of all the fear engendered by the sickness and death
around us, O what divine consolation there is for the believer in
the Lord Jesus Christ!

"Destroy him that had the power of death, that is, the devil."
What a precious truth is here brought before us! Indeed, the Lord

Jesus *has* overcome sin, Satan, death and the grave. Satan is unquestionably a conquered foe. But he is still active in the world in harassing the living family of God. O how painfully we experience in our daily lives, the stirring up of that sin which so easily besets us and the temptations to which we are subject. Satan is still a very active foe. But though a powerful foe, he is wholly under the power of our Lord and Saviour Jesus Christ. Did not Jesus assure John of this on Patmos, when he said to him, "I am he that liveth, and was dead; and, behold, I am alive for evermore, Amen; and *have the keys* of hell and of death" (Rev. 1:18). They are not in the hands of the devil, blessed be the Lord's name. The keys of hell and death are in the hands of our Lord Jesus Christ. He has delivered his people from death.

You say, but every believer must die unless the Lord returns first. Yes, they will die, but in a real sense they do *not* die. The body dies but the redeemed soul lives. And Paul says that to be absent from the body is to be present with the Lord. Human nature fears death. But as we rightly view these things in the light of God's word, does the believer have just cause to fear death? Fallen human nature is apprehensive of what will be the means and manner of our death but are we not assured the Lord will give grace for that hour? He giveth "grace and glory" (Ps. 84:11). He has upheld and provided for us thus far in life's journey. Will we then be denied dying grace in a dying hour? The Lord said to Paul, "My grace is sufficient for thee: for my strength is made perfect in weakness" (2 Cor. 12:9). That is true in all the path the Lord appoints his people as they journey on through life. But surely it will be so in that last hour. Friends, cannot we look to the Lord and trust in him? What is the gift of God-given faith for, if it is not for us to trust wholly in the Lord? Yes, very real fears afflict us. But see what the Lord says here: "to deliver them who through fear of death were all their lifetime subject to bondage." The Lord Jesus assures us he "hath abolished death, and hath brought life and immortality to light through the gospel" (2 Tim. 1:10). It is in the gospel that all our hope is found. It tells us who Jesus is and what he has done for us. Are we not therein assured, "The LORD also hath put away thy sin; thou shalt not die"? (2 Sam. 12:13).

"If sin be pardoned, I'm secure;
Death has no sting beside."

Though we pass through the portals of death, Paul says, "absent from the body" is "to be present with the Lord" (2 Cor. 5:8).

We know there is rejoicing when a babe is born into this world. And though in the death of the believer there is sadness and sorrow for those who are left behind but surely the scriptures remind us that "the day of death [is better] than the day of one's birth" (Eccl. 7:1). For the day of the believer's death is the entering into glory in the immediate presence of our Lord Jesus Christ.

"Forasmuch then as the children are partakers of flesh and blood, he also himself likewise took part of the same; that through death he might destroy him that had the power of death, that is, the devil. And deliver them who through fear of death were all their lifetime subject to bondage." Though the devil harries the people of God he can never destroy them. Though he seeks to undermine our confidence in our Lord Jesus Christ and what he had done for us, yet blessed be God, our Jesus lives and prays for us. As he said to Peter, "I have prayed for thee, that thy faith fail not" (Luke 22:32). All our encouragement is in the fact that Jesus lives. He is still our great high priest over the house of God. He ever liveth to make intercession for us. He is able to save us even unto the uttermost.

Friends, the day is fast hastening when the devil shall be bruised under the feet of God's people. The assurance is given us that as Jesus overcame, so his people are more than conquerors through him that loved them. "Who through fear of death were all their life time subject to bondage." That fear often prevails over us. But O friends, I say again, remember the consolation of which the gospel assures us. Though we die, Jesus lives, and his people most assuredly shall live with him, live through him and unto him to all eternity, to the praise of the glory of his great and holy name. Are not these things well summed up in the words of Jesus to Martha, "I am the resurrection, and the life: he that believeth in me, though he were dead, yet shall he live: and whosoever liveth and believeth in me shall never die. Believest thou this?" (John 11:26). Glorious truth! In a real sense, the believer never dies. His body is laid in the grave. There is the separation of soul and body but the redeemed soul enters immediately into the presence of their Lord. What a glorious prospect is that! What a blessed heritage is ours! On what ground are we assured of it? Are we deserving of it? No. It is because of what Jesus Christ is and has done for us.

In the opening verses of this epistle, we are told that, "When he [Jesus] had by himself purged our sins, [he] sat down on the right hand of the Majesty on high." And as *he* has overcome, so every poor sinner brought through his grace to believe and trust in him, is more than conqueror through him that loved us. Where Jesus is, there shall they be also. Is it not then vitally important that we not only know about these things but, through grace, are brought as poor sinners to *know him* and to *trust in him* only? Ah friends, fears prevail but our Lord Jesus Christ, blessed be his name, "is the same yesterday, and to day and forever" (Heb. 13:8). We are assured that he is still our great, glorious, merciful and faithful high priest in all things pertaining to God. He has made reconciliation for the sins of his people and is able to succour them that are tempted. May the Lord Jesus Christ grant us the rich consolations that are treasured up in him. To his name alone be all the praise.

The Lord add his blessing. Amen.

27

WE HAVE A GREAT HIGH PRIEST

Lord's day evening 24 May 2020

"Seeing then that we have a great high priest, that is passed into the heavens, Jesus the Son of God, let us hold fast our profession. For we have not an high priest which cannot be touched with the feeling of our infirmities; but was in all points tempted like as we are, yet without sin. Let us therefore come boldly unto the throne of grace, that we may obtain mercy, and find grace to help in time of need" (Hebrews 4:14–16).

What great and precious things are set before us in our text concerning our Lord Jesus Christ, the great high priest who has entered into heaven to appear in the presence of God for us. The assurance is given that he is not remote from us. As needy sinners blessed with living faith, we are accepted by him when we come to the throne of his grace.

I want to consider the context of these words. First of all, notice to whom the apostle writes. In the opening verse of chapter three, he says, "Wherefore, holy brethren, partakers of the heavenly calling, consider the Apostle and High Priest of our profession, Christ Jesus." Yes, this epistle was first addressed to the people of God among the Jews. But it is the word of the Lord to his church and people still. "Holy brethren, partakers of the heavenly calling." What a distinguishing mark this is of sinners saved by grace, brought to the solemn realisation that they are ruined by sin, and their salvation is only by the person and finished work of the Lord Jesus. All is of God's appointing and providing. All is only made known to them by the sovereign operations of the Holy Spirit. It is certain they are not "holy brethren, partakers of the heavenly calling" of themselves. All is entirely the work of God's grace in them to his praise. How great and high are the privileges of divine grace in those whom the Lord owns as his children, having loved them with an everlasting love and *called* them with an heavenly calling.

Paul gives gracious instruction to these brethren in the situation in which they were found. How best could that be described? "Without were fightings, within were fears" (2 Cor. 7:5). Is that not often the case with the church of God and with us personally as believers going forward in the path appointed for us? *Without are fightings* in our distresses by outward circumstances, and *within are fears* through the temptations of the evil one and the working of sin which so easily besets us. Notice in these chapters three and four the emphasis placed on the word *"today."* "To day if ye will hear his voice, harden not your hearts."

Some would speak of this *today* as if it is a day of grace which may pass away for ever if we reject the word. That is Arminian freewill rubbish, not the apostle's teaching. This is the word of the Lord *to his people* for all times and circumstances. It is a word to which we still need to give heed and most certainly in our circumstances at present. Where were these brethren directed in all their troubles? Where are we directed? To "consider the Apostle and High Priest of our profession, Christ Jesus." He is the one greater than Moses. He is the great head of the church to whom all authority and power is given in heaven and earth. He is the great high priest who is not remote from us but is personally involved in everything concerning each of his own. The Lord our God, our Lord Jesus Christ, though throned in heaven, is present with his people. Have we not the promise that he is present with us through the indwelling of the Holy Spirit? The Lord assures us that his eye is ever upon his people. He knows all their circumstances.

In these chapters there is reference to the journeyings of Israel in the wilderness. Did not the Lord provide for them? Was not his presence manifestly with them in the cloudy pillar by day and the pillar of fire by night? Did he not deliver them from all their enemies? But what was their response? Here is a warning to us today in all the troubles which beset the church of Jesus Christ and believers personally. The instruction is: let us not be moved away from the glorious hope of the gospel.

"To keep our eyes on Jesus fixed,
And there our hope to stay,
The Lord will make his goodness pass
Before us in the way."

What a great fight of faith it is to look to, and trust only in, the Lord Jesus Christ in all our afflictions, temptations and fears! Even when we cannot trace him we are still to trust him. The Lord's dealings are often strange and mysterious to us. They may be so in our present situation. Human reasoning cannot fathom out the Lord's dealings. But there is a warning here. "Harden not your hearts, as in the provocation, in the day of temptation in the wilderness." How they provoked God. O may the Lord truly deliver us from all the sinful staggerings of unbelief. Of ourselves, we are no better than they. How this emphasises that we must trust in the Lord alone in all our difficulties. Is it an easy thing to commit our way and concerns into his hands? Is it an easy thing for us to trust only in the Lord when confronted with the issues that may be in our path? O how we suffer the temptations of the evil one and the working of our fallen nature. Is it easy for us to believe, to look and cleave alone to the Lord? Friends, we find it impossible if left to ourselves. But, blessed be the Lord's great and holy name, his people are not left utterly to themselves. Yes, there is much waywardness, much forget-fulness with us, much lack of appreciation of the Lord's kindness, care and mercies lengthened out towards us. We still possess a fallen nature with its innate tendency to turn away from God and to look to man and created things. But here we are directed and encouraged to look to the Lord alone.

He says, "To day if you will hear his voice, harden not your hearts" as did those fathers of these Hebrew brethren. O how they forgot God. As soon as difficulties and troubles arose, they murmured and complained and even prepared to return to Egypt. The implication was that God was unfaithful. Though he had promised much he did not appear to be fulfilling his promises, particularly the great promise he had spoken to Abraham that he would bring his posterity into the land where he had lived as a stranger. Great was the prospect set before them in the possession of the land of Canaan, a land flowing with milk and honey. It was a great contrast to their experience in Egypt and to the wilderness through which they were passing. Was that prospect a small thing? Surely not. Yet what do we find? As soon as difficulties and trials arose they despised God's word and promise. Sadly, we see their unbelief. They did not believe They did not trust in the Lord. And here the apostle gives a warning to these holy brethren, partakers of the heavenly calling, against unbelief. It is not that a true believer can come short of what God has promised. But we can lose much enjoyment and peace in our souls through the workings of unbelief rooted in our fallen nature. O these are not unimportant matters for the spiritual welfare and peace of the living family of God and for the showing forth the praises of him who hath called us "out of darkness into his marvellous light" (1 Pet. 2:9). How do we show forth his praises? Is it not in daily seeking grace to humbly trust him, to rest upon his word and promise? Is it not to contend earnestly against the working of our fallen nature which draws us away from trust in the Lord God of our salvation?

The apostle also tells us that in the wilderness the gospel was preached to them as it is preached to us. The Lord gave Israel great promises of his care and provision in the wilderness. How much more so is that for the people of God in his full revelation to us in the gospel. The Lord made known his goodness to those Israelites by outward forms and signs. How much more is the goodness and mercy of our God opened up to us in the glorious truth of the gospel. For it sets before us, not only the promise of the life that now is, but also of that which is to come. Our Lord Jesus Christ, the great high priest over the house of God, is one whom we can trust. He has loved us and washed us from our sins in his own blood. He laid down his life for us. Can he then turn away from one of his weak, fearful people, beset with fightings without and fears within? Is there no consolation, no word from the Lord for them? One says,

> "He who has helped me hitherto,
> Will help me all my journey through."

The whole emphasis here is on warning us against departing in any way from the living God. How sad it was when our Lord Jesus Christ had been affirming that they must eat his flesh and drink his blood spiritually. Many said, "This is an hard saying; who can hear it?" Many "went back, and walked no more with him." "Will ye also go away?" he asks (John 6:67). Is not that still a question for the people of God? As Haggai spoke to the remnant discouraged by the difficulties they encountered in Jerusalem: "Thus saith the LORD of hosts, Consider your ways." Is that not still the word of the Lord to us? O friends, amidst all the fightings without and fears within, we are here directed to the precious truth of the gospel, to the Lord's constant care, kindness and provision for his people. As Paul said, "My God shall supply all your need according to his riches in glory by Christ Jesus" (Phil. 4:19). Yes, not one of the Lord's people shall ever be finally left destitute of the promised grace of God to help in every time of need. What a sure provision is in Jesus! O there is no failing in his grace. In every situation in which they are found he assures his people of his help, his upholding, his keeping and preserving them, his enabling them to persevere even unto his heavenly kingdom. Does not *this* assurance uphold the Lord's people? It is *not* their own abilities, wisdom and strength. It is as they are brought increasingly to realise their utter dependence on the Lord. How weak we are in ourselves, and truly so in all spiritual things. What a mercy if we are brought to increasingly realise, not only our weakness and unprofitableness, but that:

"Weak in myself, in him I'm strong;
His Spirit's voice I hear.
The way I walk cannot be wrong,
If Jesus be but there."

Though weak in myself, yet if the Lord Jesus Christ is with me, have I not a friend who loveth at all times, a brother born for adversity? (Prov. 17:17). Have I not one to whom I am ever encouraged to look, one whom I can lean hard upon? O to cleave closer, by the Lord's enabling grace, to him who has loved us. Is his love to his people fickle, variable? Does it depend on their response to the love of the Lord to them? No. His love is full, free, and everlasting.

How oft we have provoked him. How often have we experienced his chastening hand as did Israel in the wilderness. Yet did he forsake them utterly? Has he forsaken his people? Will

260 NORMAN ROE—SERMONS MARCH–JULY 2020

he forsake us? No, we are assured of his faithfulness to all he has spoken. And so the apostle warns us not to harden our hearts in unbelief. "Let us therefore fear, lest, a promise being left us of entering into his rest, any of you should seem to come short of it. For unto us was the gospel preached, as well as unto them: but the word preached did not profit them, not being mixed with faith in them that heard it." Friends, how important that we not only hear with our outward ear the gospel preaching but faith be mixed with what we hear, to believe and receive the word. This is truly the work of God's grace. O may we daily ask the Lord for his word to come to us not "in word only but also in power, and in the Holy Ghost, and in much assurance" (1 Thess. 1:5). O may the word abide in us in "all wisdom and spiritual understanding" (Col. 1:9). What is the fruit of it? It brings us to increasingly realise that,

> "I am a sinner and nothing at all,
> But Jesus Christ is my all and in all."

The apostle goes on to say, "we which have believed do enter into rest." The prospect before the children of Israel was the rest of Canaan, the land flowing with milk and honey which God had promised them. How much greater is the rest set before us in the gospel. Therein is pardon, peace and eternal life as we are brought by the teaching of the Holy Spirit to believe and trust alone in the Lord Jesus Christ. He, the great high priest, has obtained eternal salvation for us by his life, sufferings, death and resurrection, as set forth so beautifully by Paul in this epistle! The high priest was to deal for men in things pertaining to God. How essential that he offer a sacrifice to God for the sins of the people! O the glorious fulfilment of this in our Lord Jesus Christ "who through the eternal Spirit offered himself without spot to God"! (Heb. 9:14). He fully satisfied all the demands of God's holy law for all the sins of his people. When they were enemies, they were reconciled to God by the death of his Son.

The apostle speaks here of a rest that remains to the people of God. The entering of Israel into rest in Canaan was all of God. He had gone before them and was with them. Though Joshua was raised up as the instrument in the Lord's hand to lead them into the land of Canaan, yet the attaining of that rest was all of God, according to his promise. But there is another rest spoken of here, not an earthly but an eternal inheritance. We are here assured that "there remaineth therefore a rest to the people of God." What is *this* rest? He goes on to say, "For he that is entered into his rest, he also hath ceased from his own works, as God did from his." *Who* has entered into his rest? Surely it is our Lord Jesus Christ who *finished* the work his Father had given him. Salvation is *sure*. It is a *finished* work. It meets all the demands of a holy God in the redemption of his people, to the glory of his name. It speaks to the Lord's people, sinners such as you and me, not of something we have to do but something which is *done*. In this alone the soul, blessed with God-given faith, finds true rest and peace. It is not in what I can do, though we desire by grace to be true followers of Jesus in the exercise of faith which worketh by love. But the whole of my salvation, my standing before God, my acceptance with God *is wholly in what Jesus Christ has done for me*.

God finished the work of creation in six days and rested on the seventh day satisfied with all that he had created. And God is well pleased with the finished work of our Lord Jesus Christ, and well pleased with all for whom Jesus lived and died and rose again. "He [Jesus] that is entered into his rest, he also hath ceased from his own works, as God did from his."

The apostle then says, *"Let us labour therefore to enter into that rest,* lest any man fall after the same example of unbelief." That is, cease from all our own works, bad or good. Faith brings us to look not to anything in ourselves. What is so rooted in our fallen human nature, to which even the Lord's people are prone to look, and from which we need the grace of God to ever keep us? *Self-righteousness.* O we think there is something we must do to obtain or maintain the favour of God. Friends, the favour of God, his mercies to his people come *freely* to us. By enabling grace, may we be a people that know and love the Lord, and seek to know and do his will in our day. But that does not commend us to God. Our hope is not based on that foundation. No, it is upon what Jesus is and what he has done for us. "Let us labour therefore to enter into that rest." Let us cease from our own labourings, from our own works, bad or good, and trust only in

Jesus Christ. Friends, there is no other foundation for you and me as sinners except Jesus Christ and what he has done for us. All the fulness of the blessings of this rest that "remaineth" is founded in him. What did God the Father say? "This is my beloved Son, in whom I am well pleased" (Matt. 3:17). And that embraces all who are made partakers of Christ. They are one with him in an eternal union, blessed be the Lord's great name.

"Let us labour therefore to enter into that rest, lest any man fall after the same example of unbelief. For the word of God is quick, and powerful, and sharper than any two-edged sword, piercing even to the dividing asunder of soul and spirit, and of the joints and marrow, and is a discerner of the thoughts and intents of the heart. Neither is there any creature that is not manifest in his sight: but all things are naked and opened unto the eyes of him with whom we have to do." What a description is this of our great high priest, the Lord Jesus Christ. For the expression "word of God" embraces both the written and, essentially, the incarnate Word. Friends, here is a word of solemn warning. May each one of us ever know its searching power in the sense that there is nothing that concerns us, within or without, which is not known to the Lord. He sees all things which man does not see, even the innermost motives of our hearts. He sees all our situations and needs. Are you troubled and distressed? Do not think this is unknown to the Lord. This word of God is searching yet also encouraging. For look what follows: "Seeing then that we have a great high priest, that is passed into the heavens, Jesus the Son of God, let us hold fast our profession. For we have not an high priest which cannot be touched with the feeling of our infirmities; but was in all points tempted like as we are, yet without sin."

O friends, the Lord understands our every need and concern. He knows our outward fightings and the inward fears that possess us. Where are we directed? Not to seek to hide or cover things. We cannot succeed. May we know true openness and honesty in coming before our God, in pouring out our hearts before him in true confession of our sins, and in bringing to him all that is found in our situation. What is one of the Lord's important commands to his people? Though a command, it is often little considered as such. Remember, his commandments are not grievous. This command surely speaks to his tried, exercised, fearful people. *Come!* "Come unto me, all ye that labour and are heavy laden, and *I will give you rest*" (Matt. 11:28). I know that is often described as a gospel invitation. But it is much more. It speaks to the tried, exercised, needy and burdened of the Lord's people no less today than in generations past. "Come unto me." Where can we go? O what a mercy to realise more and more that in Jesus Christ is all our help and hope. Can we obey this gracious command to come to the Lord Jesus of ourselves? No, but it is the fruit of his grace. And the evidence of that grace of living faith in the life of a child of God is a continual coming to the Lord Jesus Christ. It is a coming to him every step of life's journey, ever as needy sinners in ourselves, yet possessing all things as one with him. So we are commanded: "Casting all your care upon him; for he careth for you" (1 Pet. 5:7).

"Seeing then that we have a great high priest, that is passed into the heavens, Jesus the Son of God, let us hold fast our profession. For we have not an high priest which cannot be touched with the feeling of our infirmities; but was in all points tempted like as we are, yet without sin." Friends, what encouragement is given us here. The Lord knows all the secret things in your life which nobody else knows and over which you may be mourning before him. You cry to him but at times no answer seems to come. Yet he knows, his eye is on his people, his compassion toward them fails not. He is faithful to the word and promise he has spoken. What encouragement then is thus given us to come to Jesus. Let us therefore come to him.

"Today if ye will hear his voice, harden not your hearts." What is the Lord's voice to his people? It is not *depart* but *come*. What is the Lord's voice to us today? Here it is: "Let us therefore *come* boldly unto the throne of grace, that we may obtain mercy, and find grace to help in time of need." That is the Lord's word to us today, blessed be his name. It does not change with changing circumstances. His word to us is still, "Come unto me, all ye that labour and are heavy laden." Come to him, as directed here, "that we may obtain mercy, and find grace to help in time of need."

We do not come as those who have merited mercy. For surely the words *mercy* and *grace* are counter to any idea of worth or merit. You know, Satan is very active by fightings without and fears within to trouble us with such thoughts as this: 'See what you are and where you are. Look at those sins in your heart and life. How can you expect the Lord to hear or answer? Yes, if things were different with you, if there was some improvement in your behaviour, if you turned away from this, that or the other, then there might be some hope for you.' Friend, remember Satan is a liar. He plays on the unbelief rooted in our fallen nature. O Lord, deliver us from the workings of the evil one upon our fallen nature! "Today if ye will hear his voice, harden not your hearts." Hear what *the Lord says,* not what Satan says, not what unbelief says.

The Lord says, "Come unto me." "Let us therefore come boldly unto the throne of grace, that we may obtain mercy, and find grace to help in time of need." This is not merely an invitation. It is the word of the Lord to us. And what the Lord says, he means and will most graciously fulfil. No sinner that comes seeking mercy is ever sent empty back. What a blessing to be brought to live on his full, free, bountiful grace, having nothing in ourselves, but increasingly realising our deep indebtedness to the Lord and our whole dependence on him.

"Seeing then that we have a great high priest, that is passed into the heavens, Jesus the Son of God, let us hold fast our profession. For we have not an high priest which cannot be touched with the feeling of our infirmities; but was in all points tempted like as we are, yet without sin." "Let *us.*" The apostle here includes himself. He realises *his* daily need of mercy and grace. O may we walk in the footsteps of those that have gone before, yea, in the footsteps of the great and good Shepherd himself.

"Let us therefore come boldly unto the throne of grace." O there is no rejection, no possibility that the poor, needy, burdened, exercised child of God should ever be sent empty away. Look *not* to your deservings. You are never deserving and never will be deserving of the mercy and favour of the Lord. Remember, Jesus Christ is the friend of sinners.

"Sinners are high in his esteem,
And sinners highly value him."

O may we increasingly value our Lord and Saviour Jesus Christ in all that he reveals of himself to us in his holy word.

I will leave the remarks there. The Lord add his blessing. Amen.

28

WHAT IS THAT TO THEE?
FOLLOW THOU ME

Tuesday evening 26 May 2020

"Jesus saith unto him, If I will that he tarry till
I come, what is that to thee? follow thou me"
(John 21:22).

Particularly upon my mind are the words the Lord repeated to
Peter, "Follow thou me." For this is the word of the Lord to each
sinner brought through grace to hear his voice, and whom he
brings from death in trespasses and sins into the light, life and
liberty of the gospel. "Follow thou me." If we profess to be those
who have been brought to know, believe, love and trust alone in
the Lord Jesus Christ, surely that *"following"* should be evident
in every aspect of our lives. The Lord put to Peter this very
searching question three times, "Lovest thou me?" Well might
that question be put to you and me. In speaking of these things
tonight, I trust I speak as much to myself as to you. May that
question search my heart and yours also. May it bring us low at
the Saviour's feet, conscious of how far short we come. How
much there is still found with us that might well cause us to
question whether we really do love the Lord Jesus Christ or not.
See in Peter the fruit of the life of God in the soul, *even after* his
expressing his devotion to the Lord but grievously failing by
denying him in the way he did. Yet *even after his restoration* we
see this questioning by the Lord. It draws forth God's work, that
is, the fruit in Peter's soul of the love wherewith the Lord had
loved him even when he was dead in trespasses and sins. "Lord,
thou knowest all things; thou knowest that I love thee." Friends,
though we have nothing to say for ourselves, yet what a mercy
we have ground to appeal with Peter to the Lord Jesus who knows
all things. He searches the inward thoughts of each one of us,
solemn consideration as that is, and he knows, and never will
reject, the work of his own hands in his people.

But leading up to these words of our text, I want to notice a few things from this chapter. We are told this was the third time that Jesus shewed himself to his disciples after his resurrection. Only a few weeks had passed since that momentous day when, early in the morning, the Lord rose from the dead. Those women had gone as they thought to minister to his body, but found the stone rolled away. The angel said to them, "Fear not ye: for I know that ye seek Jesus, which was crucified. He is not here: for he is risen, as he said. Come, see the place where the Lord lay" (Matt. 28:5–6). What wonder they experienced at that empty tomb. O how it filled them with solemn fears as they hurried to tell the disciples and were met by the Lord himself. The Lord showed himself to Mary Magdalene in the garden and said, "Go to my brethren, and say unto them, I ascend unto my Father, and your Father; and to my God, and your God" (John 20:17). He met Peter on that first day of the week and revealed himself to those two on the road to Emmaus. What a journey those two men had, what wondrous words they heard as the Lord communed with them by the way. Yes, there was faithful loving reproof. "O fools, and slow of heart to believe all that the prophets have spoken: ought not Christ to have suffered these things, and to enter into his glory? And beginning at Moses and all the prophets, he expounded unto them in all the scriptures the things concerning himself" (Luke 24:25–27). And when he revealed himself to them in the breaking of bread they hurried back to the disciples in Jerusalem. And there that very evening the Lord stood in their midst! What were his words to them? "Peace be unto you."

O how wondrous is the Lord's love and grace manifest to his own! There is no word of reproach for what had happened. Yes, he had been taken by wicked hands, crucified and slain and, even though he had forewarned them, they had all forsaken him and fled and Peter basely denied him. But when he appeared to them on that first occasion there was no reproof, no bringing them into judgment. He still manifested his mercy towards them, as those whom he had loved with an everlasting love, despite all their weakness, infirmities and needs. Why, the very purpose of the love and grace of Jesus to his own is to save them from their sins, to redeem them from all iniquity and to bring them into blessed fellowship with himself, by faith here and in glory hereafter.

Eight days later, he appeared to them again as they were gathered in that upper room. Thomas, who had been absent on the previous occasion, was present this time. See the Lord's loving dealings with Thomas. Yes, there was reproof of him, yet O what a manifestation of Jesus. "Behold my hands and my side." "My Lord and my God." "Thomas, because thou hast seen me, thou hast believed: blessed are they that have not seen, and yet have believed" (John 20:24–29). Did not the Lord manifest there his grace, love and mercy to his disciples? Friends, as with them so it is with his people still. "He knoweth our frame; he remembereth that we are dust" (Ps. 103:14). How graciously he deals with us! What does the Lord look for in us? Nothing but what he himself has first imparted to us for his glory.

And now he meets with them on this third occasion as we read, "After these things Jesus shewed himself again to the disciples at the sea of Tiberias; and on this wise shewed he himself." It appears that these disciples whose names are given here had returned to Galilee. The angel had said, "He goeth before you into Galilee: there shall ye see him, as he said unto you" (Matt. 28:7). We know there was a gathering of more than five hundred brethren at once when the Lord showed himself at some time during the forty days between his resurrection and ascension into heaven (1 Cor. 15:6). On this third occasion we find them here in Galilee. Between his resurrection and this occasion, we might say his disciples were at a loss as to what to do in their circumstances. O how much had taken place in such a short time. What wonders had they experienced, as none other before or since have experienced. Yet we find them here, not really knowing what to do or which way to turn at this time. Peter makes the decision, "I go a fishing. They say unto him, We also go with thee." They return to their old trade of fishermen. But the point I would make here is that though it might be said they were at a loss to know what to do, not only was the Lord's eye upon them but his love was upon them as we see on this occasion. O blessed be the Lord's name, in every circumstance in which his people are found, even when they may not know what to do in many things which distress them, yet what a mercy it is that the Lord's eye is upon them. The Lord knows every detail of their situation, as he did of the disciples here. And comes to them. He comes as expressed in the Song of Solomon: "The voice of my beloved! behold, he cometh leaping upon the mountains, skipping upon the hills" (Song of Sol. 2:8). And the Lord does come over all the mountains of sin, guilt, difficulty, temptation and trial. O there is no barrier that can be raised, but the Lord is able to come over it or break through it. As the Lord declares by Isaiah, "I will break in pieces the gates of brass, and cut in sunder the bars of iron" (Isa. 45:2). Nothing can hinder the Lord's coming to his own at his appointed time.

What a mercy also that when the Lord reveals himself to his people, as to his disciples here, he always does so as he does not unto the world. What did the world experience of what the disciples experienced here? What does the world know of the experience of the living family of God, Jesus revealing himself in pardoning love and supporting them in all their needs, even though his chastening hand may be upon them? O friends, how gracious is the Lord in *all* his dealings with his children. I would emphasise the outworking of his love towards them.

See it in this account. Peter says, "I go a fishing. They say unto him, We also go with thee" and they toiled all night and took nothing. Early morning as they were drawing to shore, they hear a voice saying to them, "Children, have ye any meat?" No. "Cast the net on the right side of the ship." They did so and inclosed a great catch of large fishes, "an hundred and fifty and three." Must not this have directed the minds of the disciples to the event, some three years before, when they were first brought to forsake all and follow the Lord Jesus? The Lord had used Peter's boat to speak to the people on the land. Afterwards he said, "Launch out into the deep, and let down your nets for a draught." Peter said, "Master, we have toiled all the night, and have taken nothing: nevertheless at thy word I will let down the net." They did so and inclosed a great catch of fish. Peter seeing this, fell down at Jesus feet saying, "Depart from me; for I am a sinful man, O Lord. For he was astonished, and all that were with him, at the draught of the fishes which they had taken" (Luke 5:4–9). Conscious he surely was that he was not in the presence of a mere man, for the very Godhead of our Lord Jesus Christ shone forth in gracious measure there. O how deeply affected was Peter. Remember the words of the Lord to him, "Fear not; from henceforth thou shalt catch men" (Luke 5:10). And they left all and followed the Lord Jesus.

And in this incident in which our text is found, similar important lessons were brought home to them, which also speak to us, especially in what our Lord says to Peter, "Follow thou me." They knew not at first that it was Jesus who stood on the shore. But after that great catch of fish, John said, "It is the Lord." As they came ashore, "they saw a fire of coals there, and fish laid thereon, and bread." Jesus said, "Come and dine." See how he had provided for them even early that morning. See again the kindness and care of the Lord over his own. Was there one word of reproof to them? See how gracious is the Lord in his dealings with his people!

We know the Lord's judgments are abroad in the earth. And there are times in the Lord's dealings with his people when they are brought to realise the solemn fact that it is "an evil thing and bitter" to sin against the Lord (Jer. 2:19). But what are the Lord's dealings with them even when the defilement of sin lies heavy on the conscience? Does he manifest himself in bringing judgment upon them? Yes, as I said, the Lord chastens his people *but it is always in covenant love*. That does not excuse them. They are brought to realise the evil of sinning against the Lord and that if we sow to the flesh, we do indeed reap corruption, sad and solemn as that is. Yet friends, the love of God in Jesus Christ prevails over all the sins and failings of his people. As he himself says, and he means what he says, though I know it is easy for us to repeat his words: "I have loved thee with an everlasting love: therefore with lovingkindness have I drawn thee" (Jer. 31:3). And is the lovingkindness of the Lord ever rescinded in all his subsequent dealings with his people? Is not his lovingkindness at the root of all his dealings with his people? Yes it is, blessed be his name. See this in how kindly he dealt with his disciples. No word of reproof but vitally important lessons.

Yes, on that first occasion they were brought to forsake all and follow him. *Now* in a much mightier way they were to forsake all and follow him in that work to which he had appointed them and for which they were to be equipped by the Holy Spirit on the day of Pentecost. After the event in this chapter, we do not find them ever returning to their old trade. From henceforth, and particularly following Pentecost, we find them wholly devoted to the work to which the Lord had called them. Yes, they were men of like passions as we are. All the apostles of our Lord Jesus Christ were sinners saved by grace and not without their infirmities. But one thing manifest in them is that they were brought to hear the Saviour's voice and to follow him, as he said here to Peter, "Follow thou me." Did they go back on that? Did they not prove the grace of God sufficient for them in all that lay before them in the unknown way? O they could not fully conceive what difficulties they would face. The Lord had warned them. He had spoken to them in the upper room and as he went forth to Gethsemane and Calvary. But subsequently they proved what the Lord told them. "In the world ye shall have tribulation: but be of good cheer; I have overcome the world" (John 16:33). Yes, they proved the Lord's grace sufficient for them.

Do not overlook what the Lord displayed to them in that great catch of fish. These men were poor fishermen. They had no great personal resources. We do not know what families they had. We know Peter had a wife and we read of his wife's mother as well. We know very little of the families of the others. We do not need to know. How would they be provided for in future days as they followed the Lord Jesus Christ? Was there not an indication in this great catch of fish, that the Lord was able and would provide? Friends, that is still a precious truth for every child of God brought to follow him.

What is involved in following him? It is being made willing to leave all and follow the Lord Jesus Christ. Very real sacrifices are involved. The Lord Jesus said on another occasion, "If any man will come after me, let him deny himself and take up his cross and follow me" (Matt. 16:24). And also he put that important question: Were they willing to forsake all? How that comes very close. Are we willing to forsake *all?* I am sure of this, that whatever we may be called upon to part with for Jesus' sake in the path he has appointed for us, he will never be our debtor. No, as indicated in this great catch of fish, he would provide for them. What a testimony to them and to the Lord's people still, that the Lord *will provide*. Paul could say to the Philippians, "My God shall supply all your need according to his riches in glory by Christ Jesus" (4:19). Yes friends, as called by his grace and made willing, whatever is involved, to truly follow the Lord, to forsake all and follow him, is no easy thing to our fallen nature. O how it rebels against it.

Let us come to this point. What is the chief concern for you and me this evening? What are our affections truly fixed upon? These words of our Lord Jesus Christ had a particular application as addressed to Peter. "Lovest thou me?" I repeat again, what a searching word is that. What is our response this evening? This is not asking, 'what do we *know?*' I trust we *know* much. Peter says here, "Lord, thou knowest all things; thou knowest that I love thee." There must be that knowledge, the being brought to believe in the Lord Jesus Christ, for *faith* and *love* are intimately connected though distinct graces. Faith, hope and love are ever intertwined but as Paul tells us, the greatest of these is *love*, the love of Christ and the love to Christ as "shed abroad in our hearts by the Holy Ghost which is given unto us" (Rom. 5:5). And friends, this is at the root of all true following and service of the Lord in our day and generation. O that we might know more of the living reality of it, its sanctifying influence in our daily lives as we journey on, particularly if called to a distinct work and office in the church of Jesus Christ. To *know* about the Lord Jesus Christ is very necessary, but the essential thing is, do I *love* the Lord Jesus Christ? I say again, all true service and following of the Lord by the light and teaching of the word, is rooted in the love of Jesus Christ. And if we love him, blessed be his name, it is "because he first loved us" (1 John 4:19).

As I said earlier, Peter appeals here to the Lord. *What* does he appeal to? To the work of God's grace in his own soul. Yes, he had nothing of which to boast. He dare not say he loved the Lord more than all the others or would go further than any others as he once boasted. No, he now knows his own weakness and sinfulness, and himself as a needy sinner ever wholly dependent on the

Lord. Friends, how painful is that to our fallen nature! But O how truly spiritually profitable it is to be kept low at the Saviour's feet, looking to him alone in whom is all our hope for time and eternity.

The Lord also speaks another word to Peter before our text. He informs him, "Verily, verily, I say unto thee, When thou was young, thou girdest thyself, and walkest whither thou wouldest; but when thou shalt be old, thou shalt stretch forth thy hands, and another shall gird thee, and carry thee whither thou wouldest not. This spake he, signifying by what death he should glorify God. When he had spoken this, he saith unto him, Follow me." He spoke to Peter of things wherein he should glorify God, in the outworking of the Lord's appointments for him. Yes, as called by the grace of God to be an apostle of Jesus Christ, how faithful was Peter in that work subsequently. What cause we have to be thankful to the Lord for the writings of Peter in his first and second epistles. They communicate what he had learned of himself, and what he had received of the Lord's wondrous love to him. How he was thus constrained as a servant of Jesus Christ to serve him on the earth, not for reward, but out of love to the Lord and love to those who love the Lord Jesus in sincerity and truth. Friends, as I have said, should not this love be the root of all true following of our Lord and Saviour? He told Peter that he should glorify God by dying a martyr's death, bearing witness to the Lord Jesus Christ and the Lord's love to him. And it is in the face of such a prospect that the Lord says to him, "Follow me."

To follow the Lord means that the Lord would be with him, indeed would go before him, for we *follow* one who goes *before* us. And it is a precious truth the Lord declares to his people when he says, "I am with thee." We may not always have the felt sense of it, but *"I am with thee"* is an abiding reality for the people of God. As he is with us, so he instructs us here to follow him because he goes before us. In all that may be faced by a child of God, they do not face it alone. The Lord goes before them in the way. All the enemies that beset them must first contend with the Lord who rules and overrules all events for the good of his people. He assures them "I will never leave thee, nor forsake thee" (Heb. 13:5). The Lord goes before. What a mercy to be made willing to follow the Lord whithersoever he goeth. To follow him is to believe him, to trust him above all others, to love him in the realisation of the greatness of his love made manifest to us.

Is there greater love than that revealed to us in the precious truth of the gospel? The apostle John knew much of the blessed love of God revealed in Jesus Christ to a poor sinner. Could he not say, "Herein is love, not that we loved God, but that he loved us, and sent his Son to be the propitiation for our sins" (1 John 4:10). O precious truth!

Peter, turning to John, asks, "What shall this man do?" No doubt he had a concern for his friend John. How significant is the response of Jesus to him, not only for Peter but also for the Lord's people still. "If I will that he tarry till I come, what is that to thee? follow thou me." What is the Lord emphasising to Peter, and to all his people, particularly to any he calls to an office in his church? We are to give full attention to what the Lord appoints for us. In the situations to which he calls us, he says "Let thine eyes look right on, and let thine eyelids look straight before thee" (Prov. 4:25). I am not saying we should be unconcerned for the welfare of our fellow servants in the Lord. We are to pray for one another. But our accountability to the Lord is not one of questioning or curiously enquiring into the Lord's will and purposes for others. Our accountability to the Lord is to attend to what he has called us. I believe I can say personally how deeply through the years has this been impressed on me. I am not unconcerned for the welfare of others, but I am accountable to the Lord for that to which he has called *me* in the place where he has placed me. Though often conscious of my weakness and infirmities, I trust my desire is to be faithful to the Lord in the preaching of the word to which he has appointed me, even though that word may condemn myself. I trust I preach as much to myself as I do to you. With Bunyan I would say, "Let me rather die with the Philistines than handle the word of God deceitfully." I trust we seek grace to handle the word of God aright, to be a witness even in our infirmities, to the truth as it is in Jesus.

"If I will that he tarry till I come, what is that to thee?" 'Peter, be not concerned so much with what my purposes are for John.

Pay attention to what I have appointed for *you.'* How deeply Peter learned that principle in his life and followed it out through the Lord's grace towards him. *"Follow thou me."* The Lord comes back to this point for Peter and us. How prone we are to listen to one voice or another. O may our ear be open to what the Lord says to us in his holy word. Surely should not all things in our life and circumstances be brought to the touchstone of 'What saith the Lord?' O for grace to enable us to address every issue in this light. What is the mind and will of God in his holy word regarding every matter? There is no other criterion for us. We profess, do we not, that the word of God is our only rule for what we believe and practice. All is rooted in what God has revealed to us in his word. As the prophet said, "To the law and to the testimony: if they speak not according to this word, it is because there is no light in them" (Isa. 8:20).

"What is that to thee? follow thou me." O friends, may this word still sound in our ears by the grace of God given us. "Follow thou me." And who it is that spoke to Peter and still speaks to us? He that loved us and died for us and rose again. O the glorious reality of the resurrection of our Lord Jesus Christ from the dead and his ascension into heaven, all authority and power being given him in heaven and earth! 'To follow *him?'* Why friends, he is the Lord of life and glory. He has all power and authority given him. Is not all that concerns us, whatever that may be, safe in his hands. As we by grace are brought to follow him, to believe and trust in him alone, can we perish? We are assured by his word, that the soul thus brought to follow him out of love to him, as the fruit of his grace, can never perish, blessed be his great and holy name.

"Follow thou me." May that word come again and again to your soul and mine. May we know its application and outworking in our lives as rooted in that question, *"Lovest thou me more than these?"*

But I will leave the remarks there. The Lord add his blessing. Amen.

29

HAPPY IS HE THAT HATH THE GOD OF JACOB FOR HIS HELP

Lord's day morning 31 May 2020

"Happy is he that hath the God of Jacob for his
help, whose hope is in the Lord his God:
which made heaven, and earth, the sea, and
all that therein is: which keepeth truth for
ever" (Psalm 146:5–6).

And truly *happy*, or blessed, *is* the person whose God is the Lord,
the God of Jacob. And may *we* know the God of Jacob by the
riches of divine grace. For it is only by the sovereign grace and
mercy of God that he is made known to us, as he was to Jacob.
Jacob was given the blessing of the one and only true God, the
God of his father Isaac and his father Abraham. God manifested
himself to Jacob as his God, his Saviour and his all, in everything
that concerned him. All was appointed by his God. Thus the Lord
spoke to him when he met him in the lonely place where he lay
down that night to rest when he fled from Esau. He had no
anticipation whatsoever of what would be made known to him on
that occasion. What a manifestation of sovereign and saving
grace was given to Jacob! And as it was with Jacob, so it is the
same sovereign, distinguishing grace that brings any sinner into
the believing realisation of the blessing set before us in this
psalm, that the God of Jacob is *their* God. He, the God and Father
of our Lord Jesus Christ, is the God and Father of every sinner
called by divine grace. They are one with Jesus Christ, "who of
God is made unto us, wisdom, and righteousness, and sanctification and redemption" (1 Cor. 1:30).

"Happy is he that hath the God of Jacob for his help." We read
in an earlier verse, "Put not your trust in princes, nor in the son
of man, in whom there is *no help.*" That word can be rendered
"salvation." Yes, there is no salvation in princes or any man,
whoever they are, whatever they may claim. No salvation is

found in what man is, none in the supposed great and mighty of this world. It is alone found in the Lord our God who has revealed himself in the person of our Lord and Saviour Jesus Christ as set forth in the precious truth of the gospel. O friends, how great is this blessedness! Truly happy are they that know the God of Jacob as their salvation. They are brought through divine grace to realise there is salvation in none other. There "is none other name under heaven given among men, whereby we must be saved" (Acts 4:12). And this embraces all that pertains to us as we journey on through life, all the difficulties, temptations, dangers and pressing needs that beset us. Ultimately, is help to be looked for in anything other than the Lord our God?

O friends, how great is the Lord's goodness in all his appointments for his people in the outworking of his providential mercies. Is not the Lord truly the God of our salvation, our help, our deliverer, our upholder, our keeper and our provider in all the difficulties and dangers confronting us? Above all, to the praise of the glory of his name, what assurance is given us of his provision for the eternal welfare of our never-dying souls. Do we not experience his salvation, his gracious deliverance from self, from guilt and from the working of sin in our lives? As I said, is there salvation for us in any other but in the Lord our God? Friends, I trust that these things may be more and more impressed upon us, particularly in all we may be passing through at this present time. May we be increasingly thankful to the Lord for his providential mercies upholding us from day to day. But above all, may we be thankful for the wonders of his sovereign, saving grace revealed to us by the Holy Spirit in all that the Lord Jesus is and has done. "Happy is he that hath the God of Jacob for his help, whose hope is in the LORD his God."

As many of the psalms of David, so this psalm calls forth praise and thanksgiving to the Lord our God: "Praise ye the LORD. Praise the LORD, O my soul." Here David not only calls upon all who know the blessings of saving grace and mercy to lift up their hearts in thankful praise to the Lord, but he particularly says, "Praise the LORD, O *my* soul." Yes, it is good and right for brethren to join together in praise and thanksgiving to the Lord our God. Surely he alone is the only one to be praised. For in him, as we are reminded here, is all our help and all our hope for time and eternity. I say it is good to join with brethren and exhort one another to praise the Lord, but especially we must consider the personal implication of it for ourselves. As the psalmist says, "Praise the LORD, O *my* soul" (Ps. 146:1).

How is it with us individually? What do we know of the living reality of the God of Jacob as *our* God, *our* help and hope, for time and eternity? Has God through divine grace revealed himself to us as he revealed himself to Jacob at Bethel? Friends, surely if we know something of the living reality of what Jacob there experienced, we have cause to praise the Lord *continually!* Surely for every redeemed sinner brought to know and love the Lord Jesus Christ in sincerity and truth, the whole of eternity will be taken up with praise and thanksgiving to the God of our salvation. Are we are not assured that this is the occupation of the redeemed before the throne? "Not unto us, O LORD, not unto us, but unto thy name give glory, for thy mercy, and for thy truth's sake" (Ps. 115:1). They praise God for his greatness and glory as revealed in Jesus Christ set forth in the glorious truth of the gospel. Yes, the child of God has cause every day to praise the Lord. "Oh that men would praise the LORD for his goodness, and for his wonderful works to the children of men" (Ps. 107:8).

I have said many a time, that the crying sin of fallen sinful men and woman all down the generations is that they do not acknowledge God neither are they thankful. Should we be surprised at that? Sadly *not,* if we believe what the word sets before us of the state of men and women dead in trespasses and sins as a result of the fall. Though the word of God is sounded forth, is there any hearing and heeding of it? Sadly, solemnly *not,* apart from the going forth of God in sovereign grace and mercy. What alone can impart life to that which is dead? What imparted life to those dry bones shown to Ezekiel? He was commanded to preach to those dry bones, but what made that word effectual? What imparts life to those that are dead? It is the power of the Lord the Holy Spirit who, by his word, accomplishes his purposes of sovereign saving grace in those he loved from before the foundation of the world.

"Praise ye the LORD. Praise the LORD, O my soul. While I live will I praise the LORD: I will sing praises unto my God while I have any being." O friends, may we know this gracious determination of the psalmist. Yes, we have many things that greatly distress us, not the least of them being the working of the sin which does so easily beset us. Is not that ever a cause of distress to the child of God? As Paul expressed it, "O wretched man that I am! who shall deliver me from the body of this death?" (Rom. 7:24). What a trial, what a trouble to Paul was the working of his fallen nature. Yet even in that, had he not still cause to bless God, as does every child of God who is distressed by things without and within? As Paul said, "I thank God through Jesus Christ" (v. 25). May our soul be established in the believing realisation of this provision of God. Blessed indeed is the man who knows the God of Jacob as his help and hope. Blessed is that poor soul to whom God has revealed himself in the person of the Lord Jesus by the sovereign ministry of the Holy Spirit. This God, the God and Father of our Lord Jesus Christ, is the God and Father of every poor sinner brought through grace, as was Jacob, to trust in the Lord alone. What a glorious provision has he made in the person of his only begotten and dearly beloved Son!

Yes friend, in all the trials and difficulties of life and in what you still find of the working of sin and its daily defilement, is there no help, no hope, no remedy in what has God revealed to us in the precious truth of the gospel? Blessed be God's name, *there is*. As oft as sin daily defiles us (and what a mercy to be humbled to realise it) where shall we turn, to whom can we go? "Turn thy eyes to Jesus' blood." Look to *that* which the gospel makes known. O may the Lord the Holy Spirit bring this afresh to your soul and mine. For no true peace can be found in anything less than "the blood of Jesus Christ his Son [which] cleanseth us from all sin" (1 John 1:7). O in the face of all we may meet in life, *that* truth does not alter. Unbelief may question our personal interest in Jesus. Satan may say we have no part in God. But remember, unbelief *is* unbelief. Satan is a liar. The word of God is true and faithful: "Happy is he that hath the God of Jacob for his help"! We can come to the God of Jacob. With all that may burden, distress and trouble us, we are encouraged to come to the footstool of mercy. His ear is open to the cry of his people, his eye is ever upon them.

Let us look a little deeper into these words before us: "Happy is he that hath the God of Jacob for his help, whose hope is in the LORD his God." Look at the case of Jacob as we read in Genesis chapter 28. An essential point brought before is that Jacob did not seek the Lord, but the Lord sought him and came even where he was. So it is with every sinner brought to know the blessedness of the God of Jacob as his help and hope. Jacob, brought up in the family of Isaac and Rebekah, was not without the knowledge of the one true God nor ignorant of what God had promised to Abraham and confirmed to Isaac. Indeed, Jacob sought and obtained the promised blessing from Isaac by stealing it from Esau. He was well called Jacob, a *supplanter* who supplanted his brother Esau on two occasions. What deceitfulness was seen with Jacob.

The fact is that Jacob and everyone to whom the Lord reveals himself, as he did to Jacob, is a lost and ruined sinner, ruined in the fall, black with original sin and actual transgression. There is no exception to this. The wonder is that this God, the God of Jacob, does not have to do with good men, not with those supposedly righteous in themselves, but with *sinners*. Remember, the gospel of the grace of God is not for the righteous but for sinners, sinners taught of the Holy Spirit to solemnly realise their sinnership. Every one of them is helpless, ruined, utterly lost and undone of themselves. They have *nothing* which in any way can commend them to God or incline him to be favourable to them. As I said, did Jacob first seek the Lord? He left his father's house under a cloud. Going towards Haran he did not know what lay before him. Until God met with him at Bethel, surely he viewed the blessing which Isaac bestowed on him, as merely referring to the land of Canaan which God promised to Abraham and his seed after him. But the essence of that blessing of Abraham, confirmed to Isaac and to Jacob, was that "in thy seed shall all the nations of the earth be blessed" (Gen. 22:18). O how the gospel was preached in the word of promise to Jacob! But there was no true receiving, no realisation of the need of this gospel, until the Lord met with him at Bethel. We do not read he prayed to God or had any thoughts towards God, though as I said, he was not unaware of the God of his father Isaac. See here *sovereign distinguishing grace*. As the Lord Jesus Christ himself declared, "I came not to call the righteous, but sinners…" (Mark 2:17). It is for sinners lost and ruined that the Lord Jesus came and still comes by the sovereign operations of the Holy Spirit. No sinner brought to believe and trust in Jesus Christ does so from anything in themselves. In every instance it is *God coming* just where they are, as he came here to Jacob, not when they seek him, but even when *dead* in trespasses and sins. It is God alone who quickens them into spiritual life and until he does so, there is certainly no going out of the soul after the Lord Jesus Christ. "The dead know not any thing" (Eccles. 9:5). Those dead in trespasses and sins know nothing savingly, spiritually. They have no desire for the blessings of pardoning love and mercy. They are solemnly ignorant of the need of it.

O the wonders of sovereign, distinguishing grace. *God came* to Jacob. And what a revelation he gave to him! In that dream he saw a ladder set up on the earth and its top reached to heaven. The angels of God were ascending and descending upon it, and the Lord spoke to him from heaven itself. O what did that set forth? God alone was able to open a way in which to reveal himself to ruined, guilty sinners, as a God, "merciful and gracious … abundant in goodness and truth … forgiving iniquity and transgression and sin" (Exod. 34:6–7). What wondrous provision is made in our Lord Jesus Christ for guilty sinners to be delivered from the curse and condemnation justly due to them! Remember there is but *one* way of acceptance by God. It is that which he himself has provided in the person and work of our Lord Jesus Christ. Jesus himself declared, "I am the way, the truth, and the life: no man cometh unto the Father, but by me" (John 14:6). He also declared, "I am the door" (John 10:7,9). I emphasise, there is but one way of access and acceptance with God and it is what he himself hath provided in Jesus Christ. Shown to Jacob was the *one way* wherein God comes to a sinner in saving grace and mercy. That way *is* the person and work of the Lord Jesus Christ *alone*.

"Happy is he [blessed indeed] who hath the God of Jacob for

his help, whose hope is in the LORD his God." How did he come to Jacob? A truth is beautifully opened up to us here. The Lord came to Jacob, not in wrath but in mercy. Jacob was a sinner. I am sure he was brought to the solemn realisation of it. How did the Lord come to him? He comes to Jacob in saving grace and mercy, setting before us that our God is a sovereign God. He is sovereign in all his ways and dealings, sovereign essentially in the manifestation of the blessings of salvation to sinful men and women. As we read, "Jacob have I *loved,* but Esau have I *hated"* (Rom. 9:13). The sovereign, distinguishing grace of God is evidenced in those two brothers. What was different between them? Why should Jacob be chosen and loved of God and Esau not so? Was there anything in them, is there anything in the sinner, in you and me, that God should thus be favourable to us? Why friends, we must ever come back to this place again and again:

> "What was there in me that could merit esteem
> Or give the Creator delight?
> 'Twas even so, Father! we ever must sing,
> Because it seemed good in thy sight."

The Lord's coming to Jacob was not because Jacob was deserving of it or better than his brother Esau. In many respects, Jacob was worse than Esau looked at from the human standpoint. But the Lord comes to him in mercy flowing out his eternal love towards him. O what a wondrous display of sovereign, distinguishing grace in pardoning love and mercy, comes to Jacob as God reveals himself to him! "I am the LORD God of Abraham thy father, and the God of Isaac" (Gen. 28:13). O wonder of wonders that God should thus make himself known to a sinner. 'I am thy God, thy Saviour and thy all.' Well might the psalmist call forth praise and thanksgiving for being so blessed as to have the God of Jacob for his help, his hope and his salvation, a salvation wholly in what God is and has provided.

The Lord, I say, comes to Jacob in mercy on that occasion. The word he gave to Jacob applied throughout the providences God appointed for him in his journey to Haran and in all the years that followed. But this was not all. For, as I said earlier, was not the substance of the blessing of Abraham in the fact that the gospel was preached to him as it was preached here to Jacob, the gospel revealed in all its wondrous fulness in the person and finished work of Jesus Christ? "In *thy seed* shall all the families of the earth be blessed" (Gen. 28:14). This was the great hope and expectation of all those to whom the Lord revealed himself in saving grace and mercy throughout the old testament dispensation. For them, this was ever cause for rejoicing in thankfulness and praise to God. Blessed with living faith, they found true rest for their souls in looking alone to the promised seed, even the Lord Jesus Christ.

Likewise with his people still, is not their hope and rejoicing in *him who has come?* Is it not in him who is set before us in the precious truth of the gospel? Is it not in him who has accomplished redemption and salvation for his people and has ascended into heaven and is seated at the right hand of the Majesty on high? Friends, "Behold your God" (Isa. 40:9), God as revealed to us in the person of Jesus Christ, Jacob's God, your God, my God! May we be blessedly taught of the Holy Spirit, as poor, needy, ruined, guilty sinners, to receive the testimony God has given of his only begotten Son. Truly blessed is your soul and mine if the God of Jacob is our help and hope. For surely, whatever we may meet with as we journey on through life, if this God, the Lord Jesus Christ, is made known to us by the blessed teaching of the Holy Spirit, he can never be taken away from us. Did God ever leave Jacob? Did he ever forsake him or turn away from him in all the ups and downs, ins and outs, difficulties and disappointments of Jacob's life? No. We see the gracious provision the Lord made for him, even in the most severe trials of his life and when he feared all things were against him. Until made clear to him, how little he realised that the things which appeared to be against him, were the workings out of the covenant purposes of God for his good and for the glory of the Lord's great name.

As I have said, when the Lord revealed himself to Jacob on that night it was not in judgment but in mercy. O the wonder of it! That's the blessing of the gospel! It comes to sinners deserving wrath as everyone of us does. The gospel comes to us to reveal the mercy of God in Jesus Christ. Unless the Lord does come to us in mercy where is our help, our hope, our salvation? Behold the ministry of our Lord Jesus Christ here on earth, the cases to whom he revealed himself. It was not in judgment but in mercy. All the Lord's dealings with sinners were in mercy, in healing bodily sicknesses and diseases and casting out devils, and especially in those to whom he declared the forgiveness of their sins. We see those who laid the man sick of the palsy in the midst before Jesus. What were the Lord's first words to him? O what mercy is there manifest! "Son, thy sins be forgiven thee" (Mark 2:5). *That* was made known to him even before the Lord's dealing with his physical condition. "Thy sins be forgiven." *There* is the great mercy of the Lord. *There* is the salvation of God made known to the soul by the blessed teaching of the Holy Spirit. Friends, if we have that, we have everything! We have God as *our* God and Father. He has reconciled us to himself through the redemption that is in Christ Jesus. He has forgiven our sins and brought us, with Jacob, into the blessings of an eternal covenant relationship with himself.

And see that bound up with it is all that pertains to life and godliness, for time and for eternity! See what the Lord spoke to him. "I am the LORD God of Abraham thy father, and the God of Isaac: the land whereon thou liest, to thee will I give it, and to thy seed; and thy seed shall be as the dust of the earth, and thou shalt spread abroad to the west, and to the east, and to the north, and to the south: and in thee and in thy seed shall all the families of the earth be blessed" (Gen. 28:13–14). As I said earlier, this is the very heart, the glorious essence of the blessing of God to Jacob. Yes, God gave to Jacob's descendants the land of Canaan as he promised to Abraham. But, O friends, what spiritual, eternal realities are bound up in those words, "In thee and in *thy seed* shall the families of the earth be blessed."

And the Lord goes on to say, "And, behold, I am with thee, and will keep thee in all places whither thou goest, and will bring thee again into this land; for I will not leave thee, until I have done that which I have spoken to thee of" (v. 15). O to be able to rightly view these words of our Lord to Jacob in the light of new covenant mercies. What blessings the Lord assures to Jacob of his care over him and his kindness towards him in all he would meet in the way he was called to walk. And truly Jacob experienced it. The Lord did not leave him, did not forsake him in all he subsequently experienced. The words of the Lord were borne out, to the praise of his holy name.

He says, "I am with thee, and will keep thee." Is not this one of the great blessings of the Lord? The Lord assures his people, needy sinners as they are and always will be, *"I am with thee."* Is not everything bound up in that word? O may that truth not only sound in our ears but be sealed unto us. Cannot we then face whatever may be found in our life and path? In *all* the Lord's appointments for us, he is with us. Yes, we are brought to realise our weakness, our sinfulness, our continuing need. But the Lord says, "I am with thee, and will keep thee in all places whither thou goest." Can we keep ourselves? Are we proof against temptation? Can we ever boast that we can deal with our own affairs and concerns? What a mercy to be kept in the realisation that, "I am poor and needy; yet the Lord thinketh upon me" (Ps. 40:17). "My help cometh from the Lord, which made heaven and earth" (Ps. 121:2). "I will not leave thee, until I have done that which I have spoken to thee of."

"Happy is he that hath the God of Jacob for his help, whose hope is in the LORD his God." O friends, behold how the Lord our God is set before us here! O surely what confidence we can have in him! As the psalmist goes on to say. "Whose hope is in the LORD his God: which made heaven, and earth, the sea, and all that therein is: which keepeth truth for ever." Such is the God of Jacob. Such is our God as he was Jacob's God, as brought by grace to believe and trust in him only. For he who is the God of Jacob, the God and Father of our Lord Jesus Christ, the God and Father of everyone who trusts in Jesus, is set before us here as the one who "made heaven, and earth, the sea, and all that therein is: which keepeth truth for ever." Is not this a firm foundation for the faith and hope of the living family of God? If God is my God, if he has revealed himself to me as my God and Saviour in Jesus Christ by grace through faith in his name, have I not a sure ground for my hope? For our trust is in the Lord God who "is able to do exceeding abundantly above all that we ask or think, according to the power that worketh in us" (Eph. 3:20).

By the Lord's mercies towards us, O may we be more and more drawn to Jesus, and kept looking only to him who is all our help and hope. And we are assured that in all our weakness, sinfulness and failings, the Lord faileth not, blessed be his name. His word of promise can never be undermined. What God has said he most surely fulfils. Jacob proved it so. Every poor sinner to whom he reveals himself as their God will ever prove it so too. And all is to the praise of the glory of his name.

I will leave the remarks there. The Lord add his blessing. Amen.

30

CHRIST WAS ONCE OFFERED TO BEAR THE SINS OF MANY

Lord's day evening 31 May 2020

"And as it is appointed unto men once to die, but after this the judgment: so Christ was once offered to bear the sins of many; and unto them that look for him shall he appear the second time without sin unto salvation" (Hebrew 9:27-28).

The apostle opens this epistle with the words, "God, who at sundry times and in divers manners spake in time past unto the fathers by the prophets, hath in these last days spoken unto us by his Son." And what the Lord spake to the fathers by the prophets is no different to what the Lord speaks to us through his beloved Son, as set forth in the glorious truth of the gospel. In the shadows of the old testament dispensation there is one essential theme. It was revealed when our first parents came under condemnation as transgressors against God. It was in the promise he spoke to them that the seed of the woman should bruise the serpent's head though it should bruise his heel. This is the only hope for sinful men and women through the sovereign mercy of God. And this promise was further unfolded in the following generations until its full realisation in the person of Jesus Christ. In all God's manifestations of himself to his people at sundry times and in divers manners by the prophets in the old testament there was but the *one* theme of the wonders of his sovereign grace and mercy to sinners. So it was with Jacob at Bethel as we considered this morning. Brought to solemnly realise their sinnership as transgressors of God's holy law, all their hope and salvation was in the Lord their God, the God against whom they had sinned. And he is the God against whom *we* have sinned and *our* salvation is only found in the blessedness of knowing the God of Jacob to be *our* God, *our* help, *our* salvation, and *our* hope.

"Happy is he that hath the God of Jacob for his help, whose hope is in the LORD his God" (Ps. 146:5).

In this epistle to the Hebrews, the apostle Paul fully opens up how salvation is all of grace from beginning to end. He does not direct us to what man can supposedly contribute to his salvation. He directs us to what God has provided in Jesus Christ, the fulness and freeness of redeeming love manifest through the riches of divine grace to sinners even *in* their sins. Friends, that is a vitally important point. The Lord manifests his grace by the sovereign operations of the Holy Spirit to sinners *dead in trespasses and sins*. For it is grace alone that quickens them into spiritual life, bringing them to cry to the Lord for mercy, and unfolding the wonders of his saving grace to them. Does not the word of God still declare, and may the Lord bring it home afresh to your soul and mine, "Look unto me, and be ye saved, all the ends of the earth: for I am God, and there is none else"? (Isa. 45:22). None but he who is the one true God can ever save such sinners as you and me! And he has revealed himself in the person of his only begotten and dearly beloved Son. Behold in all the scriptures the unfolding of the wonders and blessedness of that covenant of grace wherein God alone is glorified and the salvation of sinners assured. I repeat, salvation is not in what the sinner is supposed to be able to do, but in what God in Christ has done for them and sovereignly reveals to them. All is gloriously unfolded to us in the precious truth of the gospel. And what a glorious gospel it is! For it speaks to such sinners as you and me. May it speak afresh to your soul and mine this evening, calling us, not to what we are to do, but to receive what God in Christ has accomplished. May we be blessed with God-given faith to find in this gospel true rest for our souls and the peace of God which passeth all understanding. How vital is this when we consider what is set before us in the words of our text.

In this chapter we see how the apostle's emphasis is on showing sinners, called by God's grace, how all that pertains to the salvation of our souls flows to us through the person and finished work of Jesus Christ. There is *no* salvation apart from this, no other help for us as guilty sinners to meet the just demands of God's holy law. Our *only* hope is in what Jesus Christ is and what *he* has accomplished as the word here assures us. The emphasis is on what Jesus has accomplished as a *surety, substitute and high priest* for his people. O the wonders of this! Behold him here not only as the high priest, but the high priest who *sacrifices himself* through the eternal Sprit, without spot to God! O what precious, glorious things are set before us! The emphasis is always placed on the one sacrificial "offering of the body of Jesus Christ, once for all" (Heb. 10:10). For all that the holy law demanded was fully satisfied by the perfect life, obedience and sacrifice of our Lord Jesus Christ. There we see the law fulfilled for all whom his Father had given him. Divine justice demands their condemnation as transgressors of the holy law of God. But here we see divine justice satisfied by the one offering of Jesus Christ. All the law's demands were satisfied, not by the sinner, but by Jesus, the sinner's surety and Saviour.

As I said, the glorious truth of the covenant of grace is increasingly revealed in the old and new testament scriptures until the full wondrous manifestation of redeeming love and mercy in the person and work of Jesus Christ. To this, all the prophets of old pointed. As Peter reminds us, they "testified beforehand the sufferings of Christ, and the glory that should follow" (1 Pet. 1:11). As taught of God the Holy Spirit, Paul follows in their footsteps when he says to the Corinthians, "I determined not to know any thing among you, save Jesus Christ, and *him crucified*" (1 Cor. 2:2). May *we* be followers of the prophets and apostles. Friends, nothing less than this will do. Is not the glory of the true church, the glory of God as it shines unto us in the face of Jesus Christ? Here we are brought to rest, not in what we can do, but in what God in Christ has done for us. Can anything else bring true peace and joy to your soul and mine? When brought to solemnly realise we are transgressors of God's holy law, O to be brought also to see the law fulfilled by him who lived and died for us! The word of God assures us that it is so for each sinner the Lord calls by his grace. Our text underlines that the law is fulfilled *for us*.

You know, David could say, "O how love I thy law! it is my meditation all the day" (Ps. 119:97). Paul says, "I delight in the law of God after the inward man" (Rom. 7:22). How can that be? Was not true love manifested to God as they saw, and as we see, the law *fulfilled in the person of Jesus Christ?* As taught of the Holy Spirit, the believer delights in the law *there alone*. It is to see it fulfilled by Christ who is the maker, the upholder and the *fulfiller* of the law. O glorious truth! May our souls delight with David in the law as fulfilled by the Messiah. May we thus delight with Paul in the law of God in the inward man even though we find the law of sin and death still working in our fallen nature. O friends, as Paul says, what cause we have to thank God for Jesus Christ! He has fulfilled the law for us and brought in everlasting righteousness. He assures us, and may it be sealed afresh to your soul and mine, 'son, daughter, thy sins that are indeed many (who can number them?), are forgiven thee!' Ah what a wondrous truth is sins forgiven, not for what I have done, but for what another, even Jesus Christ, has done for me. I am assured in our text that the full price was paid and that Christ who died is risen again and ascended into heaven, there to appear in the presence of God for me.

The apostle says, "For Christ is not entered into the holy places made with hands, which are the figures of the true; but into heaven itself, now to appear in the presence of God for us: Nor yet that he should offer himself often, as the high priest entereth into the holy place every year with blood of others; For then must he often have suffered since the foundation of the world: but *now once* in the end of the world hath he appeared to put away sin by the sacrifice of himself." Notice the emphasis in the words *"now once."* What cause to truly bless God has the sinner who trusts in Jesus Christ! As Paul said, "I thank God through Jesus Christ our Lord" (Rom. 7:25). See how this opens up those words of our morning's text: "Happy is he that hath the God of Jacob for his help, whose hope is in the LORD his God" (Ps. 146:1). O what help for us needy sinners has the Lord laid upon Jesus Christ, the mighty one of God. None but he could ever be a help to sinners such as you and me. Remember that "his help" can also be rendered "his salvation." Yes, I repeat, salvation is in none other. "There is none other name under heaven given among men, whereby we must be saved" (Acts 4:12). But *that* salvation is certain. God said, "I have laid help upon one that is mighty; I have exalted one chosen out of the people" (Ps. 89:19). See how Paul reminds us of this in chapter two of this epistle, "Verily he took not on him the nature of angels; but he took on him the seed of Abraham. Wherefore in all things it behoved him to be made like unto his brethren," sin excepted (Heb. 2:16–17). Glorious truth!

We now consider this twenty-seventh verse, "And as it is appointed unto men once to die, but after this the judgment." Might we not justly tremble before such a word? Solemn realisation! It *is appointed* unto men once to die. Friends, not one of us can avoid meeting that appointment in the outworking of God's purposes. None can escape it. It is true for all, believers and unbelievers. All must die. "It is appointed unto men once to die." That is the fruit of sin. "The soul that sinneth, it shall die" (Ezek. 18:4,20). Did not that sound forth at the very beginning? "In the day that thou eatest thereof thou shalt surely die" (Gen. 2:17). The only ground of hope for sinful men is in the promise God spoke to our fallen first parents.

"It is appointed unto men once to die." Well we might tremble. Death is a scourge of the human race. What fears it engenders, whether men acknowledge it or not. We see it in relation to the virus abroad in the earth at present. Very sadly and solemnly, many have succumbed to death. Well might we fear and tremble in the solemn realisation of it. And we must so tremble, apart from sovereign distinguishing grace. For it says here that it is not only appointed unto men once to die, *but after this the judgment*. That is true of all who die, believer and unbeliever. As the woman of Tekoah said to David, "For we must needs die, and are as water spilt on the ground, which cannot be gathered up again; neither doth God respect any person." But, blessed be God, "yet doth he devise means, that his banished be not expelled from him" (2 Sam. 14:14). And we have this beautifully opened up to us in the verses before us.

But let me emphasise how great is the contrast between the believer and the unbeliever. Both must die. But never lose sight of this (the Lord the Holy Spirit ever seal it to our hearts). though all believers will die subject to the Lord's appointment, yet in their death is nothing *penal!* Blessed be the Lord's name, the word assures us that, "The sting of death is sin; and the strength of sin is the law. But thanks be to God, which giveth us the victory through our Lord Jesus Christ" (1 Cor. 15:56–57). Yes, blessed be God who hath thus delivered us from all curse and condemnation. O friends, from our human standpoint we may well tremble at the prospect of death but to the believer there is nothing penal in it, blessed be the Lord's name. The penalty due to sin, the *wages* of sin, is *death*. But have not those wages been paid by Jesus for his people? See how the apostle blessedly sets this before us: "Who shall lay any thing to the charge of God's elect? It is God that justifieth. Who is he that condemneth? It is Christ that died, yea rather, that is risen again, who is even at the right hand of God, who also maketh intercession for us" (Rom. 8:33–34). Blessed be the Lord's great name!

Yet to the unbeliever, death is penal. O what a solemn fact. To die in our sins is to die under the curse and condemnation of God's holy law and there can be no escape from the solemn consequences. O the wonder of sovereign, distinguishing grace! Surely, if you and I as sinners have been brought to hear the voice of our God speaking in the gospel with blessed power to our soul, O what cause we have to bless God for Jesus Christ. For the gospel thus made known, assures us that though we die, yet that death is not penal. The redeemed spirit of the believer enters immediately into the very presence of their God and Saviour! Who can comprehend the wonder of it! But the certainty of it is assuredly set before us in the word of God.

It says here that after death is the *judgment*. What is this judgment? All must be brought to judgment. All will be manifest in that last great day. The apostle says, "So Christ was once offered to bear the sins of many; and unto them that look for him shall he appear the second time without sin unto salvation." This word clearly sets before us that the Lord is coming again a second time in power and great glory to receive his own unto himself and to judge the world in righteousness. How sinners may well tremble, not only in the face of death, but of the judgment to follow. Where shall the sinner who dies in his sins stand in that day? He will be judged and justly condemned as a transgressor of God's holy law. God is holy, righteous and just and his condemnation of the sinner who dies in his sins manifests his justice in all its fulness and solemnity.

But as the believer's death is not penal, how will *they* appear in the judgment at the last great day? It will not be a judgment of condemnation, but it will be the Lord's bearing witness that he hath loved them and redeemed them with his own precious blood, and that they are *one with him*. He will say, "Come, ye blessed of my Father, inherit the kingdom prepared for you from the foundation of the world" (Matt. 25:34). What encouragement is in these truths for the child of God, amid all the circumstances in which we may be found and in whatever things the unknown future may hold for us. If Jesus is ours then all is ours, in time and to all eternity. O friends, he that hath loved us and washed us from our sins in his own blood, will never forsake us! Death cannot separate us from him. The judgment will declare that the righteousness of God's holy law has been vindicated. The testimony will be given for each believer that Christ has fulfilled the law for them. He has satisfied *all* the claims of divine justice. God *declares* that he is well pleased with his beloved Son, Jesus Christ, and with all that are found in him. What a *declaration* is that. The Lord speak it afresh to us. Even this side of the grave, it is true of every believer as found in Jesus Christ. The Lord says, "Thou art all fair, my love; there is no spot in thee" (Song of Sol. 4:7). O, says the child of God, 'How can this be? Look at what I am. Look how I sadly find myself so often defiled by sin.' O friends, faith which is the gift of God, looks to what he has revealed to us in his word. It keeps our eyes fixed alone on our Saviour Jesus Christ. For it is only *there* that we find real encouragement and consolation. It is in Jesus and flows from him in his manifestation of pardoning love and mercy.

"It is appointed unto men once to die, but after this the judgment." Well might the sinner tremble before these words. But how blessed they are for the believer in Jesus. Whatever their outward circumstances, whatever may be the circumstances of their departing from this world at death, yet the assurance is given us that *all is well*. If Jesus Christ is ours, all is well. It cannot be otherwise, for God himself by his very promise and oath in the word assures us of it. Are not *the oath and promise of God* a sure foundation for faith? "God, willing more abundantly to show unto the heirs of promise the immutability of his council, confirmed it by an oath; that by two immutable things, in which it was impossible for God to lie, we might have a strong consolation, who have fled for refuge to lay hold upon the hope set before us: which hope we have as an anchor of the soul, both sure and stedfast, and which entereth into that within the veil; whither the forerunner is for us entered, even Jesus, made an high priest for ever after the order of Melchisedec" (Heb. 6:17–20). "Which hope we *have,*" not only *shall* have, but *do now have*. This indeed is an anchor of the soul to hold us, a firm and sure hope set before us. It entereth into that within the vail. For we are here assured that as Jesus, our great high priest, has entered into heaven to appear in the presence of God for us, so shall his people be found with him at the appointed time. All is to the praise of the glory of his great and holy name.

"So Christ was once offered to bear the sins of many." There we have assurance. It emphasises that *full satisfaction* has been given to divine justice. God's holy law has received from our Lord and Saviour Jesus Christ the perfect obedience it demanded. O, as one says:

> "To see the law by Christ fulfilled,
> And hear his pardoning voice,
> Changes a slave into a child,
> And duty into choice."

O may we know more of the living reality of these things in the Lord's mercy towards us.

"So Christ was once offered to bear the sins of many; and unto them that look for him shall he appear the second time without sin unto salvation." *"Look for him."* Is not this surely the true outworking of God-given faith in a believer's life? What is faith? It is the looking unto Jesus in anticipation that what he has promised he will most surely fulfil. Faith has its sure foundation in the word and promise of our God. God is glorified in the life and experience of the believer as faith rests on his word and promise.

O you know, what a distressing and debilitating thing is unbelief. How grievous is the sin of it. Friends, let us not overlook it at all, but tremble in confession before our God when we find its working. *O, it is not unbelief but faith that glorifies God.* Faith is the gift of God. It is from God and returns to God. In its outworking in the life of a child of God, though so easily beset with the working of the sin of unbelief, yet through the Lord's rich mercies to us, may we still be found looking in faith to Jesus. May we ever look for him in believing anticipation of what he hath promised. "Unto them that look for him shall he appear the second time without sin unto salvation." What a precious truth this opens up to us! O, what a glorious day that will be when the Lord comes the second time in power and great glory! Before an assembled world, he will then manifest his greatness and glory. All judgment will be seen as given unto him. And in that great day, the living family of God, believers through his rich grace, will find in Jesus the everlasting unfolding of that great love wherewith he has loved them, even when they were dead in trespasses and sins. They will for ever have the desire to show forth the praises of him who has loved them and called them by his grace.

"It is appointed unto men once to die, but after this the judgment." Solemn truth, certainly to the unbeliever. But for the poor sinner brought to believe and trust in Jesus Christ what a glorious, assured prospect is here! "Christ shall appear the second time without sin unto *salvation.*" Does this not then bring us to this vital point? Where do we stand with regard to these things? Where is our help? Where is our hope? To whom are we looking? To whom have we been brought? Have we been brought to truly cry unto the Lord for mercy? Surely where that is so, there is the evidence of the work of God's grace in the soul of the sinner. And he will never leave undone that which is the work of his grace. No. As the word reminds us, "He which hath begun a good work in you will perform it until the day of Jesus Christ" (Phil. 1:6). And what a good work it is! It is the work of God alone. The glorious day of Jesus Christ! What a prospect is before the believer, even at death, and in that final manifestation of the glory of God in the coming of our Lord Jesus Christ the second time without sin unto salvation!

I leave the remarks there. May the Lord add his blessing. Amen.

31

THE HERITAGE OF THE SERVANTS OF THE LORD

Tuesday evening 2 June 2020

"No weapon that is formed against thee shall prosper; and every tongue that shall rise against thee in judgment thou shalt condemn. This is the heritage of the servants of the Lord, and their righteousness is of me, saith the Lord" (Isaiah 54:17).

Though I have taken this verse by way of a text, yet this evening I want to consider in some measure the three chapters I have read in Isaiah's prophecy—fifty-three, fifty-four and fifty-five. In fifty-three there is the glorious testimony to the gospel of the grace of God in the sufferings of our Lord Jesus Christ, in whom all the blessings of pardoning love and mercy are found. Then in chapters fifty-four and fifty-five we are assuredly shown that these blessings flow to sinful men and women, even as many as the Lord our God shall call.

Chapter fifty-three indeed reveals the gospel provided through the suffering Saviour. O what a glorious provision! Consider who it is that suffered and the purpose for which he suffered, that God might be glorified in the redemption and salvation of sinful men and women such as you and me! O may we not only *hear* this precious truth, but by the gracious, inward teaching of the Holy Spirit may we *know* for ourselves that he who thus died and rose again to fully atone for all the sins of his people, is *our* Saviour, *my* Saviour, *your* Saviour. Friends, how vital is this for us in life, death and eternity. Whatever we may attain to, what are we if we are destitute of a saving interest in the person and work of our Lord and Saviour Jesus Christ?

The greatest blessing that we sinners can ever be given is the believing realisation that Jesus Christ the Son of God is *my* Saviour, and the Father has reconciled *me* to himself by the redemption that is in his Son. Thus the Lord Jesus declares, "Behold I and the children which God hath given me" (Heb. 2:13). And his children have the witness of the Holy Spirit "whereby we cry, Abba, Father." "The Spirit itself beareth witness with our spirit, that we are the children of God...and joint-heirs with Christ" (Rom. 8:15–16). This glorious gospel is proclaimed throughout the whole ministry of the prophets. The apostle Peter declares that they spake of "the sufferings of Christ, and the glory that should follow" (1 Pet. 1:11). And we see the "sufferings of Christ" in this fifty-third chapter and "the glory that should follow" in chapters fifty-four and fifty-five.

In this chapter fifty-four we see gospel promises which are sure and certain to the children of God. God has had a people, a remnant according to the election of grace, at all times since the fall of our first parents. In the days of the patriarchs was there not a people who, by almighty sovereign grace, were brought to believe and receive the words and promises given by God? And we come to the time of Moses and the children of Israel. True, Israel was brought into a relationship with God as a nation. How great were the privileges afforded them. The lively oracles of God were delivered to them. Through his servant Moses, God established the Levitical order for his worship and service in those days. O how the glorious gospel of the grace of God was shadowed forth in those appointments. But though Israel as a nation was brought into that relationship with God, not all Israel, were of Israel (Rom. 9:6). None were the children of promise simply by being descendants of Abraham. But *within* that nation God had a people who were brought to know the blessings of the sure covenant wherein God graciously manifests himself in eternal mercy. And he further revealed himself through the ministry of the prophets until the promises were gloriously fulfilled in the coming of our Lord Jesus Christ. The glorious gospel was then proclaimed by those whom God raised up and endued with power from on high to go forth preaching and teaching Jesus Christ.

The point I make is that God has always had a people, and not only amongst the Jews. Even in old testament days, were there not Gentiles brought to know the blessings of a covenant relationship with God, not by their own endeavours but by sovereign distinguishing grace? As sinners, they were brought to realise their need of salvation which is found in him alone whom God has set forth as his salvation from the foundation of the world. It was set forth in the promise to Adam, confirmed to Abraham, Isaac and Jacob, and further confirmed through Moses and the prophets. The sole object of the faith of those men and women of God in the old testament period was the one whom God had promised would come. Of him the prophet here speaks in chapter fifty-three. Behold the gospel, the wonders of grace, in the suffering Saviour! True, those men and women of God in the old testament period, though brought to believe and receive the promise God had given, did not live to see the full fruition of those things. But they were fully persuaded of the reality of them as blessed with living faith.

Remember, as we read in Hebrews chapter eleven, faith is the gift of God and "without faith it is impossible to please him: for he that cometh to God must believe that he is, and that he is a rewarder of them that diligently seek him" (v. 6). And in that chapter we see the reality of true faith, in the acts, sufferings and persevering of those men and women of God. They cleaved to the Lord. They waited upon him in expectation of all he had promised. We are told, "These all died in faith, not having received the promises, but having seen them afar off, and were persuaded of them, and embraced them, and confessed that they were strangers and pilgrims on the earth" (v. 13). O may we be "followers of them who through faith and patience inherit the promises" (Heb. 6:12).

Yes, the light shines brighter in the days in which we live. For the fulness of it shone forth in the coming of the Lord Jesus Christ and the outpouring of the Holy Spirit on the day of Pentecost. *Then* the gospel went forth in the unction and power of the Spirit, effecting his sovereign work in the hearts and lives of sinners, even as many as he called by grace. What a glorious light it was and still is! Surely have we not cause, I trust, to praise and thank the Lord our God, for the wonders he has provided for us in the gospel? Truly, it is good news! What is that good news? It is *not* what the sinner can do. Indeed, it solemnly sets forth our helplessness as transgressors under the curse of God's holy law. In the glorious truth of the gospel the Holy Spirit speaks to our souls of God having reconciled poor sinners to himself "through the redemption that is in Christ Jesus" (Rom. 3:24). See how God declares this gospel here in chapter fifty-three. There we see the accomplishment by our Lord Jesus Christ of all that pertained to the salvation of his people in all its fulness and freeness.

And as we come into this fifty-fourth chapter, we see what may well be described as the application of this salvation to the mystical body of our Lord Jesus Christ, his one true church. This includes all the people of God throughout the old testament period and down the generations to our own day. We see here what promises are spoken to the people of God. They undoubtedly had application to the people of God, the remnant according to the election of grace, in the days of Isaiah. The church was then in a languishing state. The nation of Israel was eventually taken into captivity for seventy years because of their sin in forsaking what God had made known to them. All that pertained to the outward worship and service of God appeared to come to nothing when Israel was taken into captivity in Babylon.

But these things speak to us in our own day. Is not the church of God still in a languishing state? Does not this also have application to the Lord's people individually and personally? Do we not often find ourselves in a languishing state in the sense of being cast down, fearful and tried through what is found in our individual path. Questions arise. How active is Satan in stirring up the unbelief in our own soul. What are we to look to? Whom can we go to? Does not the word of the Lord here speak? O what gracious promises he speaks to his people collectively and individually, even when feeling in a barren state, tried, fearful and at times dead as well. Friends, does not the Lord promise that we shall not be left in that condition? Even in this chapter he speaks of his coming again. And indeed, the Lord the Holy Spirit does come. When there is the reviving and refreshing of us collectively or personally, is it of human efforts? No. Does it not arise from the gracious outpouring of the gracious ministry of the Lord the Holy Spirit? What a mercy to be brought to realise our condition and to cry to the Lord. And in this fifty-fourth chapter the Lord speaks of what he will do, and of those blessings that are assured to his people in spite of what they might feel. Though maybe, in a sense, in a barren, languishing condition, the Lord here declares they are not forsaken of him. And *he will not forsake them*. He goes on to set forth their blessed relationship to himself. O how close it is! He assures us it cannot be broken.

He says, "For thy Maker is thine husband; the LORD of hosts is his name; and thy Redeemer the Holy One of Israel; The God of the whole earth shall he be called." And hear what he further says! "For the LORD hath called thee as a woman forsaken and grieved in spirit, and a wife of youth, when thou wast refused, saith thy God. For a small moment have I forsaken thee; but with great mercies will I gather thee." The Lord does not come here to those who are deserving and have brought themselves near by their own endeavours. He comes to those who are afar off, those in a languishing state, those who have nothing of their own to commend themselves to the Lord. See how he comes just where they are, in all their sinfulness and need, blessed be his great and holy name. How he testifies of the relationship between himself and his people: "Thy Maker is thine husband"! O this cannot be over-emphasised! If through grace the Lord is thus ours, if we are one with him, and he is one with us, surely this is the foundation for all the consolation of his people. O what a God is the one and only true God, God as revealed in the person of Jesus Christ, he who made all things, upholds all things and, above all, has loved us and washed us from our sins in his own blood! As the psalmist could say, "This God is our God for ever and ever: he will be our guide even unto death" (Psalm 48:14).

And the Lord here continues to testify to the mercy wherewith he embraces his people individually and his church collectively. "In a little wrath I hid my face from thee for a moment; but with everlasting kindness will I have mercy on thee, saith the LORD thy Redeemer. For this is as the waters of Noah unto me: for as I have sworn that the waters of Noah should no more go over the earth; so have I sworn that I would not be wroth with thee, nor rebuke thee." And what a word we find in verse ten. What precious sure promises are here. O friends, may it speak to your soul and mine afresh tonight. "For the mountains shall depart, and the hills be removed; but my kindness shall not depart from thee, neither shall the covenant of my peace be removed, saith the LORD that hath mercy on thee. O thou afflicted..." Ah, the Lord comes just where his people are. What a mercy that is so. "O thou afflicted, tossed with tempest, and not comforted, behold, I will lay thy stones with fair colours, and lay thy foundations with sapphires..." and so on. The Lord is speaking of his gracious appointments and purposes for his people. See the foundation for their hope, encouragement and consolation. *It is the word that he has spoken, the promises he has made.* All is yea and amen in Christ Jesus our Lord and all to the glory of his name.

Surely you and I cannot take real encouragement merely from how things appear one way or another with us, even if prosperous, nor in thinking about how things might work out in our lives. The ground of encouragement and consolation for the people of God is in the word and promise of our Lord and his unchanging love and faithfulness. O friends, *these things* do not alter, even amid all the changing scenes of life to which we are subject, even in the situation in which we are found at this present time. These things do not affect the sure foundation laid for the faith and hope of the living family of God.

Look what is found in verses eleven to twelve: "I will lay thy stones with fair colours, and lay thy foundations with sapphires. And I will make thy windows of agates, and thy gates of carbuncles, and all thy borders of pleasant stones." Look at this as it applies to the church of Christ. Where is this glory and blessedness that God has bestowed on his people fully revealed? Is it not in the wonders of the free grace of God proclaimed by the Holy Spirit in the gospel? O are not these precious things indeed? Are they not things of true value? It is not for no reason that the Lord exhorts us to "earnestly contend for the faith which was once delivered unto the saints" (Jude 3). How we need to be very jealous to hold closely to the glorious doctrine God has revealed to us in the precious gospel. Let us not be moved away for one moment from the hope of the gospel.

You know, Satan is ever active in seeking to undermine the confidence of the Lord's people in the absolute veracity of what God has revealed to us in his word. Are we not beset in our generation by men's proclamations which are far removed from the mind and will of God given us in holy scripture? See the errors that abound in our day. See how we are confronted on every hand by what scientists declare concerning evolution and its outworking in society, and such like. I surely do not have to go into detail. Are not these things directly contrary to the word of God? Do they not raise questions? Most surely they do. Friends, as taught of God the Holy Spirit where do we desire to be found? Rejecting those things entirely and seeking by the Lord's enabling grace to receive and rest alone in the word he has spoken. "Let God be true, but every man a liar" (Rom. 3:4). Yes, we have the assurance that the word of God shall stand, come what may, blessed be his name.

And now we come to the words of our text: "No weapon that is formed against thee shall prosper; and every tongue that shall rise against thee in judgment thou shalt condemn. This is the heritage of the servants of the LORD, and their righteousness is of me, saith the LORD." The Lord is here saying that the welfare, preservation and persevering of his church in this world is of himself. According to his own gracious appointments and provision for them, not all that may come against the church shall ever prevail over them. The Lord assures us of this.

Remember when the Lord asked his disciples, "Whom do men say that I am?" Various were the current ideas. "Whom do ye say that I am?" Peter said, "Thou art the Christ, the Son of the living God." "Blessed art thou, Simon Barjona: for flesh and blood hath not revealed it unto thee, but my Father which is in heaven. And I say also unto thee, That thou art Peter, and upon this rock I will build my church; *and the gates of hell shall not prevail against it"* (Matt. 16:13–19). Is not that the very testimony given in our text? The Lord has said, "I will build my church; and the gates of hell shall not prevail against it." And blessed be the Lord's name, his word, the truth of the gospel, can *never be overthrown* whatever the opposition often raised against it and against the work of grace in the hearts of his people. We are weak in ourselves but remember who is the Lord our God. As I said a little earlier, the psalmist could testify that, "This God is our God for ever and ever: he will be our guide even unto death." And will he fail? No, we are assured he hath not failed. For he is the one who still has that glorious name, "mighty to save." And our Lord Jesus Christ is indeed "mighty to save" (Isa. 63:1).

"No weapon." See how *all the opposition* that may be brought against the faith of God's elect, the church of Jesus Christ in every generation, is subject to the Lord. He will use it and overrule it as seems good in his sight. We may be assured that all will redound to his glory. And as I have said many a time, what is for the glory of God, cannot but be for the true good of his people. Has he not said, and Paul testifies of it, "We *know* that all things work together for good to them that love God, to them who are the called according to his purpose" (Rom. 8:28). It is not a speculative truth but a blessed reality Unbelief says, 'How can that be?' Unbelief questions it. Faith says, 'I *know* it, for the Lord has assured us of it in his holy word. How it will be worked out, I cannot necessarily perceive, but the day will come when it will be gloriously manifest that what God has spoken, what he has assured us, is truth. The day will indeed reveal it, to the praise of the glory of his great and holy name.'

But see the blessedness of the church of Jesus Christ in chapter fifty-five. See the gospel proclaimed for the needy. What a glorious gospel it is for guilty sinners. O may it be a word to any troubled, exercised, needy soul here tonight. See how the Lord still comes, comes in his word, in the glorious gospel of his grace. O may it come to you and be heard in your heart by the application of the Holy Spirit: "Ho, every one that thirsteth." Is that not expressive of great and pressing need? "Ho, every one that thirsteth, come ye to the waters, and he that hath no money; come ye, buy, and eat; yea, come, buy wine and milk without money and without price." O the fulness and freeness of the glorious grace of God revealed to us in the gospel! He does not come demanding, does not come looking for something in us for which he can be favourable. No, he comes bringing what every needy, guilty sinner needs and which only he can impart. He assures us here that he will do so, according to his unchanging love and faithfulness.

He says in chapter fifty-four: "All thy children shall be taught of the LORD; and great shall be the peace of thy children." And all taught of God, indeed *only* those who are taught of him, "come to the waters." As Jesus himself declared in John chapter six, "Every man…that hath heard, and hath learned of the Father, *cometh unto me"* (John 6:45). Is not that the reality of true, vital religion? Is not that the very effect of the work of God the Father by the teaching of the Holy Spirit? We are brought as a needy sinner to *come,* and indeed to be continually coming to the Lord Jesus Christ who is "mighty to save"? O he has never yet turned away a needy sinner.

Ah, see here the fulness and freeness of the grace of God in pardoning love and mercy to us in the truth of the gospel. "Ho, every one that thirsteth, come ye to the waters, and he that hath no money; come ye, buy, and eat; yea, come, buy wine and milk without money and without price. Wherefore do ye spend money for that which is not bread? and your labour for that which satisfieth not? hearken diligently unto me, and eat ye that which is good, and let your soul delight itself in fatness."

Of the Lord's love for his people, his preserving them through life's journey, his blessing them with all the treasures of the gospel, we can say, *"This is the heritage* of the servants of the Lord." What a glorious heritage it is for the Lord's people, each poor sinner brought through grace to serve him as a true follower in their generation. *This* is their glorious heritage. It is not what they deserve but it is what God himself has appointed and provided for them.

"And their righteousness is of me." Are we not assured that the Lord will ever take the part of each one of his people, because he has already taken their place and satisfied every claim of divine justice against them? So he still speaks *for them. His* righteousness testifies *for them* as that in which God is well pleased, for his own glory.

"No weapon that is formed against thee shall prosper." I say again, the Lord safely preserves his people. He keeps them, he provides for them. And as he has brought them thus far unto himself, so he will bring them to the perfect fulness of his presence at his appointed time. To him be all to the praise.

I leave the remarks there. May the Lord add his blessing. Amen.

32

THERE IS NONE HOLY AS THE LORD

Lord's day morning 7 June 2020

"And Hannah prayed, and said, My heart rejoiceth in the Lord, mine horn is exalted in the Lord: my mouth is enlarged over mine enemies; because I rejoice in thy salvation. There is none holy as the Lord: for there is none beside thee: neither is there any rock like our God" (1 Samuel 2:1–2).

In this prayer of Hannah how much praise and thanksgiving there is unto the Lord her God, for what he is in himself and for what he had made known to her of his mercy as a prayer-hearing and prayer-answering God. There is much in this account for our instruction and, as helped, I will touch on one or two points in the first chapter which we read this morning. But I particularly want to direct our attention to the testimony given in this second verse, that "There is none holy as the LORD: for there is none beside thee: neither is there any rock like our God." Hannah certainly bore testimony to this truth. And if we know anything of the teaching of the Lord the Holy Spirit, cannot we also bear testimony likewise, and bow before the Lord our God in worship and adoration of him as the one and only true God? "There is none holy as the Lord…neither is there any rock like our God."

Let us then notice one or two points brought before us in this passage. Under the blessing of the Holy Spirit surely we shall find instruction and encouragement for the living family of God as in all the scriptures. So Paul writes, "Whatsoever things were written aforetime were written for our learning, that we through patience and comfort of the scriptures might have hope" (Rom. 15:4). Is there not much therein to draw out our souls in thankfulness and praise to the Lord? Whatever may be the concerns in our lives, is there not much to encourage us to seek, like Hannah, to one place, to one person, even unto the Lord our God? Are we not encouraged to pour out our hearts before him and to commit all that troubles and distresses us and all the desires and exercises of our souls, into the hands of our covenant-keeping God? So the Lord exhorts us through the apostle: "Be careful for nothing; but in every thing by prayer and supplication with thanksgiving let your requests be made known unto God" (Phil. 4:6).

Ah, I speak here for myself, do we not often have to come before the Lord in confession of how neglectful we are of prayer? We also find that prayer is no easy thing. How our fallen nature often rebels against it. O may we know the mercies of the Lord in pouring out upon us a true spirit of grace and supplications, not only as we meet together for the public worship of the Lord, but in our private devotions also. Do we find prayer an easy thing? Do we find that of ourselves we can fully and truly commit and cast all our concerns into the hands of our Lord? Can we of ourselves wait upon him, as Hannah did, in the expectation that he will hear and answer according to his sovereign will and good pleasure? Friends, may we increasingly know our weakness and how great is our continual need of the grace of our Lord Jesus Christ. May we know the mercy of the Lord in saving us from all the defilement of our sins and indeed from ourselves, both sinful self and righteous self. O to be kept low at the Saviour's feet as ever needy and dependent on him. The Lord deliver us from all that is of self, for his own great name's sake.

Let us look then at this case of Hannah. We see that Elkanah and Hannah were not without their infirmities. And where is one of the Lord's people who is without infirmities? Can one of us claim we have no sin, we have not sinned and there are not things in our personal lives which we must be brought to confess before the Lord? May he grant us grace to do so. No, not one of us can claim we are without sin. O friends, though no excuse for our sinful infirmities, but what a mercy is the Lord's provision for us in the person and finished work of the Lord Jesus Christ. Blessed be his name, he therein ever manifests the wonders of his sovereign, saving grace as being just and the justifier of them that believe and trust alone in Jesus.

See this beautifully brought before us by the apostle John writing in his first epistle, when he says, "if we walk in the light, as he is in the light, we have fellowship one with another, and the blood of Jesus Christ his Son cleanseth us from all sin" (1 John 1:7). What a glorious reality that is—to walk in the light! What is the light? It is the light in which God has revealed himself. And wherein has God revealed himself? In the person of our Lord Jesus Christ, in the precious truth of the gospel. It is only in that light we can see and receive by the Spirit's teaching, the wonders of his sovereign saving grace to us needy sinners. But John goes on to say, "If we say that we have no sin, we deceive ourselves, and the truth is not in us. If we confess our sins, he is faithful and just to forgive us our sins, and to cleanse us from all unrighteousness. If we say that we have not sinned, we make him a liar, and his word is not in us." What a mercy to be brought daily by God the Holy Spirit, not to claim we have no sin, but in true godly sorrow to confess our sins. As John also goes on to say, "My little children." What an endearing statement is that! Surely it embraces the living family of God, needy and dependent as they ever are upon their Lord and Saviour. "My little children, these things write I unto you, that ye sin not. And if any man sin, we have an advocate with the Father, Jesus Christ the righteous: and he is the propitiation for our sins." And friends, that truth *never* alters, blessed be the Lord.

But to continue here with Hannah. We see her distressed through being childless, and troubled by the provocations of Peninnah. We see her longing for a man child. Now I will not dwell upon the particular problem which distressed her but would direct our thoughts to whatever concerns us in our own personal lives. Surely there are times when matters press heavy upon us, when things trouble us from within or without. Things may press heavily upon us as we come under the sound of the word this morning. O friends, may the Lord grant us the grace he gave to Hannah.

Where did she go with this trouble which weighed so heavily and distressingly upon her? She went to *the one place only*, the one glorious person, even the Lord her God. And there she poured out her heart before *him*. See how she wrestled in prayer with the Lord, committing concerns into his hand. We see her openness, honesty, straightforwardness as she addresses her petitions to him. We see in the pouring out of her heart before the Lord that she was one who truly believed that God *is* God, and that none but God could grant her what she desired. What a mercy it is to be brought off from looking to any creature for help, any arm of flesh in times of trouble. The only place to which the needy sinners of the living family of God are ever directed is to the Lord our God at the throne of grace.

And notice here, as with Hannah, does not the Lord assure us that there is ready access for his needy, exercised children unto himself? He is *not* a God afar off, *not a God whose ear is closed against the cries of the poor and needy*. No, he assures us that he has gloriously opened up the way of access to himself through the person and work of the Lord Jesus Christ as revealed in the precious truth of the gospel. We have access by grace through faith in Jesus' name. 'Come,' he says, 'come unto me, come to the throne of grace to obtain mercy and find grace to help in time of need.' Is one ever sent empty away? We may not immediately obtain all we seek for, but we may be assured that the Lord does hear the cries of his people. And he will answer them in his own good time and way according to his own purposes which are ever for the good of his children and the glory of his name.

We see a further point here with Hannah. She wrestles in prayer before the Lord, but Eli misjudged her. How prone we are to judge others by outward appearance. How little we know of the heart exercises of another. But the mercy is that the Lord knows. Eli, though the priest of the Lord, was mistaken. He thought she was drunk. Was not that a comment on the situation that prevailed in the very precincts of the house of God at Shiloh in those days? There *were* those that went genuinely to worship God. But there was much evil around the worship of God at Shiloh as evident in Hophni and Phinehas, the wicked sons of Eli. He mistook Hannah. Man judges by the outward appearance but what a mercy that "the Lord looketh on the heart" (1 Sam. 16:7).

Now we see that Hannah not only pours out her heart trouble before the Lord, but she *leaves it* with the Lord. She was one who truly believed that God "is able to do exceeding abundantly above all that we ask or think" (Eph. 3:20). She pours out her heart before the Lord and leaves her case with him, waiting on him to answer, consistent with his holy and sovereign will. We read, "Now Hannah, she spake in her heart; only her lips moved, but her voice was not heard: therefore Eli thought she had been drunken. And Eli said unto her, How long wilt thou be drunken? put away thy wine from thee. And Hannah answered and said, No, my lord, I am a woman of a sorrowful spirit: I have drunk neither wine nor strong drink, but have poured out my soul before the LORD. Count not thine handmaid for a daughter of Belial: for out of the abundance of my complaint and grief have I spoken hitherto. Then Eli answered and said, Go in peace: and the God of Israel grant thee thy petition that thou hast asked of him. And she said, Let thine handmaid find grace in thy sight. *So the woman went her way, and did eat, and her countenance was no more sad"* (1 Sam. 1:13–18). *She left it with the Lord* in the confidence of God-given faith that he would answer consistent with his own will in his own time and way. O friends, what an important matter is that! Yes, we are to pour out our heart before the Lord, as Paul says, "Be careful for nothing; but in every thing by prayer and supplication with thanksgiving let your requests be made known unto God" (Phil. 4:6). And Peter says, "Casting all your care upon him; for he careth for you" (1 Pet. 5:7). O for grace to not only *commit* but to *leave* the matter with him, believing and trusting in the Lord that he will answer according to his own will and good pleasure. And we may be assured that what is according to his will cannot but be ultimately for our true profit.

But we see that the Lord not only graciously answered the prayer of Hannah for her *personally*. Was there not a wider aspect in the Lord's fulfilling what he promised? Was not the Lord's gift of Samuel to Hannah for the ministry of the word of God in that generation? For we see how Samuel was raised up and used of God in his day. How little we comprehend the outworking of God's purposes in all his dealings with each one of his people, not only for them personally but also for his cause in the earth.

To come then to the words of our text. "Hannah prayed, and said, My heart rejoiceth in the LORD, mine horn is exalted in the

LORD: my mouth is enlarged over mine enemies; because I rejoice in thy salvation." She rejoices in the Lord, not only in what he had given her in answer to her prayer, but in the Lord *himself*. Surely should not that be the concern of the people of God? If we know anything of his mercies towards us, his pardoning grace and love sealed to us by the gracious ministry of the Holy Spirit, we should indeed be thankful for that, but above all, thankful for what *he is*. As the apostle said, "Rejoice *in the Lord* alway" (Phil. 4:4). This continual cause for thanksgiving and praise is particularly brought out in the second verse. "There is none holy as the LORD: for there is none beside thee." He has revealed of *himself* in his word which sets forth the outworking of his purposes for *the glory of his name* in the salvation of sinners whom he calls by grace. O is not that ever cause for praise and thanksgiving unto the Lord?

"My heart rejoiceth *in the LORD,* mine horn is exalted *in the LORD:* my mouth is enlarged over mine enemies; because I rejoice in thy salvation." Notice that she rejoices in *"thy* salvation," that is, not in what she had done but in what God in Christ has done. That is true for all the people of God. She rejoiced in God's salvation, not only in the practical matters which concerned her, but surely also in the salvation of her soul. You may say, what did she know of the salvation which is wholly by the person and finished work of Christ? Friends, do not overlook this important fact with respect to the men and women to whom God manifested his sovereign grace in old testament times. Their hope of salvation was founded on his faithfulness to fulfil his promise of him who was to come. This was confirmed in the covenant he made with Abraham: "In thy seed shall all the nations of the earth be blessed" (Gen. 22:18). Though they did not have the full light of the glorious gospel which we have in our day, yet they saw those things afar off. They rejoiced in them. Their faith centred in what God had promised and in his faithfulness to fulfil it. And they did not die disappointed though they did not live to see the fulfilment in the coming of the Lord Jesus Christ. They died in faith and entered into the blessed fulness of what God hath promised for every sinner saved by his grace through the person and finished work of the Lord Jesus

Christ. O this salvation is realised by us personally as brought by divine grace and mercy to believe and trust alone in Jesus.

Now let us look at this second verse. "There is none holy as the LORD: for there is none beside thee: neither is there any rock like our God." *Three* distinct points are here brought before us in reference to the Lord our God, the only true God.

Firstly, *"There is none holy as the LORD."* O what cause have the people of God for rejoicing that the Lord our God is holy, just, and true. You say, surely as sinners must we not fear and tremble at the very remembrance of the holiness of God? In one sense that is true. But be assured that unless the Lord is holy, just and true there would be no hope for such sinners as you and me. How can that be, you say? Well, God has revealed his holy nature throughout the holy scriptures but we see the fullest revelation of this in the person and work of our Lord Jesus Christ in the gospel. There we see the holiness of God as one righteous, just, and true, one upon whom we can implicitly rely as taught by the Holy Spirit. We are assured that he will never deceive us. He has never said what he does not mean. "God is not a man, that he should lie; neither the son of man, that he should repent: hath he said, and shall he not do it? or hath he spoken, and shall he not make it good?" (Num. 23:19). Blessed be his great and holy name! O the rejoicing surely for his living family, is that their God is indeed holy, just, and true. And, through the riches of his grace, he brings every one of his people to realise what he is and to know that he has reconciled them unto himself through the redemption that is in Christ Jesus.

"There is none holy as the LORD." O may the solemnity of this ever be upon us in the concerns of our daily lives. And does this not bring us to increasingly perceive what we are and where we are of ourselves and that apart from sovereign, saving grace there is no hope whatsoever for us?

I mentioned a little earlier what John writes in his first epistle: "God is light, and in him is no darkness at all." The light in which God reveals himself is the precious truth of the gospel. And the gospel ever displays the holiness of our God. Friends, as that light shines into your soul and mine through the ministry of the Holy Spirit, does it not bring us to realise our sins and sinfulness? Does it not reveal that there is no hope for us as needy sinners except in the fulness of the grace of God, manifested in the blood of Jesus Christ his Son, which cleanseth us from all sin? God is holy, just, and true. He cannot look upon sin without just displeasure. "The wrath of God is revealed from heaven against all ungodliness and unrighteousness of men" (Rom. 1:18). And that never changes. God declares, "I change not; therefore ye sons of Jacob are not consumed" (Mal. 3:6). Wherein does God not change? He changes not in his attitude to sin, to hardened, impenitent sinners. Such shall not escape the righteous judgment of God, no. "I am the LORD, I change not." And what cause we have to bless God that he changes not in what he, the holy God, has appointed to manifest his saving grace and mercy to sinful men and women. He manifests his wisdom, power, grace and goodness in his provision of the person and work of the Lord Jesus Christ. By him, he pardons sin, cleanses from all iniquity, and imputes righteousness, even the perfect obedience of his Son, to every sinner brought to trust in Jesus alone for acceptance by God.

Secondly, "There is none holy as the LORD: *for there is none beside thee."* Ah, there are many gods that men worship. Sadly, solemnly it has been so in every generation. But the glory of the people of God is that the Lord our God is the one and only true God, the sovereign creator of the heavens and earth. Friends, I know we are familiar with these truths but may we increasingly realise their important implications for every issue that concerns us personally and the church of Jesus Christ collectively. There is none like unto our God. The prophet says: "Who is a God like unto thee, that pardoneth iniquity, and passeth by the trans-gression of the remnant of his heritage? he retaineth not his anger for ever, because he delighteth in mercy. He will turn again, he will have compassion upon us; he will subdue our iniquities; and thou wilt cast all their sins into the depths of the sea. Thou wilt perform the truth to Jacob, and the mercy to Abraham, which thou hast sworn unto our fathers from the days of old" (Micah 7:18–20). Blessed be his holy name, *there is none like unto him.* We see that surely displayed in all his works of creation, nature, providence and grace. O may we know more and more what it is to meditate on the works of our God in thankfulness and praise to him, seeking to "shew forth the praises of him who hath called us out of darkness into his marvellous light" (1 Pet. 2:9). Is that not one of the greatest works of our God—the work of his grace in the hearts and lives of sinful men and women whom he calls by grace?

"There is none like unto him." As Hannah goes on to say: "Talk no more so exceeding proudly; let not arrogancy come out of your mouth: for the LORD is a God of knowledge, and by him actions are weighed." Nothing can be hid from him. That solemn fact must be realised by us in our own lives. O may we not to try to hide things from him but always be willing to confess them to the Lord. David prays, "Search me, O God, and know my heart: try me, and know my thoughts: and see if there be any wicked way in me, and lead me in the way everlasting" (Ps. 139:23–24). Yes, have we not continual cause to pray, 'Lord, search me; Lord, thou knowest all that is found in and with me.' O what cause we have to fall down in confession at the Lord's feet, yet believing that he who searches the heart knows all our concerns and *"there is none like unto him,"* a prayer hearing, prayer answering and sin pardoning God.

Thirdly, *"Neither is there any rock like our God."* In what way is our God a rock? It is his ever being the place of refuge for his people. As a rock, he is the one foundation that is laid for the faith and hope of the living family of God. And further, remember what Paul writes of the Lord's dealings with Israel in the wilderness. Moses smote that rock as God commanded him and water gushed out. Paul says, *"that rock was Christ"* (1 Cor. 10:4). And I say that when Hannah states here "neither is there any rock like our God," this certainly directs us to the person of our Lord Jesus Christ. "That rock was Christ." That rock *is* Christ. That rock is the one foundation on which all the glory of God in the salvation of his people is founded. "Other foundation can no man lay than that is laid, which is Jesus Christ" (1 Cor. 3:11). O do we know the blessedness of this foundation? What is your hope, what is my hope founded on? Surely unless by divine grace our hope is founded on, not what we are or have done, but what Jesus Christ is and has done, how sad and solemn is our condition. "Neither is there any rock like our God," one faithful and true, one who is the sure refuge of his people, one upon whom we can rely for time and for eternity. *He never fails.*

Hannah rejoices in the Lord as her salvation. And we poor sinners taught of the Holy Spirit, ever have cause to rejoice in our Lord Jesus Christ as the rock, the one foundation of our salvation. O the blessedness of those who are founded on that rock! As Jesus himself said to Peter when he put that question to them, "Whom do men say that I the Son of man am?" Varied were the ideas that were abroad. "But whom say ye that I am?" "Thou art the Christ, the Son of the living God." *"Blessed* art thou, Simon Barjona: for flesh and blood hath not revealed it unto thee, but my Father which is in heaven" (Matt. 16:13–17). And friends, flesh and blood never reveals *that* to sinners. It is solely revealed by the sovereign work of God's grace in their hearts. The sinner is brought to receive the testimony God has given of his beloved Son. He is brought to believe and trust in Jesus alone. Jesus went on to say: "Upon this *rock,"* referring to himself as the Son of God, God manifest in the flesh. "Upon this rock I will build my church; and the gates of hell shall not prevail against it." Blessed be the Lord's great and holy name!

I will leave the remarks there. May the Lord add his blessing. Amen.

33

I AM THE LORD THAT HEALETH THEE

Lord's day evening 7 June 2020

"And when they came to Marah, they could not drink of the waters of Marah, for they were bitter: therefore the name of it was called Marah. And the people murmured against Moses, saying, What shall we drink? And he cried unto the Lord; and the Lord shewed him a tree, which when he had cast into the waters, the waters were made sweet: there he made for them a statute and an ordinance, and there he proved them, And said, If thou wilt diligently hearken to the voice of the Lord thy God, and wilt do that which is right in his sight, and wilt give ear to his commandments, and keep all his statutes, I will put none of these diseases upon thee, which I have brought upon the Egyptians: for I am the Lord that healeth thee" (Exodus 15:23-26).

It is particularly the latter part of verse twenty-six which is upon my mind for this evening: "for I am the LORD that healeth thee." Obviously in considering what the Lord sets before us here it is profitable for us to notice one or two things about this situation of the children of Israel.

How wonderfully had God wrought for them. We see the mighty works of our God in bringing Israel out of Egypt and in the great deliverance he wrought for them at the Red sea. Those great works were remembered throughout all succeeding generations. Testimony was ever given to the power, faithfulness and mercy of the Lord, exercised towards his people. God had begun with the children of Israel and he did not forsake them. He fulfilled his promise to them in spite of all their unbelief and sad failings. All who were twenty years old and under were brought into the land which God had promised them. This reminds us that though man fails, God never fails.

We see such sad things with the children of Israel in their journeying through the wilderness. We see their forgetfulness of God and their complaining against his dealings with them. And all this was in spite of the continual manifestation of the power and goodness of God in guiding them and providing for them even in that wilderness. They had manna every day for their food. Quails were given to them when they lusted for flesh. Water from that rock followed them throughout their journeyings. But it is not the history of Israel from the Red sea to their entering into Canaan I want to deal with this evening.

Let us look at the background to these words the Lord spoke on this occasion. In chapter fourteen we read of the wonderful manifestation of the greatness and goodness of our God to them and his righteous judgment upon their enemies. Remember the Lord has declared, "I am the LORD, I change not; therefore ye sons of Jacob are not consumed." And God changeth not in his wrath "revealed from heaven against all ungodliness and unrighteousness of men." Hardened and impenitent sinners shall not escape the righteous judgment of God. But also we see the goodness, mercy and pardoning grace of God manifested to a sinful, rebellious people according to his own sovereign will and good pleasure. He comes to them, not as a deserving people, but in all their sins and needs. And he reveals himself to them as a God "merciful and gracious…abundant in goodness and truth…forgiving iniquity, transgression and sin" (Exod. 34:7).

We see then the great deliverance God wrought for Israel. And in this fifteenth chapter we have the song of Moses, a song of praise, rejoicing and thanksgiving unto the God of their salvation. Likewise, friends, what cause there is for us to join in the song of praise to God and the Lamb for the redemption he has accomplished for his people. Great was the glory of God in his deliverance of Israel at the Red sea, but how much more glorious is his deliverance of poor sinners through the person, work, life, sufferings and death of our Lord and Saviour Jesus Christ. He has delivered us from a greater bondage than Israel in Egypt. He has delivered us from the curse which is upon us as lost, ruined, undone sinners by nature and as transgressors of his holy law. O I say, how great and glorious is the work of God in the redemption of his people by the person and finished work of Jesus Christ. If anything calls forth the praise and thanksgiving of the living family of God surely it is what the gospel makes known to us of the fulness and freeness of redeeming love and mercy. Why friends, eternity itself will not be long enough to express thankfulness to the Lord and to set forth the greatness and glory of him, "that loved us, and washed us from our sins in his own blood, and hath made us kings and priests unto God and his Father" (Rev. 1:5–6).

God delivered Israel from all their enemies at that time and so the Lord delivers his elect people from all their enemies. Though enemies oppress the living family of God, though Satan actively opposes them and they suffer distress within and without, yet assurance is given that deliverance is accomplished, victory is ours. O may the Lord bring it home afresh to us this evening. Yes, victory is ours as believers, not by what we do or have done, but by what Jesus Christ has done for us. As the apostle wrote to the brethren in Rome: "the God of peace shall bruise Satan under your feet shortly" (Rom. 16:20). God has wrought out a blessed peace for each of his own, peace through the blood of the cross. *Therein* he has reconciled his sinful people to himself through the redemption that is in Christ Jesus according to the riches of his grace. May the Lord the Holy Spirit seal this to us, so that we truly know the blessedness of the "peace of God, which passeth all understanding" (Phil. 4:7).

We see that Moses and the children of Israel joined in a song of joy, praise and thanksgiving to the God of their salvation. He had delivered them by making a way through the Red sea. They went over dry-shod and saw their enemies dead on the seashore. O friends, what is our God not able to do! And he is the same God still. Men may scoff at the records given in God's word of his dealings in the past. But our assurance is founded on the veracity of our God. These things were most surely accomplished and they speak to the church of God still. What God was, he still is, and ever will be. There is no issue in the life of the people of God from which his ability, wisdom, goodness, grace, mercy and power cannot deliver them and provide for them.

O friends, I say again, what cause Moses and the children of Israel had to rejoice in the God of their salvation. And, through the wonders of almighty grace, may *we* also know true thankfulness and praise to him who has loved us and washed us from our sins in his own blood.

We find then that they journeyed from the Red sea three days in the wilderness of Shur and came to Marah but could not drink of the waters of Marah for they were bitter. The children of Israel were six hundred thousand men beside women and children and a mixed multitude went up with them. They had flocks and herds. This was a great company and for them to travel three days in the wilderness and have no water was no small thing. They had come to Marah weary and thirsty. Did not the waters of Marah promise them refreshment? Yet what they find is bitterly disappointing, not refreshing. O what bitter things there are at times in the experience of the child of God. But you know, those things call forth trust and confidence in the Lord our God as much as do things more pleasant and comfortable. O for grace to trust the Lord even where we cannot trace him and when all things seem against us.

Is not the natural reaction of our fallen nature like that of Jacob when his sons returned and told him what they had experienced in Egypt when they went to buy corn? Jacob said, "All these things are against me" (Gen. 42:36). Ah, what bitterness for Jacob. But was not the hand of the Lord in those bitter things though he did not see it at that time? And through the Lord's gracious dealings, things which *we* greatly fear to be against us prove ultimately to be for our good.

They came to Marah and found the waters bitter. What a disappointment. We see the natural reaction of fallen human nature. They cried out unto Moses, "what shall we drink?" And friends, we often find ourselves in a similar situation, crying, "what shall we do?" And as Israel, that is often not the cry of faith but the cry of unbelief rooted in our fallen nature. We need the Lord to continually deliver us from self and all that is of the creature. We need the continual reminding of what *we* are of ourselves, but also of what *he* is. Can what God did for them at the Red sea be so soon forgotten? In all the issues pressing upon them, was God at a loss to know what to do? Is he who made a way through the Red sea and drowned all their enemies, less able to meet their need at this present time? O one thing so sadly evident with us is our forgetfulness of the Lord and his mercies to us. The Lord have mercy on us!

They murmured saying, "What shall we drink?" Where does Moses turn? Remember what we noticed this morning concerning Hannah. Where did she turn, to whom did she go? So here with Moses. "He cried unto the LORD." Let us not lightly pass over this. *"He cried unto the LORD."* What a mercy it is that the Lord assures us in the precious truth of the gospel that he has provided a way of acceptance by him. I should not need to remind you, yet I need continually reminding *myself,* that the Lord our God still calls his burdened, exercised and needy ones to himself. "Come unto me," he says. Where shall we go? What shall we do? *"Come unto me"* (Matt. 11:28). He alone is able, be assured of that.

See here his willingness to provide in spite of all their murmurings. They might complain, but despite all their undeservings, we find the Lord is still merciful to his own. In all the ups and downs and ins and outs of their life, in all their weaknesses, infirmities and needs, they still find that the Lord never forsakes the good work of grace he began in a poor sinner's heart. Yes, his chastening hand may often be upon them for their profit as the word declares. But O friends, never has he yet and never will he forsake his own.

Moses cried to the Lord. Here again we are reminded that the Lord our God is a prayer-hearing and prayer-answering God. He shows Moses a tree which when cast into the waters made them sweet. I know much has been said about what this tree signifies. I do not intend to go along that line this evening. All I can say is that Moses obeyed the word of the Lord and we see the wonderful working of God. Was it not similar to the time when they were at the Red sea, shut in on every hand, and with their enemies behind them? God said to Moses, "Speak unto the children of Israel, that they go forward…lift thou up thy rod, and stretch out thine hand over the sea, and divide it" (Exod. 14:15–16). Did the stretching out of Moses' rod part the sea? Did Moses' casting this tree into the water of itself cause those waters to be sweet? The point I make is that though he is pleased to use means, let us not forget, this is the wonderful working of our God.

To illustrate this thought a little further, remember what the Lord said to his disciples when five thousand had been gathered hearing his ministry for many hours. He would not send them away hungry. "Give ye them to eat." We have "five barley loaves, and two small fishes: but what are they among so many?" "Bring them hither to me." (Matt. 14; John 6). With or without means is not our Lord sovereignly able to perform what is for his glory and the good of his people? So here, the waters were made sweet. Remember as I said, at Marah were *six hundred thousand men* beside women and children and a mixed multitude with them. And these bitter waters were made sweet so that *all* were refreshed!

It is said that the Lord here proved them, he tried them at the very beginning of his leading them through the wilderness. Friends, is that not so in his dealings with his people still? Issues are brought into our path which are very trying and distressing as it was with the children of Israel. But what is the Lord's purpose in these things? Peter writes, *"If need be,* ye are in heaviness through manifold temptations" (1 Pet. 1:6). O do not think in these things that the hand of the Lord has gone out against you. Unbelief is ever ready to suggest it is so and Satan will certainly back that up. But,

> "Judge not the Lord by feeble sense,
> But trust him for his grace."

Here he tried and proved them as to whether they would heed his word and believe what he had promised them. Here was an important lesson for what they would experience in their further journeyings as the Lord led them on. Indeed, what a long journey lay before them. Little did they realise at this juncture that it would be forty years before they entered the land of Canaan, because of the unbelief of most of them.

But the point I make is that here the Lord tried and proved

them. And what is said in this twenty-sixth verse? "If thou wilt diligently hearken to the voice of the LORD thy God, and wilt do that which is right in his sight, and wilt give ear to his commandments, and keep all his statutes, I will put none of these diseases upon thee, which I have brought upon the Egyptians: for I am the LORD that healeth thee." O may the Lord ever grant us grace to heed what he speaks to us in his word. Should not the holy scriptures be our only guide in all our concerns as we journey on through life?

We hear many voices and how ready we are to give ear to them, but may our ears be opened to hear, not so much what men say, but what God says. May we not be directed by our natural feelings, not by our estimation of things as viewed from the human standpoint, but by what God sets before us in his holy word. Here he calls unto us and what a mercy it is that he imparts grace to his people to heed what he says. O may we be obedient children brought to follow him through grace. As he himself declared, "My sheep hear my voice, and I know them, and they follow me: and I give unto them eternal life; and they shall never perish" (John 10:27–28). May it be your chief concern and mine to give ear to the Lord, to follow the Lamb, the Lord Jesus Christ, the great and good shepherd "whithersoever he goeth" (Rev. 14:4).

He says, "I am the LORD that healeth thee." What a precious word is that! "I am the LORD." I am Jehovah-Rophi, that is, the Lord that healeth thee. O see who is speaking! It is the one and only true God, in whom Hannah could rejoice and say, "There is none holy as the LORD: for there is none beside thee: neither is there any rock like our God" (1 Sam. 2:2). It is the Lord Jehovah, the sovereign ruler of heaven and earth, who speaks here. It is the one who brought the children of Israel out of Egypt and led them through the Red sea and the wilderness. And he is the same almighty God still. Behold him, our Lord Jesus Christ, Jehovah Jesus, to whom all authority and power is given in heaven and in earth. *He* is "the LORD that healeth thee."

Hymn 420 we have just sung sets forth the precious truths in Psalm 103. The psalmist, blessing God for his grace and mercy towards him, says, *"Who forgiveth all thine iniquities; who healeth all thy diseases."* O friends, what grace and mercy has the Lord set before us in the precious truth of the gospel. All that meets the deepest needs of the souls of poor sinners is found in what the gospel makes known of the person and finished work of the Lord Jesus Christ.

Yes, we may have physical illnesses. We know that these things are in the hand of the Lord. Our lives are not subject to chance and fortune. No. Our lives are in the hand of the Lord our God. Is the Lord not able to heal us from sickness of body and mind, subject to his sovereign will? Yet the Lord has not promised us perfect heath throughout our life. Indeed, we may suffer the weaknesses and infirmities of advancing years. But in all the Lord may be pleased to bring upon us, let us not forget that the voice of our heavenly Father is in these things, the hand of him that loves us. And his love for his people knows no change, no end, blessed be his holy name.

"He forgiveth all thine iniquities." Is not that the greatest mercy, the greatest blessing the Lord imparts, the forgiveness of *all* thine iniquities, every one of them, not one left unforgiven? The precious blood of Jesus Christ cleanseth from *all* sin. The words mean what they say. They come from the Lord our God. "Who forgiveth *all* thine iniquities; who healeth *all* thy diseases." Yes, behold our Lord Jesus Christ as the great and good physician who healeth all manner of sicknesses and diseases of his people. And friends, sin is not merely a sickness but it defiles the *soul*. But we are assured that in the precious blood of Jesus Christ there is power to cleanse us.

"I am the LORD that healeth thee." See who it is that speaks, speaks still to his church, speaks still to us. "I AM." "I am the Almighty God," as he said to Abraham (Gen. 17:1). And so the Lord still speaks to his people, as God over all, God all sufficient, blessed be his great and holy name. May the Lord seal these precious things to your soul and mine. We find in the Lord Jesus Christ alone, all that meets the deep need of our souls for time and eternity. He delivers us from all evil and cleanses us from all the defilement of our sins. He imparts to us the imputed righteousness of our Lord Jesus Christ, the glorious robe of his righteousness, which alone fits us for the presence of God.

See what is brought before us in the book of the Revelation. John sees the redeemed before the throne. "What are these which are arrayed in white robes? and whence came they?" "These are they which came out of great tribulation, and have washed their robes, and made them white in the blood of the Lamb" (Rev. 7:14). "I am the LORD that healeth thee." All grace and truth, mercy and love, are treasured up in our Lord Jesus Christ in all fulness and freeness for needy sinners still, even as many as the Lord our God doth call. The Lord seal to us personally that he is indeed the God of our salvation.

I will leave the remarks there. The Lord add his blessing. Amen.

34

YE ARE OF MORE VALUE THAN MANY SPARROWS

Tuesday evening 9 June 2020

"Are not two sparrows sold for a farthing? and one of them shall not fall on the ground without your Father. But the very hairs of your head are all numbered. Fear ye not therefore, ye are of more value than many sparrows" (Matthew 10:29-31).

It is particularly verse thirty-one which is on my mind as helped this evening, "Fear ye not therefore, ye are of more value than many sparrows." These words were spoken in the first instance to his own disciples as he sent them forth to preach and teach in the various places where he himself would eventually come. Their ministry was confined at this time within the borders of Judea and Galilee. It was after his resurrection that the Lord gave them a commission to wait until the Holy Spirit be poured out upon them. Then they were to be witnesses to him, beginning at Jerusalem and in Judea and Samaria and to the uttermost parts of the earth. He raised them up by the gracious operations of the Holy Spirit to preach to sinful men and women the glorious truths of redeeming love and mercy set forth in the gospel of the grace of God. And by the Spirit's teaching, the blessings of those truths were to be realised by as many as the Lord God would call, those ordained to eternal life.

What a commission was given to the disciples! Though weak as all men in themselves, how great was the change wrought in them at Pentecost when they were endued with power from on high and began to preach with boldness in faithfulness and love. The Lord the Holy Spirit owned and used their word to the calling of many as we see in the account of Peter's first sermon and what followed as recorded in the Acts of the Apostles. And subsequently down the generations has not the Lord been pleased to raise up men to go forth in the ministry of the word? Has he not fulfilled his promise to bless the word to the ingathering of his elect according to his sovereign purposes? And this work of God is still going forward in our day.

Surely we see the miracle of sovereign grace in the case of every sinner brought from darkness to light, from the power of Satan unto God, to know the forgiveness of their sins through faith in Christ Jesus. Yes, what a wondrous work of God is this, particularly when we consider how poor and weak are the instruments the Lord is pleased to use for the preaching of the gospel. Surely every true sent servant of the Lord Jesus Christ is brought increasingly to realise his utter inadequacy of himself. How poor and needy they are as empty earthen vessels of themselves, wholly dependent on the grace of God. What a mercy to be kept in the realisation of having nothing in ourselves but possessing everything in Jesus Christ.

Surely then this word of the Lord was not only for his apostles but for his church and people still. Yes, it has particular reference to those called to the work of the ministry, but it also speaks to every child of God in the path he has appointed them. One thing I trust we are brought to realise with all the Lord's people down the generations, is that we are strangers and pilgrims on the earth. How great is the mercy that we have here no continuing city and are among those who look for that city promised to us by God who cannot lie. How sure is the foundation laid for the faith and hope of his living family as strangers and pilgrims on the earth in all generations. How we are brought to realise that fact in our lives and daily situations.

We may not be subject to exactly the same distresses and needs which the Lord said would be the experience of his disciples, but surely every child of God must walk a thorny path? Trouble arises from outward things and from ungodly men in a world that lieth in the wicked one. Every generation has particular oppressing distresses. But O what trouble and distress the child of God has from the working of his own fallen sinful nature! Yes, it is a trying, tribulatory path the Lord has appointed for his people and shall one of his be exempted? I do not say we are all brought to walk in exactly the same path or be subject to the same experiences. The Lord's ways and dealings with his people are varied according to his sovereign will. But in the measure the Lord appoints, everyone of them is brought to realise that in the world they shall have tribulation. What a mercy it is that the Lord blessedly says: "These things I have spoken unto you, that in me ye might have peace. In the world ye shall have tribulation: but be of good cheer; I have overcome the world" (John 16:33). O friends, in the sure victory of our Lord Jesus Christ over sin, Satan, death, hell and the grave, his people are assured *they* shall overcome and "are more than conquerors through him that loved us" (Rom. 8:37).

The Lord not only points out to his disciples what they were to expect from an ungodly secular world but even, and more particularly, from the religious world of his day. So it was with himself. And has that not been the experience of the church and people of God down the generations? What are we to expect, what can we look for from man, whether secular or religious? Can we expect anything that promotes the glory of the Lord and the spiritual welfare of his people? We know that the Lord in mercy overrules, but men's intentions do not of themselves promote the cause of God in any generation. Satan is ever active to stir up opposition one way or another. How often we see that *by the Lord's overruling providence,* things which appear to be so against the people of God have proved to promote his glory and further his cause in their spiritual welfare.

Yes, the Lord sets before his disciples how very difficult would be the path he appointed for them, humanly speaking. But let us also particularly notice how rich and full is the consolation of which he assures them. They were weak in themselves. And that is true of all the Lord's people as insufficient for all he appoints them. But though weak in themselves, what a fulness, what a sufficiency we are assured is in our Lord Jesus. Many may oppose us but does not he surely testify in our text that no matter how many may be against us, he is ever for us and will be always with us? How beautifully brought out in these verses of our text is the reality of the love and constant care of the Lord for his own. In all his providential dealings, we see the one overriding principle that *all* is according to his divine appointments and purposes.

As I have reminded you many times recently, *all things are in the hand of our God and Saviour.* He says here, not only does a sparrow not fall to the ground without your Father's leave, "but the very hairs of your head are all numbered." Are not these things beautifully expressive of the Lord's knowledge, love and care of his people? Many oppose them but they are in his hand and under his care and "if God be for us who can be against us?" (Rom. 8:31). We may fear at times as did Jacob that "all these things are against me" (Gen. 42:36). Looking at the circumstances in which he was found from a human standpoint, everything was so dark and distressing, so much so that he said they would bring down his grey hairs with sorrow to the grave. But the patriarch lived to prove that those very things were working for his good, though unseen by him. After he had concluded that Joseph was torn to pieces by wild beasts, could he have ever expected to behold him as the ruler in Egypt, foreordained of God to preserve Israel by such abundant provision? O friends, the greatness, goodness and glory of the Lord our God is surely evidenced in all his ways and dealings. He is the God of all providences, be assured of that. We sometimes sing,

"My life's minutest circumstance
Is subject to his eye."

Do we believe it? We acknowledge it. We sing it oftentimes. O for grace to walk it out in our daily lives by viewing the issues in our path as under the control of our God. For he calls us to look to him for everything, to trust in him implicitly, to commit all to him, and as he directs us in his word, to cast all our care upon him. Has he not said, "he careth for you"? (1 Pet. 5:7). How that is underlined in the Lord's words in our text.

Just one further thought before we come to look more particularly at verse thirty-one. One thing was vitally important for his disciples at this juncture and later when they went forth following the day of Pentecost. And this has its application to the Lord's servants still and to all the people of God collectively and individually. That is, *that a man be found faithful.* O friends, the vital importance of being found faithful to our God in hearing, receiving and seeking to walk out all he sets before us in his holy word in the day in which we live. O may we be guided, not by what men say, but by what the Lord sets before us in his word. "It is required in stewards, that a man be found faithful" (1 Cor. 4:2). Even in what the Lord says here the emphasis was *not* on success in the work he appointed them. Yes, all he appointed through them would be accomplished but success is not necessarily the great end in view for the people of God. We seek the Lord's blessing upon his word. May there be increasingly the gracious evidence of its working in the hearts and lives of all whom the Lord our God shall call. But for us individually and personally the Lord calls us to be faithful to him and not be afraid or ashamed to bear witness to him, to confess him in our day and generation. Whether men approve or disapprove is not the criterion by which to judge things. What is the will of God? What is his word to us? "To the law and to the testimony: if they speak not according to this word, it is because there is no light in them" (Isa. 8:20). We see, in the Lord's discourse here, how very searching this requirement to faithfulness would be in the difficulties, distresses, dangers and opposition they should meet. And it is in this light that the Lord speaks the words of our text. He says, "Are not two sparrows sold for a farthing? and one of them shall not fall on the ground without your Father."

When I awoke early this morning, as it was getting light, there was a family of sparrows twittering away in the hedge nearby, and it brought to my mind these words of our text. The sparrow, so insignificant a little bird as it is, yet the Lord says not one of them shall fall to the ground without your Father. O does the Lord care for the sparrows, even the most insignificant of his creatures? His word assures us that he does. His outworking of his providence is manifest in every aspect of his creation, in nature all around us, whether men acknowledge it or not. O surely what encouragement is this for the child of God. Even the most insignificant of God's creation is *his* handiwork, and *his* appointments and care are manifest in the time and place in which they are found.

He says, "Are not two sparrows sold for a farthing?" A farthing is an insignificantly small amount of money. The Lord's emphasis here is that if he cares for his most insignificant creatures as men view it, will he not care for you, "O ye of little faith"? He says "that one of them shall not fall on the ground without your Father. *But the very hairs of your head are all numbered*"! See how precise and distinct this is. See how close it comes. Does the Lord care so much that the very hairs of our head are all numbered? O friends, what intimate knowledge the Lord has of his own, not only of outward things in our lives but inward things as well. The word says that "the heart is deceitful above all things, and desperately wicked: who can know it? I the Lord search the heart, I try the reins" (Jer. 17:9–10). How solemn that is! Brought to the solemn realisation of it under divine teaching, will it not lay us low at the Saviour's feet in the realisation of our unfitness and unworthiness and cause us to cry out, "Can ever God dwell here?" Can such a heart as mine be the dwelling place of the Lord the Holy Spirit? But such is the wonder of sovereign, distinguishing grace that the Lord *dwells* with his people. *He dwells in their hearts* by faith through the sovereign operations of the Holy Spirit.

"The very hairs of your head are all numbered. *Fear ye not therefore.*" What! In spite of all that the Lord set before his disciples here? In spite of all found in the life and path of the Lord's people? In spite of all the ups and downs, ins and outs, trials, difficulties, distresses, sins, afflictions and sorrows? "Fear ye not therefore"? What! Nothing to fear? Are we not creatures of fear? One says,

> "Creatures of fear, we drag alone,
> And fear where no fear is;
> Our griefs we labour to prolong!
> Our joys in haste dismiss."

O what fickle creatures we are of ourselves. O may the Lord's gracious "fear not" in our text come to any troubled exercised soul this night. Hear the voice of the Lord. May it be spoken home by the gracious power of the Holy Spirit. "Fear ye not therefore." In spite of all you may be experiencing or passing through at this present time, does not that *"therefore"* encompass everything? "Fear ye not *therefore.*" O may the Lord grant us grace to heed his word, to find that resting place for our souls. Where? Low at the feet of the Saviour in the conscious sense, as one rightly says, that "My times are in thy hand" (Ps. 31:15). Can they be in any better hands? And are not those kind hands strong to uphold and keep his people safe, to provide for them and to bring them safe home at last as he has promised? Blessed be his great and holy name, most certainly they are.

He says, "Ye are more value than many sparrows." This particularly came home to me: *"more value than many sparrows?"* As taught of God the Holy Spirit, surely one thing we are brought to realise of ourselves and to confess is how unfit and unworthy we are! Yet the Lord should speak of us here as being of more *value* than many sparrows? How can this be? What is man! What are sinful men and women, such as you and me? What value are we? As regards ourselves there is certainly nothing in us to commend us to God that he should in any way look favourably on us, let alone speak of us as being valuable, even valuable to him. Yet the Lord blessedly testifies that every one of his own is valuable to him through the riches of his grace!

Peter says, to "you which believe, *he* is precious" (1 Pet. 2:7). I trust we can enter into the blessed reality that the Lord Jesus Christ is precious, yea so precious that he is the one we cannot do without. But to think that the Lord's people, poor needy sinners as they are, *are precious to him?* Why friends, this is what the glorious truth of the gospel bears witness unto! See the estimation the Lord our God has of the value of every one of his own, sinners as they are, yet sinners saved by grace. Why, the Lord speaks of them as his jewels. See what we read in Malachi. "They shall be mine, saith the LORD of hosts, in that day when I make up my jewels" (Mal. 3:17). Are they so precious to him? Does he so look on them as those in whom he delights? Blessed be his holy name, he does indeed delight in them as they are found in Jesus Christ. They are as beloved of God and as precious to God the Father as his only begotten and dearly beloved Son.

"More value than many sparrows." Yea, he has loved his people with an everlasting love. And the gracious outworking of that love is surely revealed to us in the precious truth of the gospel. We see the wonder of it displayed in the coming, the person, the life, ministry, sufferings, death and resurrection of the Lord Jesus Christ. So valuable are they, so loved of the Lord, that he spared not his only begotten Son but delivered him up for them all! So valuable are they that to save them from their sins, he paid such a price, even his own heart's blood for their redemption! As Peter tells us, "ye were not redeemed with corruptible things, as silver and gold, from your vain conversation received by tradition from your fathers; but with the precious blood of Christ, as of a lamb without blemish and without spot" (1 Pet. 1:8–9). O how invaluable is that blood! And the word assures us that the ones for whom that blood was shed are these whom the Lord declares are of more value to him than many sparrows. They are those who the Lord owns and loves. They are so valuable to him that he not only cares for them but they are never out of his sight. As our text blessedly says, "the very hairs of your head are all numbered." How they are under his protection! Enemies may and do rise up against them. Much distresses them. But none can pluck them out of the hands of their God and Saviour. To him alone be all the praise.

"Fear not therefore, ye are more value than many sparrows." Why, as I have said, these of whom the Lord testifies as being his own, as precious to him, *he has loved with an everlasting love*. He gave them to his only begotten and dearly beloved Son, our Lord and Saviour Jesus Christ, in that everlasting covenant ordered in all things and sure. They are one with Jesus Christ. What can separate us from the love of God in Christ Jesus our Lord? Shall anything the child of God meets in his life accomplish it? We are well aware how Paul concludes the eighth chapter of his epistle to the Romans with those beautiful words of that glorious testimony: "For I am persuaded [what a blessed persuasion], that neither death, nor life, nor angels, nor principalities, nor powers, nor things present, nor things to come, nor height, nor depth, nor any other creature, shall be able to separate us from the love of God, which is in Christ Jesus our Lord" (Rom. 8:38–39).

"Fear not therefore, ye are of more value than many sparrows." And if this is so, O friends, what is the implication for you and me? Is it not in what immediately follows when he says, "Whosoever therefore *shall confess me before men*, him will I confess also before my Father which is in heaven." The "fear not" is joined to our confession. This is to live to him, to not be afraid or ashamed to testify whose we are and whom we serve. That may well often result in much scorn from without and assaults from Satan within, as the people of God have experienced down the generations. But these are they whom the Lord will and does own.

"Whosoever therefore shall confess me before men, him will I confess also before my Father which is in heaven. But whosoever shall deny me before men, him will I also deny before my Father which is in heaven. Think not that I am come to send peace on earth: I came not to send peace, but a sword." The faithful preaching of the gospel of God's grace is that which always causes division, be assured of that. Paul wrote to the Corinthians that the preaching of the gospel is either the savour of life unto life or of death unto death. Where it does not come in blessing, through the sovereign operations of the Holy Spirit, it will most surely end in the curse and condemnation of all unbelievers. These are solemn things.

But to his people he says, "Fear ye not therefore, ye are more value than many sparrows." O for grace to be followers of our Lord Jesus Christ in faith and love as dear children, not afraid or ashamed to bear witness to whose we are and whom we serve in the day in which we live. Nor may we be afraid or ashamed to own the Lord Jesus as our God and Saviour. Our ultimate and full loyalty is not to man, but to the Lord our God whom we profess to know, to love and to serve. The Lord grant us grace in the outworking of it in our daily lives.

I will leave the word there. The Lord add his blessing. Amen.

35

TURN YOU TO THE STRONG HOLD, YE PRISONERS OF HOPE

Lord's day morning 14 June 2020

"Rejoice greatly, O daughter of Zion; shout, O daughter of Jerusalem: behold, thy King cometh unto thee: he is just, and having salvation; lowly, and riding upon an ass, and upon a colt the foal of an ass. And I will cut off the chariot from Ephraim, and the horse from Jerusalem, and the battle bow shall be cut off: and he shall speak peace unto the heathen: and his dominion shall be from sea even to sea, and from the river even to the ends of the earth. As for thee also, by the blood of thy covenant I have sent forth thy prisoners out of the pit wherein is no water. Turn you to the strong hold, ye prisoners of hope: even to day do I declare that I will render double unto thee" (Zechariah 9:9-12).

What words of grace and truth the Lord here speaks through his servant the prophet to his people. We must never lose sight of the fact that all such words throughout the scriptures are addressed to the church of God, the people the Lord calls his own. There is but one church of God, one people of God. Whether Jew or Gentile, the word blessedly testifies that they are all one in Jesus Christ. They are those whom God has loved and chosen from before the very foundation of the world, and in his appointed time manifests himself to them in sovereign, saving grace.

He had a people which comprised his church throughout the old testament times. They were a people brought to know the blessings of the covenant of which David spoke as being the sum and substance of the whole teaching of the word of God. It is well described as the covenant of grace ordered in all things and sure.

David's dying testimony as a child of God, as a sinner saved by grace, was that this covenant was all his salvation, all his desire, though he had to say, "although my house be not so with God" (2 Sam. 23:5). Are not our souls led into the solemn realisation that *our* house is not so with God? What are we to look to, what have we to boast of in ourselves? Our very lives surely witness to us that we have no ground for encouragement or consolation arising from ourselves? We solemnly realise that we are sinners and still find the daily working of sin in our fallen nature. And unless God has revealed himself to us in saving grace and mercy, as he did to David, where should we be, what must be our portion?

O how blessed is the portion of those who, through divine grace, are brought like David to solemnly confess before God that our house is not so with God. 'Lord, how much there is to mourn over and to humble myself before thee, under thy mighty hand, in confession of my sins and shortcomings. Surely no encouragement can be drawn from myself for any hope of finding access and favour with thee. But ah, thou hast made with me an everlasting covenant.' O what does David look to, what is his hope founded on? It is not what he had done for the Lord, but what the Lord had done for him in this everlasting covenant and had made known to him by the sovereign operations of the Holy Spirit. And that is the portion of every sinner whom he calls by grace and brings to saving faith in the Lord and Saviour Jesus Christ.

So it was with all the people of God in the old testament dispensation as brought through almighty grace to believe and receive the testimony God gave in the promise spoken from the time of man's fall in Eden. That promise was further unfolded by the word of God to Abraham, to the patriarchs, to the psalmist and to the prophets. *All centered in him who was to come, our Lord Jesus Christ*. The divine purposes which God determined from before the foundation of the world are unfolded in that covenant made with David. Yes, it was made *for* sinful men and women even as many as the Lord our God shall call. But it was made *between* the eternal Three, made in the person of our Lord Jesus Christ. He was to come in the fulness of time as God manifest in the flesh, the one mediator between God and men, the man Christ Jesus. I repeat, it was made *for* man, not *by* man. Man, as a fallen sinful creature, could not perform what that covenant demanded for the glory of God and the salvation of sinners. It was *Jesus,* God's only begotten and dearly beloved Son, who undertook the cause of those whom his Father had loved, chosen and given to him. He delighted in the work his Father had appointed him. O what love, what willingness we see in him to fulfil the engagements of that covenant! He comes forth to perform all that was required for the glory of God and the redemption of his people. He does so by his incarnation, his life, his sufferings, his death, his glorious resurrection and his ascension to the right hand of the Majesty in the heavens.

As taught of God the Holy Spirit, all the people of God in old testament times were brought to believe in this salvation. Their faith centered in him whom God set forth as his salvation to the ends of the earth. Remember that the people of God were not only Israelites. Even in the old testament dispensation there were Gentiles brought to the saving knowledge of the truth that God had revealed in his word. All were brought as sinners to believe, receive and trust in him and his unchanging faithfulness to all he had promised. We read that "these all died in faith, not having received the promise" (Heb. 11:13). That is, they did not live to see the glorious fulfilment of the promise in the coming of the Lord Jesus Christ but their whole salvation was founded in it. "Not having received the promises, but having seen them afar off, [they] were persuaded of them, and embraced them, and confessed that they were strangers and pilgrims on the earth." Their entire hope and expectation was founded on the promise. And not one of them died disappointed. Every one of them has entered, by divine grace, into the glorious presence of their God and Saviour.

In consideration of these truths I take the verses of our text in Zechariah's prophecy. See what words of grace the Lord spoke through the prophet to his people in those days. According to his promise, God had delivered them from seventy years' bondage in Babylon and had brought them back to Jerusalem. They had rebuilt the temple. God had brought the Israelites, as descendants of Abraham, into a special relationship with himself as he had promised. He separated them from all the nations of the earth, through the form of worship he established by his servant Moses for the succeeding generations. But remember that God's main purpose in view was the coming of our Lord Jesus Christ in human nature. O we see there the outworking of God's sovereign purposes. How wonderful are the works of our God displayed in creation, in nature and in providence, but *exceeding all* is his sending his Son, Jesus Christ. All that was spoken by the prophets through those generations, led up to that great event when the Lord Jesus was born of Mary and laid as a babe in a manger at Bethlehem. Is not the most wonderful work of God, the manifesting of his sovereign saving grace in Jesus?

I know we are familiar with the truth of the incarnation of the Lord Jesus Christ. But I trust we are brought more and more to bow before God in admiration and thankfulness to him for the wonder of his being manifest in the flesh. Does not Zechariah call on the church to rejoice in this? Yes, even in that old testament dispensation the people of God had cause to rejoice and give thanks to him for the certainty of the promises to be accomplished. They were called upon again and again to do so. Look at these words here before us: "Rejoice greatly, O daughter of Zion; shout, O daughter of Jerusalem: behold, thy King cometh unto thee: he is just, and having salvation; lowly, and riding upon an ass, and upon a colt the foal of an ass." In those days many things distressed the people. Haggai and Zechariah were servants of God raised up to minister to the remnant which had returned to Jerusalem, to direct and encourage them in the work God had appointed them for the glory of his name. Yes, no doubt much confronted them at that time. The church of Jesus Christ has always been in a wilderness condition. We are strangers and pilgrims on the earth. Do we really know it? Are we brought to realise increasingly that "here have we no continuing city"? (Heb. 13:14).

We have much for which to be thankful to God in his providential provisions. But friends, is this our rest? Is this what we ultimately seek and desire to receive of the Lord? Surely as taught of God the Holy Spirit, as made alive unto God by the riches of his grace, are we not *brought to realise* that we are journeying through a wilderness in which we have no continuing city? Thankful as we are to the Lord for his mercies in providence, there is nothing in the things of this present world that ever truly ministers to the spiritual welfare of our soul. Wherein is true peace to be found in this troubled world? Is true eternal happiness to be found in the things of this life? As I said, though we have much to be thankful for, yet as taught of the Holy Spirit we are brought to realise that true peace is alone in the Lord our God. True peace and happiness for us needy sinners is only found in what is revealed to us in the glorious gospel of his grace. It is not in what we possess here, but in what we possess through divine grace as one with Jesus Christ. Our peace is in what God's precious word unfolds to us of his divine appointments for the glory of his name in the redemption, salvation and glorification of every one of his own.

He says here, "Rejoice greatly, O daughter of Zion." What is she to rejoice in? What has the church of God to rejoice in? See to whom our attention is here directed: "Behold thy king cometh." We are not left in the dark as to whom these words direct us and in whom they are gloriously fulfilled. Behold the man Christ Jesus! See how these words were literally fulfilled shortly before Jesus went to Gethsemane and Calvary, when he rode into Jerusalem sitting on a colt, the foal of an ass. See him acclaimed by the multitude which a few days later cried, "crucify him, crucify him…not this man, but Barabbas" (John 19:6; 18:40). See how fickle is human opinion. What a mercy to be brought by divine grace from confidence in anything of man, to trust, rest and glory in the Lord Jesus Christ alone. For it says here, "Thy king cometh unto thee: *he is just, and having salvation; lowly,* and riding upon an ass, and upon a colt the foal of an ass."

"Thy *king* cometh." Do not these words speak to the church and people of God? Who is our king? Who is the one in whom we are brought by the Holy Spirit to believe and place all our trust and confidence? Who is the one before whom we bow as our Lord, our Saviour and our all, the one to whom alone we owe *all* loyalty? Only one has supreme authority in the church. It is our Lord and Saviour Jesus Christ. O may we truly know what it is to bow before him, to give ear and heed, not to what men say, but to what our Lord Jesus Christ makes known to us in the word of God. Should not all things which concern the people of God *be judged,* not by man's opinions, but by what the Lord reveals to us in his holy word? Surely this should be the rule in every aspect of the believer's life. As we read in the prophecy of Isaiah, "To the law and to the testimony: if they speak not according to this word, it is because there is no light in them" (Isa. 8:20). That applies to everything that pertains to the welfare of the church and the individual walk and conversation of the people of God.

O friends, what a mercy that we are here assured that our Lord Jesus Christ, the glorious King in Zion, has all authority and power in heaven and earth. There ever will be much that is against the people of God. There shall never be a time in this world when they will be out of difficulties, dangers and distresses that cause fears and doubts and a conscious sense of their own weakness, sinfulness and need. But O friends, "Behold, thy King *cometh"* having supreme power over all things. He ever comes forth for the salvation of his people in every aspect of their lives and for the welfare of his church. Paul could say, "he hath delivered, he doth deliver and we trust that he will yet deliver us" (2 Cor. 1:10). O how unchangingly faithful is our God, he upon whom alone we should ever implicitly rely. Whoever *may* fail, our Lord Jesus Christ will *never* fail. His promises remain firm and sure because he is the glorious almighty King.

"He cometh *unto thee."* And he did come into this world in the fulness of time. I refer you again to the glorious reality of the incarnation of our Lord Jesus Christ. O the wonder of it! Behold your King in the person of Jesus Christ, the man Christ Jesus. We are told, "he took not on him the nature of angels; but he took on him the seed of Abraham" (Heb. 2:16). He was made in all points like unto us, yet without sin. *"He cometh unto thee."* He shall be found in fashion as a man! He shall come in the place of his people to fulfil all that was required of him! He shall willingly enter into a covenant for the redemption of his people! He shall *himself* be made an offering and a sacrifice unto God for them! O friends, he cometh indeed, he has come and he still comes in the glorious truth of the gospel! He comes in the wonders of his sovereign, saving grace as one able to save unto the uttermost, one full of grace and truth! O the love and compassion of our Lord and Saviour Jesus Christ! His church is called upon to continually rejoice and give thanks unto God for the salvation he has provided for us in his Son.

So we see our Lord Jesus Christ *coming forth* for the redemption of his people. Having accomplished our salvation, behold him entered into heaven itself "now to appear in the presence of God for us" (Heb. 9:24). Behold him, the same glorious King in Zion, the same man Christ Jesus! O friends, he took sinless human nature into union with his divine nature and that same glorious man appears *now* in the presence of God for us! And the word assures us, "Wherefore he is able also to save them to the uttermost that come unto God by him, seeing he ever liveth to make intercession for them" (Heb. 7:25).

The prophet goes on to say, "And I will cut off the chariot from Ephraim, and the horse from Jerusalem, and the battle bow shall be cut off: and he shall speak peace unto the heathen: and his dominion shall be from sea even to sea, and from river even to the ends of the earth." This word assures us that he would most surely accomplish all that he came forth from the Father to do according to the everlasting covenant of grace. And he *has* accomplished all. He *has* overcome sin, Satan, death, hell and the grave. He *has* put away the sins of his people by the sacrifice of himself. He *has* brought in everlasting righteousness. He indeed proclaims the glorious reality that God has reconciled his people unto himself through the redemption which is in Christ Jesus. Ah, is not the peace which passes all understanding, in the reality that such sinners as you and me have acceptance with God through the riches of his grace? For God declares he is well pleased with all his beloved Son accomplished in the redemption and salvation of sinful men and women. He is well pleased with all those found one with Jesus.

Our text says, "He shall speak peace unto the heathen." As Paul says, God "justifieth the *ungodly*" (Rom. 4:5). O friends, the wonder of that! He speaks peace to the heathen? Is there not a solemn matter here for sinners such as you and me? We are heathen by nature, by original sin, by our own actual trans-gressions. We are far off from God, ignorant of God, at enmity to God. Our very lives bear witness to it. And remaining in that condition, what solemn judgment and consequences there are for us, apart from the fact that *he cometh,* speaking pardon and peace to such ruined sinners, to the glory of his name.

And this is further opened up here: "As for thee also, by the blood of thy covenant I have sent forth thy prisoners out of the pit wherein is no water." Here is the mighty outworking of the peace he speaks to the heathen. Consider those the Father gave to his beloved Son, those Jesus loved and for whom he lived, died and rose again, those for whom he ever intercedes as the great high priest at the right hand of the Majesty on high. Are they not all by nature in the pit wherein is no water? Does not this surely set before us the solemn truth of what we are and where we are as sinners? O what a solemn situation to be in that pit from which there is *no* deliverance by ourselves nor by help from any other of the sons of men. It is indeed a pit wherein there is no water, nothing to meet the deep needs of guilty sinners. But "by the blood of thy covenant I have sent forth thy prisoners out of the pit wherein is no water."

"The blood of thy covenant," that covenant signed, sealed and ratified by the precious blood of our Lord and Saviour Jesus Christ. O friends, it is the blood that makes atonement for our sins. The precious blood of Jesus Christ cleanseth us from all sin. The life, sufferings, death and resurrection of our Lord Jesus Christ deliver us from the curse and condemnation of God's holy law and bring us the "the peace of God, which passeth all understanding" (Phil. 4:7). All comes to us by the blood of the covenant made between the eternal Three. As I have said, it is a covenant for those whom God hath eternally loved and in his appointed time calls by his grace. He brings them to know the blessings which flow from that covenant, even pardon, peace and eternal life to undeserving sinners. They are brought increasingly to realise they have nothing of their own to look to or rest on in any way. They are brought by divine grace to believe and trust alone in Jesus Christ, to whom is all the glory.

"Turn you to the strong hold, ye prisoners of hope: *even to day do I declare that I will render double unto thee."* O see here the word of grace ever going forth in the precious truth of the gospel. As it has been down the generations, should not the church always be concerned to proclaim the gospel of Jesus Christ? The Lord says in his word, "ye are my witnesses...that I am God" (Isa. 43:12). What is the witness of the church of Jesus Christ? What are we are called unto as the people of God in our day? Is it not to "shew forth the praises of him who hath called us out of darkness into his marvellous light"? (1 Pet. 2:9). How do we show forth his praises? Is it not by preaching, teaching and bearing witness to the glorious truth of the gospel of his grace? Let us not be afraid or ashamed, and certainly not in this generation, to bear witness to the glorious gospel of the grace of God which lays the sinner in the dust and ever exalts a precious Saviour. The gospel places no weight on what the sinner can do. It justly condemns all transgressors of God's holy law, but also reveals what God in Christ has done in the sovereignty, wonder, fulness and blessedness of his grace. Is not the Lord's church brought to rejoice in a salvation all of grace from beginning to end, and all to the praise of the glory of our triune God?

"Turn you to the strong hold, ye prisoners of hope." Ah friends, here is surely a word for every needy, tried, exercised soul. As sinners taught of the Holy Spirit, are we not deeply acquainted with our helplessness, ruin and continual need? Is that your daily experience? *"Turn you to the strong hold."* Here we are directed to one glorious person, for this strong hold is found alone in our Lord Jesus Christ. He is "the refuge the gospel makes known." He is the one whom God hath appointed as his "salvation unto the ends of the earth" (Acts 13:47).

And what a glorious refuge, what a mighty Saviour is our Lord Jesus Christ! He is not only mighty to save, though that is a glorious blessed truth, but he is "a *willing* Saviour too." "Turn you to the strong hold, ye prisoners of hope," having *no* hope in yourselves but brought by the Holy Spirit to hope and trust in Jesus alone, going forth to him as a needy sinner, crying "God be merciful to me a sinner" (Luke 18:13). Can we ever get away from that cry? Is it our daily exercise? And friends, what do we find? Is any poor sinner, brought to cry to the Lord for mercy, sent empty away? No. The Lord says, "even to day do I declare that I will render double unto thee." O the blessings of redeeming love and mercy! May our souls be more and more established in the glorious truth of the person of our Lord Jesus Christ and in the glorious gospel of his grace. May our whole concern and desire be to bear witness unto him that loved us, and gave himself for us. O may that truth be sealed afresh upon your soul and mine this day.

I will leave the remarks there. The Lord add his blessing. Amen.

36

THE WORK OF RIGHTEOUSNESS SHALL BE PEACE

Lord's day evening 14 June 2020

"And the work of righteousness shall be peace;
and the effect of righteousness quietness and
assurance for ever" (Isaiah 32:17).

Our text this evening may not seem to follow on from the subject this morning. But as we consider what is essentially brought before us in these words as well as the context in which they are found, we shall find an opening up of the promise in our morning's text from Zechariah. "Turn you to the strong hold, ye prisoners of hope: even to day do I declare that I will render double unto thee" (Zech. 9:12). What words of grace and truth! And God's rendering double to his people is here opened up by Isaiah in the peace, quietness and assurance flowing from the work of righteousness. And the Lord still speaks through his word to needy sinners. Therein we are assured of the glorious reality of salvation in the Lord Jesus Christ alone. In him, all the deepest needs of guilty, sinful men and woman are fully met for time and eternity. By almighty, sovereign grace we are brought to know true union and fellowship with our Lord and Saviour Jesus Christ.

In leading up to this verse I would make reference to the context. Our attention is again drawn in the opening verses to the great King, the glorious Man, our Lord Jesus Christ. I know some suggest this refers to king Hezekiah and what he accomplished in Jerusalem by the hand of God upon him. But surely we have to look far beyond Hezekiah to see the fulfilment of these glorious prophecies. I do not deny that the ministry of Isaiah had application to his day, but he essentially set forth spiritual eternal realities. For what is the sum and substance of the ministries of these men of God in old testament scriptures? They spake of "the sufferings of Christ, and the glory that should follow" (1 Pet.

1:11). Brought to the true spiritual understanding of the scriptures written by all the prophets and apostles, they always direct us to what God has promised and fulfilled in the person and finished work of Jesus Christ. Therein the blessings of salvation are treasured up and, by the sovereign operations of the Holy Spirit, made known in the hearts and lives of chosen sinners, to the praise of the glory of our God.

So this chapter points to the great King, our Lord Jesus Christ! O his authority and power! May we be truly subdued by sovereign grace to bow before him, acknowledging him as our Lord and Saviour. As led and taught of the Holy Spirit, may we be concerned to be obedient children, followers of our Lord Jesus Christ, blessed with faith which is the gift of God, the faith which works by love.

This chapter also describes the situation which prevailed in the days of Isaiah, and sadly still prevails in this fallen world. Men and women are indifferent to the saving truths of redeeming love and mercy set forth in the precious truth of the gospel. What is Jesus Christ, what is the name of Jesus Christ, to this fallen generation in which we live? We hear so much of many things around us in the nation and world at this time, but one thing is still very evident and has been all down the generations. Fallen human nature, the natural man, has no time for Jesus Christ. The glorious words of redeeming love and mercy always fall on deaf ears apart from the sovereign saving operations of God the Holy Spirit quickening sinners dead in trespasses and sins.

What is the hope of the church of Jesus Christ? What encouragement have the servants of Jesus Christ to still go forward preaching and teaching the word of God? Is it because they have the ability to apply that word so as to truly influence men and women? No. The encouragement is that the Lord directs us in his word not to be afraid or ashamed to proclaim the glorious gospel of his grace, knowing what he has said. "My word…shall not return unto me void, but it shall accomplish that which I please, and it shall prosper in the thing whereto I sent it" (Isa. 55:11).

Yes, there is the solemn warning to sinners that they, as transgressors of God's holy law, are under its curse. There is no escaping God's righteous judgment apart from what he himself has provided in the riches of divine grace. O may the awakening power of the Holy Spirit be known in the hearts of sinners dead in trespasses and sins, and they be brought to cry unto the Lord! What an evidence of the life of God in the soul is a sinner being brought to cry to the Lord for mercy. O that never arises from the working of fallen carnal nature. No, it is by the sovereign, quickening power of the Holy Spirit convicting of sin and revealing Jesus Christ. None but the Spirit can reveal Jesus Christ to us. "No man can say that Jesus is the Lord, but by the Holy Ghost" (1 Cor. 12:3).

See in these words leading up to our text, the gracious promise and assurance of the ministry of the Lord the Holy Spirit. We read, "Until the spirit be poured upon us from on high." His ministry was evident in the entire old testament dispensation and most gloriously so in a fuller, more wondrous way in new testament scriptures. For following the resurrection and ascension of our Lord Jesus Christ we see the outpouring of the Holy Spirit on the day of Pentecost. What a work of God was there displayed! And is not that work of God's grace in the operations of the Holy Spirit going forward still? In the case of every sinner brought to cry to the Lord for mercy and to receive the blessings of pardoning love and mercy, there is surely the evidence of the sovereign work of the Lord the Holy Spirit.

When the Lord Jesus promised the gift of the Holy Spirit the Comforter, he said that "he [shall] abide with you for ever" (John 14:16). And the Lord has never rescinded that gift. Viewing things from the human standpoint, we may not see what earlier generations have witnessed of the outpouring of the Holy Spirit, his quickening and convicting power, his revealing of Jesus Christ to guilty, needy sinners and its fruit in their lives. We may not see the depth and extent of the Spirit's work as in previous days. Yet still I say that in the case of every soul brought to cry unto the Lord for mercy there is the evidence that the ministry of the Holy Spirit still goes forward.

And how indebted are the people of God to the Holy Spirit in his leading, teaching, sustaining mercies and his convicting us of our sins. What need we have to be *daily* brought to humbly fall at the Lord's feet in true confession of sin. And we still have the promise that the Lord the Holy Spirit shall receive of the things of Jesus to show them unto us. Does anything minister true spiritual encouragement and consolation to the tried, exercised, burdened souls of the Lord's people, but that which the Holy Spirit is pleased to make known of Jesus? He alone can reveal the wonder of Christ's love and the greatness and glory of his person as one able to save, a God not afar off but near to us. He alone can reveal him as our great high priest who cannot but be touched with the feeling of our infirmities, having been tempted in all points like as we are, yet without sin. It is alone by the gracious ministry of the Holy Spirit that we are brought to know that the Lord Jesus is able to save to the uttermost, able to strengthen and encourage every one of his own. I trust we are increasingly brought to realise personally and collectively, how we need to know more of the outpouring of the Holy Spirit. We need his quickening influence to draw out of our hearts in faith and love to our Lord and Saviour Jesus Christ.

The promise then is thus given in this chapter, "Until the spirit be *poured* upon us from on high." And then we see described the fruits and effects of the gracious ministry of the Holy Spirit. We are assured that true spiritual prosperity comes alone by his gracious leading, teaching and inditing. Why, the apostle wrote to the Romans that "we know not what we should pray for as we ought: but the Spirit itself maketh intercession for us" (Rom. 8:26). O friends, how indebted we are to the sovereign ministry of the Holy Spirit to indite prayer which is acceptable in the sight of the Lord and which he shall assuredly answer in his own time and way.

But to come more particularly to this verse before us, "And the work of righteousness shall be peace; and the effect of righteousness quietness and assurance for ever." This righteousness is blessedly manifested to needy guilty sinners by the sovereign operations of the Holy Spirit. "The work of righteousness shall be peace." Now we need to make very plain what this *righteousness* is which "shall be peace." It is the only righteousness God will accept, for it is the only righteousness which meets *all* the demands of his holy law. Friends, let us not forget that each one of us is subject to the law of God. And that law is holy, just and good. It reveals what God justly demands. When our Lord Jesus Christ was here on earth a lawyer asked him this question to tempt him: "Master, which is the great commandment in the law? Jesus said unto him, Thou shalt love the Lord thy God with all thy heart, and with all thy soul, and with all thy mind. This is the first and great commandment. And the second is like unto it, Thou shalt love thy neighbour as thyself. On these two commandments hang all the law and the prophets" (Matt. 22:36–40). That sums up the just demands of God's holy law as he is the creator, and as all his creatures are wholly dependent on him in every detail of their lives, their every breath, indeed for life itself. Did not Paul proclaim to those in Athens that, in God "we live, and move, and have our being" (Acts 17:28). And friends, not only are we *indebted* to God but *accountable* to him also. Now the righteousness of our text, which God accepts, is that which meets *every* demand of his holy law.

The point I make is that this "work of righteousness which is peace," certainly cannot in any way refer to what man can do of himself, neither before he is a subject of divine grace *nor even afterwards*. No. Our upright, godly walk, by the grace of God enabling us, is not the righteousness that can work the peace spoken of here. Paul wrote to Titus, "Not by works of righteousness which we have done, [not by man's righteousness] but according to his mercy he saved us, by the washing of regeneration, and renewing of the Holy Ghost; which he shed on us abundantly through Jesus Christ our Saviour" (Titus 3:5–6). Before the Lord called him by grace on his way to Damascus, did not Paul presume he had a righteousness of perfect obedience to the law of God? None could persuade him out of it. Why, he could say he went further than any other man in his supposed obedience. But he was brought to see that all his righteousness, though it might be approved by men, was certainly not that which is approved by God. It rather sadly evidenced, not one that was near to God, but one far off from God. The Lord Jesus Christ said that publicans and sinners enter into the kingdom of God before those who are righteous in their own eyes.

So when it speaks here of the work of righteousness which is peace, the effect of which is quietness and assurance for ever, it speaks of something altogether beyond what men can ever accomplish of themselves. It speaks of the only righteousness God will own and whereby he justifies the ungodly. And does not this chapter direct us to the Lord Jesus Christ, the great and glorious king whom God has set upon his holy hill of Zion? "Behold, a king [*the* king] shall reign in righteousness." We behold Christ Jesus as a man, and the righteousness of our text is the perfect righteousness he wrought out as the glorious substitute for all whom his Father had given him. He did what his people could never accomplish themselves as ruined sinners. The righteous, holy, just law of God gives sinners no hope, no expectation of mercy. Indeed, the law justly demands 'pay that which thou owest.' And inability to meet that demand is no excuse. Friends, the law cannot and does not deviate one iota from the just demands it always makes on the sinner as a transgressor of its holy requirements. Their transgressions are against God himself.

But here we have a work of righteousness which is peace, a work of righteousness which meets all the law's demands, to the praise of the glory of our triune God. It is a righteousness wrought out by the man Christ Jesus, not for himself, for he needed it not, being holy, righteous, just and true. It is a righteousness wrought out by his life, sufferings, death and resurrection, a righteousness which has fully met all the demands of God's holy law for all those ruined, wretched sinners his Father had given him. It is the righteousness wrought out for those found through divine grace in *union* with Jesus Christ. He and they are one. So the Lord spoke through his servant Jeremiah in reference to his church and people: "this is the name wherewith she shall be called, The LORD our righteousness" (Jer. 33:16). And ah friends, what a glorious righteousness is this which by divine grace is imputed to us needy guilty sinners. What is the implication of this? Why, all the demands and requirements of the law are fully met for us. Every transgression against it has been fully atoned for. All the perfect obedience it demands is ours, not as wrought out by ourselves, nor in any cooperation of ours with the Lord Jesus

Christ, but *wholly* wrought out by him for his people. It is imputed to them as the gift of God. What a blessed, glorious gift is this, the blessing of salvation to sinful men and woman as you and me. It is the gift of God in the giving of his only begotten and dearly beloved Son for us. Bound up in that gift is all that pertains to life and godliness, for time and eternity, even pardon, peace and eternal life. "The work of righteousness shall be peace" our text says.

Let us look at this a little further in the light of what is described as the Lord's sermon on the mount. He there makes this solemn statement: "Think not that I am come to destroy the law, or the prophets: I am not come to destroy, but to fulfil. For verily I say unto you, Till heaven and earth pass, one jot or one tittle shall in no wise pass from the law, till all be fulfilled" (Matt. 5:17–18). Clearly brought before us there is the righteousness which alone is acceptable to the holy God. It is perfect obedience to all the law's demands. He goes on to say, "except your righteousness shall exceed the righteousness of the scribes and Pharisees, ye shall in no case enter into the kingdom of heaven." O how the Scribes and Pharisees gloried in their supposed righteousness, that they were the people of God and if anyone met the demands of his holy law it was themselves. Thus Paul in his days of unregeneracy was assured he did so. He says, "I was alive without the law once" (Rom. 7:9). He did not realise what the law of God demanded of him until, as he goes on to say, "when the commandment came, sin revived, and I died." That is the essential ministry of the law as applied by the Holy Spirit: "By the law is the knowledge of sin" (Rom. 3:20). How do we know what is transgression against God except by our understanding what is clearly set before us in his law?

As I mentioned earlier, Jesus spoke of the two great commandments. Well, look at your life and mine in that light. Do we love the Lord our God with all our heart, all our soul and all our strength? Do we love our neighbour as ourselves? Can we say we perfectly fulfil all that is demanded in that summary of God's holy law? Surely friends, if we are honest (and indeed the Lord the Holy Spirit will make us honest in this matter) we have to come before the Lord and say, 'No Lord, not only do I not meet it but I do not even come anywhere near it. There is so much in me that is so far from such obedience that if it is required of me a sinner then I have no hope whatsoever. I am utterly lost and undone and hell must be my deserved abode.'

O blessed be God, our text reveals to us a work of righteousness with which God *is* well pleased, and by which he justifies the ungodly! It is the work of our Lord and Saviour Jesus Christ which his Father gave him to do and for which he came into the world. Shortly before he went to Calvary, he could say, "I have finished the work which thou gavest me to do" (John 17:4). O glorious truth, wondrous reality! This is the work of righteousness which shall be peace, as our text says. Its fruit is peace in its imputation to sinners, through the riches of divine grace and according to God's sovereign purposes. For friends, there can only be peace for you and me with a holy and just God through the righteousness of Jesus Christ. The poor sinner must be brought to believe, receive and trust alone in this righteousness which God has provided. The very essence of God-given faith is that it brings us to rest alone on what God in Christ has done for us.

O what a great and glorious work is this work of righteousness! It *fully* meets all that a holy God demands. By it, God receives sinners. We are accepted into his very presence through the person and "work of righteousness" of our Lord Jesus Christ!

"The work of righteousness shall be [is] peace." See how this is beautifully brought before us in Paul's epistle to the Romans. See the opening verse of chapter five: "Therefore being justified by faith, we have peace with God through our Lord Jesus Christ." Of Abraham, the apostle said, "Abraham believed God, and it was counted [or imputed] unto him for righteousness" (Rom. 4:3). And "it was not written for his sake alone, that it was imputed to him; but for us also, to whom it shall be imputed, if we believe on him that raised up Jesus our Lord from the dead; who was delivered for our offences, and was raised again for our justification" (Rom. 4:23–25). As with Abraham, faith believes, receives and rejoices in what God has spoken and promised. As a sinner saved by grace, "we have peace with God through our Lord Jesus Christ."

What a glorious peace has been obtained by the Lord Jesus Christ through his finished work for his people. The reality of this peace is that God has reconciled us to himself through the redemption which is in Christ Jesus. Nothing comes between a holy God and a sinner brought by divine grace to believe and trust in Jesus Christ. As the Father delights in Jesus Christ so he delights in them as clothed in the righteousness of Jesus and washed in his precious blood.

"The work of righteousness is peace," a peace which sin, Satan, death and hell can never mar, for it is founded and cemented in the atoning work and sacrifice of our Lord and Saviour Jesus Christ. As Peter could say to Cornelius: this is "the word which God sent unto the children of Israel, preaching peace by Jesus Christ: (he is Lord of all)...and through his name whosoever believeth in him shall receive remission of sins" (Acts 10:36, 43). He is saying that the blessings of pardon, peace, and eternal life are assured to every poor sinner brought by divine grace to believe and trust alone in the Lord Jesus Christ.

And our text goes on to state that "the effect of righteousness [is] quietness and assurance for ever." Here we see the eternal realities flowing from this righteousness. We could sum it up in those words:

> "Once in Christ, in him for ever;
> Thus the eternal covenant stands.
> None shall pluck thee
> From the Strength of Israel's hands."

What can pluck one of the Lord's people from his hands, he who lived for them, died for them and rose again for them? Can one of them perish?

"The work of righteousness is peace." And the blessedness of that peace is quietness and assurance for ever. Here is the true resting place, the only resting place for the child of God taught by the Holy Spirit to realise his need as a sinner. Paul says in his epistle to the Hebrews, "There remaineth therefore a rest to the people of God" (Heb. 4:9). O what a glorious rest is that! Why, in that rest we are assured that God has reconciled us to himself by the redemption in Christ Jesus. We are assured that all the sins of every one of his people are fully atoned for by the precious blood of Christ and we have full acceptance with God through the righteousness of Christ imputed to us.

And when we are brought rightly to consider, all these blessings are of God through the riches of his grace. Nothing of man enters into the obtaining of them. There is no supposed cooperating of man with Jesus Christ. No. All is a free gift. "The gift of God is eternal life through Jesus Christ our Lord" (Rom. 6:23). Our Lord declared in his high priestly prayer: "As thou hast given him power over all flesh, that he should give eternal life to as many as thou hast given him" (John 17:2). O the blessedness, the very reality of that eternal life which is assuredly ours by grace through faith in our Lord Jesus Christ! The work of righteousness has surely been accomplished and its fruit in this glorious peace is surely what the glorious gospel of the grace of God sets before us.

"The effect of righteousness quietness and assurance for ever." To the Lord's name, be eternal praises! May he lead our souls more fully, feelingly, believingly into the reality of these things, grounding and establishing us upon this righteousness by which God justifies the ungodly. As Paul declares to the Corinthians: "For he hath made him to be sin for us, who knew no sin; that we might be made the righteousness of God in him" (2 Cor. 5:21). Friends, can you and I fully comprehend the breadth, length, depth and height of this love of God revealed in Jesus Christ our Lord? O the assurance that is given us of these blessings of pardon, peace and eternal life! And all to the praise of the glory of our God.

I will leave the remarks there. The Lord add his blessing. Amen.

37

SHE…WORSHIPPED HIM, SAYING, LORD, HELP ME

Tuesday evening 16 June 2020

"Then came she and worshipped him, saying,
Lord, help me" (Matthew 15:25).

There are two aspects in the life and ministry of our Lord Jesus Christ for which we surely have continual cause to give thanks unto his name. Firstly, he himself declared that he "came to seek and to save that which was lost" (Luke 19:10). And secondly, he did not deny but graciously witnessed that he, this glorious man, our Lord Jesus Christ, receiveth sinners, and eateth with them" (Luke 15:2).

And let us notice the emphasis on the truth that *he receives sinners.* Are we not increasingly brought to realise this as taught of God the Holy Spirit? As we look back over the path in which the Lord Jesus has taught us thus far in life's journey, we have much for which to give thanks to him. But are we not still daily taught the solemn truth that we can only come as a poor, needy sinner in ourselves, cast wholly on the Lord Jesus Christ, through the almighty grace of our God? And this is undoubtedly seen in our text.

On the face of it, in the first coming of this dear woman to the Lord Jesus Christ she did not appear to be given a very kind reception. Yet surely we see in her the wondrous work of God's grace to a sinner, a needy child of God, as she unquestionably was, even though not of the children of Israel. She could not claim, in that sense, to be in the covenant God had made with Israel. But without question, she was in that covenant ordered in all things and sure, as one whom the Lord had loved and chosen in purposes of grace from before the foundation of the world. The appointed time had surely come in her experience when the Lord would make known to her, in the fulness and blessedness of it, the wonder of his great love wherewith he had loved her from eternity. True, her circumstances were most trying. She was in great distress through the affliction of her daughter and no doubt it had continued a considerable time. We do not know the full details. It is not wise for us to speculate beyond what is revealed to us in the word. But in this record, at first it appeared that for this dear deeply distressed woman there was no hope for her in God. Yet we surely see the wonderful grace and mercy of the Lord to her.

The point I would make is that with this woman, though her faith was severely tried, yet there was the prevailing of that faith, it being the gift of God. And this speaks to us. Encouragement is given to needy, exercised, burdened souls. O friend, be not afraid, be not ashamed to come, how ever much you have to be ashamed of in yourself. Is it not true that each one of us has so much to be ashamed of every day? Can we boast of any goodness in ourselves? Can we boast we have attained by our own ability to the grace by which the Lord should be served? We trust we desire to be found followers of the Lord but are conscious of how far short we come. Even with what might be called our best things, we have to say we are unprofitable servants. I trust that is deeply impressed on us. We have nothing in self, and you will never find anything in self to commend you to the Lord, or from which you can draw any encouragement. But O friends, to the praise and glory of the Lord's name, there is everything in Jesus Christ for his people as poor, needy sinners, as this woman found. Yes, every grace, every favour is truly treasured up in our Lord Jesus Christ. And we see here, though in the first instance it appeared he was turning away from her, yet we see the manifesting to her of how gracious and kind is the Lord.

"She…worshipped him, saying, Lord, help me." Ah friends, do we know anything of the reality of that? Do we know what it is to thus come daily? As exercised and burdened with issues and situations, we increasingly find we have neither wisdom nor ability to deal with them. In the sense of our helplessness and need are we thus brought to cry? O the mercy of the Lord to needy souls brought to seek unto him. "Lord help me." No sinner will ever thus cry to the Lord in vain. Though he may not appear to immediately answer, be assured that his ear is ever open to the cry of his people. He will in his own good time and way appear for them and grant them answers of peace.

We see here with this woman, yes, her faith was tried but what blessings were in it for her. She was not only blessed with the restoring of her daughter but surely she was brought to realise yet more the wonder of that great love wherewith the Lord has loved his people. For remember, all the Lord's mercies which are manifest to his own, flow out of that great love wherewith he hath loved them even from before the foundation of the world. And how great indeed is that love, as the apostle John writing in his first epistle reminds us: "Herein is love, not that we loved God, but that he loved us, and sent his Son to be the propitiation for our sins" (1 John 4:10). What greater love is there than that? O may the Lord the Holy Spirit open up these things more and more to us and shed abroad a Saviour's love in our heart.

Let us look then at one or two points in this account of the Lord's dealings with this Syrophenician woman. Yes, we find her seeking unto the Lord and crying unto him but notice this particularly: *was it not the Lord who sought her?* It says, "Then Jesus went thence, and departed into the coasts of Tyre and Sidon." He goes outside the boundaries of Judea and Galilee. When he first sent out the seventy to preach and teach in the places whither he should come, he had instructed them to confine themselves within the boundaries of Judea and Galilee. But here the Lord himself departs out of Judea and comes into the coasts of Tyre and Sidon. For what purpose? Was this a mere coincidence in his life? No, here is the outworking of divine appointments made before the foundation of the world.

O the sovereignty of our God manifest in the salvation of each sinner whom the Lord calls by his grace. His mercy is shown to us here in that the Lord had a distinct purpose in going into the coasts of Tyre and Sidon. He knew that this woman was there. He knew her case and need. Those things were not hidden from him. As the man Christ Jesus, was there not in every aspect of his life on earth, the evidencing of one led of the Spirit of God, indeed, endued with the Spirit of God without measure as indeed he was? O in every aspect of his life, he fulfilled the work his Father had given him to do. And as I mentioned in my opening remarks, was not the great work of our Lord Jesus Christ essentially that he came to seek and save that which is lost? He comes just where this sinner is at the time of her pressing need.

O do not these things speak, I trust, to you and me? We may be troubled. We may be greatly distressed at this time with things in our circumstances and personal experience. O friends, though we may feel and fear to be afar off, though we cry to the Lord and there seems to be no answer, O be assured that our Lord Jesus Christ is not a God afar off but ever near at hand. See how in mercy (and it is in mercy that he manifests his grace) he comes even where this woman is. It appears he went to the coasts Tyre and Sidon for no other purpose, for immediately following this incident he "departed from thence, and came nigh unto the sea of Galilee." So it was evident he came here for one purpose only. O does not this remind us that the Lord's dealings with his people are individual, they are personal. Yes, the Lord's people are a great number which no man can number but the manifesting of his grace and mercy to his own is a very real and personal thing. It is the working of the great and mighty ministry of the Lord the Holy Spirit. It is very evident then, that the Lord had first begun with this woman.

You know, there is something remarkable here as well. Our text says, "she worshipped him." What is true worship? It is very evident that this woman truly worshipped him. The word of God declares that "without faith it is impossible to please him: for he that cometh to God must believe that he is, and that he is a rewarder of them that diligently seek him" (Heb. 11:6). Is not the reality of that seen in this woman? We read, "And, behold, a woman of Canaan came out of the same coasts, and cried unto him, saying, Have mercy on me, O Lord, thou Son of David; my daughter is grievously vexed with a devil." See here the faith which the Lord highly commends as a fruit of his grace. He says to her eventually, "O woman, great is thy faith: be it unto thee even as thou wilt." I say again, from whence did this woman receive this faith? Surely we see the work of God's Spirit, the evidence of the life of God in the soul. Yes, she was a woman of Canaan, a Gentile sinner. She was greatly troubled and distressed. But O see how she is brought here to the Lord.

And with whatever may concern us at present, what a mercy likewise for us to know as did this woman, the one place, the one person who can help us. She does not come to the disciples but to the Master himself. O are we not thus directed and encouraged to come, not through intermediaries, but immediately to our Lord and Saviour Jesus Christ. His word ever proclaims "come unto me," not go to this or that, or look to this or that person, no, but "come unto me" (Matt. 11:28). What a mercy thus to be taught of God the Holy Spirit! Jesus says that all those taught of God come unto him. The work and teaching of the Lord the Holy Spirit, will never leave us destitute of the coming to the Lord Jesus Christ, as did this woman. Yes, her need is great, her situation is pressing. She could not deal with it, nor could any other fellow creature help her. So it was with that man of God, Hezekiah, generations before, when he prayed, "O LORD, I am oppressed; undertake for me" (Isa. 38:14).

This woman was greatly oppressed. Her "daughter is grievously vexed with a devil." You know, we cannot fully comprehend what was involved for her in that situation. But the point I would notice is that, yes, her need was great, but O the goodness and mercy of God! She comes to him who alone is able to deal with her trouble. She is fully persuaded he is able to do what she needed. As I said, "without faith it is impossible to please him: for he that cometh to God must believe that he is, and that he is a rewarder of them that diligently seek him." Here see the reality of that faith in this woman. She *did* believe that Jesus is the Christ, the Son of God. You say, is not that going too far? Well, why does she express herself in the way she does? Did all the others who heard him and saw his miracles? No. Many saw his miracles, heard his words and may even had been healed by his miracles, and yet did not truly believe on him as did this woman. See the evidence in her language: "Have mercy on me, *O Lord, thou Son of David."*

There is something remarkable here. What does she behold with her natural eye? A man, a Jew, a Jewish teacher. But she sees far more in this man. As the apostle reminds us, *"no man can say that Jesus is the Lord, but by the Holy Ghost"* (1 Cor. 12:3). Ah, the very essence of the faith which is the gift of God is that it receives the testimony God has given, that Jesus is the Christ the only begotten Son of God. She comes to him as one who by faith looks to him as God, God manifest in the flesh. I am not saying she comprehended all the fulness and depth of that glorious and wondrous truth, but she believed that Jesus was the Christ, the Son of God. I say again, this is not the working of fallen human nature. It was the work of God the Holy Spirit who quickened her soul into spiritual life to truly know herself as a sinner, and to draw her in all her need to the Saviour.

"Have mercy on me, O Lord, thou Son of David; my daughter is grievously vexed with a devil." In this cry to the Lord see, if we might put it this way, she does not beat about the bush. She comes immediately with what distresses her. It is as the psalmist says: "Trust in him at all times; ye people, pour out your heart before him: God is a refuge for us" (Ps. 62:8). O let us beware of pouring out our inward troubles and exercises into a fellow creature's ear. But let us never be afraid to pour our heart out before the Lord, into the ear of the God of our salvation.

"My daughter is grievously vexed with a devil." "But he answered her not a word." Does not this appear to be a rebuff? Is there not the trying of faith here? She is brought to cry to him in her distress. And we know that the scriptures set before us the kindness and compassion of our Lord Jesus Christ. That is undoubtedly evidenced again and again in his ministry. Surely then he will not pass her by? "But he answered her not a word." Is this the dealing of the Lord Jesus, full of grace and truth, with a needy sinner? Ah friends, let us not judge things by how they may appear outwardly in our situation. The purpose of the Lord is to further draw out her soul to him, to manifest more fully the reality of the work of grace in her, that it was not the work of man but the work of God. And all is to the glory of his great and holy name. Jesus said, "Every man therefore that hath heard, and hath learned of the Father, cometh unto me" (John 6:45). Here was one who had unquestionably heard and learned of the Father.

"But he answered her not a word." The disciples "besought him, saying, Send her away; for she crieth after us." What a reaction of the disciples! These men had been followers of the Lord Jesus Christ for some time. They were good men, sinners saved by grace, apart from Judas. They surely knew something of the reality of grace and mercy towards them. But we see their attitude to a needy sinner! 'Send her away; for she crieth after us. This is hindering us. It is a burden we do not need to be troubled with.' Friends, O for grace to drink more deeply into the spirit of our Lord Jesus Christ, to be followers of *him* as dear children. I speak these things as much to myself as I do to you.

"Send her away; for she crieth after us. But he answered and said, I am not sent but unto the lost sheep of the house of Israel." Who are these lost sheep of the house of Israel? We may say, well, those who are the immediate children of Abraham. The Jews prided themselves as such. Surely God had no purposes outside the boundaries of the kingdom of Judea whose inhabitants could claim immediate descent from Abraham? But John the Baptist told them, "think not to say within yourselves, We have Abraham to our father...God is able of these stones to raise up children unto Abraham" (Matt. 3:9). To rest on the fact that they were by natural descent the children of Abraham availed them nothing, without the faith which is the gift of God, as evidenced in this woman. So with ourselves. No outward advantages of themselves, no natural relationships, avail us for acceptance with God. May we be thankful for God's providential dealing with us in these things, but that is not the saving faith. without which it is impossible to please God. How blessedly is the grace of saving faith evidenced in this woman.

Jesus said, "I am not sent but unto the lost sheep of the house of Israel." Does not this appear to be a further rebuff? O how it draws out the grace of faith in this woman. On another occasion the Lord Jesus said, "men ought always to pray, and not to faint" (Luke 18:1). He reminds us of the case of the widow and the unjust judge, and how by her continuing coming she wearied him. "Hear what the unjust judge saith. And shall not God avenge his own elect, which cry day and night unto him, though he bear long with them? I tell you that he will avenge them speedily." This woman kept knocking, she kept coming, she would not give over, she did not go away. I believe it was not only because of the depth of her distress that she kept coming, but the believing realisation of who he was to whom she cried for mercy. "O Lord, thou Son of David." The Lord was the only one that could address her need and therefore she would not let him go.

Why, it was surely the same with Jacob when he was left alone, fearful of his brother Esau whom he sought to appease with the presents he sent him. Left alone that night he wrestled with the Lord, saying, "I will not let thee go, except thou bless me" (Gen. 32:26). There we see the very fruit of the work of grace in the heart of a poor sinner and O what grace and mercy was shown him: "and he blessed him there." So here with this woman. "Then came she and worshipped him, saying, Lord, help me." She worshipped him. As I mentioned earlier, can there be true worship without faith which believes that God is, and is a rewarder of them that diligently seek him? Friends, whatever men may say concerning worship, unless there is real, genuine faith, can their supposed worship be acceptable to God? Does it glorify him alone and meet the sinner's needs? No.

Remember what the Lord Jesus said to that Samaritan woman when she raised the question about whether God was to be worshipped in Jerusalem or mount Gerizim? What does Jesus reply: "the true worshippers shall worship the Father in spirit and in truth: for the Father seeketh such to worship him. God is a Spirit: and they that worship him must worship him in spirit and in truth" (John 4:23–24). This woman of Canaan was one whom the Father sought. Here was the reality of true worship. She worshipped him as a needy sinner coming to a full Christ, destitute of any good in herself.

Friends, how this speaks to us. With her pressing need she comes crying unto him, fully persuaded that only he can help her situation. *That* is the reality of true worship. It is the coming to him with nothing in our hand. It must be ever so with ourselves. For in all our approaches unto the Lord, we come as a sinner looking wholly unto the Lord Jesus Christ. O we are not required to find something in ourselves to assure us of acceptance by God when we approach him. No, our coming must always be as taught of God the Holy Spirit, as one said:

> "Nothing in my hand I bring;
> Simply to thy cross I cling;
> Naked, come to thee for dress;

> Helpless, look to thee for grace;
> Foul, I to the fountain fly;
> Wash me, Saviour, or I die."

"She worshipped him, saying, Lord help me." How brief is this prayer but what a fulness is in it. Here is the life of God in the soul which brings a poor sinner such as you and me, not merely now and again, but continually crying, "Lord, help me." In each situation which arises, do we have a supply of wisdom and ability to deal with it, let alone to deal with the working of sin in our heart and life? No. As we go on from day to day, even moment by moment, how appropriate is this prayer. O may we know the blessed reality of it. "Lord, help me."

"But he answered and said, It is not meet to take the children's bread, and to cast it to dogs." Does the Lord speak of her as a Gentile dog? See how she falls under it. 'True, Lord, I cannot say anything for myself. It is true what you say. Ah, yet the dogs eat of the crumbs which fall from their master's table.' "O woman, great is thy faith: be it unto thee even as thou wilt." Great faith? We see the reality of great faith here in a poor, needy sinner coming with all the discouragements that appear in the way, yet still coming, still pressing on, still pressing forward, still coming to the throne of grace.

And friends, it is an open way, be assured of that, opened through the person and work of our Lord Jesus Christ. He assures us that, coming this way, we will obtain mercy. Did not she obtain mercy and grace to help in her time of need? He is still our Lord Jesus Christ, "the same yesterday, and to day and for ever" (Heb. 13:8). We see the power and authority he displayed on earth in healing all manner of sicknesses and diseases and casting out devils. Behold him now upon the throne on high, the same Jesus, full of grace and full of truth. Here then we find this woman coming to the Lord upon the ground of what he had revealed of himself in the two great truths I mentioned at the beginning of the sermon. "The Son of man is come to seek and to save that which was lost." And "this man," this glorious man, our Lord Jesus Christ, "receiveth sinners, and eateth with them." Friends, if that is not so, there is no hope for sinners such as you and me. But blessed be his great and holy name, it is true, blessedly true, and no sinner coming seeking mercy for Jesus' sake shall ever be sent empty away.

I will leave the remarks there. The Lord add his blessing. Amen.

38

HE LED THEM FORTH BY THE RIGHT WAY

Lord's day morning 21 June 2020

"O give thanks unto the Lord, for he is good: for his mercy endureth for ever. Let the redeemed of the Lord say so, whom he hath redeemed from the hand of the enemy; And gathered them out of the lands, from the east, and from the west, from the north, and from the south. They wandered in the wilderness in a solitary way; they found no city to dwell in. Hungry and thirsty, their soul fainted in them. Then they cried unto the Lord in their trouble, and he delivered them out of their distresses. And he led them forth by the right way, that they might go to a city of habitation" (Psalm 107:1-7).

We have recorded in this psalm what may well be described as the Lord's manifold providences in his ways and dealings with his people, collectively and individually. And surely the great mercy for which the psalmist shows we have continual cause to give thanks unto the Lord is that all the concerns of his people are according to his divine appointments and purposes. What a mercy it is to be brought to believingly see the hand of the Lord in all the matters that concern us, even in things adverse and troubling. Remember how it was with Job, that dear man of God, when brought into distressing circumstances. What was his response to those calamities that came upon him one after the other? "The Lord gave, and the Lord hath taken away; blessed be the name of the Lord" (Job 1:21). So it was with Eli, "It is the Lord: let him do what seemeth him good" (1 Sam. 3:18). O may we be blessed with grace which brings us, in all the matters which confront us, to lie low at the Lord's feet, submissive to his will, seeking to cast all our cares upon him. This psalm reminds us that the Lord's ear is ever open to the cry of his people. In his providential dealings described here, the dangers and difficulties so troubling and distressing to the people of God, we find one thing again and again brought before us: "Then they cried unto the Lord in their trouble, and he delivered them out of their distresses." I say, his ear is ever open to their cry and his hand "is not shortened, that it cannot save" (Isa. 59:1). How great is the goodness of our God for which we have continual cause to bless his great and holy name.

Well, I want as helped this morning to look at the things brought before us in the first seven verses of this psalm. And surely the first is this exhortation: "O give thanks unto the Lord, for he is good: for his mercy endureth for ever." What cause we have for thankfulness that the Lord our God is the one and only true God, Father, Son and Holy Spirit, blessed for evermore. What cause for thankfulness that he has revealed himself as good and that his mercy endureth for ever! Is not his goodness seen in all the works of his hands in creation and nature? Truly, we can say the Lord is good and he doeth good. Are not all men accountable to God to give thanks to him because he is good and they are recipients of his goodness in his providential dealings? The crying sin of fallen unregenerate men and women is that they neither acknowledge God nor are thankful. Well might we mourn that such is increasingly the situation today. What a mercy if we have been made to differ, not through anything in ourselves, but wholly by the Lord's sovereign grace bringing us to give thanks to him "for his mercy endureth for ever."

"He is *good.*" This is indeed manifest in his providential dealings in all his benefits daily bestowed upon us. But O friends, is not the goodness of God revealed supremely in the precious truth of the gospel? What a provision he has made in the person and work of our Lord Jesus Christ, wherein he manifests his glory and mercy in the redemption and salvation of sinful men and women such as you and me! O may the Lord the Holy Spirit seal to us our personal interest in his saving mercy.

"His mercy endureth for ever." *Is not our Lord Jesus Christ the mercy promised?* See *him* in the very first promise God gave to our first parents following their sinful disobedience in Eden. What mercy God promised them! The *seed of the woman* should bruise the serpent's head though it should bruise his heel. And the mercy promised is gloriously unfolded throughout the old testament by patriarchs and prophets led and taught of God the Holy Spirit. They spake of "the sufferings of Christ, and the glory that should follow" (1 Pet. 1:11). Yes, in old testament times every believer blessedly experienced what is set forth in these verses of our text.

You say, but did it not apply to the people of Israel after the flesh, who were brought into a covenant relationship with God and separated from all other nations? Undoubtedly they were set apart by God to know all that pertained to his worship. To them were delivered the lively oracles of God. What a favoured people they were. But remember, they were not all Israel that were of Israel. In that nation there was but a remnant according to the election of grace. And in the lives of that remnant we see the sovereign work of God's grace in calling them and revealing to them the wonders of pardoning grace and mercy. Their faith and hope were fixed on the word of promise that God had spoken. They were looking for and hasting unto the coming of the Lord Jesus Christ who would accomplish all that God had promised for the salvation of his people. Their faith and hope centred wholly in Jesus Christ as the Lamb slain from the foundation of the world. O did they not believe and trust in God? Was not their faith and hope founded upon his word?

How that should surely be so still with the Lord's people, through the grace of God given us. Is our faith and hope founded upon our feelings? No! It is upon what God has revealed to us in his holy blessed word as it centres in the person of our Lord Jesus Christ. Yes, I want right and comfortable feelings. I want to feel the wonders of the grace and mercy of God to me. But friends, the faith and hope of the child of God is founded upon a *sure* foundation—not feelings but Jesus Christ our Lord. The elect sinner is always led by the sovereign operations of the Holy Spirit to the Lord Jesus Christ alone, in whom is all their salvation. We shall not be left to rest in anything else, anything less than Jesus. Though we find the working of our fallen nature is in the opposite direction, yet the Holy Spirit will bring us to where we need to be continually brought, that is, the glorious person of our Lord and Saviour Jesus Christ. In him alone do we know the blessedness of the rest that remains for the people of God.

"Let the *redeemed* of the Lord say so." Truly, the Lord's people are a people redeemed by grace "from the hand of the enemy." And the Holy Spirit brings them to the blessed believing realisation of the wonders of redeeming mercy in what the gospel reveals of the person and work of Jesus Christ. And if ever a people should be a thankful people, it is sinners saved by grace, brought to know the redeeming love and mercy of the Lord. O may we not be afraid or ashamed to bear testimony unto him. O may the Lord the Holy Spirit seal these truths afresh unto us and enlarge our hearts in the love and praise of our God who hath redeemed us from all iniquity.

That very word *"redeemed"* implies a people purchased from hard bondage. When the Lord appeared in the bush to Moses, the Israelites were in bitter bondage in Egypt. Their deliverance was not by their own ingenuity or by rebellion against the Egyptians. That would have availed them nothing. They were delivered by the Lord manifesting his mercy toward them. He says to Moses, "I have surely seen the affliction of my people which are in Egypt, and have heard their cry…and I am come down to deliver them" (Exod. 3:7–8). O the wonders of that grace! The Lord comes down, as he has come in the person of our Lord Jesus Christ, to redeem and deliver his people for himself. And how great was the price he paid for the redemption of his people! O this is no insignificant matter. No. How great is their redemption! *Full* satisfaction has been rendered, a *full* price paid! The Lord Jesus has redeemed his people by his own precious blood.

Friends, what wonders of grace are unfolded to us here in that which you and I as sinners could never do. How greatly we are in debt to God as transgressors of his holy law. We are not merely five hundred talent debtors but ten thousand times ten thousand talent debtors. Yet the Lord himself, God in the person of his Son, has redeemed his people from the curse of a broken law. The Lord Jesus has most surely satisfied all that the holy God justly demanded of them in his holy law. He fully satisfied for them as their substitute. What we could *not* do he himself has fully accomplished. And what he has once done is done forever! The redemption price has been paid! O as the word of God ever testifies, the precious blood of Jesus Christ cleanseth us from all sin, blessed be his great and holy name.

What then is the standing of the believer as redeemed by the precious blood of the Lord Jesus Christ? "There is therefore now no condemnation to them which are in Christ Jesus, who walk not after the flesh, but after the Spirit" (Rom. 8:1). What is it to "walk not after the flesh, but after the Spirit"? To walk after the Spirit is ever set before us in the word as the very life of God in the soul. "The just shall live by faith" (Rom. 1:17). That was true of old testament believers and it is ever true of all taught of God the Holy Spirit. "The just shall live by faith," and *they do live by faith*. Their whole life is bound up in what they receive out of the Lord Jesus Christ who loved them and washed them from their sins in his own blood. Where is their sure ground of hope? Where is their trust? *Alone in the Lord*. O that we may know increasingly the living reality of these things in our own soul's daily experience.

"He hath redeemed [them] from the hand of the enemy; and *gathered* them out of the lands, from the east, and from the west, from the north, and from the south." Yes, the Lord's people are a people gathered out by the Holy Spirit. The Lord said of Israel in Egypt, "I am come down to deliver them." And he does come down to gather his people, "from the east, and from the west, from the north, and from the south." Does this not surely clearly indicate that the people of God are not the national Israel of old? Yes, God had separated Israel from the nations of the earth. Through them the divine purposes were fulfilled in the coming of our Lord Jesus according to his human nature. But essentially the people of God, both then and always, are a people saved by grace, a people whom God has loved, chosen, called out and *gathered,* as indicated here, from all nations.

Is not this fully opened up to us in the new testament scriptures by the words of our Lord Jesus Christ himself as he commissioned his disciples? He says "ye shall be witnesses unto me both in Jerusalem, and in all Judaea, and in Samaria, and unto the uttermost part of the earth" (Acts 1:8). They were commissioned to go forth preaching and teaching Jesus Christ, ingathering his people by the sovereign operations of the Lord the Holy Spirit, not only from the Jews but also from all the Gentile nations of the earth. All was according to his own divine appointments, to the praise of the glory of his great and holy name. O friends, how little we comprehend the fulness of the wonders of redeeming love and mercy! Yes, in the world the Lord's people are a remnant. In every generation it has been so. But we read that the Lord's people are a number "which no man could number, of all nations, and kindreds, and people, and tongues" (Rev. 7:9). Glorious truth indeed!

This *gathering* of a people refers not only to the church of Jesus Christ collectively but to each individual sinner whom the Lord brings to himself out of death in trespasses and sins. Essentially brought before us here is the sovereign work of God the Holy Spirit. Remember the words of our Lord Jesus Christ when he informed his disciples he was going away, He knew how distressed they would be. But he says, "If I go not away, the Comforter will not come unto you; but if I depart, I will send him unto you" (John 16:7). What a promise, and that fulfilled in the wonderful coming of the Lord the Holy Spirit on the day of Pentecost! And the Holy Spirit's work seen on the day of Pentecost is manifest in every sinner *gathered* from death in trespasses and sins, into the light, life and liberty of the gospel. For the means the Lord has appointed is *the preaching of the gospel,* bringing the blessings of salvation to sinners such as you and me through the sovereign application of God the Holy Spirit. Without that sovereign work no person can ever know anything savingly of the truth as it is in the Lord Jesus Christ.

We see here then a people *redeemed* by the precious blood of Jesus Christ and *gathered.* "He gathered them." What a mercy! The Lord knows just where each sinner towards whom he has purposes of love and mercy is to be found. They are a people scattered afar off even to the very ends of the earth. But as taught by the sovereign gracious operations of the Holy Spirit, they are brought to the solemn conviction of their sin. And in his appointed time he reveals himself to them in Jesus Christ as a "God, merciful and gracious…abundant in goodness and truth…forgiving iniquity and transgression and sin" (Exod. 34:6–7). He blesses them with pardon, peace and eternal life.

We read, "They wandered in the wilderness in a solitary way; they found no city to dwell in. Hungry and thirsty, their soul fainted in them." O how true that is in the experience of the living family of God when he first awakens them by the sovereign operations of the Holy Spirit. He brings them to know themselves as transgressors of his holy law, justly deserving to be cut off for ever if he were to deal with them according to their sins. But it is also true of the people of God as we journey on through this wilderness world, even after the Lord has brought us to know himself as our Saviour.

As I have said, we have very much for which to be thankful to the Lord in his daily providential mercies, his care and kindness over us. Yet what can this world yield of any spiritual welfare to our never dying souls? What can meet the spiritual needs of the living family of God? Do earthly things? Friends, are we not brought to realise increasingly that our rest is not in earthly things? O how trying and troubling is the path in which the Lord's people are called to walk. "They found *no* city to dwell in." No, *nothing* can truly satisfy a living soul, except the salvation the Lord has provided according to his word of promise. To this sure foundation we are brought to look by the Holy Spirit. As one says of worldly things,

> "These can never satisfy;
> Give me Christ, or else I die."

Friends, is that your soul's longing desire? O what a mercy if it is so. Such longings will not go unsatisfied, though there is an appointed time when Christ will reveal himself. And not only does he reveal himself once, but again and again in gracious dealings towards us.

"Hungry and thirsty, their soul fainted in them." The Lord Jesus said, "Blessed are they which do hunger and thirst after righteousness: for they shall be filled" (Matt. 5:6). One said,

> "I thirst, but not as once I did,
> The vain delights of earth to share;
> Thy wounds, Immanuel, all forbid
> That I should seek my pleasure there."

Yes, I trust, through the Lord's mercies towards us, we hunger after the bread which comes from heaven and thirst for the living water which the Lord Jesus Christ promised the woman at the well of Samaria. May our longings be to know him and have more communion with him. Nothing can meet the desires of a living soul apart from the manifestation of the Lord Jesus Christ in grace and mercy, blessing his precious gospel to us as preached with the anointing of the Holy Spirit in faithfulness and love. Are not these the means God has provided to nourish the souls of his hungry and thirsty living family? Do we not feed upon the promises of God in his holy word? What brings health, healing, pardon, strength and encouragement to us? Is it not the word of the Lord in mercy applied to us by the unction of the Holy Spirit? What a mercy to have a spiritual appetite for the spiritual and eternal truths of the glorious gospel, the word of his grace through which he speaks to us.

The Lord fed Israel for forty years in the wilderness with manna that came down from heaven. It failed not all the years they were in the wilderness, despite all their unbelief and the rebellious spirit which they evidenced repeatedly, sadly even loathing the very bread God provided for them. O we see there the faithfulness of God to his word. But O friends, what a humbling truth! Are we any better than Israel of ourselves? I trust we are brought to increasingly realise what needy sinners we are, utterly indebted to the goodness and mercy of the Lord towards us. "He hath not dealt with us after our sins; nor rewarded us according to our iniquities" (Ps. 103:10). Has not the Lord provided for the spiritual welfare of his people in all that Jesus is and all he has done as made known to them by the Holy Spirit?

The Lord Jesus said to the woman of Samaria, "If thou knewest the gift of God, and who it is that saith to thee, Give me to drink; thou wouldest have asked of him, and he would have given thee living water" (John 4:10). She says, "From whence then hast thou that living water?" O does not Jesus Christ direct her wholly to himself? And still the Holy Spirit directs us wholly to the Lord Jesus as set forth in the word of the truth of the gospel. As I have said many a time, the gracious leading of the Holy Spirit of each one of his own, is always according to, and through, the word of God given us in holy scripture. How vitally important that is. Can you and I find any encouragement, any spiritual nourishment for our souls, that is not founded on what the Lord reveals to us in his word? One of old said, "Thy words were found, and I did eat them; and thy word was unto me the joy and rejoicing of mine heart" (Jer. 15:16).

"Hungry and thirsty, their soul fainted in them. *Then they cried unto the Lord* in their trouble, and he delivered them out of their distresses." O friends, what a mercy that the Lord's ear is ever open to the cry of his people. He is more ready to hear than we are to call upon his name. What an evidence of the life of God in the soul is the cry of a poor sinner unto the Lord. "No man can say that Jesus is the Lord, but by the Holy Ghost" (1 Cor. 12:3). None are brought truly to cry unto the Lord except as taught of the Holy Spirit to increasingly realise their need as sinners and to know the fulness of grace in Christ Jesus our Lord.

"And *he led them forth* by the right way, that they might go to a city of habitation." Who led them forth? The Lord the Spirit was with Israel and went before them. Every sinner brought to the saving knowledge of the truth, whether patriarchs, prophets, men or women, were subjects of the Spirit's sovereign gracious ministry and operations. And our Lord Jesus Christ himself promised, "I will pray the Father, and he shall give you another Comforter, that he may abide with you for ever; even the Spirit of truth; whom the world cannot receive, because it seeth him not, neither knoweth him: but ye know him; for he dwelleth with you, and shall be in you" (John 14:16–17). "He shall take of mine, and shall shew it unto you" (John 16:15). Glorious truth! How vitally important is this for the true welfare of the people of God, individually and personally, as we journey on through life. What a mercy we are not left to ourselves and our own devices but are the subjects of the leading and teaching of the Lord the Holy Spirit, directing, keeping and providing for us. For are we not a needy, dependent people? O what a mercy to ever be brought to increasingly realise how needy and dependent we are upon the Lord alone. The psalmist said, "I am poor and needy; *yet the Lord thinketh upon me"* (Ps. 40:17). How descriptive is that of the living family of God.

"He led them forth *by the right way.*" The Lord the Holy Spirit leads in no other way. Therein are the blessings of salvation to the glory of God. It is well described as the *right* way. It is the *only* way. And what is the way in which the Lord the Holy Spirit leads? It is in the Lord Jesus alone, through faith in him. When his disciples said that they knew not the way, Jesus said, "I am the way, the truth, and the life: no man cometh unto the Father, but by me" (John 14:6). And the leading of the Holy Spirit is never apart from what he reveals of the Lord Jesus Christ in the fulness and freeness of his sovereign grace and mercy to his own. What a mercy to be kept "looking unto Jesus, the author and finisher of our faith" (Heb.12:2), led daily of the Holy Spirit, in all that burdens and exercises us, to the Lord Jesus Christ, to the throne of his grace "that we may obtain mercy, and find grace to help in time of need" (Heb. 4:16).

And see the culmination of this leading. "He led them forth by the right way, *that they might go to a city of habitation.*" What a promise was that to his people of old, as they looked forward to the first coming of the Lord Jesus Christ as the fulfilment of all God had promised. So with his people still. He leads them forth. They go to a city of habitation. And what a city, what an abiding place is that for the living family of God as found in Jesus Christ our Lord! They have "the promise of the life that now is, and of that which is to come" (1 Tim. 4:8), that eternal inheritance appointed for them. To this all believers look and never has one died disappointed. All *will* be brought home, as our Lord Jesus Christ himself has promised, for none can pluck them out of his hand. He says, "All that the Father giveth me shall come to me; and him that cometh to me I will in no wise cast out" (John 6:37). Glorious, precious truth!

"He led them forth by the right way, that they might go to a city of habitation." What a glorious prospect there is for the church and people of God! O friends, may we be found looking for and hasting unto the coming of our Lord Jesus Christ.

The Lord add his blessing. Amen.

39

FEAR NOT: BEHOLD, YOUR GOD WILL COME

Lord's day evening 21 June 2020

"Strengthen ye the weak hands, and confirm the feeble knees. Say to them that are of a fearful heart, Be strong, fear not: behold, your God will come with vengeance, even God with a recompence; he will come and save you" (Isaiah 35:3-4).

These words of the prophet were spoken to the people of God in his day against the background of the righteous judgments of God on Israel and Judah. And as we see in the thirty fourth chapter, have not the judgments of God always been abroad in the earth? For as we look back over the whole history of mankind, has there been a time when the judgments of God have not been evident in one form or another on a fallen sinful world? And certainly it is no less so today. In our present circumstances, is there not the evidence of the judgments of God upon a sinful wicked generation?

But friends, the important point I want to emphasise tonight is that in the midst of these righteous judgments of God we also see his mercy manifest in his grace towards his church and people. In these promises, the prophet set forth the rich consolations in Jesus Christ for believers in his day and surely for us today. Here is the precious grace and truth of the glorious gospel of our Lord and Saviour Jesus Christ. This commission of the prophet seen in our text this evening is more fully expressed in chapter forty of his prophecy: "Comfort ye, comfort ye my people, saith your God. Speak ye comfortably to Jerusalem, and cry unto her, that her warfare is accomplished, that her iniquity is pardoned: for she hath received of the Lord's hand double for all her sins." Was not that a glorious setting forth of the wondrous grace and mercy of God? See there the fulness of God's grace in all he has appointed, promised and gloriously fulfilled in the coming of the Lord Jesus Christ at his appointed time, to the praise of the glory of his name. These were not empty words, nor are they ever so to the true people of God. O may we be increasingly blessed by the Holy Spirit revealing to us the things of the Lord Jesus Christ.

Here again we see the commission of the prophet. The Lord says to him, "Strengthen ye the weak hands, and confirm the feeble knees." This was the word of the Lord to the remnant in those days and it is so to his people in our day. It has been blessed to the Lord's people all down the generations. It has been proved by them in their times of difficulty, temptation and trial. The Lord gave the same commission to Peter on the shores of the sea of Galilee following his resurrection: "Feed my lambs…feed my sheep…feed my sheep" (John 21:15–17). Is that not still a vital aspect of the faithful ministry of the word of God? O yes, there are words of reproof and rebuke in that faithful ministry. How needful they are and what a mercy it is if we know them being applied to us in the situations in which we may be found. But remember that all are words of grace and truth. O see in them the purposes of our God and Saviour in the outworking of his gracious love towards his own. As that great high priest over the house of God, our Lord is not one remote from us. He is not indifferent to our needs and situations. We are told that he was "in all points tempted like as we are, yet without sin" (Heb. 4:15). He is able also to comfort those that are tempted. He blessedly does so. I say, he is not a Saviour afar off from his people but one ever near to them.

See this comfort in the fourteenth chapter of the gospel recorded by John. How greatly troubled were the disciples at the prospect of his going away from them, they not being fully conversant with what that implied. They could not even begin to contemplate the removal of his physical presence from them. See how the Lord dealt so graciously and tenderly with them. See what encouragement he gives them and still speaks to his church and people in the most troublesome and distressing times: "Let not your heart be troubled: ye believe in God, believe also in me" (John 14:1). And is that not still the testimony of our Lord and

Saviour Jesus Christ? Does he not lead and direct us, by the inward teaching of the Holy Spirit, to believing trust and reliance on himself alone in all our needs? Does he not cause us to seek to walk in the light of his holy word? He goes on to say to his disciples, "I will not leave you comfortless: I will come to you. Yet a little while, and the world seeth me no more; but ye see me: because I live, ye shall live also" (John 14:18–19). O friends, what a fulness is in those words as they set forth the constancy of the love and care of the Lord to his own! The Lord's whole purpose in setting forth his mind and will through the prophets and apostles is to minister to his people the glorious reality of the rich consolation which flows to them from our Lord Jesus Christ.

It was not without reason that the psalmist expressed it in this way: "he knoweth our frame; he remembereth that we are dust" (Ps. 103:14). Ah indeed, are we not brought to realise our weakness, sinfulness and need? Remember that all these things are known to our Lord Jesus Christ. See what gracious provision he has made for all the weakness, needs and infirmities of his people. This is not excusing their weaknesses, not dismissing them as unimportant. But in the very midst of those things, the Lord here sets before his remnant in all generations, a gracious, glorious prospect. He reveals who he is and what he will manifest of himself in the life of his church and people. Yes, even in times of danger, when the judgments of God are abroad in the earth, as they were then and are today, yet see what is here set forth for his people. We may be greatly troubled and cast down by reason of the way. We may think things are deeply troubling and exercising to us. O for grace to look up as directed here, "behold your God." That is what I particularly want to be able to set forth in some measure this evening.

Let us look firstly at these words, "Strengthen ye the weak hands, and confirm the feeble knees." How descriptive is that of the people of God in themselves. Surely if we know anything of the gracious teaching of the Lord the Holy Spirit, are we not increasingly brought to realise that we are *nothing* and have *nothing?* How weak we are of ourselves. Can we attain to anything which meets the deep needs of our souls apart from the gracious ministry of the Holy Spirit? Weak hands and feeble knees? Here is a fearful trembling people and is not that often true of the people of God? We sing in our hymn what is sadly often true with us:

> "Creatures of fear we drag along
> And fear where no fear is
> Our griefs we labour to prolong!
> Our joys in haste dismiss."

O how prone we are to only view from a human standpoint the issues which appear to be in our life and path at the present time. Things so often seem dark. How helpless we find ourselves to be. And so we are. But see how the Lord comes in the ministry of his word as applied by the Holy Spirit. What alone can strengthen the weak hands and confirm the feeble knees? Is it not Jesus Christ revealed to us by his word "in power, and in the Holy Ghost, and in much assurance"? (1 Thess. 1:5). As I mentioned this morning, does not the Lord provide for his people? Is there not spiritual meat and drink for them? And what is it provided for? Is it not for the nourishment of their souls, the strengthening them with might in the inner man by the gracious indwelling and teaching of the Lord the Holy Spirit? Wherein is the ministry of the Spirit truly realised? Is it not by the word as brought home to us? O what cannot the word of the Lord accomplish! Surely we are not strangers to it in our own experience when at times very much cast down as may be so at present? Wherein have we found and still do find that which is for the lifting of us up? Is it not as the Lord comes in his word? How much is contained in *one* word, one word of promise! It truly puts strength into the souls of the Lord's people, enabling them to rise up and go forward in the strength which the Lord imparts to them, trusting in him alone.

Consider the situation in the life of Abram when he returned from the slaughter of the kings, and Melchisedec met him and blessed him. What a remarkable victory the Lord gave him over those who had taken Lot and many others captive. Yet we then read, "After these things the word of the Lord came unto Abram in a vision, saying, Fear not, Abram: I am thy shield, and thy exceeding great reward" (Gen. 15:1). Would the Lord speak a "fear not" to him if there were not fears and apprehensions in his servant? The Lord not only knows the way his people take, he knows what is in their hearts. What a mercy it is that the Lord does not deal with us as we deserve. O how he comes over all that offends and grieves, comes in the power of the Holy Spirit through his own word and says, "Fear not, I am thy shield, and thy exceeding great reward." O how Abram lived to prove the blessed reality of that promise as a source of encouragement and consolation to him in those circumstances and in the subsequent path the Lord had appointed for him.

So the Lord still comes in his word. He comes here through his servant the prophet, proclaiming those things that pertain to his glory and the true spiritual welfare of his people. What a glorious prospect is set forth here in the language of this thirty-fifth chapter of Isaiah! To what does it direct us? Wherein was it fulfilled and is so still for the church? Is it not in the glorious gospel of the grace of God? You know, the gospel was preached to brethren in the old testament period as much as it is preached by the grace of God in our generation. There were those who, through the grace of God, were truly brought to believe and receive the testimony God had given as it centred in the promise of him that was to come. How much greater is the light given us in our day of the things spoken by the prophet. For we see the certain fulfilment of them as accomplished in the coming of the person of the Lord Jesus Christ and by his finished work. We have the blessings that flow from it in the fulness of redeeming love and mercy to poor sinners. Are these not great and glorious things?

There may be much in our present circumstances that troubles, distresses and casts us down. O friends, is there not much more in what God sets before us in his holy word, for which to give thanks to him and take encouragement in the most trying circumstances? Are we not brought to realise that the Lord our God is faithful and true? He doesn't speak to us what he does not mean and what he will not in his appointed time fulfil. Was not what he spoke to his disciples in John 14 for the strengthening of their weak hands and confirming of their feeble knees in their distressing circumstances? "Let not your heart be troubled: ye believe in God, believe also in me. In my Father's house are many mansions: *if it were not so, I would have told you.* I go to prepare a place for you." Does that have no resonance with us? Does not that speak, I trust, to your heart and mine? If our Lord Jesus Christ bore such witness to his disciples, why am I so cast down, why so troubled by the present circumstances? If Christ is mine and heaven is mine by the riches of divine grace, O how great and glorious is the prospect! The Lord Jesus did not set those things before his disciples (and his people still) for no reason. As I said already, "he knoweth our frame; he remembereth that we are dust." So he comes as he promises through Isaiah, even where his people are. For what purpose? Why, to draw them unto himself.

"Strengthen ye the weak hands, and confirm the feeble knees. Say to them that are of a fearful heart, Be strong, fear not: behold, your God will come with vengeance." *"Say to them that are of a fearful heart."* Yes, does not the Lord speak in the ministry of the word? The commission was given to the prophets and apostles to sound forth the word of the truth of the gospel. *"Say unto them."* Does not the word still speak? O friends, may we know it, not only sounded in our ears, but coming to us by the unction of the Holy Spirit in a very personal way.

"Say unto *them."* See how the Lord speaks to the needy, exercised, burdened, weary, fearful and fearing of his people: "Say unto them *that are of a fearful heart"* I say again, how that describes what is so often experienced in the path of the living family of God. Some might say, Well surely if one believes they should have no fears. But people who say that cannot be truly acquainted with the plague of their own hearts. Even if made alive unto God by the riches of divine grace, we are not free from a body of sin and death as we journey on through life. How troublesome is this to us, not only in things outwardly but things inwardly as well. O friend, how active is Satan. How active is the working of our own fallen and sinful nature and that sin which does so easily beset us. Looking at ourselves, what can we say? Is there anything good to be said? Is there any encouragement to be drawn from it? Look to ourselves? 'O how can I, how can such a heart as mine be the dwelling place of the Holy Spirit? Surely if I was one of the Lord's people would it not be very different with me? I find so much that troubles me through the working of sin in my heart and life.' There is no excuse for these things, neither as taught of God the Holy Spirit, will we be left to make excuse for them. O friends, remember this and the Lord the Holy Spirit seal it afresh to your heart and mine, "Say to them that are of a fearful heart, Be strong, fear not."

What have we therefore to say to the fearing ones of the Lord's people? *This man, our Lord Jesus Christ, receives sinners and eats with them.* Does not this address the situation? Do not these words of grace and truth proclaimed by Isaiah declare what the Lord Jesus said: "Come unto me, all ye that labour and are heavy laden, and I will give you rest"? (Matt. 11:28). Does not the unction of the Holy Spirit accompany the words to bring us fearing and needy to the footstool of mercy? Friends, remember that the fulness and freeness of the mercy of our Lord endureth for ever, blessed be his great and holy name.

"Say to them that are of a fearful heart, *Be strong,* fear not." Strong in what? In my own determination to make the best of my situation? No. Be strong, not in our own strength, for what strength have we? Why, we are utter weakness but "strong in the Lord, and in the power of his might" (Eph. 6:10). Ah, how wondrous is the grace of God in upholding and keeping his people amid all the trials, temptations and difficulties experienced in their daily lives. This upholding is essential for the people of God, as Peter only too well experienced. Without it he would have fallen, never to rise again. As he says in his first epistle, the Lord's people are "kept by the power of God through faith unto salvation" (1 Pet. 1:5). If that was not so, how easily and quickly would we succumb to all the opposition we meet with from without and within. Without the Lord's keeping would not every one of his own soon fall away? But blessed be his name, he says, "Be strong, fear not: behold, your God will come." O "to keep our eyes on Jesus fixed," who is "the same yesterday, and to day, and for ever" (Heb. 13:8).

"Behold your God." Ah, is there not something very precious in this word for the people of God? O may we know its personal application. "*Your* God." O how blessed if we are indeed brought to say that this God is *my* God. What a wonder it is that the Lord should ever bring such a sinner into this relationship with

himself! Surely is not this all of grace, to his praise alone? Ah yes, we truly have to say "brethren, we are debtors," debtors to the grace and mercy of God (Rom. 8:12). When it says, "Behold your God," do we see God as it were standing aside, viewing our case from afar? No, it clearly states, "behold your God" *coming*. "Behold your God *will come* with vengeance, even God with a recompense; he *will come* and save you." Yes, what a mercy if we behold him as *my* God, as *your* God, not as one standing afar off, but as coming to us, his eye ever being on his people, and his ear ever open to their cry.

As our heavenly Father, he knows what things we have need of even before we ask him. Nothing can be hidden from him. We pray to be honest before our God as we come to his throne of grace, confessing our sins before him, and pleading his promise "that we may obtain mercy, and find grace to help in time of need" (Heb. 4:16).

The promise, "Behold thy God *will* come," is not empty speculation. O is not all the encouragement and consolation of his people founded upon the *shalls* and *wills* of our triune God. We cannot rely implicitly on the word of man. How often we find their word fails and we fail as well. But the word of the Lord can never fail. He is faithful and true. "Your God *will* come with vengeance, even God with a recompense."

This vengeance is manifest against his and his people's external *and internal* enemies. For he comes to deliver his people from the working of that sin which does so easily beset them. Friends, what a mercy that the Lord does thus come. Yes, he comes in his word of reproof by the Holy Spirit, to bring and keep us low at his feet. And he *will* come with vengeance to deliver his people from their enemies. What a word of promise the Lord gave to his servant Paul for the brethren at Rome when he says, "the God of peace shall bruise Satan under your feet shortly" (Rom. 16:20). Yes, we shall live to see the day when all the enemies of himself and his people will be ultimately brought under the feet of our Lord Jesus Christ. We shall truly realise full and final deliverance, to the praise of the glory the Lord's great and holy name.

While we journey on through this world, we are subject to

trouble, as the Lord said to his disciples: "In the world ye shall have tribulation: but be of good cheer; I have overcome the world" (John 16:33). Is it not often a rough and thorny path the Lord's people are called to walk? That may be so, yet the Lord is ever with them. Indeed, he says, "I will never leave thee, nor forsake thee" (Heb. 13:5). There will not always be the felt comfort, but the word of the Lord still remains faithful and true: "your God will come with *vengeance*, even God with a *recompence*; he will come and save you."

I take *"recompense"* as being the Lord's gracious dealings with his people, not only in delivering them from all their enemies, but also in giving them rich encouragement and consolation. And that surely comes through the word applied by the gracious ministry of the Holy Spirit, whereby he manifests his love and mercy to them.

"He will come and save you." Friends, what a word is that! "He *will* come and *save* you." Yes, not one of his own shall be left destitute. We may indeed fear and feel to be afar off. Satan may harass as he does. Unbelief, trouble, distress, doubts and fears arise. "He will come" and he does come. Does not the Lord Jesus assure us of this when he says, as I mentioned already, "Let not your heart be troubled." Read again that fourteenth chapter of John in the context of these words of Isaiah. O what a glorious prospect is therein brought before the church and people of God, not only for the present but also in that which is to be realised in the fulness of it. What the Lord revealed to the brethren in Isaiah's day strengthened and encouraged them at that time. It also set a glorious prospect before them to be realised in the coming of our Lord Jesus Christ and the fulfilling of all God had promised from before the foundation of the world. And still, as it concerns his church and people, "He will come and save you." Is not that surely the blessed expectation of the living family of God: "He will come"? As surely as he came the first time, so in all their needs and situations he still comes to his people by the ministry of the Holy Spirit through the word. In the Lord we find one that is *able* to save and *willing* to save as well. O the word of grace to his people can never fail, blessed be his great and holy name.

He hath come, he does come and, blessed be his name, he will come in that day appointed of God. He will come in the clouds of heaven, in power and great glory, to receive his own unto himself and to judge the world in righteousness. How glorious will be that coming of the Lord Jesus Christ! Blessed is his coming to us in the manifestation of his pardoning love and mercy as we journey on through life. And gloriously blessed will be the final coming of the Lord. Even though we may not live to *that* day, yet even his coming at his appointed time, when we pass from this time state into eternity, is a glorious coming for the living family of God. What a deliverance is surely wrought at that time for the eternal welfare of each one of his own, to the praise of the glory of our God. Friends, blessed be his great and holy name, these things are *true*. These things *can never fail* in the experience of the living family of God. O may our souls be led more and more fully and feelingly into the blessed realities set forth in these words of our text and in John chapter fourteen. What a glorious revelation of himself, God full of grace and truth, is given us in the precious truth of the gospel, as it all centres in the person of our Lord Jesus Christ.

But I will leave the remarks there. The Lord add his blessing. Amen.

40

MINE HOUR IS NOT YET COME

Tuesday evening 23 June 2020

"And when they wanted wine, the mother of Jesus saith unto him, They have no wine. Jesus saith unto her, Woman, what have I to do with thee? mine hour is not yet come. His mother saith unto the servants, Whatsoever he saith unto you, do it" (John 2:3-5).

We are told in verse eleven that, "This beginning of miracles did Jesus in Cana of Galilee, and manifested forth his glory; and his disciples believed on him." There is much gracious instruction in what is said here about this first miracle of our Lord Jesus Christ at the beginning of his public ministry. We must not overlook how this event is closely related to what we read in the opening chapter of this gospel concerning the witness of John the Baptist and the testimony given by our God himself in those opening verses. "In the beginning was the Word, and the Word was with God, and the Word was God. The same was in the beginning with God. All things were made by him; and without him was not any thing made that was made. In him was life; and the life was the light of men." O what a glorious manifestation there is of the glory of God as revealed in the face of Jesus Christ! How great is the wonder of that grace whereby sinners such as you and me are brought by the sovereign work of the Holy Spirit to behold that glory and to believe on Jesus to everlasting life.

We see the testimony John the Baptist gave to the Pharisees that asked him who he was. He said that he was not the Christ but was the one sent before him. O what a testimony he gives to the Lord Jesus Christ. "He that sent me to baptize with water, the same said unto me, Upon whom thou shalt see the Spirit descending, and remaining on him, the same is he which baptizeth with the Holy Ghost. And I saw, and bare record that this is the Son of God." See what he declared as he beheld Jesus of Nazareth, a real man, coming unto him. What was there to outwardly distinguish Jesus from his fellowmen? Yet John, by the witness of the Holy Spirit, testified as he did. O what cause we have to bless and praise our God that what John declared is as true today as it was when he testified, "Behold the Lamb of God, which taketh away the sin of the world." And does not this word of God, by the gracious power of the Holy Spirit, wholly direct us as ruined, guilty sinners to the Lord Jesus Christ alone? Does it not bring us to look to him, to bow before him, to fall at his feet in true confession and godly sorrow over our sins, and to receive out of the fulness of his grace? As the apostle John assures us, "the Word was made flesh, and dwelt among us, (and we beheld his glory, the glory as of the only begotten of the Father,) full of grace and truth." How great is the blessedness of thus beholding our Lord Jesus Christ, "the same yesterday, and to day, and for ever," still full of grace and truth (Heb. 13:8). Has not every needy sinner, brought by grace to call upon his name, found *that* to be true, at the appointed time of God's manifestation of it to them? O the fulness of grace and truth that flows out of the person of our Lord and Saviour Jesus Christ.

We see his grace at the beginning of his public ministry in his calling those early disciples to follow him. In this miracle at Cana, we see the gracious confirmation to them that Jesus of Nazareth is indeed the Son of God, the one promised to the patriarchs and prophets, the glorious Messiah that was to come. They beheld the one in whom the glory of God is revealed in the wonders of redeeming love and mercy to guilty, needy sinners, even as many as the Lord our God shall call.

Well, we see these disciples and his mother Mary with others of her family, called to this marriage in Cana of Galilee. Just a word here with regard to Mary the mother of Jesus. As the scriptures declare, Mary was highly favoured among women and yet she is not exalted to the position that Rome would have her to be. It is grievous blasphemy to speak of her as being divine or equal with our Lord Jesus Christ. But in rejecting that, let us not overlook how favoured Mary was. Indeed, she was a sinner saved by grace. Did she not herself declare, "my spirit hath rejoiced in God *my Saviour*" (Luke 1:47). Yes, wonders of divine grace were manifest in her. But Mary was highly favoured as the one to whom the Lord Jesus Christ was born according to the flesh. Friends, how wondrous are the works of God! What divine mysteries are here! What occasion is given for the faith of the living family of God to bow before the Lord with wonder, love and praise.

But speaking of Mary, you remember what was said to her by the angel Gabriel in announcing the coming birth of the child which was to be born unto her. He should be called the Son of God, and God would give to him the throne of his father David according to promise. Then after the birth of our Lord Jesus Christ, she and Joseph took the child to the temple to do to him according to the law. And dear old Simeon, who had been waiting for the consolation of Israel, came into the temple and took up the child in his arms and blessed God and said, "Lord, now lettest thou thy servant depart in peace, according to thy word: for mine eyes have seen thy salvation" (Luke 2:29–30). Remember what Simeon spoke directly to Mary, "Behold, this child is set for the fall and rising again of many in Israel; and for a sign which shall be spoken against; (yea, a sword shall pierce through thy own soul also,) that the thoughts of many hearts may be revealed." Anna the prophetess likewise spoke of him to all that looked for redemption in Israel. Referring to these events described in the gospel according to Luke, it is said that Mary pondered those things in her heart. We are not to speculate, but surely, she was moved by them, though not fully knowing what the final outcome of those things would be.

See here at the beginning of the Lord's public ministry, she and others followed him, together with those disciples whom he had called. We do not know the particular circumstances of this marriage in Cana, but we are told that they wanted wine. And we read of Mary: "And when they wanted wine, the mother of Jesus saith unto him, They have no wine." As I said, we are not to speculate. But keeping in mind the things I have just mentioned concerning Mary, was it out of place for her to approach the Lord Jesus and inform him of the problem? During all those years in Nazareth up to this beginning of his public ministry, we do not read that Jesus performed any miracle. We are told that after his visit to the temple when twelve years of age, he went down to Nazareth and was subject to his parents. The point I am making is that when there was here a real need for wine, does it not appear that there was something in her that felt Jesus would be able to supply that need? So far, so good.

The response of Jesus to her might seem harsh on the face of it. "Woman, what have I to do with thee?" But the Lord Jesus did not speak disparagingly to his mother, far from it. This word *woman* was commonly used in addressing married women. No, the Lord Jesus always fully obeyed the law of God in honouring his earthly parents. Most certainly he did. But in these words to Mary, he is saying that it was not for Mary to suggest what, or when, or how he should do those things. Yes, she was highly favoured. And our Lord Jesus Christ had been subject to his parents but the time had come when that was ended. Even in that, is there not instruction for us likewise? While we are young, we are called upon to honour our parents, and even in after years we are certainly not to speak disparagingly of them. Far from it. But there comes a time, as we develop into adulthood, that we are no longer subject to the authority of our parents. We have each, to put it this way, to stand on our own feet and be responsible for our own actions as before God and man. It is important also that parents remember that as well. As their children grow and increase in years, we cannot hold on to them all their life. We cannot dictate to them what they should or should not do. We have to leave them with the Lord, remembering that each is responsible for their own actions as they go forward in life. We would ever endeavour to pray for them, seeking their true spiritual welfare, as well as for all that pertains to the necessities of this present life. While on this point, surely with parents and children, whatever issues may arise between them, should not the tie of mutual love one for another ever prevail? I just leave those thoughts with you, believing they are fully consistent with the word of God.

But these words the Lord says to Mary here: "Woman, what have I to do with thee? mine hour is not yet come." On the face of it, it may appear difficult to fully understand the meaning of our Lord in these words. I believe we can express it in this way.

He is saying, 'Leave the matter in my hands.' Did not Mary take it in that way? For she said to the servants, "Whatsoever he saith unto you, do it."

'Leave the matter in my hands.' The point is that the Lord knew what he would do. Those things were not unknown to him. He was fully aware of the whole situation. Does not this still speak to the church collectively and ourselves personally? Whatever may be the issues we are confronted with at this present time, none are unknown to our Lord Jesus Christ. He is fully aware of the whole situation. Indeed, we are encouraged, not only to bring all unto him, but to leave all in his hands. Is that an easy thing? I do not find it so. Do you find it an easy thing? Yes, it is a mercy to be enabled to bring our concerns in prayer to the throne of grace and pour out our hearts before him. We are ever directed and encouraged to do so in his word. As the psalmist says, "Trust in him at all times; ye people, pour out your heart before him: God is a refuge for us" (Ps. 62:8). I say, it is a mercy to be enabled to pour out our hearts before him, but friends, in doing so, do we also seek to leave the matter with him? How often we find ourselves returning again and again to anxious care over the issues that confront us. We increasingly realise we cannot deal with them. We do not have the answer to them and we do not have the wisdom or grace to handle them. How utterly dependent we are upon the Lord. O what a mercy to be brought and kept low at the Saviour's feet, conscious of our weakness, our foolishness, our need. Though realising *we* know not what to do, blessed be the Lord's name, *he* is not at a stand to know what to do! You remember how Jehoshaphat, when that great company was coming up against him, poured out his heart before the Lord. "O our God...we have no might against this great company that cometh against us; neither know we what to do: but our eyes are upon thee" (2 Chron. 20:12). Ah friends, is not that surely where we ever desire to be found? Yes. 'Leave the matter in my hands.'

"What have I to do with thee? mine hour is not yet come." We can interpret that in the sense that the Lord knew what was needed and would deal with it in his own time. And friends, how true that is of the Lord's dealings with his people still. With us, our time is always ready. But the Lord's time is best and right and will also manifest forth his glory as it did here in Cana in this beginning of miracles. "And his disciples believed on him." Though we may feel the Lord delays his coming and we call upon him with no apparent answer, yet is he deaf to the cry of his people? Remember, the Lord waits "that he may be gracious unto you" (Isa. 30:18). He knows what he is doing and will appear in his own good time and way. His time is always the right time, be assured of that. Therein will be evidenced in gracious measure the manifesting forth of his glory. And surely, by the Lord's blessing, it will be for the strengthening of the faith of his people, the drawing out of their hearts in love to him, the confirming of them in that blessed hope which maketh not ashamed.

"What have I to do with thee? mine hour is not yet come." There is a further aspect to these words. Was there not an appointed hour for the Lord Jesus himself? From the very beginning of his incarnation, did he not always have before him *that* hour. Was it not at the forefront of all his life and ministry throughout the years he was here upon earth? Did not all culminate in *that hour?* Thus we read in John chapter thirteen, "When Jesus knew that his hour was come that he should depart out of this world unto the Father, having loved his own which were in the world, he loved them unto the end." Ah friends, what an hour was that! What an appointment for our Lord Jesus Christ when he who knew no sin, was made sin for us, that we might be made the righteousness of God in him? In *his* hour, was the full consummation of the purpose of his coming into this world. He laid down his life that his people might live. He put away their sins by the sacrifice of himself. He brought in for them an everlasting righteousness founded upon the perfect obedience he rendered to the holy law of God. He met all its demands, not for himself for he was holy, righteous, just and true, but for all those his Father had given him. O what glories of God's grace were set forth in *that* hour.

"Mine hour is not yet come." We see the response of his mother. Did she not fall under that word of the Lord? And so she says to the servants, "Whatsoever he saith unto you, do it." You know, here was displayed the glory of his Godhead. Yes, though veiled in human nature, the Lord never set aside his divine glory.

See that manifest in turning this water into wine. He did not speak to it. He did not touch it. By *his will* that water was turned into wine. He simply gave the servants instructions to fill the waterpots with water, to draw forth, and to take to the governor of the feast. And it was good wine, most assuredly. As the governor said to the bridegroom, not knowing its origin, "thou hast kept the good wine until now."

See here the power of the Godhead of our Lord Jesus Christ. What is he not able to do, not only in what he did in turning water into wine? O friends, is not the glory of his Godhead manifest in the case of every sinner brought from death in trespasses and sins into the life, light and liberty of the gospel? Is that not a mighty work which only our God in Christ is able to accomplish, through the sovereign operations of the Holy Spirit? Can man do it? Can man turn water into wine? No. But here we see the display of the glory of God. And, as we read here, it was but the beginning of miracles which displayed the glory of Jesus. They witnessed to those whose eyes were opened to behold his glory. Their hearts were wrought upon by the Holy Spirit to receive him, in the exercise of God-given faith, believing that he was the Christ, the Son of God.

I refer again to the testimony of John the Baptist when those Pharisees asked him who he was and why he was baptizing. He said, "he that sent me to baptize with water, the same said unto me, Upon whom thou shalt see the Spirit descending, and remaining on him, the same is he which baptizeth with the Holy Ghost. And I saw, and bare record that this is *the Son of God.*" O friends, the emphasis on *that* truth. Is not the reality of God-given faith that which always receives and embraces Jesus as the Christ, the Son of God? As I have mentioned many a time, John later in this gospel testifies to the same truth. "Many other signs truly did Jesus in the presence of his disciples, which are not written in this book: but these are written, that ye might believe that Jesus is the Christ, the Son of God; and that believing ye might have life through his name" (John 20:30–31).

"Whatsoever he saith unto you, do it." Was it not a strange thing that Jesus directed these servants to do, to fill those waterpots with water and then to draw out and bear to the governor of the feast? This miracle was not done in a particularly public way. Few were aware of what had taken place. The governor of the feast did not know. Many at that marriage were ignorant of it. His disciples were aware of it as was Mary and the servants who took the water that was made wine to the governor of the feast. It was not a public demonstration at this stage in the life of our Lord Jesus Christ. But what a witness to that little band of disciples he was drawing around him to be his followers! O what a confirmation of the things that they had heard and witnessed with regard to the person of Jesus Christ. Friends, see how gracious the Lord is with his disciples here and to his people still. See his gracious words and dealings with them, the very confirmation of his care for them, his love of them and his assured provisions for them.

Notice here as well, what an abundant supply of wine was given. It says, "And there were set there six waterpots of stone, after the manner of the purifying of the Jews, containing two or three firkins apiece." Ah, there was abundance here. Does it not speak to us as well of the Lord's dealings with his people? Friends, there's nothing niggardly in the Lord's dealings with his people. O his mercies towards them! What a fulness! What a freeness! How gracious is our Lord and Saviour Jesus Christ! How full and free are the mercies he bestows upon his own. The Lord Jesus Christ is ever ready and willing to receive every poor needy sinner brought through his grace to call upon his name. None are turned away empty. Far from it. This man, blessed be his great and holy name, still receives sinners and eats with them. O what encouragement is here given for the needy, burdened, exercised soul this evening. Here in the Lord Jesus Christ, is one who is mighty to save, able to save to the uttermost, and willing to save too! As the hymnwriter says,

> "Power and love in Christ combine,
> An able, willing Saviour too;
> Is he a Sun? On thee he'll shine.
> Is he thy God? He'll bring thee through."

He'll bring his people through, in spite of all that opposes them. Our Lord Jesus Christ is the one whom we can trust implicitly. See his goodness and mercy still lengthened out here to his people. "This beginning of miracles did Jesus in Cana of Galilee, and manifested forth his glory; and his disciples believed on him." Ah, I come back to that point. It has, I trust, been a word to myself today. *'Leave the matter in my hands.'* Friends, O for grace enabling us so to do. "Commit thy way unto the Lord; trust also in him; and he shall bring it to pass" (Ps. 37:5).

I will leave the remarks there. The Lord add his blessing. Amen.

41

THIS IS MY BELOVED SON, IN WHOM I AM WELL PLEASED

Lord's day morning 28 June 2020

"And after six days Jesus taketh Peter, James, and John his brother, and bringeth them up into an high mountain apart, and was transfigured before them: and his face did shine as the sun, and his raiment was white as the light. And, behold, there appeared unto them Moses and Elias talking with him. Then answered Peter, and said unto Jesus, Lord, it is good for us to be here: if thou wilt, let us make here three tabernacles; one for thee, and one for Moses, and one for Elias. While he yet spake, behold, a bright cloud over-shadowed them: and behold a voice out of the cloud, which said, This is my beloved Son, in whom I am well pleased; hear ye him. And when the disciples heard it, they fell on their face, and were sore afraid. And Jesus came and touched them, and said, Arise, and be not afraid. And when they had lifted up their eyes, they saw no man, save Jesus only" (Matthew 17:1–8).

In the previous chapter we read the dealings of the Lord Jesus with his disciples, particularly Peter. Jesus asks them, "Whom do men say that I the Son of man am?" Various were the ideas put forward, but he then asks, "But whom say *ye* that I am?" We have Peter's confession: "Thou art the Christ, the Son of the living God." Jesus said, "Blessed art thou, Simon Barjona: for flesh and blood hath not revealed it unto thee, but my Father which is in heaven." O friends, the wonder and blessedness of being brought personally by the gracious ministry of the Holy Spirit, to truly believe that "Jesus is the Christ, the Son of God; and that believing we might have life through his name" (John 20:31). O the wonder of the grace which brings a sinner into the blessedness of union with Jesus Christ, he being one with them and they one with him, as set before us in the precious truth of the gospel.

But afterwards, when Jesus told them that he should be taken by wicked hands, crucified and slain, Peter says, "Be it far from thee, Lord." See how the Lord severely rebuked him: "Get thee behind me, Satan...for thou savourest not the things that be of God, but those that be of men."

And yet in the latter part of that sixteenth chapter, we read that Jesus said unto them, "Verily I say unto you, There be some standing here, which shall not taste of death, till they see the Son of man coming in his kingdom." And amongst those was *Peter,* Jesus taking him with James and John, "and bringeth them up into an high mountain apart."

O friends, the wonder of the grace and mercy of the Lord to his own. And after all Peter had witnessed of Jesus, especially as recorded in our text, yet he afterwards denied his Lord and Master! Ah friends, well do we have to say, What is man. What is any child of God of themselves? Can we keep ourselves? Are we proof against temptation? Are we not wholly dependent on the Lord? Peter could well write years afterward, we are "kept by the power of God through faith unto salvation ready to be revealed in the last time" (1 Pet. 1:5). Ah, if ever one realised his need, and the blessedness of that keeping by the Lord, it was certainly Peter! May we know, not only our need of keeping, but the blessedness of it. We cannot keep ourselves from temptation. We have to truly confess before the Lord, "I am poor and needy" (Ps. 40:17), always poor and needy, wholly dependent upon the Lord. O through the rich mercies of the Lord towards us, may we be more and more delivered from trust and confidence in self and in created things, that Jesus Christ may truly be all in all unto us.

The Lord had said that some of them should not taste of death until they saw the Son of man coming in his kingdom. And was there not a blessed confirmation of that given to the three disciples before whom the Lord was transfigured on that mountain? Peter surely remembered this all his days, particularly when he came towards the end of his life, very aware that his days were numbered, as he wrote in his second epistle. "Yea, I think it meet, as long as I am in this tabernacle, to stir you up by putting you in remembrance; knowing that shortly I must put off this my tabernacle, even as our Lord Jesus Christ hath shewed me. Moreover I will endeavour that ye may be able after my decease to have these things always in remembrance. For we have not followed cunningly devised fables, when we made known unto you the power and coming of our Lord Jesus Christ, but were eyewitnesses of his majesty. For he received from God the Father honour and glory, when there came such a voice to him from the excellent glory, This is my beloved Son, in whom I am well pleased. And this voice which came from heaven we heard, when we were with him in the holy mount. We have also a more sure word of prophecy; whereunto ye do well that ye take heed, as unto a light that shineth in a dark place, until the day dawn, and the day star arise in your hearts" (2 Pet. 1:13–19).

The word of God continually directs us to the truth contained in Peter's letter. We may not be favoured with the manifestation the disciples had on the mount of transfiguration but Peter tells us, *"we have also a more sure word of prophecy."* That more sure word is what God sets before us throughout his holy scriptures. Therein a blessed testimony is given us of the greatness, glory and goodness of God revealed in the precious truth of the gospel, centering as all does, in the person of our Lord and Saviour Jesus Christ.

What precious things are here set before us in the trans- figuration of our Lord Jesus Christ on that mount! O that we may have an ear to hear what the Spirit saith unto us, and our souls be led into the believing receiving of these things. What a found- ation for the hope and expectation of the living family of God through the riches of divine grace!

It is said that "he bringeth them up into an high mountain apart." We are not told what mountain it was. It does not matter. We read, he "was transfigured before them: and his face did shine as the sun, and his raiment was white as the light." We cannot even begin to describe what is set forth in these verses, but may we know what it is to truly receive the testimony here given.

Surely here set forth is the very glory of God manifest in the flesh, in the person of Jesus Christ. And he is the same Jesus still. He is the one John beheld on the isle of Patmos. I want to emphasise that in the description here given us, we behold the glory of God in the person of our Lord Jesus, that glorious man. While here on earth the glory of his Godhead was veiled in human nature. But this man now reigns in heaven above as one with the Father and the Holy Spirit, and as one with all the brethren his Father has given him.

See how the prayer of Jesus in John seventeen bears testimony to his oneness with the Father and with all whom his Father has given him. They are one in him in a blessed union, never to be severed. It is so with every poor sinner brought to believe and trust in Jesus Christ. Journeying on through this wilderness world, with all the sorrows, difficulties, temptations and trials that beset them, yet the blessedness of this is sure to each one of them. They are one with Jesus Christ now and to all eternity, to the praise of the glory of his great and holy name.

He "was transfigured before them: and his face did shine as the sun, and his raiment was white as the light. And, behold, there appeared unto them Moses and Elias talking with him." Does not this bring something very wonderful before us? As it were, there is the lifting of a corner of the veil that separates time from the glorious realities of eternity. And Peter reminds us that these are not cunningly devised fables. They *are* glorious realities. Is not a glimpse given us here of the glory that awaits every believer, through the riches of divine grace? We are bowed down with much that distresses us, not least the sin which so easily besets us. We have trials, difficulties, temptations. But friends, look up and behold our Lord Jesus Christ who is set before us here. That same glorious man who suffered to save us from our sins and bring us into acceptance by God now reigns in heaven. And we are here given a glimpse into the glory of that eternal inheritance that awaits us.

You say, what is to be drawn from the appearance of Moses and Elias talking with Jesus? Moses had been dead fifteen hundred years. It was nine hundred years since Elias was taken up by a whirlwind into heaven. Does not this assure us of the reality of life after death? God's word ever bears witness to the glorious truth that there is life after death for every believer, through the riches of divine grace. Glory most surely awaits them. O the solemnity of those who die in their sins. They continue for ever under the just curse and condemnation of God against all transgressors of his holy law. But for believers there is most surely deliverance from what is described as the second death. Yes, though death removes them from this earth, yet the redeemed soul enters immediately into the joy of their Lord. These things speak to us of the certainty of life after death and the glory of the resurrection as well.

Elijah did not pass through death but was immediately translated into heaven, as was Enoch generations before. Does not this speak of the life to come? And as surely as our Lord Jesus Christ rose from the dead, so shall all who die in Christ. Their body is laid in the grave, sees corruption and returns to the dust from whence it was taken. Yet as the Lord Jesus redeemed his people, body and soul, so shall that body rise again at the last day, made like his glorious body. These are not cunningly devised fables. They are glorious realities confirmed to us again and again in the word of God.

Also notice that though the disciples had never seen Moses and Elias before, yet they immediately recognized them. The question arises of the mutual recognition of believers in heaven. We know that the one central object for the church in eternal glory is God as revealed in the person of Jesus Christ. Yet as there is surely union between Christ and his people, and they one with another while here on earth, will that be so different with believers in heaven? We cannot comprehend this with our finite understanding but faith believes the testimony God has given of the certainty of the glory which awaits us. As the word says, "Eye hath not seen, nor ear heard, neither have entered into the heart of man, the things which God hath prepared for them that love him" (1 Cor. 2:9).

O friends, may we truly be found as those who are waiting and looking for the blessed appearing of our Lord and Saviour Jesus Christ, being made ready and willing to go to him when he calls. Is not this the work of God's grace in the hearts and lives of his people in preparation for what he has appointed for them, to the praise of his great name?

We are told in another account that Moses and Elias talked with him and "spake of his decease which he should accomplish at Jerusalem" (Luke 9:31). O does not this open up to us the wonder of the great work of our Lord Jesus Christ in redeeming his people from all their sins by the offering and *sacrifice of himself?* Could anything less than divine wisdom have devised this and divine power accomplished it? Did not all blessedly flow from the everlasting love of God? Surely this fills all heaven with praise to the glory of our God in his redemption and salvation of sinners to whom Jesus Christ is truly made all and in all. Friends, I know we are familiar with these things, but how little do we truly enter, I fear, into the wonders of redeeming love and mercy. O the fulness and the freeness of it!

They were talking with him of his decease that he should accomplish at Jerusalem, as appointed even from before the foundation of the world. Therein is founded all the hope and expectation of every poor sinner brought to believe and trust in Jesus Christ. Therein alone is the certainty of their eternal salvation, to the praise of the glory of our triune God. May we truly bow in worship and praise of God revealed in the person of Jesus Christ. For surely if ever a people should be a thankful people, it is sinners saved by grace. Yes, we should be thankful for his mercies as we journey on through life but especially for the wonders of sovereign saving grace in that the Lord had purposes of mercy to such sinners as you and me! Is not this one of the greatest wonders of all? One says,

> "Wonder above wonders,
> To see one black as I,
> White without spot and blemish
> Before God's throne on high."

Yes, it will be an eternal wonder that such as you and me are found there. But friends, if *we* are found there it will be entirely through the grace of God revealed in Jesus Christ in what he has done for us. This was the subject of conversation between Moses, Elias and our Lord Jesus on the mount.

In response to these things, Peter said to Jesus, "Lord, it is good for us to be here." Indeed it was good. We might desire to have been there to see and hear what they witnessed. But Peter reminds us "we have also a more sure word of prophecy." O for grace to give heed to what the Lord speaks to us in his holy word. The vision the disciples beheld on the mount of transfiguration quickly passed away, but the word of the Lord abideth for ever. This is the ground upon which the faith of the living family is founded.

> "What Christ has said must be fulfilled;
> On this firm rock, believers build;
> His word shall stand, his truth preveil,
> And not one jot or tittle fail."

But the account given us here is faithful and true. We receive it through the gracious teaching of the Lord the Holy Spirit, not merely as a vision from heaven, but as the solid ground established by the word of our God in holy scripture.

Just an aside at this point. Why does Peter emphasise that *"we have also a more sure word of prophecy"?* I believe it is important to remember that our experience of these spiritual, glorious realities is always founded on, and in accordance with, the light and teaching of the word of God. O let us not seek to *found* the interpretation of his word on what we may feel to experience. Many put emphasis on dreams and visions and such like things. We do not say God cannot use them, but friends beware of them. Are the things we might think we receive in a dream in accordance with the word of God? *All things must be brought to the law and the testimony.* Whatever it is, "If they speak not according to this word, it is because there is no light in them" (Isa. 8:20). That is a standing warning to the people of God. Yes, we want more of the blessed experience of the word of his grace and fellowship with the Lord Jesus Christ in our daily experience. But O friends, remember our salvation is not founded on what we feel, though we want right feelings, but on what God has revealed in his word concerning Jesus Christ. Yes, faith has a sure and solid foundation as it receives the testimony God has given of his only begotten and dearly beloved Son.

"Then answered Peter, and said unto Jesus, Lord, it is good for us to be here: if thou wilt, let us make here three tabernacles;

one for thee, and one for Moses, and one for Elias." Peter did not realise what he was saying. Moses and Elias represented the law and the prophets. One thing is essentially set before us here in the transfiguration. Moses and Elias had their place but Jesus Christ is the one to whom all the law and all the prophets bore witness. And he is here manifested as having come. As that bright cloud overshadowed them and they feared as they entered into the cloud, God the Father himself spake to them: "This is my beloved Son, in whom I am well pleased; hear ye him." Moses and Elias were faithful servants of God but Jesus is the Christ, the Son of God, the fulfilment of all to which the law and prophets bore witness. As it were, Moses and Elias here fade away. Jesus Christ only is set before us as the *one* in whom God is well pleased. As Paul writes to the Hebrews, "God, who at sundry times and in divers manners spake in time past unto the fathers by the prophets, hath in these last days spoken unto us by his Son" (Heb.1:1). The same testimony is here given. God has spoken to us and still speaks to us through his Son.

He says, "This is my beloved Son, in whom I am well pleased." What glorious truth is unfolded to us in those words. The Father testifies that his Son Jesus is one with himself and the Holy Spirit, one God over all, blessed for evermore. He testifies that his beloved Son, the man Christ Jesus, is the one mediator between himself and men. Is not this testimony of God the Father to his Son, the great foundation for the faith and hope of the living family of God?

I refer again to the words of John at the close of his gospel. "Many other signs truly did Jesus in the presence of his disciples, which are not written in this book: but these are written, that ye might believe that *Jesus is the Christ, the Son of God; and that believing ye might have life through his name"* (John 20:30–31). Can there be a surer foundation for the faith and hope of the living family of God than the witness of God himself that Jesus, his beloved Son, is the Christ in whom he is well pleased?

He doesn't say *with* "whom I am well pleased." That was true but he says *"in* whom I am well pleased." What does this convey to us? Remember that the life and ministry of Jesus Christ, the beloved Son of God manifest in the flesh, was not merely as a private person, but as the representative of his people. He is their head, surety and substitute. Do not overlook the reality of the oneness of Christ with all that his Father has given him. He himself testifies, *"Behold I and the children which God hath given me"* (Heb. 2:13). All the life and ministry of our Lord Jesus Christ was not only *on behalf of* those his Father had given him but as *one with them* in an indissoluble union. The testimony is here given us that as God is well pleased with his beloved Son, so he is well pleased with all that are found *in* Jesus as one with him now and to all eternity.

Friends, what great and glorious things are set before us here! You and I, poor, guilty, needy, hell-deserving sinners are *one* with Jesus Christ as brought to believe and trust in him! The Father says, "this is my beloved Son, *in* whom I am well pleased" and all that are in Jesus Christ come under that same blessed witness that God the Father gave here of his Son. As pleased with his beloved Son so he is pleased with all that are given to his Son, who are *in* his Son, and for whom his Son lived, died, rose again and entered into heaven itself to appear in the presence of God for them. Blessed union! Blessed reality, to see ourselves, poor guilty needy sinners, one with Jesus Christ. And what does the Father testify, "Thou art all fair, my love; there is no spot in thee" (Song of Sol. 4:7), as clothed in the righteousness of Jesus Christ and washed in his precious blood.

"This is my beloved Son, in whom I am well pleased; *hear ye him."* Friends, what a word is that which still speaks to us today. *"Hear ye him."* Moses and Elias depart from the scene. Jesus alone remains. As taught of God the Holy Spirit, it is to him alone we must be concerned to give heed, in what he sets before us in the precious truth of his word. As believers, to whom are we to be devoted? Who commands our loyalty? Is it not ultimately our Lord Jesus Christ? Is he not our Lord, our Master, our Saviour and our Redeemer, blessed be his great and holy name? Do not we owe all to him?

Look what the Lord Jesus says at the end of chapter sixteen "Then said Jesus unto his disciples, If any man will come after me, let him deny himself, and take up his cross, and follow me. For whosoever will save his life shall lose it: and whosoever will lose his life for my sake shall find it. For what is a man profited, if he shall gain the whole world, and lose his own soul? or what shall a man give in exchange for his soul? For the Son of man shall come in the glory of his Father with his angels; and then he shall reward every man according to his works." To whom then are we to be wholly devoted? To whom are we to render our complete loyalty and alone follow? To whom alone are we to give ear and heed? It is not what men say but what Jesus Christ sets before us in his holy word.

Yes, the Lord appoints and raises up those whom he sends into the ministry, to bear testimony to himself in the glorious truths of redeeming love and mercy set forth in the gospel. But in the ministry of the word it is not to the preacher, but to Jesus Christ alone that *all* should point. "This is my beloved Son, in whom I am well pleased."

"And when the disciples heard it, they fell on their face, and were sore afraid." Surely is not that ever the reaction whenever the Lord thus manifests himself in the word of truth as there declared? So it was with John on the isle of Patmos when he beheld the risen and ascended Lord. "I fell at his feet as dead" (Rev. 1:17). That is always the response of the sinner when God thus reveals himself in the wonders of his grace. So it was with Isaiah: "Woe is me! for I am undone; because I am a man of unclean lips, and I dwell in the midst of a people of unclean lips: for mine eyes have seen the King, the Lord of hosts" (Isa. 6:5).

And so it was here with the disciples. When they heard that voice, "they fell on their face, and were sore afraid." O see here the wonder of the grace and love of our Lord Jesus Christ to his own. "And Jesus came and touched them, and said, Arise, and be not afraid." He spoke the same to John on Patmos: "And he laid his right hand upon me, saying unto me, Fear not; I am the first and the last: I am he that liveth, and was dead; and, behold, I am alive for evermore, Amen; and have the keys of hell and of death."

O friends, the rich compassion of our Lord Jesus Christ! He "came and touched them, and said, Arise, and be not afraid." O the wonder of that grace, that compassion, of our Lord Jesus Christ as he comes to his needy people. "It is I; be not afraid"

(Matt. 14:27). O then, whatever issues may be confronting us in our path at this present time, whatever may be before us in the days that lie ahead: *"It is I; be not afraid."* O that we might know the Lord's gracious touch, his blessed presence with us according to his promise. "For he hath said, I will never leave thee, nor forsake thee" (Heb. 13:5). The Lord never goes back on what he speaks to his people, though it may have been spoken in years past. He meant it then and it still stands true today, blessed be his holy name.

"And when they had lifted up their eyes, they saw no man, save Jesus only."

> "To keep our eyes on Jesus fixed,
> And there our hope to stay,
> The Lord will make his goodness pass
> Before us in the way."

But I will leave the remarks there this morning. The Lord add his blessing. Amen.

42

THEY SAW NO MAN, SAVE JESUS ONLY

Lord's day evening 28 June 2020

"And Jesus came and touched them, and said,
Arise, and be not afraid. And when they had
lifted up their eyes, they saw no man, save
Jesus only" (Matthew 17:7-8).

The fear that overcame those disciples is surely not surprising
when they were overshadowed by that bright cloud, and heard
that voice speaking, "This is my beloved Son, in whom I am well
pleased." And surely all manifestations of the greatness and
holiness of the heart-searching God, brought home to a sinner,
cannot but bring them to solemnly realise what they are, and
where they are, before him. It cannot but engender very real fear
and dread in the souls of sinners. How solemn it was so here with
the disciples. They were followers of the Lord Jesus Christ. They
had been brought into an acquaintance with him. More, through
what they had received of him, they had been brought to believe
in him. But in a conscious realization at this time of what they
were of themselves how could they (or any sinner) stand before
the holiness of God revealed in his word and brought home by
the power of the Holy Spirit?

They fell upon their faces when they heard that voice speaking
to them. But the Lord Jesus came to them, and touched them, and
said, *"Arise, be not afraid."* We see here a most blessed precious
vitally important truth set before us. As sinners there is but one
way of access for us to God and acceptance by him. Without a
mediator, where are we? Can we ever stand before God? Are we
not brought under his righteous judgment, and that justly because
we are sinful men and women? But the Lord Jesus Christ is our
mediator and advocate with the Father. Surely we have continual
cause to give thanks unto the Lord that through the sovereign

operations of the Holy Spirit we are brought to believe on Jesus Christ unto eternal life.

The disciples heard the Father's testimony: "This is my beloved Son, in whom I am well pleased." And we, as sinners are brought to hear that same testimony, and to believe and trust alone in him of whom God the Father speaks, even his only begotten and dearly beloved Son, God manifest in the flesh. Friends, here we see what the Father himself, the very God against whom we have sinned, has provided. We see it in the precious truth of the gospel in which is manifest the outworking of the wisdom, power, goodness and love of God. Therein we see the love wherewith he loved his people from before the foundation of the world. And in his appointed time, he calls them by his grace and reveals the wonders of his sovereign saving love to them.

Here we see the unchanging love of our Lord Jesus Christ to his people. It is not founded in any way upon their worth, merits or behaviour. Consider Peter's weaknesses, infirmities, failings, even his grievous denial of his Lord. See how this was brought home to Peter when the Lord looked on him and he went out and wept bitterly through the conscious sense of what he had done. The Lord's look was not one of condemnation, not "I told you so." It was a look of love. And such is the love of the Lord Jesus Christ to his own. Not that there is the approving of their failings and sins. The Lord's chastening hand is known by his people. But it is always in love. It is never outside the covenant of his grace. Therein the Lord embraces his people in never-failing love, collectively, individually, personally. He says, "I have loved thee with an everlasting love: therefore with lovingkindness have I drawn thee" (Jer. 31:3). O may the Holy Spirit seal those words afresh to your soul and mine, to any trembling needy exercised soul before him this evening.

See here again the compassion of our Lord Jesus Christ to his own. Remember who it is that came and touched them! Jesus, he whom they beheld transfigured before them, that same glorious man, the God-man, unquestionably our Lord Jesus Christ. And when that scene had passed away, they found Jesus still as he ever is to his people, "the same yesterday, and to day, and for ever" (Heb. 13:8). Yes, and now we behold with wonder that same glorious man in glory, our Lord Jesus Christ who is entered into heaven itself, there to appear in the presence of God for us. The Lord the Holy Spirit reveal it more and more unto us. Still he testifies, as he does here in effect to these disciples, "It is I; be not afraid" (Matt. 14:27).

Ah yes friends, there is much to be afraid of from the working of sin in our hearts and lives and the many issues we meet with from day to day. They do occasion fears with us. We do not say those things are to be looked on lightly. Far from it. They effect us greatly, as the disciples were here affected. But O let us never lose sight of where the encouragement and consolation of the living family of God is to be found in every situation. It is found in the truth that Jesus lives, that Jesus saves, that Jesus, to whom all authority and power is given in heaven and earth, still reigns and rules on Zion's hill as the great head of the church.

You remember that occasion in the days of Elisha when the Syrian army surrounded the city of Dothan. The following morning, Elisha's servant perceiving how they were besieged, says, "Alas, my master! how shall we do?" Elisha replies, "Fear not: for they that be with us are more than they that be with them" (2 Kings 6:15–16). He prayed the Lord to open the young man's eyes and he beheld the mountain full of horses and chariots of fire round about Elisha. The true church of Jesus Christ ever testified, and every believer likewise can truly say, that there are more that be with us than with them. With them is an arm of flesh but with us is the Lord our God to save us, deliver us and provide for us. Is not the Lord ever thus known to his people?

Was not this made known to Abraham on mount Moriah when he offered up his son Isaac at the command of God, and a ram was offered in the place of Isaac? And he called "that place Jehovah-jireh...In the mount of the Lord it shall be seen" (Gen. 22:14). What Jehovah-jirehs the Lord's people experience in their own lives when they can truly say that the Lord doth provide, blessed be his name! Is there any situation in which the Lord's people are found when he leaves them utterly to themselves? He may indeed in mercy bring them to realize their utter ruin, helplessness and need. But he never leaves them to perish in their sins. He always graciously appears for them.

He comes to his disciples here. He touched them. O friends, the blessedness of that touch of our Lord Jesus Christ. And he said, "be not afraid." They lifted up their eyes and saw no man save Jesus only. O remember, it is the Lord alone who, by the gracious ministry of the Holy Spirit, brings true encouragement and consolation to his people. "He touched them."

Remember that time early in the ministry of our Lord Jesus Christ when a leper came to him, saying "Lord, if thou wilt, thou canst make me clean" (Matt. 8:2). Did Jesus turn away from him? Ah, others would have nothing to do with him. A leper was an outcast from society, going about, crying, "unclean, unclean." But see the wonder of the grace and mercy of the Lord to that poor, needy, sinful, afflicted man. The Lord did something for him that no other would have done. He "put forth his hand, and touched him." What grace and mercy was in that touch. In it, the man experienced healing from his leprosy and, I believe, the realization of the love and mercy of the Lord Jesus Christ to him. Yes, the Lord did what no other could do. He cleansed him of his leprosy. But O, was there not more than the cleansing of the body? Did not the Lord bring peace and pardon into his soul, so that he surely went on his way rejoicing, and could not refrain from setting forth the praise of him who manifested such grace and mercy to him! May we know the living reality of the same for ourselves. For a touch from the Lord, his word brought home to us in the blessed power and unction of the Holy Spirit, O can it not impart true spiritual strength to our souls? Can it not raise up those that are cast down and strengthen us to still go forward in the path the Lord has appointed for us? Certainly we prove we are not sufficient of ourselves.

You know, how arduous was the work of the ministry to which Paul was appointed of God. How involved he was in it. What a conscious sense he always had of his weakness, his need and his dependence on the Lord. But could he not bear testimony that though not sufficient of himself, he ever proved his sufficiency was of the Lord? For it was not in his own strength he went forward, nor of his own abilities was the word used to the salvation of so many. It was alone through the grace of God given to him. As the Lord himself had promised, "My grace is sufficient for thee: for my strength is made perfect in weakness" (2 Cor. 12:9).

He "came and touched them, and said, Arise, and be not afraid." What gracious lifting up there is for those that are cast down. What can lift up the soul burdened by the guilt of their sins and transgressions pressing heavy upon them? Their only deliverance is by what flows from the Lord Jesus himself. Through the riches of his sovereign grace, his pardoning love and mercy is brought home to us by the word and power of the Holy Spirit.

He said, "Arise, and be not afraid." How many times in the word does the Lord thus speak to his own, "Be not afraid." Surely it is not because there in nothing to be afraid of. The Lord "knoweth our frame; he remembereth that we are dust" (Ps. 103:14). He knows our weaknesses and infirmities and how we are greatly affected by issues in our personal situation, or which we may perceive to be before us at this present time. The fears of the Lord's people are oftentimes very real. O let none say, and surely if taught of the Holy Spirit none will claim, they are never afraid. It could be said, 'What is there for a true believer to be afraid of, if the Lord is indeed their God?' In one sense that is so. But fears often beset us, we being still in a body of sin and death and still experiencing our weakness and infirmities and our daily needs. But here we see that only the Lord himself can lift us up and deliver us from those fears. "Arise and be not afraid."

Remember the occasion of the disciples on the sea of Galilee. The Lord Jesus had sent them over before him. They were overtaken by a great storm and Jesus came to them walking on the water. They thought it was a spirit and cried out for fear. But Jesus spake! O friends, the word of the Lord comes not in word only but in power, in the Holy Ghost, in much assurance. "It is I; be not afraid." *Is not everything in that?* "It is I." Ah, it is the Lord, blessed be his name. He never overlooks, he will not forsake those that are his own. What a mercy that is. On that occasion, though the disciples perceived it not, the Lord knew just where they were. His eye was upon them. He knew all their circumstances. All was under his control. Is it any less so in our day as it concerns each one of his own? No. O for grace, not only to perceive more of the hand of the Lord, believingly and feelingly, but to know blessed rest in his love that knows no change and no end.

We read, "when they had lifted up their eyes, they saw no man, save Jesus only." Friends, what a word is that! They heard that voice speaking to them from heaven, saying, "This is my beloved Son, in whom I am well pleased." Moses and Elias had gone. Jesus alone remained. Though Moses and Elias were faithful servant of God in their generation, it could not be said of them what God the Father said here, "This is my beloved Son, in whom I am well pleased." Remember, though faithful servants of God, Moses and Elijah were yet sinners, sinners saved by grace alone. There is but one man, one man only, of whom it could truly be said that in him was no sin, and that is the man Christ Jesus. Well might we say of him, "Behold the man" (John 19:5). Pilate knew not what he said, when Jesus came forth, crowned with thorns and clothed in a purple robe. O, but poor sinners, taught of God the Holy Spirit, by precious faith behold that man, the man Christ Jesus who is now exalted at the right hand of the Majesty on high. For he entered into heaven itself, there to appear in the presence of God for us. The disciples beheld him on the mount of transfiguration. We poor sinners, behold him set before us in the word, in the reality of his sufferings and death on Calvary. O friends, this glorious man, the man Christ Jesus! "This is my beloved Son, in whom I am well pleased." In *none other* is God well pleased, as testified here.

As I mentioned this morning, God's being well-pleased embraces all who are found *in* Jesus Christ, and he *one* with them. They were given to him in the covenant ordered in all things and sure. The Lord Jesus Christ, in all his life and ministry here on earth, did not act as a private individual, but as *the* great head and representative of his church. The Lord Jesus was one with his people, not only then, but now and to all eternity, to the praise of the glory of his name. The union of Christ with his own, is an indissoluble union. Every individual believer, as one with Jesus Christ, is as safe now, as precious to God now, as they shall be to all the ages of eternity. Yes, we shall change our place from earth to heaven. We shall lay aside this body of sin and death.

But be assured that the union of Christ with his people is an abiding reality. "This is my beloved Son, *in* whom I am well pleased."

When they had lifted up their eyes, they saw no man, save Jesus only." May *we* increasingly see no man, save Jesus only. *This is vital.* What has troubled the church of Jesus Christ all down the generations? What did the apostle so contend against in his day, when he wrote to the Galatians and also to other churches? What error has Satan ever sought to promote, which is so engaging to fallen human nature? It is to say, 'Yes, Jesus Christ and what he accomplished is needful for salvation but something else must also be added to it, even the obedience of the individual. Jesus Christ alone is not sufficient.' O how acceptable is that to fallen human nature, being what we are of ourselves. O what grace is needed to teach us our utter nothingness, and to bring us as a sinner to be wholly dependent on the Lord Jesus Christ alone. What grace we need to realise that our salvation is not partly on what Jesus Christ has done and on something we must add to it. No, salvation is wholly founded on what he has done. O to be made willing to be saved by grace alone. What a great work of God is this. Such is the pride of our fallen nature, that we do not like, even naturally, to be wholly dependent on another. And does not this pride so often intrude into spiritual things? O may the Lord deliver us from all that is of self, sinful self and more so, righteous self. Nothing of our own can ever contribute to the believer's acceptance with God. Our acceptance is not founded on what we have done or can do in any way, but alone on what Jesus Christ has done for us.

Is not that the glory of the gospel? It declares that salvation is all of grace. It is without money, without price. It is a free gift of God in Jesus Christ. If it is the gift of God, does it then require something to be supplied by those who are the recipients of it? If we are the recipients of a gift, that gift is free. If it is not, it is not a gift. But salvation *is* the gift of God. The gift of God is eternal life through Jesus Christ our Lord, blessed be his name. O for grace, to ever hold firmly on to this, as blessedly taught and enabled of the Lord the Holy Spirit.

"Hear ye him." May that *always* be so with us. We are so

prone to give ear to this, that or the other. May our ear be opened only to what the Lord speaks as set before us in his word. God the Father directed them, "hear ye *him*." Does not that blessedly underline the important fact, that it is not what man says, but what God in Christ has declared. That is to be the criteria by which all is judged and all obedience to the Lord determined, not by what man says accompanying it but what God has plainly revealed to us in his word. He speaks to us through our Lord Jesus Christ and we are to give heed wholly to what the Lord says to us in his holy word.

"Hear him…no man save *Jesus only.*" Friends, how precious is that word. See Jesus only as all our righteousness, Jesus only as all our sanctification, Jesus only as our redemption, Jesus only, from whom the blessings of pardon and peace flow to us, Jesus only, the glorious object of the faith, hope, and love of the sinner, of your soul and mine as taught of the Holy Spirit. I trust we can say in the language of Peter, "Unto you therefore which believe he is precious" (1 Pet. 2:7). For he is the one we cannot do without. He is the only one in whom all the blessings of salvation for us are found in all their *fulness,* and manifest to us in all their *freeness.* Yes, Jesus Christ is the sole object of the faith, hope and love of his people. "They saw no man, save Jesus only."

I closed this morning with those words,

"To keep our eyes on Jesus fixed,
And there our hope to stay,
The Lord will make his goodness pass
Before us in the way."

"Jesus only." O to see all our concerns wholly in the hands of the Lord Jesus Christ, all subject to his sovereign will and good pleasure. *"Jesus only."* O I say, may that ever be so in every aspect of our personal lives and in the life and company of the church and people of God. "To him give all the prophets witness" (Acts 10:43). And may we likewise bear witness to him, that Jesus is ours, and there is none like him and none beside him. In him only is found the fulness and freeness of redeeming love and mercy, and all our hope and expectation in time and to all eternity.

You know, *Jesus only* is the whole object of the praise and thanksgiving of the redeemed before the throne and will be so to the living family of God through the ages of eternity. They worship God as revealed in the person of Jesus Christ. O the glorious realisation of this when brought to see him face to face! As the apostle John could say, "Beloved, now are we the sons of God, and it doth not yet appear what we shall be: but we know that, when he shall appear, we shall be like him; for we shall see him as he is" (1 John 3:2). O what a glorious promise is that! *"See him as he is,"* the Lamb, the fulness of the glory of God as revealed, not just in the precious truth of the gospel, but face to face throughout the ages of eternity. All will be to the praise of the glory of his name and the eternal welfare of all he has loved, chosen, redeemed and called by his grace to believe and trust *alone in him.*

I will leave the remarks there. The Lord add his blessing. Amen.

43

I HAD FAINTED, UNLESS I HAD BELIEVED TO SEE

Tuesday evening 30 June 2020

"I had fainted, unless I had believed to see the goodness of the Lord in the land of the living. Wait on the Lord: be of good courage, and he shall strengthen thine heart: wait, I say, on the Lord" (Psalm 27:13–14).

Through the prophet Isaiah, the Lord declares, "Behold my servant, whom I uphold; mine elect, in whom my soul delighteth; I have put my spirit upon him: he shall bring forth judgment to the Gentiles" (Isa. 42:1). And undoubtedly, the same servant of the Lord is set forth in this psalm. I know it is described as a psalm of David, and no doubt David wrote out of his own experience as taught of God the Holy Spirit. But he was one of those holy men of old who were moved by the Holy Spirit to set forth the coming of Jehovah's righteous servant, even our Lord Jesus Christ in his sufferings and the glory that was to follow. And certainly this is the word of the Lord to us in our day.

Essentially, our Lord Jesus Christ is the only one of whom we can say that all set before us in this psalm was fulfilled. That glorious man, the man Christ Jesus, Jehovah's righteous servant, fully walked out this psalm in his life and ministry here on earth. The Spirit was given without measure to him. He was perfectly obedient to the will of his Father. He accomplished all that his Father had appointed him. In that work was all that pertained to the glory of God in the redemption of sinful men and women whom the Lord our God has chosen. Have not those to whom these blessings are made known, *daily* cause to bless God for Jesus Christ?

Remember what the apostle expressed in his letter to the Romans. He *daily* experienced the working of sin so easily besetting him. And it besets us likewise. For if we know anything of saving, distinguishing grace, we will know the conflict between the flesh and the Spirit, that which is born of God and that which is born of the flesh. The apostle was brought to cry, "O wretched man that I am! who shall deliver me from the body of this death?" What was his answer to that question? "I thank God *through Jesus Christ our Lord"* (Rom. 7:24–25). And surely if the saving mercy of God is made known to us, will it not be a *daily* exercise with us to be thankful to God for Jesus Christ?

As Jehovah's righteous servant, see what the fulfilment of his Father's work involved for him. The scriptures tell us that he was "a man of sorrows, and acquainted with grief" (Isa. 53:3). O what contradiction of sinners he experienced against himself. Yet, as we see in this psalm, it is blessedly evident that he delighted in the work his Father gave him to do. Indeed, we are told of him, "who for the joy that was set before him endured the cross, despising the shame, and is set down at the right hand of the throne of God" (Heb. 12:2).

Some might question, Can you really say that this psalm brings before us the personal life, ministry and sufferings of our Lord Jesus Christ here on earth? Well, look at the second verse. "When the wicked, even mine enemies and my foes, came upon me to eat up my flesh, they stumbled and fell." Go to the garden of Gethsemane. See what was witnessed by the disciples when the Lord took three of them and went further into the garden. We see there the prayer and agony of our Lord Jesus Christ. O friends, what conflict our Saviour endured. Can we even begin to comprehend what was involved for him who knew no sin, being made sin for us? He took the cup his Father gave him to drink, a cup filled with the wine of the wrath of God, justly poured out without mixture against all the sins of those whom his Father had given him. Ah friends, can we even begin to comprehend the awful depths and fulness of that cup. But behold, it was for sinners such as you and me. May the Lord the Holy Spirit, seal to us the pardon of our souls through the Lord's drinking that cup.

> "For love of me, the Son of God,
> Shed every drop of vital blood,
> For me, amazing anguish felt,
> The wrath of an offended God."

He did so, that we sinners who are brought by divine grace to believe and trust in him, should never experience the wrath of God. He delivered us from the just curse and condemnation of God's holy law, else hell would have been our deserved abode. So it must have been, apart from the wonders of grace.

Jesus prayed three times, "O my Father, if it be possible, let this cup pass from me: nevertheless not as I will, but as thou wilt" (Matt. 26:39). Wondrous grace was seen there in this faithful servant of God, our Lord Jesus Christ. And when that band of soldiers led by Judas came to apprehend him, he went forth to meet them. He said, "Whom seek ye?" They reply, "Jesus of Nazareth." He said, *"I am he."* What was the effect? "They went backward, and fell to the ground" (John 18:4–8). It was just as said in this psalm, "When the wicked, even mine enemies and my foes, came upon me to eat up my flesh, they stumbled and fell." Was such a thing ever known before? Here was the *man* Christ Jesus but in that incident we see his Godhead shine forth in the manhood.

We spoke on Sunday morning of the transfiguration of our Lord Jesus Christ on that mountain. The disciples saw that wondrous revelation of the glory of God manifest in the flesh. Well, his glory was displayed in a different way in the garden. None of that band of soldiers sent to apprehend him, could lay one finger on him without his being willing to allow them to do so. We see how willing Jesus was to die. He said, "No man taketh [my life] from me, but I lay it down of myself. I have power to lay it down, and I have power to take it again. This commandment have I received of my Father" (John 10:18). How vital was that in the offering and sacrifice of Jesus for the redemption and salvation of his people. Under the law, what was offered to God for the remission of sins, the blood of the animal, had to be a free-will offering. Such was the offering of our Lord Jesus Christ, "who through the eternal Spirit offered himself without spot to God" (Heb. 9:14). I say again,

> "How willing was Jesus to die,
> That we wretched sinners might live!
> The life they could not take away
> How willing was Jesus to give!"

O these wonders flow out of the love of God. And that love is revealed in Jesus Christ our Lord to sinful men and women such as you and me. By the grace of God, the Lord reveals himself to us in pardoning love and mercy. O that this love may be more and more known in felt experience in our own soul and its sanctifying influence manifest in our lives. Friends, may we be truly those who believe and trust in the Lord alone.

In our text we read, "I had fainted, unless I had believed to see the goodness of the Lord in the land of the living." Surely, here again, we see our Lord Jesus Christ as Jehovah's righteous servant. Here was one that truly believed God, one that trusted in God, going forward in the work his Father had given him to do. The scriptures tell us how he steadfastly set his face to go to Jerusalem. He well knew all that lay before him in the path appointed him, but did he flinch or turn aside from it? No. We see all the opposition he met from wicked men and devils. See how he was reproached and derided. Yet we behold our Lord Jesus Christ going forward, believing and trusting in his heavenly Father. They said, "He saved others; himself he cannot save…let him now come down from the cross, and we will believe him. He trusted in God; let him deliver him now" (Matt. 27:42–43). O friends, what reproach was heaped on Jesus. Remember that for such sinners as you and me, he "endured the cross, despising the shame." And so in our text, he says, "I had fainted, unless I had believed to see the goodness of the Lord in the land of the living."

See what our Lord Jesus Christ always had in view. It was said by Isaiah, "He shall see of the travail of his soul, and shall be satisfied: by his knowledge shall my righteous servant justify many" (Isa. 53:11). The glorious end to be accomplished was ever before our Lord Jesus, even the glory of God in the redemption of his people. We see that truth in his high priestly prayer: "I have finished the work which thou gavest me to do. And now, O Father, glorify thou me with thine own self with the glory which I had with thee before the world was" (John 17:4–5). O behold there the glory of the God-man, the Lord Jesus Christ, the mediator between God and men, the man Christ Jesus, the great head of the church. Ah, *"he* believed to see the goodness of the Lord in the land of the living." In the face of all he endured, the certainly of his full, final victory over sin, Satan, death, hell and grave, was ever before him. He trusted in God as to the certainty that all would be successfully accomplished to the praise of the glory of our triune God.

Now I will not go further into the many other things that could be brought out of this psalm relative to the personal life of our Lord Jesus Christ on earth. I have said that David undoubtedly wrote out of his own experience. And these things apply to the people of God today, those who are the sheep of his pasture, and who are brought, through his grace, to follow in the footsteps of their Lord and Master Jesus Christ. O friends, how wondrous is the grace which brings such a sinner as you and me, to be a follower of the Lord Jesus Christ. Not only are we brought to know *about* him but to own him as our Lord and Saviour, because he has owned us and manifested his love to us. As John says, "We love him, because he first loved us" (1 John 4:19).

"I had fainted, unless I had believed to see the goodness of the Lord in the land of the living." What gracious application this has to the church and people of God in every situation in which they may be found today personally or collectively. What fears abound around us in society at large, ourselves also not unaffected. Notice our text does not say, "I had fainted unless I had *seen to believe.*" No, it says, *"I believed to see."* Remember, faith is a gift of God. Paul defines it as "the substance of things hoped for, the evidence of things not seen" (Heb. 11:1). Faith receives what is sovereignly imparted by God to the sinner through the riches of divine grace. Surely its essence is, "He that believeth on the Son hath everlasting life" (John 3:36). Yes, faith receives the testimony God has given of his only begotten and dearly beloved Son. O to *"believe to see"!* For faith has a true perception to receive what God reveals to us in his holy word, *all centering* in our Lord and Saviour Jesus Christ. In him we see "the goodness of the Lord" appointed and provided for his people. It is not perceived by the natural eye. The light with which we see these things is given to us by the Holy Spirit's gracious application of the word of God. These things are real and precious. They are not some cunningly fables. No. Does not the Lord the Holy Spirit teach his people by the light he sheds on his word in applying it to them?

Friends, what upholds, strengthens, helps and encourages us as we go forward in the path the Lord has appointed for us, in the face of all the trials, difficulties, temptations and fears that beset us? If we were left to ourselves, having nothing else to look to or rest upon, surely faith would, as it were, perish under our trouble. O see the gracious provision the Lord had given his church and people, which upholds, keeps and strengthens them in the face of all the issues that arise in their life and circumstances. O remember the word of the Lord to Paul, "My grace is sufficient for thee: for my strength is made perfect in weakness" (2 Cor. 12:9). Remember that the resources of the Lord for his people never diminish. Blessed be his name, what a fulness there is. How ever much is drawn out of that fulness, it never diminishes one iota, for it is the fulness of our infinite God as revealed in Jesus Christ. Hear how Paul expresses this in writing to the Philippians: "My God shall supply all your need according to his riches in glory by Christ Jesus" (Phil. 4:19). Can we estimate those riches of glory in Christ Jesus? The Lord promises, not merely to supply your needs out of those riches, but *according to those riches* in all the fulness, wonder, blessedness and freeness of them! O friends, the goodness of God as made known to his people! Why, one rightly says,

> "He that has made my heaven secure
> Will here all good provide;
> While Christ is rich, I can't be poor;
> What can I want beside?"

Do we really believe these things set before us in the word? Are we so affected by the issues we meet at this particular time as to be so fearful, so trembling, so forgetful of the Lord our God? Do we lose sight of the constancy of his love and care for us? Can I not trust my life in his hands? Am I so fearful to go forward in the path appointed for me because 'this, that or the other' might come or not come, when the word assures me that my life's minutest circumstance is subject to his eye? We profess to believe it. We sing it. Friends, do we really believe it in the walking out of it in our lives?

"I had fainted, unless I had believed to see the goodness of the Lord in the land of the living." I read the fourth chapter in the second epistle to the Corinthians this evening. I did so because Paul there sets forth the same important principles concerning the people of God, in walking the path the Lord has appointed for them and in whatever matters concern them. Paul surely opens up this psalm when he says, "as we have received mercy, *we faint not*" (2 Cor. 4:1). If the Lord has been merciful to us, will he ever go back on what he has made known to us of his pardoning grace and mercy? Is the Lord so changeable, like ourselves and all men? Blessed be his name, he assures us: "I am the Lord, *I change not;* therefore ye sons of Jacob are not consumed" (Mal. 3:6). What important application that has to the people of God, directing us to where our help and hope is found. Has the Lord our God ever failed us, whatever may have been our situation? Can we not then still trust him for all that may yet come?

"As we have received mercy, we faint not." Paul, later in the chapter, goes on to say, "We having the same spirit of faith, according as it is written, I believed, and therefore have I spoken; we also believe, and therefore speak." And what does he speak? "Knowing that he which raised up the Lord Jesus shall raise up us also by Jesus, and shall present us with you." See what a foundation is laid for the faith and hope of the living family of God in the life, sufferings, death and resurrection of our Lord Jesus Christ. Are there things that oppose us, that distress us and occasion fears which so prevail with us? O behold our Lord Jesus Christ who has overcome sin, Satan, death, hell and the grave, blessed be his great and holy name. He goes on to say, "For all things are for your sakes, that the abundant grace might through the thanksgiving of many redound to the glory of God. For which cause *we faint not;* but though our outward man perish, yet the inward man is renewed day by day."

"I had fainted, unless I had believed to see the *goodness* of the Lord." See that goodness of the Lord in the person of the Lord Jesus and in what he has done for his people, as set before us in the gospel. It can never be undone, though sin and Satan seek to overthrow it. Not all the enemies of God and his people can ever prevail against them while Jesus lives. We read in the scriptures,

"If God be for us." Does not the Lord testify that he is for his people, and not only for them but loves them with an everlasting love? Can *everlasting* love cease? Blessed be his name, no. "If God be for us, who can be against us? He that spared not his own Son, but delivered him up for us all, how shall he not with him also freely give us all things?" (Rom. 8:32–32). O friends, the fulness and wonders of the grace and mercy of the Lord to his own!

Paul goes on to say to the Corinthians, "For which cause we *faint not;* but though our outward man perish, yet the inward man is renewed day by day. For our light affliction, which is but for a moment, worketh for us a far more exceeding and eternal weight of glory." "I had fainted, unless I had believed to see the goodness of the Lord." His goodness set before us in the precious gospel, is pardon, peace and *eternal life*. As the hymn I quoted a few moments ago, "He that hath made our heaven secure." Has he indeed done so? Is our hope and trust found there, wholly in Jesus Christ our Lord? Has he assured us of a heavenly inheritance? Whatever we may be called to pass through in this life, and the circumstances in which we come towards our end, can they change this inheritance? No. His word testifies that the Lord is ever with his people. His love and care for them never changes and knows no end. Paul goes on, "For our light affliction, which is but for a moment, worketh for us a far more exceeding and eternal weight of glory; while we look not at the things which are seen, but at the things which are not seen: for the things which are seen are temporal; but the things which are not seen are eternal."

How greatly we are affected by the things which *are seen* in our present circumstances. O friends, are we as much affected by the things which *are not seen?* For those things are far more real than the things of time and sense in that they are *eternal* realities. These *things* are the glories of the redeeming love and mercy of God who has reconciled us to himself through the redemption that is in Christ Jesus. If God then is my God, if through his grace I am a child of God, an heir of God and joint heir with Christ Jesus, O how blessed I am! Does this have any real influence on us in our whole attitude to all that concerns us at present? "The things which are seen are temporal." Even for the longest living of any of us, how soon shall these things be done and finished with. "But the things which are not seen are eternal." They are eternal realities.

So what is the implication of this for us? Look at the last verse of this psalm. "Wait on the Lord: be of good courage, and he shall strengthen thine heart: wait, I say, on the Lord." May the Lord the Holy Spirit bring this word home afresh to your soul and mine. Tried, exercised, fearful, needy child of God, where does the word direct you? To *one* place, one glorious person, our Lord Jesus Christ. He was Jehovah's righteous servant who fulfilled all the work his Father gave him to do for the redemption of his people, to the praise of the glory of our triune God. We are directed "unto him that loved us, and washed us from our sins in his own blood," he who lives and reigns in heaven and earth (Rev. 1:5).

"Wait on the Lord: be of good courage, and he shall strengthen thine heart: wait, I say, on the Lord." What is this waiting on the Lord? Why friends, it is to bring all to him, to commit all our cares into his hand. Peter assures us of this precious truth when he says: "Casting all your care upon him; for *he careth for you*" (1 Pet. 5:7). *Do we believe it?* O for grace enabling us to truly practice the things we profess to believe, by walking them out in our own lives.

"Wait on the Lord." Who speaks this? It is the word of our God himself. We hear the voice of our Lord and Saviour by the gracious ministry of the Holy Spirit. "Wait on the Lord." O what gracious direction and encouragement is given us here. We are assured of the certainty that waiting upon him, looking to him, trusting him, casting our concerns into his hands, is *never* a vain thing. Far from it! Why, from our Lord Jesus Christ alone, flows all that pertains to our spiritual and eternal welfare, and indeed our physical welfare as well.

He says, "Be of good courage, and he shall strengthen thine heart: wait, I say, on the Lord." Friends, what flows from the mercy of the Lord to us, not only addresses our outward man, but the inward man in the truest sense. "He shall strengthen thine *heart.*" O there is a fulness, a sufficiency in our Lord and Saviour

Jesus Christ. What is his word to his people still? 'Come, come unto me, come with all your needs, all your concerns, come to the throne of my grace.' What does he promise? His promise is firm and sure. We shall "obtain mercy, and find grace to help in time of need" (Heb. 4:16). It is no vain thing then to wait on the Lord. As it is emphasized here, "wait, *I say,* on the Lord." May it be so with us. Wait on him, on him alone.

I will leave the remarks there. The Lord add his blessing. Amen.

44

THOU HAST CAST ALL MY SINS
BEHIND THY BACK

Lord's day morning 5 July 2020.

"Behold, for peace I had great bitterness: but
thou hast in love to my soul delivered it from
the pit of corruption: for thou hast cast all my
sins behind thy back" (Isaiah 38:17).

Here is "The writing of Hezekiah king of Judah, when he had
been sick, and was recovered of his sickness." There were
undoubtedly outward problems in the great difficulties and
dangers which he and the inhabitants of Jerusalem experienced
through the Assyrian invasion. They had already taken the
fortified cities of Judah, and Jerusalem itself was besieged by
them. We have Hezekiah's prayer to the Lord his God on that
occasion. And the message had come from Isaiah that the Lord
would, in his appointed time, deliver them from that distress. But
it would appear that in the midst of those things the hand of the
Lord was not only seen in his dealings with the inhabitants of
Judah and Jerusalem, but with Hezekiah himself personally. And
the spiritual exercises of this man of God in the Lord's dealings
with him, and the manifestation the Lord's sovereign saving
mercies toward him, are prominently set before us here.
Particularly is this so in these words I have read by way of a text.

I will not go into the outward circumstances we read in
chapters thirty-six and thirty-seven. They are well set forth and
more detail is given us in the second book of Kings. You can read
those passages in your own time as enabled. But I want to
consider the Lord's dealings with Hezekiah personally. In the
matters of true religion are not the Lord's personal dealings with
us vital? We do not deny the Lord's hand is in all things that
concern his people collectively and in all the issues of the nations
of the world as well. We are not unconcerned with those outward
things. Far from it. As here with Hezekiah the dangers that

threatened them from the Assyrians were greatly troubling. They had no ability of themselves to successfully defend Jerusalem against those Assyrian armies. As Rabshakeh boasted, none of the gods of the nations had been able to deliver them from the hand of Sennacherib. Therefore he boasted that the God in whom Hezekiah trusted would not be able to deliver them either. What boastful blasphemy is this language of Rabshakeh, the general of this great army of Sennacherib. O friends, man may boast as he does but the word of the Lord shall most surely stand.

Likewise in our own day, it is not what man declares he will do or not do that shall come to pass but what God has appointed. In all the dealings of God among men and nations and in our individual lives, it is his word that shall stand. What a mercy it is for us to know the gracious personal dealings of the Lord with us. O that he would therein be pleased to reveal himself to us as the one and only true God, the God and Father of our Lord Jesus Christ, who has reconciled us to himself by the redemption that is in his Son. Here *alone* are found all the blessings of salvation for us as sinners.

Let us look then, as helped, at the exercises and experience of Hezekiah, king of Judah, in the issues within the nation and the Lord's dealings with him personally. It is well said that troubles often do not seem to come singly but one upon another. Hezekiah might have thought that the situation faced by the city was problem enough. But a heavier burden came upon him from the Lord's hand in his sickness. And indeed remember that all the infirmities and sicknesses to which we are subject as we journey on through life, and doubtless increasingly so the older we get, are of the Lord. But for his people, they are not sent in judgment. Yes, in measure there is the Lord's chastening hand in them according to his appointments. But how ready we are to judge the Lord's dealings with us as if his hand has gone out against us. May we be brought to realise what is expressed in the hymn we sometimes sing,

> "God moves in a mysterious way
> His wonders to perform;
> He plants his footsteps in the sea,
> And rides upon the storm."

And here it might have appeared to Hezekiah that all those things were against him. Indeed, he cried out, "O Lord, I am oppressed; undertake for me." We see that the hand of the Lord was in all those afflictions but also that what the Lord made known to his servant was ultimately for the true spiritual profit of his soul. And above all we see displayed the mighty works of God. See them in the Lord's delivering Jerusalem out of the hand of Sennacherib and his judgment on that king of Assyria. See also the remarkable phenomenon of the sun going backwards ten degrees in the sundial of Ahaz. What a mighty work of God was that! The point I make is that we must remember that the God of Hezekiah is the same God still. No change has taken place in him. He is still the almighty God. May we ever acknowledge that he holds all things in his hand. All things are under his control. What is man in comparison to the one and only true God? What are we as individuals? We are mere worms of the earth in comparison with the mightiness of the one and only true God.

And the greatest wonder of the works of God is that he looks in mercy on such sinners as you and me. That is the point I particularly want to come to this morning. Yes, the works of God are here displayed in delivering them from the armies of the Assyrians and in the wonder of the sun going backwards. But friends, the greatest wonder of all is what Hezekiah testified to in these words of our text. "Thou hast in love to my soul delivered it from the pit of corruption: for thou hast cast all my sins behind thy back." That is the greatest wonder, the greatest work of God! For remember what was involved in the manifestation of such sovereign grace and mercy to Hezekiah and to all poor guilty needy sinners God brings to know the blessed truth that, "Thou hast cast all my sins behind thy back." Ah I say, what was involved in that? The greatest wonder of all is that God reveals himself in the person and work of the Lord and Saviour Jesus Christ. Surely this work exceeds all creation! The incarnation of our Lord Jesus Christ, that great mystery of godliness, that God should be manifest in the flesh! That God, in the person of Jesus Christ, should come and be found in fashion as a man and be obedient unto death, even the death of the cross! That the Son of God should come to fulfil all righteousness and satisfy every demand of the holy law of God on behalf of all his Father had given him! He became their surety, their substitute! He laid down his life for them that they might live! Why friends, I say again that God's delivering Hezekiah and the inhabitants of Jerusalem from the Assyrians, and the sign given to Hezekiah personally were great works. But how great is this wonder, "Thou hast in love to my soul delivered it from the pit of corruption: for thou hast cast all my sins behind thy back"!

Let us look then in a little further detail at what is brought before us in this chapter. First of all, we read that Hezekiah was sick unto death. Evidently this sickness came upon him at the very time when the danger of the Assyrians was so pressing and distressing to the nation. Here we see the hand of God on him. He was sick unto death. Humanly speaking, it appeared there was no cure for him. Death must be inevitable. And added to this, Isaiah comes. And what a message he brings! "Thus saith the Lord, Set thine house in order: for thou shalt die, and not live." O how heavy were those tidings, surely adding to the great distress of Hezekiah. Very pertinent was this message to him but is it any different for ourselves? I trust we are brought solemnly to realise that we are all in a dying state. Death is inevitable for each one of us. It may not appear to be brought home to us so pointedly as here to Hezekiah, but it is just as inevitable. Friends, we know not the day nor the hour of our death, but most certainly "it is appointed unto men once to die" (Heb. 9:27). And none can avoid that appointment. The important point is that we be found ready and prepared when that day comes. What alone can give us encouragement and consolation in the very prospect of death? It is only as we are brought and taught of God the Holy Spirit, as a poor needy sinner, to *flee* to the Lord Jesus Christ alone for refuge. Escape is not through what we are or can do, but in what Jesus Christ has done for our souls. Is not this the precious truth of the gospel of the grace of God? Is not this the only hope of salvation for the sinner? Indeed, Hezekiah was brought to know this blessedness for himself as expressed in the words of our text.

But receiving those heavy tidings, it is said that he "turned his face toward the wall, and prayed unto the Lord." That is very instructive. "He turned his face to the wall." That is, he turned away from everything, not only to one place but to *one person* alone. "He prayed unto the Lord." O friends, may we ourselves know the blessedness of that. In every issue, every situation which concerns us, where shall we go, to whom shall we go? There is but one place, one person. It is to the throne of grace, and to our Lord Jesus Christ who ever occupies that throne. He has opened the way unto it for poor needy guilty trembling hell-deserving sinners. Does not his word assure us that at the throne of his grace, as Hezekiah surely experienced, we "obtain mercy, and find grace to help in time of need"? (Heb. 14:16).

This prayer then of Hezekiah. He says, "Remember now, O Lord, I beseech thee, how I have walked before thee in truth and with a perfect heart, and have done that which is good in thy sight. And Hezekiah wept sore." It might appear on the face of it that Hezekiah is here pleading what he has done for the Lord. Yes, there is a reference obviously to that. For see what a work he, as king, had wrought in Jerusalem, in casting down all the altars to vain idols and in instructing the people to worship at one altar alone. He had gone to great lengths in diligently seeking to bring reformation to Jerusalem and Judah. How needful that was. How far the people had departed from the worship of the one true God! Yet how greatly had that reformation progressed and in great measure had been accomplished. Then we see this invasion of the Assyrians. Yes, in that sense, Hezekiah mentions what he had done in Jerusalem through the hand of the Lord upon him. He said, "I have walked before thee in truth and with a perfect heart, and have done that which is good in thy sight." In those outward things there had been that which was good in God's sight.

But it says here as well, and this is the important point, "And Hezekiah wept sore." Why did he weep sore? Was it fear of death? Was it disappointment that after all he had done, he would not live to see a full conclusion of that reformation, or the full deliverance he had been promised from the Assyrians? I do not want to speculate but there may well have been some such thoughts. But I believe there was something much more concerning to him personally. "Hezekiah wept sore." Let us not forget that though Hezekiah was king in Jerusalem, yet he was a sinner, as each one of us is. And with death imminent through sickness, and the message Isaiah brought to him, did not the solemn fact of his own sins, his own unfitness in the very prospect of death, cause him to weep sore? I believe he wept sore as one humbled under the hand of God in true confession and godly sorrow over his sin, and in the conscious sense that if the Lord was swift to mark his iniquity, he could not stand before him. Where was his hope? Where is your hope and mine, as sinners, in the certain prospect of death, however near or far off that may be? Where do we stand? What particularly exercises your soul and mine? Is it to be found right with men or to be found right with God? That is the vital point.

"He wept sore." O friends, see what grace it is that brings a sinner to the footstool of mercy, to cry to the Lord for mercy, to weep sore. For indeed Hezekiah deeply felt the solemn fact of himself as a sinner before God. As I have said, we see here the inward exercises, the personal experience, of this man of God. The record in the book of Kings does not include this writing of Hezekiah. Here the Lord, through his servant Isaiah, is pleased to disclose to us the inward exercises of this man under the Lord's sovereign, yet gracious dealings with him. Painful and distressing was that situation for Hezekiah. And no doubt it is likewise in the Lord's dealings with ourselves. Yet what a mercy it is to be found low at the footstool of divine mercy.

And see what is here particularly displayed of the wonders of God's sovereign grace and mercy. In his dealings with Hezekiah, there could appear to be God's going forth in judgment against him. Yet he proved that these things were not evidence of God being against him. They were to manifest in a fuller way what Hezekiah was in himself and the fulness of God's grace and mercy towards him, treasured up in our Lord and Saviour Jesus Christ and revealed by the Holy Spirit.

Yes, he was brought very low. "O Lord, I am oppressed; undertake for me." Friends, do we know anything of that, whether in outward circumstances or in soul exercises as a needy sinner? Does not sin oppress? Is it not a troubling thing in the daily lives of the people of God? See how Paul expressed it, and surely if taught of the Holy Spirit we are no strangers to it. He cried, as we read in Romans seven, "O wretched man that I am! who shall deliver me from the body of this death?" (Rom. 7:24) What was so troubling to him? It was the consciousness that in his flesh dwelt no good thing, that defilement by sin is the sad daily experience of the living family of God. We trust that through divine grace there is the partaking of that new nature which is born of God and cannot sin. But the child of God is very conscious that though he possesses a new nature, there is also our old fallen sinful nature in us which will greatly trouble us to the very hour of our death.

"Then death, that puts an end to life,
Shall put an end to sin."

"O Lord, I am oppressed; undertake for me." Friends, what a mercy to be brought there. Is it not in some sense the daily experience the people of God? O those things that oppress and distress! We see it in the language of that Syrophenician woman, greatly distressed as she was by the affliction of her daughter who was grievously vexed with a devil. She comes to the Lord. See what we read. She worshipped him, saying, "Lord help me" (Matt. 15:25). Is that not, in a sense, the very expression of Hezekiah? 'O Lord, I am oppressed. I cannot deal with these things. They weigh heavy upon me. Indeed, they press me down. Undertake for me.'

O friends, what a mercy that the Lord's arm is indeed an almighty arm. He can and does deliver. His ear is open to the cry of his people, as seen here in the cry of Hezekiah, "Like a crane or a swallow, so did I chatter: I did mourn as a dove: mine eyes fail with looking upward: O Lord, I am oppressed; undertake for me. What shall I say? he hath both spoken unto me, and himself hath done it: I shall go softly all my years in the bitterness of my soul." He recognizes the hand of the Lord in these things, and it is important that we do so too. But, as I said earlier, is it because the hand of the Lord had gone out against him? You know, we read what Zion says later in this prophecy of Isaiah. And this embraces the Lord's people collectively but also personally. "Zion said, The Lord hath forsaken me, and my Lord hath forgotten me" (Isa. 49:14). The psalmist says, "Hath God forgotten to be gracious …Will he be favourable no more?" (Ps. 77:9,7). Is that where you are brought? O hear the language of the Lord to his people in all their needs. "Can a woman forget her sucking child, that she should not have compassion on the son of her womb? yea, they may forget, yet will I not forget thee. Behold, I have graven thee upon the palms of my hands; thy walls are continually before me" (Isa. 49:15–16).

Was Hezekiah forgotten of God? Was God departed from him? Ah, these dealings of the Lord with him, bring him low at the Saviour's feet in true godly sorrow and confession of his sins. And there we see the Lord's manifest grace in raising him up. As the psalmist said, "If thou, Lord, shouldest mark iniquities, O Lord, who shall stand? But there is forgiveness with thee, that thou mayest be feared" (Ps. 130:3–4).

We come particularly to these words of our text. "Behold, for peace I had great bitterness." It can be rendered, 'Upon my peace I had great bitterness.' When he poured out his heart before God because of the invasion of the Assyrians, the Lord had sent a message by Isaiah that he would deliver them from their hand. But it appeared that when deliverance from the Assyrians was assured, this bitterness of personal sickness came on him and death became imminent. 'For my peace I had great bitterness.' *"But."* What mercy is in this little word *"but."* *"But* thou hast in love to my soul delivered it from the pit of corruption." This can be rendered, 'thou hast loved my soul from the pit of corruption.' Is not that saving grace and mercy towards a sinner gloriously set before us in the precious truth of the gospel? I trust it is so for you and me. From whence does it flow? "Thou hast in love." O that love! The Lord has loved his people even when they were dead in trespasses and sins. Did not the Lord declare to his servant the prophet the very foundation of the manifestation of his grace and mercy to guilty needy sinners? "I have loved thee with an everlasting love: therefore with lovingkindness have I drawn thee" (Jer. 31:3).

Friends, remember that love of the Lord is not in tongue and word only but "in deed and in truth" (1 John 3:18). As I mentioned earlier, how gloriously it is demonstrated in the person and work of our Lord Jesus Christ. The very God against whom we have sinned has himself come forth, in the person of Jesus

Christ, for the salvation of ruined guilty sinners, transgressors of his holy law. Surely each one of us has offended God and continually offends him, "But thou hast in love to my soul delivered it from the pit of corruption." O what a pit of corruption that is! It applies to each of us. As Paul said, "O wretched man that I am! who shall deliver me from the body of this death?" What a pit of corruption is in each one of us! But "thou hast in love to my soul delivered it from the pit of corruption," that is, from what I justly deserve. Never lose sight of the solemn fact that, "My sins deserve eternal death." But what response to that can Hezekiah make here, and all true believers? "But Jesus died for me."

He says, "For thou hast cast all my sins behind thy back." How can God do that? How can he do it justly, meeting all the demands of his law? How can he cast all our sins behind his back and be wholly consistent with himself as holy righteous just and true? God cannot overlook sin. He doesn't overlook sin. He doesn't pass it by as something insignificant. He doesn't say, O it does not really matter. Far from it. "The wrath of God is revealed from heaven against all ungodliness and unright-eousness of men" (Rom. 1:18). *That* includes your sins and mine. As I have just said, "our sins deserve eternal death," *but* "Jesus died for me."

"Thou hast cast all my sins behind thy back." Notice, it does not say he will do it. He *has* done it. And that is true for every poor sinner who by divine grace is brought to believe and trust alone in Jesus. And that believing and trusting him is the fruit of the love of God in Jesus Christ, that everlasting love of God by which he has embraced them. Yes, "thou *hast* cast all my sins behind thy back." Not *will* do, but *has* done. The gospel ever sets before us the glorious truth of this finished work, directing the Lord's people as needy sinners to the one offering and sacrifice of our Lord Jesus Christ. As Paul so beautifully puts it in his epistle to the Romans: "There is therefore *now* no condemnation to them which are in Christ Jesus, who walk not after the flesh, but after the Spirit" (Rom. 8:1). "No condemnation" founded, not on what they have done or what they do, but on what God in Christ has done for them.

"Thou hast cast *all* my sins behind thy back." O not one of them is left unatoned for. Full redemption is assured. Was it not this wonder of mercy manifest to him that caused Hezekiah, delivered from the depths of distress, to so rejoice in free and sovereign grace? Yes, the Lord gave him a sign, both with regard to certain deliverance from the Assyrians, and also confirming his promise to add fifteen years to his life. These were great mercies. What a wonder that the sun should go backwards ten degrees in the sundial of Ahaz. It must have been a phenomenon, not only known to Hezekiah but to the whole world at that time. But the greatest wonder of all, was in God's personal dealings with him in the greatest of all blessings. *"Thou hast cast all my sins behind thy back."* O the wonder of this, the greatest of all wonders, "Thou hast in love to my soul delivered it from the pit of corruption: for thou hast cast all my sins behind thy back."

"If sin be pardoned, I'm secure;
Death has no sting beside."

O the blessedness of pardoned sin, access into God's favour and the blessed certainty of the full enjoyment of eternal life through Jesus Christ. These are the blessings of believers *now,* and they will enter into the fulness of them *hereafter.*

He goes on to say, "For the grave cannot praise thee, death can not celebrate thee: they that go down into the pit cannot hope for thy truth." Solemn things. "The living, the living, he shall praise thee, as I do this day: the father to the children shall make known thy truth. The Lord was ready to save me." Friends, how ready is the Lord to save, beyond all our expectations. For the Lord is far better to us than we ever deserve, even beyond what we can begin to contemplate. O the fulness and freeness of his grace! "The Lord was ready to save me: therefore we will sing my songs to the stringed instruments all the days of our life in the house of the Lord." What a prospect is that for *now* and for *all eternity.*

I will leave the remarks there this morning. The Lord add his blessing. Amen.

45

THINE ANGER IS TURNED AWAY

Lord's day evening 5 July 2020

"And in that day thou shalt say, O Lord, I will praise thee: though thou wast angry with me, thine anger is turned away, and thou comfortedst me. Behold, God is my salvation; I will trust, and not be afraid: for the Lord JEHOVAH is my strength and my song; he also is become my salvation" (Isaiah 12:1–2).

These six verses in this twelfth chapter of Isaiah truly comprise one of the spiritual songs of Zion. They express what the living family of God is graciously taught in faith and love by the Holy Spirit. Conscious of what they are in themselves as ever needy sinners, they are brought to know what the Lord has done for them in the person and work of Jesus Christ, for his glory and praise and their eternal salvation. All flows out of the fulness and freeness of the love of God revealed in the precious truth of the gospel. All centres in the person of our Lord and Saviour Jesus Christ.

In the eleventh chapter, Isaiah by the inspiration of the Holy Ghost, gloriously testifies of the person of our Lord Jesus Christ. He speaks of his incarnation and what he accomplished in his life, sufferings, death and resurrection. He speaks of his ascension and enthronement at the right of the Majesty in the heavens, and the wonders which flow from his person and work. This is the substance of the ministry of all the prophets. As I have mentioned many a time, they "testified beforehand the sufferings of Christ, and the glory that should follow" (1 Pet. 1:11).

And the glory that follows is surely the work of God's grace by the sovereign operations of the Holy Spirit in the hearts and lives of sinful men and women, as many as the Lord our God shall call. He gathers out of every nation, kindred, tribe and tongue from under heaven, guilty hell-deserving sinners as every one of them is, and manifests the wonders of his sovereign grace and mercy to them. That eleventh chapter also sets before us a glorious prospect for the church and people of God, when the ingathering of God's elect is complete. There will be the consummation of all things when the Lord comes the second time in power and great glory. He shall then receive his own unto himself and judge the world in righteousness.

I want as helped to look at these two verses I have read by way of a text this evening. May the Lord the Holy Spirit open them up afresh to your soul and mine. "And in that day thou shalt say, O Lord, I will praise thee: though thou wast angry with me, thine anger is turned away, and thou comfortedst me." There is frequent reference in the ministry of the prophets, particularly in Isaiah, to what is described as *that day*. What is *that day?* Without question it is the day of the coming of the Lord Jesus Christ. He was the glorious fulfilment of all that God had promised from the time of man's fall in Eden. Patriarchs and prophets had testified to his coming which had been divinely appointed before the foundation of the world. The greatest event the world has ever witnessed was the incarnation of our Lord Jesus Christ. Well might the angels declare at the birth of that child born to Mary, "Glory to God in the highest, and on earth peace, good will toward men" (Luke 2:14). O friends, the wonders of the divine appointments and purposes of God for his glory in the redemption and salvation of sinful men and women! What God promised he has most surely fulfilled. And as taught of the Holy Spirit, have not we ourselves, as ruined guilty sinners, cause to increasingly praise and thank God for such wonders of grace made known to such as us. We are ever brought to realise that all is of grace from beginning to the end. It is not by works of righteousness which we have done but according to his mercy he saved us.

The mercy of God! Mercy is for the helpless. Mercy is for the miserable. Mercy is for those who have *nothing* of their own to look to and nothing whatsoever to bring for acceptance by God. No, the wonders of God's grace are manifest in mercy which endureth for ever, mercy revealed to us in all its fulness and freeness in the precious truth of the gospel. Does not that glorious gospel of the grace of God ever proclaim mercy for the helpless and the miserable? In this provision which God appointed, he is glorified in the blessings of salvation for those who have nothing of their own to merit it in any way. All is full, all is free, all is of God.

Yes, the term *in that day* directs us essentially to what God promised in the coming of our Lord Jesus Christ. Is it not also expressive of the day of the Lord's coming and manifesting himself to sinful men and women individually, by the sovereign operations of the Lord the Holy Spirit? There is very real personal application in *that* day, in *conviction*, *revelation*, and *assurance*.

"In that day thou shalt say, O Lord, I will praise thee: though thou wast angry with me, thine anger is turned away, and thou comfortedst me." Yes, is there not here clearly indicated that *in that day* there is cause to praise the Lord because he *convicted* us as guilty sinners? He showed us the solemn consequences of our transgressions against his holy law. "Thou wast angry with me." And is he not justly angry? As I quoted this morning, "the wrath of God is revealed from heaven against all ungodliness and unrighteousness of men" (Rom. 1:18). Can we say of ourselves that we are excluded from that word? The scriptures emphatically tell us that by nature we are no different, no better than any other. In us, that is, in our flesh dwelleth no good thing. "There is none that doeth good, no, not one" (Rom. 3:12). Fallen human nature in every sinner "is enmity against God" (Rom. 8:7). We ourselves are no exception. And there never will be any exception to it, apart from sovereign distinguishing grace.

"Thou wast angry with me." Here is true conviction brought home to the soul by the quickening awakening sovereign operations of the Holy Spirit to see ourselves as ruined, hell deserving sinners. What a mercy, that though the Lord comes in convicting power, his holy law testifying against us that we have sinned and "our sins deserve eternal death," yet by that same power and unction of the Holy Spirit comes a glorious *revelation* as well. What cause then has the soul to give thanks and praise to the Lord. For in that day of the Lord's coming, by the awakening

of the Holy Spirit, the sinner is brought to the feet of the Lord
Jesus Christ. And what is the sentence that goes forth for such a
sinner? Here are wonders of grace opened up to us for which we
may well say, "I will praise thee."

Notice here a very personal application: *"I* will praise thee."
Yes, the people of God ever have cause collectively to praise the
Lord. But here is a very personal realisation: *"I* will praise thee."
Why? 'Ah Lord, for what thou art, what thou hast done, what
thou hast revealed in thy rich mercy even to such a sinner as I
am.' "Though thou wast angry with me, thine anger is turned
away, and thou comfortedst me." See here, I say, *conviction.* See
also blessed *revelation.* A revelation of what? The mercy of God
through Jesus Christ our Lord.

Yes, the soul is brought to the feet of the Lord Jesus Christ in
conviction of their sins. But friends, remember this is not only at
the Lord's first dealings with a sinner but even throughout the life
of a child of God. It is a being brought continually to the feet of
the Lord Jesus Christ, conscious of our need. And is not our need
continual, in a sense of our helplessness, our unprofitableness and
from what we still find of the working and defilement of sin in
our hearts and lives? As I have said many a time, is not the
language of the publican, the very language of each child of God?
And the further we go on, we certainly cannot get far, nor in one
sense desire to get far from it: "God be merciful to me a sinner"
(Luke 18:13). And not only is there that *conviction* but also the
revelation of mercy to us by the ministry of the Holy Spirit, as
that publican experienced. "He went down to his house justified
rather than the other."

What does it mean to be justified? Why, it is the very reality
of what Hezekiah expressed in our subject this morning, "Thou
hast in love to my soul delivered it from the pit of corruption: for
thou hast cast all my sins behind thy back" (Isa. 38:17). It is God
justifying the ungodly. Hezekiah had nothing of his own to plead.
Conscious of himself as a sinner in the immediate prospect of
death, where was his hope? In what could he trust in that
situation? Nothing in himself, not even in what he had done for
the Lord in his day. O, as brought home to him afresh in conviction and revelation, his hope was in what the Lord had done

for him. "Thou hast in love to my soul delivered it from the pit of corruption: for thou hast cast all my sins behind thy back." And this is what the prophet here declares, "I will praise thee: though thou wast angry with me, thine anger is turned away, and thou comfortedst me."

What alone delivers from the just judgment of God against us as sinful men and women? As I ever seek to emphasise, nothing that we are or what we can do, can save us. It is wholly in what the Lord is and what he has done as set before us in the precious truth of the gospel. O nothing can deliver us from that pit of corruption but the love of God as revealed in Jesus Christ our Lord. And that love is manifest, not in overlooking or passing by our sins and transgressions, but by a full atonement made for them in the person and finished work of our Lord and Saviour Jesus Christ. What is the only ground on which Hezekiah could say, "Thou hast cast all my sins behind thy back"? Or the psalmist could say, "As far as the east is from the west, so far hath he removed our transgressions from us"? (Ps. 103:12). Or Micah could say, "thou wilt cast all their sins into the depths of the sea"? (Mic. 7:19). All these words express a full glorious deliverance from our sins and from the curse and condemnation due to us. Never shall they be raised again to condemn that person who, though a sinner still in themselves, is brought by divine grace to believe and trust alone in the Lord Jesus Christ. All that comes between such a sinner and a holy God is fully satisfied, fully removed, by our Lord Jesus Christ, the great surety and substitute of his people.

Friends, these are great and glorious realities for which the soul surely has continual cause to give thanks and praise to the Lord. Yes, we are distressed oftentimes by many things from within and without, as we journey on through life. Invariably, how very trying is the path the Lord has appointed for his people. But in all his leadings and dealings with them one thing ever remains sure and certain. What God in Christ has appointed and provided in redemption and salvation can *never be undone*. God will never go back on it. Why, what Jesus Christ has wrought out for his people is that which always provides full satisfaction to the Lord our God, holy just and true as he is.

Remember what God the Father spoke at the baptism of our Lord Jesus Christ in Jordan. That voice was heard from heaven: "This is my beloved Son, *in whom I am well pleased*" (Matt. 3:17). Precious truth indeed. And he is likewise well pleased with all found by divine grace in Jesus Christ as their surety, their substitute and their great and glorious head. What Jesus Christ is, so is every poor sinner brought to believe and trust in him. How precious are those words of John in his first epistle. "Herein," he says, "is love." Yes, this love of God, this love through which Hezekiah could say, he hath delivered me from the pit of corruption and cast all my sins behind his back. "Herein is love, not that we loved God, but that he loved us, and sent his Son to be the propitiation for our sins" (John 4:10). "Herein is our love made perfect...because as he is, so are we in this world" (v.17). Wondrous truths are there set forth before us! And our text bears witness to them. Ever is there cause for God's people to give thanks to the Lord.

"I will praise thee: though thou wast angry with me, thine anger is turned away, and thou comfortedst me." What a glorious revelation then does God give to us in the precious truth of the gospel, that which speaks of pardon, peace and eternal life through Jesus Christ our Lord. Oh friends, is not this "good news from a far country" (Prov. 25:25), God reconciling us unto himself through the redemption that is in Christ Jesus? Paul could say to the Corinthians that, as a faithful servant, he was an ambassador for Christ and bore witness to what God in Christ has provided. He said, "God was in Christ, reconciling the world unto himself, not imputing their trespasses unto them; and hath committed unto us the word of reconciliation" (2 Cor. 5:19). He goes on to testify of the blessed foundation laid for the faith and hope of the people of God: "He hath made him," that is Jesus, "to be sin for us, who knew no sin; that we might be made the righteousness of God in him" (v.21). Surely we have cause to praise and bless the Lord's great and holy name for such wonders of grace revealed in the gospel. Remember, all is sure, all is the outworking his divine appointments and purposes, founded upon his unchanging love and faithfulness. And all is made known by the Holy Spirit in the life of a poor sinner.

So it was with Hezekiah amid all the trials, difficulties, temptations and fears that had come upon him, not only in the nation, but personally in the very heavy tidings Isaiah brought to him. O surely he goes on to say in effect, in praise to the Lord, "though thou wast angry with me, thine anger is turned away, and thou comfortedst me." What a blessed *revelation* it is, as brought home by the power of the Holy Spirit, that God has reconciled us to himself by the redemption in Christ Jesus. May not one of us be destitute of the blessed reality of it. Ah, is not this more than anything this world can give us? If Christ is mine and I am his, then I have the one thing that can make my soul blessed in time and to all eternity. The reality of my relationship with Christ can never be overturned.

Many things come in the life of the child of God. We meet with many disappointments. Indeed, in the relationships of the people of God one with another, we often meet disappointing things that trouble and distress us. But friends, what a precious truth it is that in what Jesus Christ is to his people, there is never any disappointments. There may well often be just cause for disappointment with ourselves, especially in our returns to the love and mercy of the Lord made known to us. We have to come continually to that place where we say we are unprofitable servants, we have only done that which is our duty to do. And we even come far short in *that*. What a mercy it is that the love of God in Christ to his people is full, free, and knows no alteration or end. All is to the Lord's praise alone.

"Though thou wast angry with me, thine anger is turned away, thou comfortedst me." It is a glorious *revelation* when the Lord comes in power, speaking pardon and peace through a Saviour's blood! See these things in what the apostle writes to the Hebrews: "Ye are not come unto the mount that might be touched, and that burned with fire, nor unto blackness...but ye are come unto mount Sion, and unto the city of the living God, the heavenly Jerusalem, and to an innumerable company of angels, to the general assembly and church of the firstborn, which are written in heaven, and to God the Judge of all, and to the spirits of just men made perfect, and to Jesus the mediator of the new covenant, and to the blood of sprinkling, that speaketh better things than that of Abel" (Heb. 12:18–24). O what a revelation is that, made known and brought home to us by the Spirit's teaching. Surely we have cause to continually praise the Lord for all that he is and all that he has done.

The prophet goes on to say: "Behold, God is my salvation; I will trust, and not be afraid: for the Lord JEHOVAH is my strength and my song; he also is become my salvation." Here is blessed *assurance* as the Lord the Holy Spirit bears witness to these things in the experience of a poor sinner. "Behold, God is my salvation." Is this presumptuous language? No. It is the language of God-given faith. This glorious testimony to the fulness and freeness of redeeming love and mercy declares, "God *is* my salvation." Not he may be, or he will be in future times, or has been in the past. It is as the psalmist expressed it in Psalm 46, "God *is* our refuge and strength, a very *present* help in trouble" (Ps. 46:1). God is ever present with his people. He is not just past or future, but he is "I AM" (Exod. 3:14). He is ever the same, ever present with his people, He is Jesus Christ, God manifest in the flesh, "the same yesterday, and to day, and for ever" (Heb. 13:8).

"God is my salvation." Salvation is all of God from beginning to end. We, as sinners, can never save ourselves. Nor can any of our fellow creatures give us what we so need as guilty sinners. *"God* is my salvation." And as I have said, what a salvation, so full and free. Though it has come to us truly free, never lose sight of how great a price was paid for the redemption and salvation of your soul and mine, as brought to trust in the Lord Jesus Christ. Peter tells us, and may we ever remember it, "Ye were not redeemed with corruptible things, as silver and gold, from your vain conversation received by tradition from your fathers; but with the precious blood of Christ, as of a lamb without blemish and without spot" (1 Pet. 1:18–19). Precious blood. "Invaluable blood," as one said. It fully atones for the believer's sins and fully meets all their needs as a sinner, to the praise of the glory of our God.

"God is my salvation; *I will trust, and not be afraid."* As I said, this is the language of God-given faith, amid all the weaknesses and infirmities of the Lord's people. Faith is the gift of God even if it be but as a grain of mustard seed. Whether faith is considered weak or whether it is strong, yet it is the gift of God. Even though in the experience of the child of God at times, faith may seem very weak and feeble, it is still the gift of God. And faith looks to find encouragement, not from what we are, fearful and trembling as we may well be, but from what God sets before us in his word of who Jesus is and what he has done. Yes, in whatever situation we are found, may we be brought in the very reality of God-given faith to turn away from everything in self and to look alone to the Lord Jesus Christ.

Look at Jonah in the whale's belly. We know his sinful folly and disobedience brought him there. Yet it was of the Lord's dealings with his servant. Terrible must have been that situation for Jonah. We cannot begin to comprehend what it must have been like to be three days in the fish's belly. How his folly and sin must have been brought home to him. Yet there, in the fish's belly, what is the language of Jonah? "I am cast out of thy sight; yet I will look again toward thy holy temple…They that observe lying vanities forsake their own mercy…Salvation is of the Lord" (Jonah 2). *"Yet I will look again."* And friends, faith, even in the deepest of trials, brings us to look to where all poor sinners taught of God the Holy Spirit are brought to look, even to "look again toward thy holy temple." That temple blessedly signified the person of our Lord Jesus Christ as the temple made without hands. Thus Jonah, testifying that salvation is of the Lord, put his trust in him who was to come, our Lord Jesus Christ, God manifest in the flesh.

And Isaiah says in our text, "I will trust, and not be afraid: for the Lord JEHOVAH *is my strength and my song."* O what a fulness is *there,* for the Lord's people, weak in themselves but "strong in the Lord, and in the power of his might" (Eph. 6:10). Ah friends, much may be against us, much within us rising up in condemnation against us. But, "if God be for us, who can be against us?" (Rom. 8:31). Look at that name, "the Lord JEHOVAH," encompassing as it does, God the Father, God the Son and God the Holy Spirit, one God over all, blessed for evermore. Was not that the very name by which he revealed himself to Moses? "I AM THAT I AM" (Exod 3:14). See the power and glory of God displayed in what he spoke and promised to Moses when he sent him to bring Israel up out of Egypt in spite of all the opposition he met. God there displayed his power, his wisdom, and his grace to his people. And the Lord our God is still the Lord JEHOVAH. He "is my strength and my song; he also is become my salvation."

I said in the words here before us are found *conviction*, *revelation* and blessed *assurance*. O may the Lord the Holy Spirit lead our souls into the blessed reality of these things. May we be brought truly to praise and bless his name, for all that he is and all he has revealed to us of his saving grace and mercy. Let us just read again this spiritual song in closing this evening.

"And in that day thou shalt say, O Lord, I will praise thee: though thou wast angry with me, thine anger is turned away, and thou comfortedst me. Behold, God is my salvation; I will trust, and not be afraid: for the Lord JEHOVAH is my strength and my song; he also is become my salvation. Therefore with joy shall ye draw water out of the wells of salvation. And in that day shall ye say, Praise the Lord, call upon his name, declare his doings among the people, make mention that his name is exalted. Sing unto the Lord; for he hath done excellent things: this is known in all the earth. Cry out and shout, thou inhabitant of Zion: for great is the Holy One of Israel in the midst of thee."

O what glorious spiritual truths and realities are these! We ever have cause to bear testimony to them. "The Lord JEHOVAH is my strength and my song; he also is become my salvation." May each one of us know the true blessedness of this salvation, to the praise of the glory of his name.

I will leave the remarks there. May the Lord add his blessing. Amen.